Social Movements

Social Movements

An Introduction

THIRD EDITION

Donatella della Porta
and
Mario Diani

WILEY Blackwell

Registered Offices
John Wiley & Sons, Inc., 111 River Street, Hoboken, NJ 07030, USA
John Wiley & Sons Ltd, The Atrium, Southern Gate, Chichester, West Sussex, PO19 8SQ, UK

Editorial Office
9600 Garsington Road, Oxford, OX4 2DQ, UK

For details of our global editorial offices, customer services, and more information about Wiley products visit us at www.wiley.com.

Library of Congress Cataloging-in-Publication Data

Names: della Porta, Donatella, 1956– author. | Diani, Mario, 1957– author.
Title: Social movements : an introduction / Donatella della Porta and Mario Diani.
Description: Third edition. | Hoboken, NJ : Wiley-Blackwell, 2020. |
     Includes bibliographical references and index.
Identifiers: LCCN 2019051993 (print) | LCCN 2019051994 (ebook) | ISBN 9781119167655
     (paperback) | ISBN 9781119167686 (adobe pdf) | ISBN 9781119167679 (epub)
Subjects: LCSH: Social movements.
Classification: LCC HN17.5 .D45 2020 (print) | LCC HN17.5 (ebook) | DDC 303.48/4–dc23
LC record available at https://lccn.loc.gov/2019051993
LC ebook record available at https://lccn.loc.gov/2019051994

Cover Design: Wiley
Cover Image: © Mary Mackey Art Denver Colorado USA

Set in 10.5/13pt STIX Two Text by SPi Global, Pondicherry, India
Printed and bound in Singapore by Markono Print Media Pte Ltd

10   9   8   7   6   5   4   3   2   1

Contents

Foreword to the Third Edition

This is the third edition of a book that was first published in English in 1999 (the Italian edition having appeared in 1997 with the *Nuova Italia Scientifica* publishing press), and then in 2006. Innumerable significant changes have taken place in the political landscape over the last decades – think of the 2011 revolts across the globe, the spread of online protest activity, or the renaissance of right-wing extremism. They have been paralleled by a constant growth of research on social movements and collective action, as witnessed by the proliferation of handbooks charting the field from multiple angles, specialized journals, or references to social movement theory in the scientific literature. Both developments have shaped the drafting of the third edition. On the one hand, we have updated many of our empirical examples, including references to recent episodes of contention and trying to add more materials from a comparative angle. We have also kept, however, many references to earlier movements, as we deem important to draw our readers' attention to the fact that some basic, core mechanisms of collective action may be found operating across movements that may differ substantially in timing and content. As for our treatment of the literature, given its fast and massive increase, it is even more selective and partial than in the previous two editions. Back in the late 1990s, the first edition of the book also served as a "literature review" of sort, bringing together, as the late Charles Tilly noted, European and American perspectives in the same introductory text. In this new edition, performing a similar mapping function would have been neither feasible, given the exponential rise in the scientific output, nor necessary, as a number of systematic accounts of growth in the field have appeared. As we have promoted some of them (della Porta 2014; della Porta and Diani 2015) and contributed to others (e.g. Fillieule and Accornero 2016; Snow et al. 2019), we know that they can do a much better job at covering the field than we could in this book. Accordingly, this edition presents itself even more neatly as an introductory text, if not one for beginners in social research.

It is also worth reminding readers that they are not being introduced to the full range of possible intellectual approaches to the theme "social movements." Significant contributions have come from fields such as history, political philosophy, anthropology, or psychology, that are almost entirely neglected here. So are important treatments of social movements by "social theory" broadly conceived (on that see Crossley 2002; Buechler 2011; Cox and Fominaya 2013; Eder 2015). The approach we refer to has established itself mainly at the intersection of sociology and political science, with the ambition of generating theory-driven systematic empirical research. For all its limitations, and despite an empirical focus that is still primarily Western centric, the conceptual apparatus introduced in this book has also proved a useful tool for many researchers investigating other areas of the world (Ellis and van Kessel 2009; Broadbent and Brockman 2011; Rossi and von Bülow 2015). Ours may not be (it certainly is not) the whole story, but it is an important story. We are delighted to be able to share its third version with our readers.

Florence and Trento, May 2019

ACKNOWLEDGMENTS

We are grateful to our editors at Blackwell for their patience and assistance, to Daniela Chironi for her careful work on the bibliography, and to Cambridge University Press for granting permission to reproduce Figure 6.1 and some sections of Chapter 6 from Diani (2015).

CHAPTER 1

The Study of Social Movements

Recurring Questions, (Partially) Changing Answers

In the late 1960s, the world was apparently undergoing deep, dramatic transformations – even a revolution, some thought. American civil rights and antiwar movements, the Mai 1968 revolt in France, students' protests in Germany, Britain, or Mexico, the workers-students coalitions of the 1969 Hot Autumn in Italy, the pro-democracy mobilizations in as diverse locations as Francoist Madrid and communist Prague, the growth of critical Catholicism from South America to Rome, the early signs of the women's and environmental movements, that would have shaped the new politics of the 1970s: all these phenomena – and many more – suggested that deep changes were in the making. In 2018, the fiftieth anniversary of 1968 has stimulated reflections on its long-term effects not only on society and politics, but also on social movement studies (della Porta 2018a).

Accordingly, the study of social movements developed to an unprecedented pace into a major area of research. If, at the end of the 1940s, critics lamented the "crudely descriptive level of understanding and a relative lack of theory" (Strauss 1947, p. 352), and in the 1960s complained that "in the study of social changes, social movements have received relatively little emphasis" (Killian 1964, p. 426), by the mid-1970s, research into collective action was considered "one of the most vigorous areas of sociology" (Marx and Wood 1975). At the end of the 1980s, commentators talked of "an explosion, in the last ten years, of theoretical and empirical writings on social movements and collective action" (Morris and Herring 1987, p. 138; also see Rucht 1991).

Today, the study of social movements is solidly established, with specialized journals, book series, and professional associations. The excitement and optimism of the roaring 1960s may be long gone, but social and political events over the last four

Social Movements: An Introduction, Third Edition. Donatella della Porta and Mario Diani.
© 2020 John Wiley & Sons Ltd. Published 2020 by John Wiley & Sons Ltd.

decades have hardly rendered the investigation of grassroots activism any less relevant or urgent. To the contrary, social movements, protest actions and, more generally, political organizations unaligned with major political parties or trade unions have become a permanent component of Western democracies. It is no longer possible to describe protest politics, grassroots participation, or symbolic challenges as unconventional. References to a "movement society" (Dodson 2011; McCarthy, Rafail, and Gromis 2013; Melucci 1996; Meyer and Tarrow 1998; Soule and Earl 2005) seem increasingly plausible, not only in the most advances democracies but even in authoritarian regimes and in the Global South (della Porta 2017a).

To be sure, there has been considerable fluctuation in the intensity of collective action over this period, as there has been in its degree of radicalism, its specific forms, and its capacity to influence the political process. However, forecasts that the wave of protest of the late 1960s would quickly subside, and that "business as usual," as represented by interest-based politics, organized according to traditional political divisions, would return in its wake, have largely been proved wrong. In different ways, and with a wide range of goals and values, various forms of protest have continued to emerge, in the Western world as well as elsewhere (Ballard, Habib, and Valodia 2006; Beissinger 2002; Bennani-Chraïbi and Fillieule 2003; Broadbent and Brockman 2011; Kriesi et al. 1995). At the start of the new millennium, possibly for the first time since 1968, the wave of mobilizations for a globalization from below (often identified as global justice movement) mounted a new, global, challenge, combining themes typical of class movements with themes typical of new social movements, like ecology or gender equality (Arrighi and Silver 1999; della Porta and Tarrow 2005; Smith 2008; Tarrow 2005). Later on, in Latin America as well as in North Africa, in Europe as well as in the United States, the Great Recession and austerity policies have triggered a broad wave of protests that have been influenced by the different times and forms of the financial crises, but also took inspiration from each other (Almeida and Chase-Dunn 2018; della Porta and Mattoni 2014; Kriesi et al. 2012; Rossi and von Bülow 2015).

In truth, speaking of "global justice movements" or "anti-austerity movements" as if they were unitary, homogeneous actors would be very misleading. The initiatives against neoliberal globalization or the elites' management of the global crisis have been very heterogeneous, and not necessarily connected to each other. They have addressed a range of issues, from child labor's exploitation by global brands to deforestation, from human rights in developing countries to military interventions by Western powers, from economic deprivation to threats to democracy. And they have done do so in a myriad of forms, from individual utterances of dissent and individual behavior to mass collective events, and from a variety of points of view.

Looking at them well illustrates what doing *social movement analysis* actually means. In their research practice, most of the people who study social movements focus either on individuals, organizations, or events, in the best instances trying to capture the interdependence between them:

- *Opposition to neoliberal policies can be looked at as the ensemble of individuals expressing opinions about certain issues, advocating or opposing social change.* Globalization has surely raised fears and hopes in equal measure, but the balance is distributed unequally across countries and socioeconomic areas. Repeatedly, public opinion surveys indicate diffuse worries about the impact of globalization over people's lives, both economically and politically. Although this may be more a diffused concern in Western Europe than in the United States or even more so elsewhere, globalization is undoubtedly at the core of public opinion's interest these days. Those who are skeptical and often hostile to it represent a distinct and vocal sector of public opinion. Their views are forged and reinforced in dialogue with a range of prominent opinion makers and public figures, exposing the costs and faults of globalization from a Western/Northern as well as an Eastern/Southern perspective, such as Indian writer Arundhati Roy, Philippine sociologist Walden Bello, Australian journalist John Pilger, or economist and Nobel laureate Josef Stieglitz. Books like Naomi Klein's *No Logo* (1999) may be safely credited with the same impact that Rachel Carson's *Silent Spring* (1962), or the Club of Rome' s report on *The Limits to Growth* (Meadows, Randers, and Behrens 1972) had on the spread of environmental concerns back in the 1960s and 1970s. Building on this sensitivity in public opinion, anti-austerity protests have also built on and fueled a widespread concern for economic inequalities and social injustice in the public opinion, that in large part started to stigmatize the elites (the 1%) as being responsible for the suffering of the people (the 99%) (Flesher Fominaya 2014; della Porta 2015a).
- *Individual opinions and concerns often turn into various forms of political and social participation.* Moral and philosophical worldviews and deeply felt convictions are then paralleled by specific attempts by individuals to stop threatening developments, redress instances of injustice, and promote alternative options to the managing of social life and economic activity. A possible way of looking at the movements for social justice and against inequalities is, then, by focusing on those individuals who actively express their opposition to neoliberal capitalism. By signing petitions calling for the cancellation of developing countries' debt, contributing money to the activities of various social movement organizations, mobilizing to stop the building of dams or the effects of extensive exploitation of land in Asia or Africa, blocking access to the European Central Bank in Frankfurt, or Occupying Wall Street, or attempting to stop ships exporting toxic waste to developing countries or trains carrying military equipment, individuals citizens may contribute to the campaigns against neoliberal globalization and its effects at domestic level. They may do so, however, also through actions that affect individual lifestyles and private behavior as

much – and possibly more – than the public sphere. Throughout the West, the recent years have seen the spread of fair trade organizations and practices that have been further fueled as direct practices aiming at the same time to criticize austerity policies and to build alternatives (Boström, Micheletti, and Oosterveer 2019; Monticelli and della Porta 2019). By consuming certain products or choosing to do business only with banks committed to uphold moral and ethical standards, individuals may try and affect the balance of economic power on a broad scale.

- *However, antiglobalization can hardly be reduced to sets of individuals with similar views and behavior.* Rather than on individual characteristics, it may also be interesting to concentrate on the properties of the events into which conflictual interactions take place between powerholders and their opponents; as well as in events in which individuals and organizations identifying with a cause meet to discuss strategies, to elaborate platforms and review their agendas. Global justice activists have been particularly good at staging events – or disrupting opponents' events – with a strong emotional impact over public opinion and participants alike. Already before Seattle, periodical meetings by international bodies associated with the neoliberal agenda, such as the World Trade Organization, the International Monetary Fund, the World Bank, or the G8, have provided the opportunity for a string of highly visible, very well attended demonstrations trying to both disrupt the specific gatherings and draw people's attention toward alternative agenda. Events promoted by global justice activists, most notably the World Social Forum gatherings in Porto Alegre and in Mumbai, their European counterparts in Florence (2001), Paris (2003), or London (2004), the corresponding meetings in the South, such as the African Social Forum that met first in Bamako, Mali, in January 2002, all confirmed the vitality and strength of the "movement of movements" (Pianta 2001). Below the global level, critics of globalization have promoted thousands of events, ranging from confrontational demonstrations to presentations of reports or press releases, from religious vigils to squatting into military buildings. Located anywhere from the national to the very local level, those events also support popular views about the existence of a distinctive anti-globalization movement. As the Great Recession spread, protests shifted in scale, with very large waves organized by national networks of organizations mobilized against home evictions, cuts in welfare, privatization of public services, and the like. Long-lost protest camps in highly symbolic public spaces became, for a while, most lively innovation in the repertoire of contention, allowing for highly visible contestation of the existing order, but also the prefiguration of a different world.

- *Other times, by* global justice movement *are actually meant, first and foremost, the* organizations *operating on those issues*. The opposition to neoliberal globalization has been conducted by broad coalitions of organizations.

Some – probably most – of them had a long history of political and social activism, well spread over the political spectrum. In Seattle as well as in Genoa or elsewhere, involved in the demonstrations were established political parties, mostly if not exclusively from the left; trade unions, farmers, and other workers' organizations; ethnic organizations representing both native populations and migrant groups; consumers associations challenging multinational companies; religious organizations and church groups; environmental groups; women's associations; radical autonomous youth centers (Italy's *centri sociali*); and the like. But the criticism of neoliberal globalization has also produced specific organizations, such as Attac, who advocate the so-called Tobin tax to reduce financial gains in the international stock market; People's Global Action, a coalition of hundreds of groups in the North and the South; or the Rete Lilliput, a net of groupings, associations, and individuals active in Italy on environmental, fair trade, and social justice issues. Beyond the global justice movement, also in other recent mobilizations. The role of organizations that are not directly political is particularly worth mentioning. The spread of fair trade practices is facilitated by the existence of extended networks of cooperatives and small retail operators in the West, who try somehow to reach a balance between ethic-driven public action and market requirements. The reproduction of countercultural networks linking radical activists from all over the place is likewise facilitated by the existence of alternative cafes, bookshops, social and cultural centers, offering meeting points – as well as at times accommodation – to people identifying with radical milieus. From a totally different perspective, the network of Islamic schools, mosques, and other institutions offering support to fundamentalist versions of Islam may also be regarded as providing the organizational infrastructure for the diffusion of that particular version of the opposition to Western globalization (Bennani-Chraïbi and Fillieule 2003). In 2011, the spreading of protest camps from Tahrir in Cairo to Puerta del Sol in Madrid and Sintagma in Athens – and then to Gezi Park in Istanbul and Maidan in Ukraine, built on existing organizational networks at various geographical levels (della Porta and Mattoni 2014). Whatever their specificity, organizations secure continuity to collective action even when the potential for spontaneous, unmediated participation somehow subsides. They also provide resources and opportunities for action to escalate when opportunities are more favorable; as well as sources for the creation and reproduction of loyalties and collective identities.

1.1 FOUR CORE QUESTIONS FOR SOCIAL MOVEMENT ANALYSIS

As the example of global justice and anti-austerity campaigning suggests, studying social movements means focusing on at least some of the dimensions we have just introduced, as well as, most important, on how ideas, individuals, events, and organizations are linked to each other in broader processes of collective action, with some continuity over time. Given their complex, multidimensional nature, it is no surprise that social movements may be approached in reference to very diverse intellectual questions. In this book, we shall focus on four sets of them, broadly articulated. We shall try to relate them to the broader theoretical and practical concerns that have inspired the analysis of grassroots political action and cultural resistance since the 1960s.

The first set of questions refers to the relationship between structural change and transformations in patterns of social conflict. Can we see social movements as expressions of conflicts? And what conflicts? Have there been changes in the main conflicts addressed by social movements? And along what lines? Is class conflict coming back as dominant cleavage? How do different cleavages interact and intersect?

Another set of questions has to do with the role of cultural representations in social conflict. How are social problems identified as potential objects of collective action? How do certain social actors come to develop a sense of commonality and to identify with the same "collective we"? And how can specific protest events come to be perceived as part of the same conflict? Where do social movement cultures and values originate from? Is the construction of collective identities hampered in liquid post-modernity, or does insecurity fuel the emergence of strong identification with larger or smaller imagined communities?

A third set of questions addresses the process through which values, interests, and ideas get turned into collective action. How does it become possible to mobilize and face the risks and costs of protest activity? What is the role of identities and symbols, emotions, organizations, and networks in explaining the start and persistence of collective action? What forms do organizations take in their attempts to maximize the strength of collective challenges and their outcomes but also to develop new knowledge and prefigure a different future?

Finally, it has frequently been asked, how does a certain social, political, and/or cultural context affect social movements' chances of success, and the forms they take? What explains the varying intensity over time of collective violence and other types of public challenges against power holders? Do the traits of political systems and their attitudes toward citizens' demands influence challengers' impact in the political arena? How do protest tactics and strategies adapt to or challenge the closing down and opening up of opportunities? And how do movements themselves construct and appropriate opportunities even in moments of extensive threats?

While these questions certainly do not entirely reflect the richness of current debates on collective action and social movements, they have surely played a significant role in shaping discussions over the last decades. Indeed, the 1960s were important because they saw not only an increase in new forms of political participation but also a change in the main conflictual issues. Traditionally, social movements had focused mainly on issues of labor and nation: since the 1960s, "new social movements" emerged instead on concerns such as women's liberation and environmental protection. These changes in the quantity and quality of protest prompted significant innovations in social scientists' approach to those questions. The principal theoretical models available at the time for the interpretation of social conflict – the Marxist model and the structural-functionalist model – both came to be regarded as largely inadequate.

In Europe, scholars confronted with the new wave of protest often relied on Marxism. However, their attempts to explain developments in the forms of conflict in the 1960s encountered a number of problems. The social transformations that occurred after the end of the Second World War had put the centrality of the capital–labor conflict into question. The widening of access to higher education or the entry *en masse* of women into the labor market had created new structural possibilities for conflict, and increased the relevance of other criteria of social stratification – such as gender relations.

Indeed, even the most superficial observer of the 1960s could not help noticing that many of the actors engaged in those conflicts (youth, women, new professional groups) could only partly be related to the class conflicts, which had constituted the principal component of political cleavages in industrial societies (Rokkan 1970; Tilly 2004a). Problems posed by Marxist interpretations did not, however, relate only to doubts about the continued existence of the working class in postindustrial society: they also concerned the logic of the explanatory model. The deterministic element of the Marxist tradition – the conviction that the evolution of social and political conflicts was conditioned largely by the level of development of productive forces and by the dynamic of class relations – was rejected. So was the tendency, particularly strong among orthodox Marxists, to deny the multiplicity of concerns and conflicts within real movements, and to construct, in preference, outlandish images of movements as homogeneous actors with a high level of strategic ability (for a critique: Touraine 1981).

In America, collective action was often seen as crisis behavior. Having reduced collective phenomena to the sum of individual behaviors, psychologically derived theories defined social movements as the manifestation of feelings of deprivation experienced by individuals in relation to other social subjects, and of feelings of aggression resulting from a wide range of frustrated expectations. Phenomena such as the rise of Nazism, the American Civil War, or the movement of black Americans, for example, were considered to be aggressive reactions resulting either from a rapid and unexpected end to periods of economic well-being and of increased expectations on a worldwide scale; or from status inconsistency mechanisms (Davies 1969; Gurr 1970). From a somewhat different but compatible point of view, the emergence of political extremism was also associated with the spread of mass society in which integrative social ties based in the family or the community tended to become fragmented (Gusfield 1963; Kornhauser 1959). Isolation and displacement produced individuals with fewer intellectual, professional and/or political resources, who were particularly vulnerable to the appeal of antidemocratic movements of the right and the left.

To some extent, these problems were shared by the most famous version of structural-functionalist approach, that of Neil Smelser (1962), that saw social movements as the side effects of overrapid social transformation. According to Smelser, in a system made up of balanced subsystems, collective behavior reveals tensions which homoeostatic rebalancing mechanisms cannot absorb in the short term. At times of rapid, large-scale transformations, the emergence of collective behaviors – religious cults, secret societies, political sects, economic Utopias – has a double meaning, reflecting on the one hand, the inability of institutions and social control mechanisms to reproduce social cohesion; on the other, attempts by society to react to crisis situations through the development of shared beliefs, on which to base new foundations for collective solidarity.

Smelser's value-added model of collective behavior consists of six steps: structural conduciveness, i.e., a certain configuration of social structure that may facilitate or constrain the emergence of specific types of collective behavior; structural strain, i.e., the fact that at least some trait of the social system is experienced by a collectivity as a source of tension and problems; growth and spread of generalized belief, i.e., the emergence of a shared interpretation by social actors of their situation and problems; precipitating factors, i.e., stressful events that induce actors to take action; mobilization, i.e., the network and organizational activities that transform potential for action into real action; operation of social control, i.e., the role of social control agencies and other actors in shaping the evolution of collective behavior and its forms (see also Crossley 2002, p. 2; Smelser 1962).

Some scholars regard as unfortunate that Smelser's work came out at the time it did, thus ending up being strongly associated with the crisis of the functionalist paradigm. Despite its problems, his was a major attempt to connect into an integrated model different processes that would have later been treated in sparse order, and to firmly locate social movement analysis in the framework of general sociology (Crossley 2002, p. 53–55). Whatever the case, Smelser's approach came to be subsumed under the broader set of approaches viewing social movements as purely reactive responses to social crisis and as the outcome of malintegration, and became the target for the same criticisms. Let us see now how the criticism of Marxist and functionalist approaches were elaborated in relation to the four questions we have identified earlier, but also how those answers where themselves challenged later on.

1.1.1 Is Social Change Creating the Conditions for the Emergence of New Movements?

Given the importance of Marxism in European intellectual debates, it is no surprise that European social sciences were the most eager to explain the rise of the movements of the 1960s and the 1970s in explicit critique of the Marxist models of interpretation of social conflict. Criticism addressed both the most structuralist currents of Marxist thinking, deriving class conflict directly from the mode of production, and those interested in the formation of class consciousness (or class *for itself*). Certainly, scholars of the new movements were not the only ones to be aware of these problems. The same difficulties had been raised by those who had studied the labor movement with the aim of explaining the formation of a collective actor, challenging the widespread idea of an almost automatic transformation of structural strains in conscious behavior (Thompson 1963).

Departing often from a Marxist background, scholars associated with the *new social movements* approach made a decisive contribution to the development of the discussion of these issues by reflecting upon the innovation in the forms and contents of contemporary movements.

Scholars of new movements agreed that conflict among the industrial classes was of decreasing relevance, and similarly that the representation of movements as largely homogeneous subjects was no longer feasible. However, there were differences of emphasis in relation to the possibility of identifying the new central conflict which would characterize the model of the emerging society, defined at times as *postindustrial, post-Fordist, technocratic,* or *programmed.* An influential exponent of this approach, Alain Touraine, was the most explicit in upholding this position: "Social movements are not a marginal rejection of order, they are the central forces fighting one against the other to control the production of society by itself and the action of classes for the shaping of historicity" (Touraine 1981, p. 29). In the industrial society, the ruling class and the popular class oppose each other, as they did in the agrarian and the mercantile societies, and as they will do, according to Touraine, in the programmed society, where new social classes will replace capitalists and the working class as the central actors of the conflict.

The break between movements of the industrial society and new movements was also stressed in the 1980s by the German sociologist Claus Offe (1985). In his view, movements develop a fundamental, metapolitical critique of the social order and of representative democracy, challenging institutional assumptions regarding conventional ways of "doing politics," in the name of a radical democracy. Among the principal innovations of the new movements, in contrast with the workers' movement, are a critical ideology in relation to modernism and progress; decentralized and participatory organizational structures; defense of interpersonal solidarity against the great bureaucracies; and the reclamation of autonomous spaces, rather than material advantages.

Another contribution to the definition of the characteristics of new movements in the programmed society came from Alberto Melucci (1989, 1996). Drawing on the image proposed by Jürgen Habermas of a colonization of lifeworlds, Melucci described contemporary societies as highly differentiated systems, which invest increasingly in the creation of individual autonomous centers of action, at the same time as requiring closer integration, extending control over the motives for human action. In his view, new social movements try to oppose the intrusion of the state and the market into social life, reclaiming the individual's identity and the right to determine his or her private and affective life against the omnipresent and comprehensive manipulation of the system. Unlike the workers' movement, new social movements do not, in

Melucci's view, limit themselves to seeking material gain, but challenge the dominant notions of politics and of society themselves. New actors do not so much ask for an increase in state intervention, to guarantee security and well-being, but especially resist the expansion of political-administrative intervention in daily life and defend personal autonomy.

It would be misleading to speak of the new social movements approach without remarking that its principal exponents have considerably modified their positions over time. Already in the late 1980s, Offe (1990) recognized the influence of traditional-style political action on the practices of the movements. Melucci increasingly concentrated on the mechanisms by which certain representations of the world and of individual and collective identities are produced and transformed over time. Moreover, he went as far as to declare the debate of the "newness" of contemporary movements to be outdated or irrelevant (Melucci 1996).

This perspective had – and still has – several merits. First, it drew attention to the structural determinants of protest, reevaluating the importance of conflict, at a time when non-class conflicts were often ignored. Compared with the then-dominant Marxist interpretations, the theoreticians of new social movements had two specific advantages: they placed once again collective actors at the center of the stage; and they had the ability to capture the innovative characteristics of movements that no longer defined themselves principally in relation to the system of production. Despite the influence of the *new social movements* perspective, attention to the relationship between social structure and collective action is by no means restricted to it. A Marxian approach has continued to inspire numerous analysts of collective action who have maintained the concept of social class a central role in their analyses. In many senses, structural approaches strongly influenced by Marxism can be regarded as the predecessors of the thriving research on global justice and anti-austerity movements (Barker et al. 2014; Barker and Lavalette 2015). Some scholars have attempted to locate the new wave of popular mobilization in the global South as well as within the Western world in the context of much larger processes of economic restructuring on a global scale, and from a long term historical perspective, broadly inspired by Wallerstein's theory of the world system (Arrighi, Hopkins, and Wallerstein 1989; Reifer 2004; Silver 2003).

In explicit critique of analyses suggesting the demise of social conflict and its individualization, and most explicitly the end of conflict about distributive stakes, many scholars regard the crisis of the workers' movement in the 1980s and 1990s, following financial restructuring at the global level, as a largely conjunctural phenomenon. Systemic failure to meet the expectations of the working class from developing countries will fuel a new wave of sustained class conflicts, that will also reflect the growing feminization of the labor force and its stronger ethnic dimension, following mass migration dynamics (Arrighi and Silver 1999). The increasing relevance of "global justice" as a central concern (della Porta 2006) seems to support these arguments. Moreover, and rather unexpectedly, social movements have developed in the South, bridging frames and organizational structures with their northern counterparts. Especially in some geographical areas (such as Latin

America and the Far East) social movement research developed, often within a Gramscian approach, stressing the role of cultural hegemony. Not only research indicated that the class conflicts was well alive in many parts of the world, with a bias view of its decline deriving from a culturally bias focus on the North–West, but what is more Marxism was revisited as a potentially useful approach also to understand the growing focus on social inequality even at the core of the capitalist system (Silver and Karatasly 2014; della Porta 2015a; della Porta 2017b; Cini, Chironi, Dropalova and Tomasello 2018).

Another important attempt to relate social structural change to mass collective action has come from Manuel Castells (Castells 1983, 1997). In an earlier phase of his work, Castell has contributed to our understanding of the emergence of urban social movements by stressing the importance of consumption processes (in particular of collective consumption of public services and public goods) for class relations, by moving the focus of class analysis from capitalist relations within the workplace to social relations in the urban community (Castells, 1983). Later, Castells has linked the growing relevance of conflicts on identity both in the West (e.g. the women's movement) and in the South (e.g. Zapatistas, religious fundamentalisms, etc.) to the emergence of a "network society," where new information technologies play a central role.

Yet another original effort to link structural analysis and social movement analysis has been inspired by French sociologist Pierre Bourdieu. Researchers engaged in the analysis of cultural habits (or the cultural predispositions produced by processes of socialization) as well as their structural determinants have used Bourdieu's insights to explore specific instances of political conflicts, stressing their cultural meanings within the specific fields to which individuals belong. Going beyond economic interests, some scholars explained indeed social movement activism as following needs and desires that derive from values and norms that are typical of specific cultures (or fields). In this sense, action is not rational, but reasonable (Bourdieu 1992). In the Bourdesian perspective, pragmatic sociology has looked at social movements as carriers of broad cultural justifications and shifting capitalist conceptions (Boltanski and Chiappello 2005; Boltanski and Thevenot 1999). From a different angle, and with explicit reference to general theory à la Smelser, Crossley (2002) has used Bourdieu's key concepts of habitus, structure, and agency to propose a new theoretical model, able to integrate the insights from European and American approaches over the years. In doing so, he has proceeded in parallel with other theoretical work in the broader framework of structuration theory (Livesay 2002; Sewell 1992).

A major criticism of new social movements theory has been that it took as foundational characteristics of new social movements certain traits that were not necessarily new and far from generalizable – such as activists' middle class origins, or loose organizational forms (see e.g. Calhoun 1993; Kriesi et al. 1995; Rudig 1990). Structural approaches in general have also been faulted for failing to specify the mechanisms leading from structural tensions to action. In fairness, this criticism does not apply to Melucci's work, and only partially to Touraine's and

Bourdieu's (in any case, the latter's overall influence over social movement studies has been quite limited); while it is surely appropriate for scholars like Offe or Castells, or world system theorists, whose focus is clearly not on micro or meso processes. Certainly, it developed general theorization upon a specific historical context, considering as broad historical trends also some contingent transformations that affected especially some specific geopolitical areas (della Porta 2015a). Whatever the case, the approaches presented here must be regarded first of all as theories of social conflict, more specifically, of the impact of structural transformations over stakes and forms of conflict. And it is fair to say that the questions more directly related to the development of collective action have been more cogently addressed by other intellectual traditions.

1.1.2   How Do We Define Issues as Worthy Objects, and Actors as Worthy Subjects, of Collective Action?

In the 1950s and 1960s, students of collective behavior tended to classify under the same heading phenomena as diverse as crowds, movements, panic, manias, fashions, and so on. Two problems arose from this. On the one hand, although many of them defined movements as purposeful phenomena, students of collective behavior placed more attention on unexpected dynamics – such as circular reactions – rather than on deliberate organizational strategies or, more generally, on strategies devised by actors. As James Coleman recalled (1990, p. 479), the hypothesis that situations of frustration, rootlessness, deprivation and social crisis automatically produce revolts reduces collective action to an agglomeration of individual behaviors. Functionalism so ignores the dynamics by which feelings experienced at the (micro) level of the individual give rise to (macro) phenomena such as social movements or revolutions.

One response to these theoretical gaps has come from symbolic interactionists close to the so-called Chicago School, credited with having developed the analysis of collective behavior as a specialist field within sociology. The concept of collective *behavior* – contrasted with that of collective psychology – indicated the shift of attention from the motivation of individuals to their observable actions. Already in the 1920s, the founders of this approach – among them, Robert E. Park and Ernest W. Burgess – had stressed that collective phenomena do not simply reflect social crisis but rather produce new norms and new solidarities, and viewed social movements as engines of change, primarily in relation to values systems. Subsequently, other students of collective behavior were to make reference to the tenets of the Chicago School, focusing their attention on situations of rapid change in social structures and prescriptions (Blumer 1951; Gusfield 1963; Turner and Killian 1987 [1957]). Tendencies toward large-scale organizations, population mobility, technological innovation, mass communications, and the decline of traditional cultural forms were all considered to be emerging conditions pushing individuals to search for new patterns of social organization. Collective behavior was in fact defined as behavior concerned with *change* (for example, Blumer 1951, p. 199), and social movements as both an integral part of the normal functioning of society and the expression of a wider process of transformation.

Rooted in symbolic interactionism, the contemporary school of collective behavior sees particular relevance in the meaning actors attribute to social structures; and the less structured the situations faced by the individual, the more relevant this aspect appears to be. When existing systems of meaning do not constitute a sufficient basis for social action, new norms emerge, defining the existing situation as unjust and providing a justification for action (Turner and Killian 1987, p. 259). As an activity born outside preestablished social definitions, collective behavior is located beyond existing norms and ordered social relations. The study of collective behavior thus concentrates on the transformation of institutional behaviors through the action of emergent normative definitions. These definitions appear when the traditional normative structure comes into conflict with a continually evolving situation. As Blumer (1951, p. 169) put it:

> *Sociology in general is interested in studying the social order and its constituents (customs, rule, institution, etc.) as they are. Collective behavior is concerned in studying the way in which the social order comes to existence in the sense of the emergence and solidification of new forms of collective behavior.*

Change, in fact, is conceived of as part of the physiological functioning of the system: social movements are accompanied by the emergence of new rules and norms, and represent attempts to transform existing norms. For example, Gusfield (1963) saw the prohibitionist movement as an area of conflict between social systems, cultures and groups of different status.

The genesis of social movements is in the coexistence of contrasting values systems and of groups in conflict with each other. These are regarded as distinctive parts of social life (Killian 1964, p. 433). Changes in the social structure and in the normative order are interpreted within a process of cultural evolution through which new ideas emerge in the minds of individuals. When traditional norms no longer succeed in providing a satisfactory structure for behavior, the individual is forced to challenge the social order through various forms of nonconformity. A social movement develops when a feeling of dissatisfaction spreads, and insufficiently flexible institutions are unable to respond.

The sociology of social movements owes many of its insights to students of the collective behavior school. For the first time, collective movements are defined as meaningful acts, driving often necessary and beneficial social change. Observations of processes of interaction determined by collective action moreover constitute important foundations for those who, in more recent times, have taken on the task of understanding movement dynamics. The emphasis on empirical research has led to experimentation with new techniques, providing through various methods of field research a valid integration of archive data. Since the 1980s, the interactionist version of the theory of collective behavior has stressed the processes of symbolic production and of construction of identity, both of which are essential components of collective behavior. This has led to a research program that has lasted over time, as demonstrated by the work of scholars such as Joe Gusfield (1963), and that has become at the same time very influential and diversified (Eyerman and Jamison 1991; Melucci 1996; Oliver and Johnston 2000; Oliver and Snow 1995).

In the 1990s, however, some researchers grew dissatisfied with a view of the role of culture in collective action that they regarded as too strategic and rationalistic, in particular by scholars like Snow and Benford (1992) that were conversant with resource mobilization theory. They started to re-emphasize again the part played by emotions in the production and reproduction of social movements. In their view, symbolic production is not only (or mainly) strategically oriented, but it involves feelings and emotions. Moral shocks developing when deeply held rules and norms are broken are often first step in the individual mobilization and, indeed, protest organizations work at transforming fear in moral indignation and anger (Jasper 1997: 107–114). Movements indeed produce condensing symbols and rhetoric oriented to rise various types of emotions in what has been defined as a libidinal economy of movements. As Jasper (1997, p. 220) observed, "Virtually, all the pleasures that humans derive from social life are found in protest movements: a sense of community and identity; ongoing companionship and bonds with others; the variety and challenge of conversation, cooperation and competition. Some of the pleasures are not available in the routines of life."

The stress on social movement as agents of normative change, that was present in the Chicago School, has been revisited in recent times of accelerated transformation within an emerging concern in social movement studies with "great transformations" as well as protests that – such as the protest camps – triggered big mobilizations (della Porta 2018b). Especially, as protests spread, new norms tend to emerge in the open spaces created by the social movements themselves. Such spaces allow for the development of intense emotions as well as the spreading of alternative visions through various forms of prefigurative politics oriented to practice changes (Wagner-Pacifici and Ruggiero 2018).

It is worth noting at least two main problems generated by the collective behavior perspective. On the one hand, despite defining movements as purposeful phenomena, many students of collective behavior placed more attention on unexpected dynamics – such as circular reactions – rather than on deliberate organizational strategies or, more generally, on strategies devised by rational, strategic actors. On the other hand, focusing on the empirical analysis of behavior, they are often limited to a description – albeit detailed – of reality, without devoting much attention to the structural origins of conflicts which subsequently well up in particular movements. While structuralist approaches like the new social movements dealt with the latter shortcoming, organizational perspective like the resource mobilization theory addressed the former. To its basic tenets we now turn.

1.1.3   How Is Collective Action Possible?

In deliberate contrast to conceptualizations of social movements as irrational, largely reactive phenomena, some American sociologists in the 1970s started to reflect on the processes by which the resources necessary for collective action are mobilized. In their view, collective movements constitute an extension of the conventional forms of political action; the actors engage in this act in a strategic way, following their interests; organizations and movement "entrepreneurs" have an essential role in the mobilization of collective resources on which action is founded. Movements are therefore part of the normal political process. Stressing the external obstacles and incentives, numerous pieces of research have examined the variety of resources to be mobilized, the links which social movements have with their allies, the tactics used by society to control or incorporate collective action, and its results. The basic questions addressed relate to the evaluation of costs and benefits of participation in social movement organizations.

In early contributions in this vein, Mayer Zald (McCarthy and Zald 1987; Zald and Ash 1966), Anthony Oberschall (1973, 1980) and Charles Tilly (1978) defined social movements as rational, purposeful, and organized actions. Collective action derives, according to this perspective, from a calculation of the costs and benefits, influenced by the presence of resources – in particular, by organization and by the strategic interactions necessary for the development of a social movement. In a historical situation in which feelings of unease, differences of opinion, conflicts of interest and opposing ideologies are always present, the emergence of collective action cannot be explained simply as having been caused by these elements. It is not enough to discover the existence of tensions and structural conflicts: we also have to study the conditions which enable discontent to be transformed into mobilization. The capacity for mobilization depends on the material resources (work, money, concrete benefits, services) and/or nonmaterial resources (authority, moral engagement, faith, friendship) available to the group. These resources are distributed across multiple objectives according to a rational calculation of costs and benefits. Beyond the existence of tensions, mobilization derives from the way in which social movements are able to organize discontent, reduce the costs of action, utilize and create solidarity networks, share incentives among members, and achieve external consensus. The type and nature of the resources available explain the tactical choices made by movements and the consequences of collective action on the social and political system (Edwards and McCarthy 2004; McCarthy and Zald 1987).

The existence of solidarity networks once again questioned a widely spread assumption at the time, namely, that movement recruits are mainly isolated and rootless individuals who seek to immerse themselves in the mass as a surrogate for their social marginalization. According to rational approaches, mobilization can thus be explained as being more than the gratification of pursuing a collective good; it also promotes the existence of horizontal solidarity links, within the collective, and vertical links, integrating different collectives. On the basis of a wide range of empirical research, one can therefore foresee this phenomenon:

> *Participants in popular disturbances and activists in opposition organizations will be recruited primarily from previously active and relatively well-integrated individuals within the collectivity, whereas socially isolated, atomized, and uprooted individuals will be underrepresented, at least until the movement has become substantial.*

(Oberschall 1973, p. 135)

Accordingly, scholars of resource mobilization concentrate their attention on how collective actors operate, how they acquire resources and mobilize support, both within and without their adherents' group.

Over the years, research on social movement organizations has extended its attention to the relations between organizations and the dynamics going on in organizational populations. Increasingly sophisticated network studies have looked at the interactions between the organizations and individuals identified with social movements (Diani 2015; Diani and McAdam 2003; Krinsky and Crossley 2014; Mische 2008). Concepts and methods borrowed from organizational theory have been applied to the study of the factors behind organizations' emergence and survival, again with reference to both the national and the global sphere (Atouba and Shumate 2010; Davis et al. 2008; Den Hond, De Bakker, and Smith 2015; Smith et al. 2018; Smith and Wiest 2012; Wijk et al. 2013).

The definition of social movements as conscious actors making *rational choices* is among the most important innovations of the resource mobilization approach. However, it has been the target of several criticisms. It has been charged with indifference to the structural sources of conflict and the specific stakes for the control of which social actors mobilize (Melucci 1989; Piven and Cloward 1992). Its emphasis on the resources controlled by a few political entrepreneurs, at the cost of overlooking the self-organization potential by the most dispossessed social groups, has also been criticized (Piven and Cloward 1992). Finally, it has been noted that in its explanation of collective action this approach overdoes the rationality of collective action, not taking the role of emotions adequately into account (Goodwin, Jasper, and Polletta 2001). In fact, as some of the most influential proponents of this approach admitted, "early resource mobilization models exaggerate the centrality of deliberative strategic decisions to social movements" (McAdam, Tarrow, and Tilly 2001, p. 7), overemphasizing similarities between social movements and interest politics. As in organizational sociology neo-institutionalism focused attention to appropriateness rather than rationality, also social movement studies tended to give more attention to the importance of norms over means and on prefiguration as anticipation of the future (Tavory and Eliasoph 2013).

1.1.4   What Determines the Forms and Intensity of Collective Action?

A most cogent and systematic response to this question has come from the perspective usually defined as "political process" (McAdam 1982; Tilly 1978). This approach shares with resource mobilization theory a strategic view of action – so much so that they are sometimes treated as a unified perspective – but pays more systematic attention to the political and institutional environment in which social movements operate. The central focus of "political process" theories is the relationship between institutional political actors and protest. In challenging a given political order, social movements interact with actors who enjoy a consolidated position in the polity. Charles Tilly (1978, p. 53) famously spoke of movements as "challengers," contrasting them to established members of a given polity. The concept that has had the greatest success in defining the properties of the external environment, relevant to the development of social movements, is that of "political opportunity structure." Peter Eisinger (1973) used this concept in a comparison of the results of protest in different American cities, focusing on the degree of openness (or closure) of the local political system. Other empirical research indicated important new variables, such as electoral instability (Piven and Cloward 1977), the availability of influential allies (Gamson 1990), and tolerance for protest among the elite (Jenkins and Perrow 1977). Sidney Tarrow integrated these empirical observations into a theoretical framework for his study of protest cycles in Italy, singling out the degree of openness or closure of formal political access, the degree of stability or instability of political alignments, the availability and strategic posture of potential allies and political conflicts between and within elites (Tarrow 1989, 1994).

To these variables others have been added, relating to the institutional conditions that regulate agenda-setting and decision-making processes. Characteristics relating to the functional division of power and also to geographical decentralization have been analyzed in order to understand the origins of protest and the forms it has taken. In general, the aim has been to observe which stable or 'mobile' characteristics of the political system influence the growth of less institutionalized political action in the course of what are defined as protest cycles (Tarrow 1989), as well as the forms these actions take in different historical contexts (Tilly 1978). The comparison between different political systems (for some pioneering works, see Kitschelt 1986; Kriesi et al. 1995; della Porta 1995) enabled the central theme of relationships between social movements and the institutional political system to be studied in depth.

The *political process* approach succeeded in shifting attention toward interactions between new and traditional actors, and between less conventional forms of action and institutionalized systems of interest representation. In this way, it is no longer possible to define movements as phenomena that are, of necessity, marginal and anti-institutional, expressions of dysfunctions of the system. A more fruitful route toward the interpretation of the political dimension of contemporary movements has been established.

One should not ignore, however, some persisting areas of difficulty. On the one hand, supporters of this perspective continue to debate delicate problems such as the choice of the most appropriate indicators to measure complex institutional phenomena. First, the lack of consensus on the relevant dimensions of the concept of political opportunities resulted in their exponential growth. Early studies of political opportunities focused on a small number of variables. Since the 1980s, however, the addition of new variables to the original set has expanded the explanatory power of the concept, but reduced its specificity. The concept runs the risk of becoming a 'dustbin' for any and every variable relevant to the development of social movements. Most of the concept's problems arise from the way in which it has been developed, picking up variables from a variety of studies on a variety of movements. This accumulation of heterogeneous variables reflecting different authors' concerns and ideas has resulted in a concept which, to quote Sartori (1970), denotes much but connotes little. Particularly in international comparative studies, it is impossible to handle the large number of variables and assess properly their explanatory power. Focus on structural variables might shift attention away from how norms and values, referring in particular to movements goals (or discursive opportunities), influence movement strategies as well as their chances of success (Goodwin 2011; Goodwin and Jasper 1999; Jasper 2018).

A second problem arises when we wish to distinguish between 'objective' reality and its social construction (Berger and Luckmann 1969). Some changes in the political opportunity structure do not have any effect on a social movement unless they are perceived as important by the movement itself. Structural availability must be filtered through a process of 'cognitive liberation' in order to unleash turmoil (McAdam 1986). For protest to emerge, activists must believe that an opportunity exists, that they have the power to bring about change and they must blame the system for the problem. Looking at structural opportunities without considering the cognitive processes that intervene between structure and action can be very misleading. It is important, therefore, to analyze activists' understandings of available opportunities, the lenses through which they view potential opportunities for their movements (Gamson and Meyer 1996). Perceptions of state response may be particularly influenced, for instance, by its more dramatic manifestations, such as repression, causing the less visible responses, such as negotiation, to be overlooked.

The political process approach has also been criticized externally for its tendency to adopt a kind of "political reductionism" (Melucci 1987, 1989). In effect, its proponents have paid little attention to the fact that many contemporary movements (of youth, women, homosexuals or minority ethnic groups) have developed within a political context and in a climate of cultural innovation at the same time (Melucci 1996; Rupp and Taylor 1987). Lastly – as we have already noted when introducing resource mobilization theories – rationalist approaches to the study of collective action have tended to neglect the structural origins of protest. Other scholars, often associated with the new movements approach, have long pointed at this limit, by raising attention to the cultural dimension, while more recently Marxist approaches have returned upon the relevance of the interaction between the state and the market within the evolution of capitalism (Barker et al. 2014; della Porta 2015a). Within this perspective, in a moment in which movements tend to proliferate even with a closing down of political opportunities, attention went to the role of socioeconomic threats as triggers for collective action (ibid.).

Faced with some relevant transformations in the two main sources of opportunities for movements – the nation-state and the political parties – research developed in two main directions. On the one hand, and especially in Europe, attention focused on the role played by movements, not just within the political system, but also within the public sphere. In this direction, the discursive opportunities – i.e., the presence of dominant public discourses on certain controversial issues, which are likely to affect movements' chances of success – have been stressed (Koopmans and Statham 1999). Moreover, more and more attention has been paid to transnational opportunities, or, better said, to a multilevel opportunity structure for movements (della Porta and Tarrow 2005). The development of the European Union as an arena for movement demands has been discussed more in depth (della Porta and Caiani 2009). Considering movements as part and parcel of the political system, an increasing number of studies has also focused on their effects, especially in terms of policy process and policy decisions (Bosi, Giugni, and Uba 2015). What is more, while social movements had been traditionally considered as 'strangers at the gate' of the political system (Tarrow 2012), in the turmoil of the Great Regression, social movements have been very effective in penetrating electoral politics through referendums from below as well as the proliferation of movements' parties (della Porta, O'Connor et al. 2017; della Porta, Fernandez et al. 2017).

1.1.5 Are These Questions Specific to Social Movement Analysis?

In this book we shall address these different questions: the social determinants of protest (chapter 2), the role of cultural and symbolic elements (chapters 3–4), the organizational dynamics (chapters 5–6), and the political context for and effects of movements (chapters 7–9). But, before doing that, we still have to discuss whether the questions – and the responses – identified above are peculiar to social movement research. In many cases, these questions address not just social movements but collective action more in general. Collective action broadly refers to individuals, sharing resources in pursuit of collective goods – i.e., goods that cannot be privatized and subtracted to any of the members of the collectivity on behalf of which collective action has taken place. Such goods may be produced within movements, but also in many contexts that normally are not associated with movements. In our notion, the idea of 'collective goods' comprises both public goods *à la* Olson and club goods. For Samuelson (1954), the key characteristics of public goods are non-excludability, and nonrivalrous consumption (i.e., no scarcity once the good is produced). A club good is nonexcludable for club members but excludable for outsiders, possibly (but not necessarily) non-rivalrous for those with access (Buchanan 1965).

For example, political parties also face the problem of mobilizing their members and providing them with incentives to join and somehow support the organization – if anything through the payment of membership fees; so do interest groups only minding the sectoral – often, very parochial – interests of their specific reference groups (Jordan and Maloney 1997; Knoke 1990). Likewise, even political parties or narrow interest groups focus face the problem of adapting their strategies and tactics to changing environments, as the context in which they operate may become more or less favorable, such as through changes in the attitudes of power holders toward specific parties or interest groups' demands, changes in legal opportunities for interest representation, or changes in the cultural models with which ordinary people make sense of their political and social world (Panebianco 1988). From a different angle, many voluntary organizations do not identify any social or political opponent to protest against, and their strategies focus entirely on service delivery rather than advocacy, political representation, or challenges to dominant norms or lifestyles. Even these organizations, however, still face problems of attracting and keeping members, securing the resources necessary to promote action, elaborate the cultural models necessary to pursue goals along the desired lines, and framing their issues in order to make them as attractive as possible to the widest audience as possible (Wilson 2000).

As it happens, analyses of social movements and analyses of collective action at large are inextricably linked. Let us say that the experience of social movements reflects phenomena with more than passing analogies to other instance or political or cultural collective action, taking place within political parties, interest groups, or religious sects. Therefore, when we analyze social movements, we deal with social processes that may also be of interest to researchers who do not define themselves at all as social movement analysts. Accordingly, we feel that a lot of what is presented here may be of interest to a much broader audience.

Recently, there have been several attempts to synthesize scholarship on social movements with the aim of linking it to broader theoretical and/or empirical concerns. Some of these attempts have aimed at integrating social movement theory with general sociological frameworks.

A most ambitious development by social movement scholars, openly criticizing the insularity of the social movements studies community, and also drawing heavily on non-Western materials, has been the Dynamics of Contention (DOC) program (McAdam et al. 2001). The main suggestion coming from this approach has been the possibility to combine the knowledge developed in the fields of social movements with those elaborated on revolutions, democratization, and ethnic conflicts, singling out a field of contentious politics, defined as "episodic, public, collective interaction among makers of claim and their objects when (a) at least one government is a claimant, an object of claims, or a party to the claim and (b) the claims would, if realized, affect the interest of at least one of the claimants" (McAdam, Tarrow, and Tilly 2001, p. 5). As Sidney Tarrow (2015, p. 90) summarized, the contentious politics approach focused on episodes of contention, rather than on individual social movements, looking at the relations of different actors within complex political processes. Advocating a dynamic rather than static use of concepts, the scholars involved in this project have tried to single out general mechanisms of contention, defined as "delimited changes that alter relations among specified sets of elements in identical or closely similar ways over a variety of situations"

(McAdam, Tarrow, and Tilly 2001, pp. 24–25). While criticized for the uncertain status of the concept of causal mechanism as well as for the lack of capacity to account for causes and effects of social movements, the contentious politics approach has rightly pointed at the importance to bridge the field of social movements to other cognate fields (see Diani et al. 2003; Tarrow 2015 for discussions of the approach).

1.2   WHAT IS DISTINCTIVE IN SOCIAL MOVEMENTS?

If the core questions addressed by social movement analysts are not necessarily specific, one can wonder whether social movements have an analytical peculiarity that justifies the development of a distinctive field of research. In order to address this question, we have to discuss the concept of social movement.

1.2.1   The Concept of Social Movement

In a number of pieces, Mario Diani (1992, 1995, 2013; Diani and Bison 2004) has portrayed social movements as a distinct social process, characterized by the fact that actors engaged in collective action:

- hold conflictual orientations to clearly identified opponents.
- connect through dense, informal networks connect them.
- share a distinct collective identity.

We can look at these actions in more detail:

- *Conflictual collective action.* Social movement actors are engaged in political and/or cultural conflicts, meant to promote or oppose social change. By conflict we mean an oppositional relationship between actors who seek control of the same stake – be it political, economic, or cultural power – and in the process make negative claims on each other – i.e., demands which, if realized, would damage the interests of the other actors (Tilly 1978; Touraine 1981, p. 80–84). Accordingly, addressing collective problems, producing public goods, or expressing support to some moral values or principles does not automatically correspond to social movement action; the latter requires the identification of targets for collective efforts, specifically articulated in social or political terms. For example, collective action challenging austerity policies in countries like Greece (Kotronaki 2013; Seferiades 2013; Diani and Kousis 2014) is conflictual to the extent that organizations like the European Commission or the International Monetary Fund are blamed not because of their officials' misconduct or specific policy mistakes, but as representatives of distinct coalitions of interests. When collective action focuses exclusively on the behavior and/or the legitimacy of specific individuals, or blames problems on the humankind as a whole, on natural disasters or divine will, then it is difficult to speak of social movement processes (Melucci 1996, Part I).

- *Dense informal networks.* Dense informal networks differentiate social movement processes from the innumerable instances in which collective action takes place and is coordinated mostly within the boundaries of specific organizations. A social movement process is in place to the extent that both individual and organized actors, while keeping their autonomy and independence, engage in sustained exchanges of resources in pursue of common goals. The coordination of specific initiatives, the regulation of individual actors' conduct, and the definition of strategies all depend on permanent negotiations between the individuals and the organizations involved in collective action. No single organized actor, no matter how powerful, can claim to represent a movement as a whole. It follows that more opportunities arise for highly committed and/or skilled individuals to play an independent role in the political process, than would be the case when action is concentrated within formal organizations.

- *Collective identity.* Social movements are not merely the sum of protest events on certain issues, or even of specific campaigns. To the contrary, a social movement process is in place only when collective identities develop, which go beyond specific campaigns and initiatives. Collective identity is strongly associated with recognition and the creation of connectedness (Pizzorno 1996; Tilly 2005). It brings with it a sense of common purpose and shared commitment to a cause, which enables single activists and/or organizations to regard themselves as inextricably linked to other actors, not necessarily identical but surely compatible, in a broader collective mobilization (Touraine 1981). For example, research on environmentalism suggested that animal rights activism were more distinctive and less identified with environmentalism in Britain than in Italy: as a result, it made much more sense to regard the two as involved in the same movement process in the latter than in the former (Rootes 2003). Likewise, not all networks between people holding similar beliefs and orientations necessarily reflect social movement processes: for example, the international Zapatista support network was not regarded by all analysts as a social movement because of the lack of a focused identity and the resulting bonds, even though resources of solidarity certainly circulated through it (Olesen 2004)). Even people who participated in major events like those that ultimately led to the demise of president Mubarak in Egypt in 2011 did not necessarily share long-term identities beyond the common goal of toppling the dictator (Sowers and Toensing 2012; Diani and Moffatt 2016).

Collective identity building also entails actors establishing connections between different occurrences, private and public, located at different points in time and space, which are relevant to their experience, and weaving them in broader, encompassing narratives (Melucci 1996; Tilly 2005). As a result, organizational and individual actors involved in collective action no longer merely pursue specific goals, but come to regard themselves as elements of much larger and encompassing processes of change – or resistance to change. For example, in 2011, participants in events as distant as the Indignados square occupations in Spain and the anti-government protests in Tunisia or Egypt might have felt to be linked together through processes of identity building based upon the shared call for greater democracy and supranational communication. Within social movements, membership criteria are extremely unstable and ultimately dependent on mutual recognition between actors; the activity of boundary definition – i.e., of defining who is and who is not part of the network – indeed plays a central role in the emergence and shaping of collective action (Melucci 1996, ch.3).

Looking at different combinations of these three elements enables us to contrast social movements to other collective action processes. Here we provide a few examples; however, we have to keep in mind that no empirical episode of collective action – those that we conventionally define as environmental movements, solidarity movements, disabled movements, or the like – fully corresponds to any pure type. To the contrary, we can normally detect more than one process within any empirical instance of collective action. The exploration of how such processes interact with each other represents a fundamental step of social movement analysis.

1.2.2   Conflictual and Consensual Collective Action

It is not rare to witness broad coalitions of charities and other voluntary associations mobilizing on solidarity issues, such as on social exclusion in domestic politics, or on development or human rights issues in an international perspective, and to refer to them as social movements. In many cases, however, they might be best characterized as *consensus movements*. In both social movement and consensus movement dynamics, actors share solidarity and an interpretation of the world, enabling them to link specific acts and events in a longer time perspective. However, in the latter sustained collective action does not take a conflictual element. Collective goods are often produced through cooperative efforts that neither imply nor require the identification of specific adversaries, trying to reduce the assets and opportunities of one's group or preventing chances to expand them. Prospected solutions do not imply redistribution of power nor alterations in social structure but focus instead on service delivery, self-help, and personal and community empowerment. Likewise, the practice and promotion of alternative lifestyles need not the presence of opponents defined in social and political terms. Collective actors may fight ethereal adversaries, ranging from bad or conventional taste, in the case of artistic and style-oriented movements, to "the inner enemy," in the case of some religious movements, without necessarily blaming any social actors for the state of things they intend to modify.

However, insisting on the presence of conflict as a distinctive trait of movements need not force social movement analysts away from the investigation of those instances of collective action where a conflict is difficult to identify, such as those oriented to personal change (e.g. the *human potential movement*, or many countercultural, alternative lifestyle networks) and those focusing on the delivery of some kind of help or assistance to an aggrieved collectivity (e.g., solidarity movements: Giugni and Passy 2001; Brown and Yaffe 2013). This perspective implies, instead, that analysts recognize the presence of several social mechanisms or dynamics within each instance of collective action, and focus their efforts on exploring how such mechanisms operate and interact with each other.

1.2.3   Social Movements, Events, and Coalitions

We have a social movement dynamic going on when single episodes of collective action are perceived as components of a longer-lasting action, rather than discrete events; and when those who are engaged in them feel linked by ties of solidarity and of ideal communion with protagonists of other analogous mobilizations. Identity building also means that a sense of collective belonging can be maintained even after a specific initiative or a particular campaign has come to an end. The persistence of these feelings will have at least two important consequences. First, it will make the revival of mobilization in relation to the same goals easier, whenever favorable conditions recur. Movements often oscillate between brief phases of intense public activity and long latent periods (Melucci 1996) in which self-reflection and cultural production prevail. The trust and solidarity links, activated in the European antinuclear movements during the mobilizations of the second half of the 1970s, for example, represented the base on which a new wave of protests gathered momentum in the wake of the Chernobyl incident in 1986 (Flam 1994a). Second, representations of the world and collective identities that developed in a certain period can also facilitate, through a gradual transformation, the development of new movements and new solidarities. For example, the close relationship existing in several countries between different waves of activism has been noted on a number of occasions (Dalton 2008; Grasso 2016; della Porta 2018b).

Reference to other examples of informal networks of collective action, such as coalitions, also illustrates why collective identity is such a crucial feature of social movements. In coalition dynamics, collective actors are densely connected to each other in terms of alliances, and identify explicit opponents, but those links are not necessarily backed by strong identity links. The networks between actors mobilizing on a common goal take a purely contingent and instrumental nature. Resource mobilization and campaigning is then conducted mainly through exchanges and pooling of resources between distinct groups and organizations. The latter rather than the network are the main source of participants' identities and loyalties. Actors instrumentally share resources in order to achieve specific goals, yet do not develop any particular sense of belonging and of common future during the process. Once a specific battle has been fought, there need not be any longer term legacy in terms of identity and solidarity, nor attempts to connect the specific campaign in a broader framework (see e.g. Lemieux 1997, 1998). Of course, nothing prevents a coalitional dynamic from evolving into a social movement one, but it is still important to recognize the analytical difference between the two processes (Diani 2015).

It is worth stressing that associating movements to a distinctive collective identity implies no assumptions about the homogeneity of the actors sharing that identity. We have a social movement identity dynamic to the extent that groups and/or individuals feel part of a collectivity, mobilized to support or oppose social change; that they identify shared elements in their past, present, and future experiences; and that other social or political actors be held responsible for the state of affairs being challenged. Whether a specific collective identity will be inclusive or exclusive, and the degree to which holders of such identity will share one or several traits, is an empirical question (see chapter 4).

1.2.4   Social Movements and Organizational Processes

Social movements have traditionally been compared with political parties and interest groups as different types of political organization (for a classic formulation: Wilson 1973), as well as with religious sects and cults (see e.g. Bromley 2016; Robbins 1988). However, the difference between social movements and these and other organizations does not consist primarily of differences in organizational characteristics or patterns of behavior, but of the fact that social movements are not organizations, not even of a peculiar kind (Oliver 1989; Tilly 1994). They are networks which may either include formal organizations or not, depending on shifting circumstances. As a consequence, a single organization, whatever its dominant traits, is not a social movement. Of course it may be involved in a social movement process, but the two are not identical, as they reflect different organizational principles: "all too often we speak of movement strategy, tactics, leadership, membership, recruitment, division of labor, success and failure – terms that strictly apply only to coherent decision-making entities (i.e., organizations or groups), not to crowds, collectivities, or whole social movements" (Oliver 1989, p. 4).

Treating specific organizations like Oxfam or Greenpeace as *movements* does not add very much to the insights provided by concepts like *public interest group*. Similarly, religious organizations like Nichiren Shoshu or Hare Krishna may be more conveniently analyzed as *sects*. This concept takes into account the greater organizational rigidity and the more hierarchical structure that these organizations display by comparison with social movement networks (Robbins 1988, pp. 150–155). It also recognizes the higher degree of social control that is exerted over members. In contrast, what both "public interest group" and "sect" do not really capture are the interaction processes through which actors with different identities and orientations come to elaborate a shared system of beliefs and a sense of belonging, which exceeds by far the boundaries of any single group or organization, while maintaining at the same time their specificity and distinctive traits.

To shift the emphasis from single organizations to informal networks allows us, furthermore, to appreciate more fully the space reserved for individuals within movements. Individual participation is essential for movements, and one of their characteristics is, indeed, the sense of being involved in a collective endeavor – without having automatically to belong to a specific organization. Strictly speaking, social movements do not have members, but participants. The participation of the individual, detached from specific organizational allegiances is not necessarily limited to single protest events. It can also develop within committees or working groups, or else in public meetings. Alternatively (when the possibility arises), one may support a movement by promoting its ideas and its point of view among institutions, other political actors, or the media. However, the existence of a range of possible ways of becoming involved means that the membership of movements can never be reduced to a single act of adhesion. It consists, rather, of a series of differentiated acts, which, taken together, reinforce the feeling of belonging and of identity.

If social movements are analytically different from social movement organizations, any organization which is involved in a social movement dynamic (i.e., which fulfills the requirements we have indicated: interactions with other actors, conflict, collective identity, and recourse to protest) may be regarded as a "social movement organization" (Diani 2012; 2015, p. 9). This may also hold for bureaucratic interest groups, and even political parties. By saying that political parties may be part of social movements we do not mean to suggest that social movements is a broader theoretical category in which several type of organizations (interest groups, community groups, political parties, and so forth) are represented as many subtypes. Rather, we suggest that under certain and specific conditions some political party may feel itself to be part of a movement and be recognized as such both by other actors in the movement and by the general public. Since the 1980s the Green parties provided a major example of political parties originating from social movements (Richardson and Rootes 1995); more recently, what are now referred to as "movement parties" (Kitschelt 2006) have grown to include political organizations originating from both left-wing and right-wing poles of the political spectrum. They have included parties close to the Indignados and anti-austerity movements like Podemos or Syriza as well as right-wing populist parties like the French Front National or the German Alternative fuer Deutschland (Kriesi and Pappas 2015; della Porta, Fernandez et al. 2017).

One could reasonably object that no matter how strong their identification with a movement, political parties actually perform specific functions at the level of interest representation and in this sense are different from social movements. That differences exist at the functional level is beyond question. Yet, the main peculiarity of social movements does not consist of their specific way of performing the function of interest representation. Of course, their networks of interaction favor the formulation of demands, the promotion of mobilization campaigns and the elaboration and diffusion of beliefs and collective identities. These factors all, in turn, contribute to redefining the cultural and political setting in which the action of interest representation takes place. However, when we focus on the function of interest representation in strict terms, we do not look at the way "the movement" performs this function. We look at the way different specific social movement organizations do this. Whether or not they decide to include participation in elections within their repertoire of action is dependent upon several factors including external opportunities, tactical and/or ideological considerations and their links to other actors in the movement. The mere fact that they decide to do so, however, will not automatically exclude them from the movement. Rather, they will be part of two different systems of action (the party system and the social movement system), where they will play different roles. The way such roles are actually shaped will constitute a crucial area of investigation (see e.g. della Porta, Fernandez et al. 2017).

1.2.5   Social Movements and Protest

Until the early 1970s, debates on social movements emphasized their non-institutionalized nature (see e.g. Alberoni 1984). Even now, the idea that social movements may be distinguished from other political actors because of their adoption of 'unusual' patterns of political behavior is still very popular. Several scholars maintain that the fundamental distinction between movements and other social and political actors is to be found in the contrast between conventional styles of political participation (such as voting or lobbying political representatives) and public protest (Rucht 1995). Protest is undoubtedly a distinctive feature of political movements, on which we shall largely focus in this book; while it is less conspicuous among movements focusing on cultural and personal change, like religious or countercultural ones (Snow 2005).

There are some objections to considering protest a core feature even of political movements. First, public protest plays only a marginal role in movements concerned with personal and cultural change, in religious movements, and the like. Cultural conflict and symbolic challenges often take forms such as the practice of specific lifestyles, the adoption or certain clothes or haircut, and the adoption of rituals that can only be regarded as protest if we stretch the concept to a very considerable degree (Snow 2005). Moreover, even in the political realm it is increasingly debatable whether protest can still be considered an "unconventional," or even violent or "confrontational" activity. Various forms of political protest have become, to an increasing degree, part of the consolidated repertoire of collective action, at least in Western democracies. In general, protest seems no longer restricted to radical sectors, but rather, an option open to a much broader range of actors when they feel their relative position in the political process to come under threat (Dalton 2008; McCarthy, Rafail, and Gromis 2013).

At the same time, however, public protest still differentiates social movements from other types of networks like those referred to as 'epistemic communities' (Haas 1992, 2015; Keck and Sikkink 1998). These communities are organized around networks of individuals and groups with specific scientific and/or managerial competences in distinct policy areas. Like social movements, their members share a common frame of reference and take side on conflictual issues. The forms of structural ties and exchange of resources within those networks are however different from those that tend to characterize social movements. Epistemic communities involve actors usually endowed with decision-making power and certified knowledge, as well as, often, electoral accountability. Instead, social movement actors usually occupy a peripheral position in decision-making processes, and need to mobilize public opinion to maintain their pressure capacity. Even if some forms of protest are "normalized," social movements tend to invent new disruptive forms of action—challenging the state on issues of law and order. It is true that, thanks to new communication technologies, forms of protest online have developed alongside more conventional ones, as illustrated by mail bombings or anonymous hackers entering protected sites of government or corporations (Coleman 2013; McDonald 2015). However, as the waves of collective mobilization at the turn of the century and from 2011 have confirmed, social movement politics is still to a significant extent "politics in the streets" (Gerbaudo 2012; della Porta and Mattoni 2014). The use of protest as a major source of pressure power has relevant effects on the structure and strategy of social movements.

1.3   IN THIS BOOK

In this chapter we identified four broad questions that have recurrently attracted the attention of analysts of social movements since the 1960s. These refer to how changes in the social structure in Western countries, most specifically the passage from an industrial to a post-industrial mode of social organization, might affect the forms of collective action (section 1.1.1); how cultural and symbolic production by social actors enables the identification of social problems as worthy objects of collective action and the construction of collective identity (section 1.1.2); how organizational and individual resources make collective action not only possible but also successful, at least potentially (section 1.1.3); how the forms of action adopted by social movements, their developments over time, and their clustering in broader waves of contention are all affected by the traits of the political and social systems in which social movements operate (section 1.1.4).

For each of these questions we have also identified some of the most influential answers provided by social movement scholars over the years. This has enabled us to introduce, if briefly, the main approaches that have characterized the field in the last decades: most particularly, if not exclusively, the new social movements, the collective behavior, the resource mobilization, and the political process approach. While none of these perspectives can be reduced to just one of the questions we identified, they all speak more neatly to one of such questions. The new social movements perspective can be regarded first and foremost as a theory of how the stakes and the central actors of social conflict are modified under changing structural conditions; the collective behavior approach mainly theorizes the role of symbolic production in shaping collective action and the conditions for the emergence of new issues and/or identities; resource mobilization theory explored the conditions leading to the emergence of collective action among people who might have more than one good reason not to engage in it; finally, the political process approach looks at the forms of collective action and their variation across different political regimes and different points in time.

In the second part of the chapter, we have showed how social movements may be regarded as distinctive social and political processes. In particular, we have identified their distinctiveness in their consisting of informal networks, linking individual and organizational actors engaged in conflictual relations to other actors, on the basis of a shared collective identity (section 1.2.1). This has enabled us to differentiate social movements from a number of other related processes and phenomena. These include collective actions oriented to non-conflictual goals, e.g. in the field of charity work (section 1.2.2); the differences between movements and coalitions, mobilizing on specific issues or events (section 1.2.3); the relationship between political organizations such as parties and traditional interest groups and social movement processes (section 1.2.4); and the role of protest in contemporary movements (section 1.2.5).

As we have repeatedly argued, the questions we have identified are neither restricted to nor specific of social movement analysis, and can be of interest to a much broader spectrum of social and political analysts. At the same time, they are surely central to social movement research as it has developed since the 1960s, hence our decision to organize the rest of the book around such questions. We start with a discussion of the structural bases of contemporary movements (Chapter 2). By this we refer, on the one hand, to the mechanisms by which new social groups and new interests take shape, while other groups and interests which previously held center stage see their relevance declining; and on the other, to the impact that structural changes such as first the growth and then the contraction of public welfare, and the expansion of higher education, have on forms of political participation and, in particular, on noninstitutional participation. The impact of globalization processes is particularly relevant to our discussion.

There follow two chapters dedicated to symbolic production. Chapter 3 shows how cultural elaboration facilitates the definition of social problems as the product of asymmetries of power and conflicts of interest, and the identification of their causes in social and political factors, which are subject to human intervention. In chapter 4, we show how the creation and reinforcement of symbols also represents the base for the development of feelings of identity and solidarity, without which collective action cannot take place.

A third important level of analysis consists of the organizational factors which allow both the production of meaning and the mobilization of resources necessary for action. We take into consideration both informal networking and the more structured component of the organizational dimension. Chapter 5 deals in particular with the analysis of individual participation. We look at the mechanisms behind individual decisions to become engaged in collective action and to sustain their commitment over time, but we also look at how individuals create, through their participation, several opportunities for the development of networks that keep social movements and oppositional milieus together. Chapter 6 concentrates on certain properties of movement organizations, discussing the factors – internal and external – which influence the adoption of certain organizational models, and the consequences that follow for mobilization. It draws in particular our attention to the difference between "organization" and more general principles of "organizing," meaning by that the broader mechanisms through which social actors coordinate their behavior.

The fourth crucial dimension is the interaction between movements and the political system. Movements represent innovative, sometimes radical, elements both in the way in which the political system works, and in its very structure. The characteristics of the political system offer or deny essential opportunities for the development of collective action. It is, furthermore, in reference principally, if not exclusively, to the political system that it becomes possible to value the impact of protest movements and their consequences in the medium term. In Chapter 7, we reconstruct some of the properties of protest cycles which have marked the history of recent decades, and the repertoires of collective action that were formed within these. In Chapter 8, we present certain aspects of the relationship between the configurations of political opportunities and the development of mobilization. In Chapter 9 we discuss, finally, the problem of the effects of movements. While the center of our analysis is represented by political change, we try, however, to pay attention also to the impact of movements on the social and cultural spheres.

CHAPTER 2

Social Changes and Social Movements

The austerity policies implemented during the financial crisis, which from the United States spread to Europe around 2008, have triggered an intense wave of protest, against cuts in public expenditures that added up to privatization of public services and the deregulation of financial and labor markets. Intensifying especially in 2011 in the so called 'Occupy movement', contention has diffused globally in the following years, involving also countries which, as Brazil or Turkey, had been considered on the winning side of neoliberal developments (della Porta 2015a, 2017a).

Beginning with Iceland in 2008, and then spreading to Egypt, Tunisia, Spain, Greece, and the United States, among others, protests targeted the corruption of the political class, seen in both bribes in a concrete sense, and in the privileges granted to lobbies and collusion of interests between public institutions and economic (often financial) powers. In the years to follow, most recently in Perù, Brazil, Russia, Bulgaria, Turkey, France, citizens took the street against what they perceived as a corruption of democracy, defined as source of inequality and people's suffering.

Data collected on the social background of those who protested do not unequivocally confirm either the thesis of the mobilization of a new precariat, or that of a middle-class movement. In all protests,

Social Movements: An Introduction, Third Edition. Donatella della Porta and Mario Diani.

a broad range of social backgrounds is represented, from students, to precarious workers, manual and non-manual dependent workers, petty bourgeoisie and professionals. Over-proportionally young in terms of generation, the protests also see the participation of other age cohorts whose high educational levels do not correspond to winning positions in the labor market. As Goran Therborn (2014, p. 16) noted, in different combinations, the critique to neoliberalism came from pre-capitalist populations (as indigenous people), extra-capitalist "wretched of the earth" (as casual laborers, landless peasants and street vendors), but also workers and emerging middle-class layers. In sum, an alliance needed to develop between pre-capitalist populations, fighting to retain their territory and means of subsistence; surplus masses, excluded from formal employment in the circuits of capitalist production; exploited manufacturing workers across rustbelt and sunbelt zones; new and old middle classes, increasingly encumbered with debt payments to the financial corporations – these constitute the potential social bases for contemporary critiques of the ruling capitalist order.

Anti-austerity protests developed indeed during the Great Recession. Beginning in the 1980s, the core capitalist states experienced a turn toward more free market in so-called neoliberal capitalism and then its crisis. First, the United States and Great Britain, led respectively by Ronald Reagan and Margaret Thatcher, moved toward cuts in the welfare state as justified by an ideology of the free market. As increasing inequalities and reduction of public intervention risked depressing the demand for goods, low interest rates were used, in a sort of private Keynesianism, to support demand – ultimately fueling the 2008 financial crisis. In fact, in that year, the failure of Lehman Brothers produced such a shock that governments decided to come to the rescue, with increasing government debt. Given economic decline in the United States and United Kingdom, coordinated market economies like the EU and Japan – where firms rely more on non-market relations to manage their activities – seemed to demonstrate equal or even superior competitiveness as compared to the liberal market economy, which relies for coordination on competitive market arrangements (Hall and Soskice 2001; Streeck 2010). However, that form of capitalism also moved toward more free market and was hit by the financial crisis. This could be seen especially in the EU, where the trend toward welfare retrenchment was aggravated, especially in the weaker economies, by the monetary union that (together with the fiscal crisis) increased inequalities both among and within member states. With the abandonment of Keynesian types of intervention, which assigned leading functions to fiscal policies, the monetarist orientation of the EU policies – with the renunciation of full employment as a goal and the priority given to price stability – was responsible for the type of crisis that developed in the union (Scharpf, 2011; Stiglitz, 2012, p. 237). The European Monetary Union (EMU) created in fact particular problems for countries with below-average growth, as interest rates proved too high for their economies.

In 2008, the evidence of the crisis at the core of capitalism became dramatic as the attempt to develop public demands through low interest rates showed its fragility. Some countries (with traditionally weak economies) were indeed much harder hit than others. In rich states as well, however, neoliberalism had the effect of exponentially increasing social inequalities, with a very small percentage of winners and a pauperization of the working class, together with a proletarization of the middle class. While the welfare state under Fordism had brought about a decommodification of some goods, subtracted to free market and defined as public services, neoliberalism brought about the privatization and (re)commodification of once-public goods together with a deregulation of the labor market that weakened workers' power. The evolution of the last 30 years or so has deeply transformed the social structures. Fordism is said to have created a two-thirds society, with new social movements emerging from the pacification of class conflict, and even the embourgeoisement of the working class, with the crisis of the 1970s producing a short but radical wave of protest by the excluded one third. The mobilizations of 2011 seem instead to reflect the pauperization of the lower classes as well as the proletarianization of the middle classes, with the growth of the excluded in some countries to about two thirds of the population (della Porta 2015a). As protest spread worldwide, its target was especially social inequality that neoliberalism had produced.

Different from the previous wave of protests against neoliberalism at the turn of the millennium, especially the Global Justice Movement, the anti-austerity protests developed mainly at domestic level, following the different timing, intensity and dynamics of the financial crisis. In fact, anti-austerity protests had very different strength and forms in the different countries with varying capacity to mobilize the heterogeneous social groups that had been hit from neoliberalism and its crisis. In particular, while protest was initially limited in the countries in which the financial crisis – and consequent Great Recession – had hit relatively less, it later spread also to countries that had looked more protected from the worst consequences of the Great Recession. Also in the latter countries, discontent emerged in different forms, in some cases through electoral earthquakes, with the breakdown of center-left and center-right parties and the growth of right-wing populism, in others taking the streets and even ending up in the development of strong electoral challenges on the Left. The constellation of protests varied in particular, between more traditional mobilization through trade unions and new forms of Occupy-type protests (della Porta 2017a). These protests have been seen as part of anti-austerity movements, mobilizing in a context of the crisis of neoliberalism. Protestors react not only to economic crisis (with high unemployment and precarious work) but also to a political situation in which institutions are (and are perceived to be) particularly closed toward citizens' demands, at the same time unwilling and incapable of addressing them in an inclusive way.

As it is often the case, this new wave of protest has revitalized social movement studies, giving new relevance to contentious politics, but also brought about some challenges for interpreting protests that did not neatly fit within existing theoretical models. In particular, it focused attention on the impact of social transformation on social movements. Strangely, in social movement studies concerns for the social bases of protest had declined, as socioeconomic claims raised through protest remained stable or even increased, with scholars talking of a strange disappearance of capitalism from the analysis (Hetland and Goodwin 2013). Similarly, in political sociology the focus on the process of mobilization has, since the 1980s, diverted attention from the relations between social structures and political participation, as well as collective identities (Walder 2009). Recently, some scholars have looked at Marxist approaches to social movements (Barker, Cox, Krinsky, and Nilsen 2013), or called to bring political economy back into the analysis of recent mobilizations against austerity (Tejerina et al. 2013). Research on the 2011 protests pointed at the grievances neoliberalism and its crisis had spread in the Arab countries as well as in Southern Europe (della Porta 2014), given cuts in public spending, deterioration of public services and related growth in inequality and poverty as sources for grievances, and therefore protests. In all of these mobilizations, a new class – the precariat: young, unemployed or only part-time employed, with no protection, and often well educated – has been defined as a main actor within broader coalitions. In order to analyze recent protests, it is indeed all the more relevant to bring attention to capitalist dynamics back into social movement research.

The short account of the anti-austerity protests stresses some of the main dimensions that have structured the debate on the interaction between societal characteristics and social movements. First of all, it indicates that movements usually refer to a base that, in various ways, is defined by some social features. Although in American social movement research, criticism of breakdown theory (see Chapter 1) has for long time (and with few exceptions, among which Piven and Cloward 1992) diverted attention from structural grievances (Buechler 2004), there is no denying that the socioeconomic structure of a society influences the type of conflicts that develop in it. Since the 1970s, indeed, European social movement scholars especially have focused on new conflicts in Western democracy: the ecological movement or the women's movement were the typical objects of this stream of research. Social movements have been considered indeed as the bearers of postmaterialistic values, while the class cleavage on which the labor movements had mobilized seemed to be pacified. Anti-austerity protests bring attention back to the relationship between changes in the social structure and collective action.

Social change may affect the characteristics of social conflict and collective action in different ways. It may facilitate the emergence of social groups with a specific structural location and potential specific interests, and/or reduce the importance of existing ones, as the shift from agriculture to industry and then to the service sector suggests. As the anti-austerity protests indicate, however, structural tensions do not directly translate into mobilization: misery can deter protest, more than facilitating it. Class conflict is considered as a central factor in determining revolutionary situations and outcomes. Together with an acute suffering, with a dramatic deterioration in living standards, with disruptions of people's daily routines, is seen as encouraging defiance of authority. In fact,

> *Economic crises, wars, and even natural disasters often provoke such disloca-tions. In these scenarios, ordinary people suffer the impact of the loss of work or income and of being sent into bloody and often unpopular wars. Significantly, the breakdown or even collapse of institutions upon which daily survival depends—work, commerce, transportation, and other services such as health and education—has the potential to thrust normally quiescent people into militant protest. In sum, one precondition for dual power consists of deep disloca-tions that break down routinized systems of social stability and control.*
>
> (Goodwin and Rojas 2015, p. 797)

Societal conditions also have important influences on the distribution of resources that are conducive to participation in collective action, such as education, and/or facilitate the articulation of interests. Globalization and deindustrialization have been seen as triggering a decline of the working class, at least in the global North (e.g. Tilly 1994; Zolberg 1995).

Keeping in mind these kinds of effects, we shall focus on three types of transformation that have interested, in different historical moments, not only Western societies since the Second World War: in the economy, in the role of the state, and in the cultural sphere. Without attempting to cover the innumerable processes which make up what is usually regarded as the transition to postindustrial (or postmodern, disorganized, post-Fordist, and so on) society, we shall limit ourselves to mention those processes of change that have been explicitly cited in the social movement literature as affecting social movements. In the next section we shall indeed focus on changes in the social structure and their reflection in political cleavages (2.1); then on the social impacts of changes in the political sphere (2.2), and on the effects of cultural changes on social movements (2.3). We shall conclude by discussing the hypothesis of social movements as actors of new class conflicts (2.4).

2.1 SOCIAL STRUCTURE, POLITICAL CLEAVAGES, AND COLLECTIVE ACTION

Linking capitalist transformations to citizens' agency is a main theoretical challenge for social movement studies. In the social sciences, the effects of socioeconomic characteristics upon social and political conflicts have often been addressed by looking at political cleavages; that is, at the main politicized conflict lines (Lipset and Rokkan 1967). Political cleavages have traditionally been associated with a model of collective action in which actors: (1) fought against each other in order to protect material or political interests; and (2) defined themselves (as members of a class, a faction, or a national group) in relation to these interests. As well known, the concept of cleavages was used by Stein Rokkan to describe the main conflict lines in the development of European societies and politics. As he stated:

> *Two of these cleavages are direct products of what we might call the* National Revolution*: the conflicts between the* central nation-building culture *and the increasing resistance of the ethnically, linguistically or religiously distinct* subject populations *in the province and the periphery; the conflict between the centralizing, standardizing and mobilizing Nation-State and the historically established corporate privilege of the* Church. *Two of them are products of* Industrial Revolution*: the conflict between the* landed interests *and the rising class of* industrial entrepreneurs*; the conflict between* owners and employers *on the one side and* tenants, laborers and workers *on the other.*
>
> (Rokkan 1999, p. 284)

In general, social movements have played a very important role in the formation, structuration and politicization of conflicts: the labor movement helped in "freezing" the class cleavage, while new social movements have been said to emerge from new cleavages. Both trends help to explain why there has been – with few valuable exceptions – a strange silence from social movement studies on the social bases of conflicts as "cleavage theory occupies a central place in literature on conventional political participation, but is remarkably absent in literature on unconventional political participation" (Damen 2013, p. 944).

Social movement studies developed, as mentioned, in a period of rejection of conceptions of the dominance of the economic sphere, pointing at the autonomy of the political or the social domains. Considering grievances, strains, cleavages, and the like as always present, social movement studies concentrated on explaining the passage from structure to action (Klandermans, Kriesi and Tarrow 1988). When cleavages are referred to in social movement studies, it is to highlight their pacification. On the other side, research on cleavages focused on their effects on electoral and party politics, disregarding the role of social movements. In fact, focusing on the environmental or women's movements, research noted that these 'new social movements' arose especially when and where the old cleavages had faded away, leaving spaces for new ones to emerge (e.g. Kriesi et al. 1995).

While Rokkan singled out the social groups on which the structuration of political conflicts developed, looking at the class cleavage in particular, Stefano Bartolini and Mair 1990 (see also Bartolini 2000) contributed to a conceptualization of cleavage as composed of three elements: (1) a sociostructural reference as empirical element; (2) a collective identity, as informed by "the set of values and beliefs that provide a sense of identity and role to the empirical elements and reflects a self-awareness of the social group(s) involved"; and (3) an organizational/behavioural element, linked to a set of individual interactions, institutions, and organizations, such as political parties, that structures the cleavage (Bartolini 2000, p. 17).

The development of cleavages as a politicized divide is therefore a process composed of various steps such as the generation of oppositions due to different interests or visions, the crystallization of opposition lines into a conflict, the emergence of alliances of political entrepreneurs engaged in mobilizing support for some policies, then the choice of mobilization strategy (community versus purpose specific) and conflict arena (electoral versus protest). The cleavage itself emerges through processes of politicization, mobilization, and democratization in the nation-state: it is, that is, translated into politics (rather than repressed or depoliticized) by the action of party translators. The work of these translators is all the more important in keeping emotional feelings of solidarity alive, as they tend to be reduced by social heterogeneity and differentiation, the separation of workplace from residence, the reduction of direct contacts with members of the group, and the development of impersonal contacts in the party (Bartolini 2000, p. 17).

Similarly, social movement studies have stressed the importance of group characteristics for their capacity to mobilize by the presence of both specific categorical traits and networks between those sharing such traits (Tilly 1978). In synthesis, collective action on the part of particular social groups is in fact facilitated when these groups are: (1) easily identifiable and differentiated in relation to other social groups; (2) endowed, thanks to social networks among their members, with a high level of internal cohesion and with a specific identity. While the past strength of the class cleavage contributed to the development of a so-called mid-century compromise between labor and capital, with the growth of welfare states and citizens' rights, new cleavages seemed to emerge.

From the perspective of social movement studies, the link between social structure, norms, and organizations can be seen as characterized by continuous feedback between those elements. As social groups are formed through processes of identification, they tend to structure themselves into various organizational formats. Organizational entrepreneurs develop new codes, often politicizing the conflict, and their framing contributes to mobilizing the social groups.

The concept of cleavage has entered the analysis of social movements, with reference to the pacification of the old class cleavage and the emergence of new ones. Research on the class bases for new social movements singled out the new middle class, in particular the highly qualified workers in the sociocultural sector as the empirical base of a new cleavage, endowed with post-materialist values and structured into sort of archipelagos (Kriesi 1993; Inglehardt 1977). As the new middle classes (especially the sociocultural profession) were considered as the 'empirical element' of the cleavage, post-materialist values were singled out as its cultural element. As Habermas observed long ago (1987, p. 392):

> [New conflicts] no longer flare up in domains of material reproduction; they are no longer channeled through parties and associations; and they can no longer be allayed through compensations. Rather, these new conflicts arise in domains of cultural reproduction, social integration and socialization; they are carried out in subinstitutional – or at least extraparliamentary – forms of protest; and the underlying deficit reflects reification of communicatively structured domains of action that will not respond to the media of money or power.

Finally, from the organizational point of view, new social movements emerged as networks of networks. Although new parties, such as the Green ones, were founded to represent emerging claims on environment protection or gender rights, they never reached the structuring capacity of the socialist or the communist party families in the case of the class cleavage (Diani 1995).

From this perspective, the central question for the analysis of the relationship between structure and action is whether social changes have made it easier to develop such social relationships and feelings of solidarity and of collective belonging, to identify specific interests and to promote related mobilization. The move toward capitalism did not only create aggregates of individuals joined together by the fact that they possessed the means of production (the capitalists) or their own labor force (the proletariat); it also created systems of social relationships which facilitated the development of an internal solidarity in these aggregates and their transformation into collective actors.

The working class was a central actor in the conflicts of the industrial society not only because of its size or the relevance of its economic function, but also as a consequence of a wider range of structural factors. In the Fordist factory, a large number of workers performed similar tasks within large productive units, where labor mobility was limited. These factors certainly facilitated identification of a specific social actor and reinforced internal cohesion. The concentration of the proletariat in large productive units and in urban areas produced dense networks in which a specific class identity developed along with a capacity for collective mass action (Thompson 1963; Calhoun 1982; Fantasia 1989; Urry 1995).

The bases of the industrial conflict have been weakened by modifications affecting the conditions described above. Within industry, the ways in which work is organized have changed. Automated technologies and small work groups have replaced the Fordist conveyor-belt approach and the related mass-worker model. Collective solidarity derived from the carrying out of the same duties has been weakened as a result. Starting in the 1980s, production began to move from large factories to smaller ones as corporations shifted production offshore and began to rely on suppliers to produce component parts of their products, rather than producing them themselves. This brought about a significant decentralization of production processes within a geographical area and led to the growth of the hidden and informal economy. Also the physical closeness of the factory and the neighborhoods inhabited by the working classes, which once represented a source of solidarity, is now broken (Lash and Urry 1987).

The importance of some productive sectors changed as well, with a noticeable decline in industrial work in favor of administrative and service occupations. Highly qualified work in the tertiary sector has grown throughout the world, creating a professional new middle class, which is very different from traditional clerical workers in industry or public bureaucracies. The change has affected both the private sector, with a marked increase in "producer services," and the public sector, with a strong expansion of "social services" related to education, health, and social care (Castells 1996, p. 208–220).

The new middle class is, however, far from a homogeneous group; indeed, there appear to be considerable differences in terms of social rewards within it. The status of the new professionals is not always comparable with that of the traditional middle-class professionals (lawyers, doctors, and so on). In the new producer service sector (such as advertising, marketing, communications) precarious and low-paid forms of work are fairly widespread and constitute marked discrepancies between the cultural capital which individuals have at their disposal, and the recognition – in terms of earnings as well as of social prestige – which is obtained from these.

Unemployment also increased in many countries, and came to be considered as a structural feature of capitalist economies. The relationship between the employed and the unemployed has also changed, in more general terms: entry into the labor market is delayed more and more, excessively prolonging a nonadult lifestyle; increasingly fewer sectors of the population can count on stable and protected forms of work. If it is difficult to determine effectively the level of unemployment, and its structural determinants, in developed countries, it is safe to state that the incidence of precarious and temporary work has risen enormously (della Porta, Andretta et al. 2016). Growing inequalities emerge not only between the North and the South (Franzini and Pianta 2017), but also within the North, even in the most modern global cities (see Sassen 2000).

Poverty is also more and more widespread. In general, socioeconomic indicators converge in pointing at the increasing misery. Research has stigmatized the extreme level of deprivation in recent times. In her book on *Expulsions*, Saskia Sassen has singled out an emergent systemic trend that allowed for extreme concentration of wealth and rapidly increasing inequalities, with the development of "predatory formations" as "a mix of elites and systemic capacities with finance a key enabler, that push toward acute concentration" (2014, p. 13). She points indeed at the exceptionally high profit-making capacity of some service industries also through new technologies that facilitates hypermobility. The degrading of the welfare state project so brings about "a shrunken space with relatively fewer firms, fewer workers, and fewer consumer households, all indicators of a system gearing toward expelling what does not fit in its evolving logic" (Sassen 2014, p. 217). As Thomas Piketty (2014) recalled, today's unequal distribution of wealth is similar to that of the end of the late nineteenth century, as the capital rate return is greater than the economic growth. This inequality in turns produces social and political instability with often dramatic existential effects of inequalities in terms of disruption of everyday life (Therborn 2013).

Together with wars and predation, demographic pressure have triggered significant migrations toward the stronger economies, promoting the expansion in Western societies but also in some area in the Global South of a subproletariat with a strong ethnic character (Castells 1996, Chapter 4, especially 233–234). While by no means a new phenomenon (Olzak 1992), the scale of migrations toward the end of the twentieth century has certainly increased the potential for racial conflicts within Western democracies and has been used for a resurgence of extreme right groups. Mobilization around migration have been influenced not only by sheer number but also by changing migrant groups, with growing concerns about the religious diversity:

> *These structural changes in the size and diversity of the immigrant population may have two consequences. On the one hand, they might increase the likelihood to observe the rise of migrants' mobilizations, all other things being equal. On the other hand, they might also increase the likelihood that other actors—especially anti-migrant ones—might mobilize, either verbally or physically.*

> (Eggert and Giugni 2015, p. 161)

Solidarity movements have in fact interacted with the collective mobilization of migrants themselves (della Porta 2018c).

Religion also assumes a public role. Challenging the vision of secularization as an unbroken trend, researcher pointed at de-secularization (Berger 1999) or de-privatization of religion (Casanova 2001) with the

> *reappearance of religion as a contentious issue in the public sphere and as a source of political protest and activism in many parts of the world in the last two decades of the twentieth century... ... Empirically this religious revivalism has been associated with diverse phenomena ranging from the Iranian revolution to terrorism associated with al-Qaeda, Pope John Paul II's support to the Solidarity movement in Poland, Catholic liberation theology in Latin America, Protestant fundamentalism in the United States, and outbursts of violence within new religious movements.*

> (Lindekilde and Kuhle 2015, p. 173)

The influence of religious groups has increased face to the retrenchment of social services as "With the pressure on welfare states and the challenges posed by ethnic and religious diversity, states are likely to be more rather than less eager to engage religious communities in providing welfare and countering alleged threats to social cohesion caused by "radicalization" (Lindekilde and Kuhle 2015, p. 176). Face to globalization and migration, with experiences of loss of cultural identity, cultural religious views (such as Salafism or Christian Evangelicalism) have provided for oppositional identities (Kühle and Lindekilde 2009). Religious spaces have worked to protect opposition in authoritarian regimes, but also to nurture claims for recognition of specific religious needs.

Additionally, generations acquired new centrality with some changes in the age distribution of the population. As Goldstone (2015, pp. 149–150) noted, socialization of new cohorts

> *tends to work smoothly when the numbers of people in society are stable or changing slowly enough for growth in the economy and institutions to accommodate the change. However, rapid change in the size of cohorts, or of particular*

social groups, can easily disrupt this process and place great strains on institutions. Sudden increases in the number of young people, or of migrants, can place a burden on schools (and on government to finance them). Rapid urbanization and educational expansion can rapidly change outlooks and loyalties as people move out of familiar and traditional settings into more fluid ones, where they have a greater variety of choices to create and join voluntary organizations, including new religious and social movements.

Research pointed in particular to the emergence of a precarious generation characterized by a sum of insecurity on the labor market, on the job (as regulations on hiring and dismissals give little protection to workers), on the work (with weak provisions for accident and illness), on income (with very low pay), all these conditions having effects in terms of accumulation of anger, anomie, anxiety, and alienation (Standing 2011, pp. 10 ff.). Guy Standing noted:

> *[The precariat] is not just a matter of having insecure employment, of being in jobs of limited duration and with minimal labor protection … it is being in a status that offers no sense of career, no sense of secure occupational identity and few, if any, entitlements to the state and enterprise benefits that several generations of those who found themselves as belonging to the industrial proletariat or the salariat had come to expect as their due.*

(Standing 2011, p. 24)

Another fundamental force of change has consisted of the massive entry of women into the paid labor force. Within Western societies, the phenomenon has been particularly pronounced in the service sector, which suggests a relationship between dematerialization of the economy and increased opportunities for women (Castells 1997, p. 163). This process has affected lines of differentiation and criteria for interest definition within social groups, which were previously perceived as homogeneous. Continuing wage differentials between men and women represent, for example, an obvious source of division and potential conflict within the salaried classes. At the same time, and not only in the Western world, the combined impact of women's growing economic independence and professional commitments has shaken the base of patriarchy both at home and within the professions and created opportunities for the development of even deeper gender conflicts in the private sphere.

All these processes have weakened the structural preconditions that had facilitated the emergence of a class cleavage, particularly in the working-class model of collective action. Overall, the size of social groups which lack full access to citizenship and its entitlements has grown, whether because they are migrants (legal or illegal), employed in the hidden economy, or engaged in low-paid work. The sense of general insecurity has been further reinforced by the growth of individual mobility, principally horizontal, as more people tend to change jobs several times in the course of their life – whether out of choice or out of necessity (Castells 1996). The multiplication of roles and of professions and of the related stratifications, and the (re)emergence of ethnicity, generational or gender-based lines of fragmentation within socioeconomic groups have made it more difficult to identify specific social categories. The greater frequency of job changes and the weaker links with territorial communities have also made relationships among those who once shared the same structural condition more unstable and fragmentary. As work seems to be gradually losing its collective nature, a process Manuel Castells has defined as "individualization of labor" (1996, p. 265), it is more difficult to deduct actors' interests from their structural position, and to organize their protection on that basis (Dalton 1988, Chapter 8).

2.2   STATES, MARKETS, AND SOCIAL MOVEMENTS

Politics and the state have experienced relevant changes. State action is capable of producing collective actors in at least two ways: by fixing the territorial limits of political action (i.e. setting borders); and by facilitating or blocking the development or the growth of certain social groups – depending on the priorities of public policy, and in particular on the destination of public spending.

2.2.1   Globalization and Protest

Structural processes influence the territorial dimension of conflict. Traditionally, social movements have organized at the national level, targeting national governments. Today's national protests are more often accompanied by transnational ones, in a process of upward scale shifts, as changes in the territorial level of action (McAdam and Tarrow 2005). The relationship between economic activities and geography has changed too, in the sense that such activities are increasingly transnational in both "strong" and "weak" sectors. The importance of the multinationals has grown: the emphasis on the international division of labor has facilitated the transfer of activities with high environmental risks to the poorest areas. Decentralization of production went hand in hand with the centralization of economic control, with the merging of firms into larger and larger corporations.

Although the process of global interdependence has its roots in the distant past (Wallerstein 1974; Tilly 2004a, Chapter 5), the technological revolution of the 1980s contributed to intensifying "both the reality of global interdependence, and also the awareness of the world as one single unit" (Robertson 1992, p. 8). In the economic system, growing interdependence has meant the transfer of production (in economic theory, the "delocalization of production processes") to countries with lower wages; a strengthening of multinational corporations; and especially the internationalization of financial markets, to the extent that some speak of an "economy without borders." Global economic interdependence has been a factor in pushing large numbers of people from the South and East of the world to its North and West, but also in transforming the division of international labor by deindustrializing the North (where the economy is increasingly service oriented) and industrializing some areas in the South (in particular in Latin America and Central Asia and now also in eastern Europe), where the economy used to be based on the export of raw materials.

The contractual capacity of trade unions has been significantly weakened by the threat of moving production to locations with lower labor costs. Economic globalization has also raised specific problems around which actors, both old and new, have mobilized. In the world's North, it has brought unemployment and especially an increase in job insecurity and unprotected working conditions, with frequent trade-union mobilization in the agricultural, industrial, and service sectors. In the South, too, the neoliberal policies imposed by the major international economic organizations have forced developing countries to make substantial cuts in social spending, triggering fierce protests (Walton and Seddon 1994; Eckstein 2001; Ayuero 2001). Again, already weak political regimes have often allowed the private exploitation of natural resources as well as development projects with major environmental impact. Native populations have mobilized against the destruction of their physical habitat – for instance, via the destruction of the Amazon forests or the construction of big dams, often sponsored by IGOs such as the World Bank or the IMF (Yashar 1996).

Traditionally, political action in the industrial society presupposed a specific concept of space and territory, which translated into the model of the nation-state. Having the monopoly of the legitimate use of force in a certain area, the state fixed its borders, and thus the "natural" limit of the complex of much wider relationships conventionally defined as society. Social relationships were, in the first place, relationships internal to a particular nation-state. There were, admittedly, many communities within states that were endowed with specific institutions and forms of self-government, but they were considered to be largely residual phenomena, destined to disappear as modernization processes advanced (Smith 1981).

Relevant collective actors were, at that time, those social groups able to influence the formulation of national policy: for example, groups with central economic and professional roles, or organized labor. Political and class conflict tended to be seen as a conflict between social groups defined on a national scale, and concerned with the control of national policy making. The existence of conflicts between the center and the periphery that were not based on class issues did not belie this perception: minority nationalities, groups bearing a particular cultural, historical, and/or linguistic identity, defined their strategies and their own images in reference to a central state and to the dominion which the state exercised on their territory, and they often aimed at building their own nation-states. In this case, the goal was not concerned with national policy but rather with the modification of the borders of the nation-state. However, actors did define themselves in terms of the state and its borders.

The correspondence of nation-state and society is nowadays weaker than it was in the past. In this sense, economic globalization has called into question not only the role of the nation-state, less and less capable of governing within its own borders, but also, in more general terms, the capacity of politics to intervene in the economy and regulate social conflict. Global capitalism has in fact breached the longstanding historical alliance among capitalism, the welfare state, and democracy (Crouch 2004). The shift from Keynesian-driven economics – with the state playing an important role in governing the market – to neoliberal capitalism implied a reduction of labor protection as well as workers' rights (Brecher, Costello, and Smith 2000). Even left-wing governments have espoused the liberal concepts of flexibilization of the workforce and cuts in social spending.

Overall, the capacity of the state to regulate behavior within a certain territory has clearly lessened. First, the importance of territorial political structures within single states has grown. In most cases this has been intertwined with the consolidation of various forms of territorial decentralization (della Porta, Keating et al. 2018). In some cases, moves toward autonomy have led to the emergence of genuine subnational entities, often in places where historical traditions of autonomy were strong, but even where they were weak. At the same time, the growing interdependence among states and the strengthening of some IGOs have weakened the idea of the states as the only relevant units in the international system. The devolution of regulatory power to IGOs such as the EU has unsettled national boundaries.

Globalization is not only a matter of new technologies but also of the political tools set in place to regulate and reproduce the mode of production through the proliferation of international governmental and nongovernmental organizations (Boli and Thomas 1999). While the national political context still filters the impact of international shifts on national politics, growing economic interdependence went hand in hand with "a significant internationalization of public authority associated with a corresponding globalization of political activity" (Held and McGrew 2000, p. 27). From this perspective, the international system based on the nation-state seems to be mutating into a political system composed of overlapping multilevel authorities with low functional differentiation and scant democratic legitimacy. In the political system, globalization has brought a transnationalization of political relationships. In fact, research into international relations has highlighted a pluralization of relevant actors (Nicholson 1998, p. 131 ff.). Since the Second World War, there has been a growth in the number of international governmental organizations with both a worldwide scope of action (like the United Nations) and a regional one (like the European Union, but also Mercosur in Latin America and NAFTA in North America); with military objectives (NATO or the now defunct Warsaw Pact) or with the declared aim of fostering economic development (the IMF, World Bank, or WTO) (Princen and Finger 1994, p. 1).

International organizations have contributed to the spread of international regulations and norms, which in some cases supersede national sovereignty. As has often been pointed out, "no official authority controls states in the contemporary world system, but many are subject to powerful unofficial forces, pressures and influences that penetrate the supposed hard shell of the state" (Russett and Starr 1996, p. 62). Furthermore, while the majority of intergovernmental organizations function as a meeting place and discussion forum where decisions are taken unanimously and then ratified by national organs, a growing number of international organizations make decisions on a majority basis that bind all member states (Russett and Starr 1996). International governmental organizations have been both tools for economic globalization, through policies liberalizing trade and the movement of capital, and a way to govern processes that can no longer be handled at the national level.

This does not mean that the state has lost its centrality, but undoubtedly the presence of simultaneous moves toward the constitution of supranational and subnational authorities has brought about significant changes in the construction of collective actors. For example, in the case of minority nationalities within multicultural states, the presence of supranational entities tends to change the criteria according to which actors define themselves, as well as their strategies. European integration has certainly contributed to the remobilization of ethnic minorities in western European states, providing them with a new interlocutor and new goals: from the construction of new states following the breakup of those already in existence, there has been, increasingly, a move toward the renegotiation of relationships between central and peripheral regions of a state, within a "regional Europe." At the same time, we have seen a shift from nationalist identities with a strong ethnic component, to identities that combine reference to the nation with greater attention to multiculturalism and the cohabitation of diverse cultural groups (Johnston 1991; Melucci 1996). The struggle for self-government of indigenous peoples addresses not only specific rights, but also the very political rights of nonterritorially bounded communities (Brysk 2000; Yashar 1996).

Moreover, not only has globalization weakened the power of politics over economics, it has generated transnational conflicts on the policies of international institutions, producing different results depending on the organization and field of intervention involved. In particular, opposition has arisen to the neoliberal policies of the so-called international financial institutions (such as the IMF or the WB), which wield strong coercive power through the threat of economic sanctions and conditionalities on international credit.

More generally, in addition to the acquisition of power by these largely nonrepresentative, nontransparent bodies, criticism has centered on their manifest democratic deficit. Similar considerations may hold for other international organs, for example, in the sphere of the United Nations, or for other types of policy enacted by the European Union itself, from environmental issues to human rights. In all of these cases, new opportunities have emerged for mobilization and campaigns conducted on a transnational scale (Marks and McAdam 1998). As governance began to involve multiple territorial levels, protestors also started to develop multilevel strategies (Imig and Tarrow 2001a and 2001b; della Porta and Tarrow 2005; della Porta 2004a; della Porta and Caiani 2006; see also Chapter 8).

2.2.2 State and Classes: The Conflicts around the Welfare State

The state does not influence the formation of collective actors only through the definition of territorial boundaries to political action. It is well known that the role of the state in the economy has increased progressively in the course of the twentieth century, peaking in the 1970s, and then, even if unequally in crossnational comparison, declining with social expenditures at the turn of the century (Crouch 1999). However considered, since the 1950s, even in many developing countries, the state moved for a while from being a guarantor of the market to managing economic activities through public enterprise; moreover, the welfare state has contained social inequalities (for a global discussion, see Rose 1984). This has led some observers to hold that the principal social cleavage was no longer based on the control of the means of production, but relates, rather, to the procurement of the means of survival either in the private market or through public intervention (Crompton 1993, pp. 103–104). Certainly, criteria for allocation of public resources, often those concerned with the satisfaction of basic needs such as housing or transport, have represented a significant area for collective action, in particular, for social groups from an urban context (Castells 1983; Pickvance 1985, 1986).

Processes of a political nature, rather than based on market dynamics, affect the existence of certain social groups. After the Second World War, the phenomenon has become more marked, with the development of the welfare state, as well as of neocorporatist patterns of interest representation (see Chapter 8). In recent decades, social movements have criticized the model of the interventionist state, as well as that of the state as mediator between the forces of production. Various factors have converged toward a further widening of the potential for conflict. First, as the active role of the state in the distribution of resources has become increasingly evident, the opportunities for mobilization to protect ever more heterogeneous social groups and interests have also grown. Second, while the expansion of social rights has certainly brought greater opportunities for those from the lowest social classes, it has also entailed considerable fiscal redistribution. This has been considered, in the medium term, as particularly heavy for the middle classes, as well as insufficient to cover the growing costs of the welfare state, particularly in the context of an aging population. The result has been a universal welfare crisis that is at the same time fiscal and political. The explicitly political nature of the criteria for the allocation of social resources has, in fact, stimulated mobilization among the middle classes, not only in the form of antitax movements, but also from a perspective that is globally critical of the welfare state (Brissette 1988; Lo 1982, 1990).

More recently, however, the global justice movement has mobilized mainly in defense of the welfare state. In differing ways in various countries, trade-union organizations have joined in protest, accusing neoliberal globalization of subordinating citizens' rights to the free market, thus increasing the inequalities both between the North and South and within their own countries. The forerunners of the Seattle protests can be found, at least in part, in the world of work. As mentioned, in various ways, depending on the prevailing patterns of interest representation in various countries, the 1990s saw a transformation of labor action. While, in general terms, the union federations in European countries accepted privatization, deregulation, and the "flexibilization" of labor, opposition grew in other sectors both inside and outside unions.

Apart from public transport, opposition to neoliberal economic policies extended particularly to education and health. In these areas, in countries with pluralist patterns of industrial relations (with various representative organizations competing with each other), new unions highly critical of the various forms of privatization arose and expanded (Sommier 2003; della Porta 2006). In the so-called neocorporative countries, with occupational representation confined to a single union, public-sector unionists took the most radical positions (for instance, first workers' union OETV and then Ver.di in Germany). It was no coincidence that these unions were the most involved in the protest campaigns against neoliberal globalization (della Porta 2006, 2005a).

As for anti-austerity protests, changing political conditions are related to some specific forms of capitalism. If capitalism is, according to Marxism, one of a set of modes of production, defined on the basis of the relations between the owners of the conditions of production and the producers, then the specific forms exploitation takes during the evolution of capitalism must be expected to have an effect on producers' mobilization (Barker 2013).

In cities, social movements have developed around claims on "collective consumption" (housing shortages, inadequate health care and education, access to water supply, sewerage systems, and electricity), but also urban planning (relocation of uses and demolition of cityscape). Critical mass, reclaim the streets, or right to the city have been important actors in city politics, addressing economic reorganization and urban redevelopment in the post-industrial global city (Salet 2007; Pruijt 2007, p. 5116; see also Chapter 3) and its hegemonic model of urban development with large-scale physical renovation projects. Going beyond the Western world, "the emergence of this model of urban development has been an international process. The privatization and commodification of urban resources, the processes of residential gentrification, the dispossession and displacement of low-income people, and the growing impact of tourism in central urban areas are increasingly prominent in cities across the world" (Andretta, Piazza and Subirats 2015, p. 203). In recent years, the global crisis "is intensifying the breaking points around which urban social movements have been rallying, suddenly validating their claims and arguments about the lack of sustainability and the destructiveness of the neoliberal growth model" (Mayer 2009, pp. 370–371).

To summarize: the growth of the role of the state has multiplied the number of social actors whose existence and opportunities seem to be linked at least partially to political decision-making mechanisms. At the same time, the processes of globalization that we have just described, have undermined the capacity of consolidated political actors to effectively mediate between the various interests. Changes in the criteria for defining actors and for determining the stakes to play for, have promoted the multiplication of collective identities and of mobilized interests and, therefore, also their segmentation.

2.3 KNOWLEDGE, CULTURE, AND CONFLICTS

Social movements also react to changes in the value system and the culture in general. We shall discuss in a later chapter the *discursive opportunities* for movements (see Chapter 8), and their effects on values, knowledge, and attitudes. In this section, we want to single out some general cultural changes that have often been mentioned in relation to movements, looking in particular at the conception of the public and the private, the growth of movement counterculture, as well as the development of global culture.

2.3.1 Shifting Boundaries between the Public and the Private

In the past, the expansion of the role of the state has contributed to the modification of the boundaries between the public and the private. The state has intervened with growing frequency in areas relating to private life, in particular, through the provision of social services and the action of welfare agencies. The principal form of support offered to citizens has been, however, accompanied by increased control over aspects of life that previously would have been left to the autonomous regulation of social actors. The extension of the public health service, for example, has favored the standardization of therapeutic methods and the treatment of crucial events in the experience of individuals, such as maternity. A tendency toward the bureaucratization and rationalization of the private sphere has followed (Habermas 1976, 1987; Melucci 1989, 1996).

In this way, definitions of criteria for determining normality and deviance in areas that were previously left to the regulation of other institutions (such as the church or the family) have become the object of public intervention. Thus, the premises have been created for the rise of new conflicts whose protagonists are social groups – for example, professionals and users of social services, or managers with responsibility for the coordination and running of public agencies (Hoffman 1989). In many cases, protest has related not only to the efficiency of services but also to their impersonality and their tendency to create and reproduce deviance and marginality instead of combating them. Similar concerns are expressed by movements that criticize private groups of professionals (for example, certain sectors of the medical establishment, pharmaceutical companies, and so on) accused of subordinating care for service users to organizational and economic logics (J. Gamson 1989; Crossley 2006).

In the industrial society, a (relatively) clear distinction between public and private allowed people to define citizenship rights as a complex of civil opportunities (relating, for example, to freedom of expression and association), political opportunities (relating to the right to vote, for example), and social benefits (relating to access to minimum levels of well-being and education) without any further qualifications (Marshall 1992). These rights, in fact, referred to the citizen as understood generically – usually male, adult, Western. Mobilization aimed at extending rights of citizenship entailed provision of the same set of entitlements to social groups that had been excluded: illiterate and nonaffluent people, but also women and ethnic minorities (Barbalet 1988).

Toward the end of the twentieth century, however, various factors have revealed the problematic nature of this notion of citizenship. Not only has it been pointed out how Marshall's model was hardly applicable in countries other than Britain (Giddens 1983; Barbalet 1988), but also a series of structural processes have undermined previously taken-for-granted understandings. With the consolidation of the presence of women in the public sphere (in both professional and political terms), the contradiction has become clear between rights formally recognized as universal, and existing forms of organization of family and professional life that have restricted women's enjoyment of those rights. Immigration waves to Western countries have made the problem more urgent of how to articulate citizens' rights in such a way as to allow for the existence of different cultural groups. Particularly, the growing number of non-national residents pushed for an adaptation of the very notion of citizenship rights, with the effects of various degrees of protection for different "shades" of citizenship (Soysal 1994; Isin and Turner 2002; della Porta 2018c).

All these examples suggest that, although the nation-state and modern citizenship rights took their inspiration from universal identities, other possible sources of collective identity and of conflict have not disappeared. Other criteria based on traits such as gender, ethnic origin, or age regularly appear alongside those of a functionalist or universal type, to define collective actors. In consequence, citizenship appears to be less a set of endowments and more a process of a conflicting nature, where what is at stake are the criteria defining what a citizen is. The fact that the state has widened its scope for intervention only makes the political nature of those asymmetries and inequalities more obvious.

2.3.2 Cultures and Countercultures

Growing differentiation in lifestyles represents another source of problematization of social identities. In a world in which class allegiances seem fragmented and political ideologies are in crisis, cultural consumption, use of one's free time, ways of organizing one's emotional life, eating habits, or styles of clothes can all represent a powerful factor for diversification and, in the final analysis, of new stratification, among social groups (Bourdieu 1984; Eder 1993). In many cases, it is simply an issue of individual consumer behavior, no different from other fashion phenomena. In other cases, however, lifestyle becomes the stake in conflicts regarding the legitimacy of emerging cultural forms or the defense of traditional ones.

Youth movements and other oppositional countercultures provide examples of how individual lifestyle may take up an antagonistic character. The emergence of punk at the end of the 1970s had elements that could easily be reduced to fashion, but also a powerful symbolic antagonism, in the sense of breaking away from consolidated canons of decorum and good taste. In other words, it also had a distinctive countercultural flavor (Crossley 2015). Similar remarks may apply to other forms of youth cultural experience, from rap to rave. More recently, alternative cultures and lifestyles have been nurtured in the Italian and Spanish squatted youth centers, as well as in the radical wing of the anti-road movement in the United Kingdom (Doherty 1998; della Porta, Andretta, et al. 2006). In the late twentieth century, various sectors of social movements have indeed reserved considerable space to action concerning consumer goods and cultural elaboration. Women's, squatters', or youth movements have promoted the construction of alternative networks offering autonomous opportunities for support and social contacts to their participants (Melucci 1984; Taylor and Whittier 1992; see Chapter 7).

In other cases, collective action on lifestyles has been concerned with the defense of values and traditions which, it was held, were threatened. Movements such as the American Moral Majority or those against the introduction of divorce in Italy in the early years of the 1970s also chose the private sphere and the criteria by which one can define a particular lifestyle as ethically desirable as their favored terrain for political mobilization (Wood and Hughes 1984; Wallis and Bruce 1986; Oberschall 1993, Chapter 13).

The growing importance of lifestyle has also led to consumerism becoming a specific object of collective action. The consumer has been increasingly identified as a political, and not simply as an economic, actor. Consumer organizations have addressed their mobilization attempts to the public in general. Structures for the production and distribution of alternative goods, for example, in the food sector, have been created; campaigns and mobilizations in favor of consumers have also been launched. They have taken forms ranging from quasi-countercultures (for example, in the alternative networks promoting and distributing organic food in the early stages of environmental movements) to classic public interest-group action (for example, in the form of mass professional organizations like Common Cause) (Baek 2010; Boström, Micheletti, and Peter Oosterveer 2019; Earl, Copeland, and Bimber 2017; Forno and Graziano 2014). Fair trade and boycotts have grown enormously in recent years, with a particularly successful trend among young people (Micheletti 2003; see also Chapter 7).

Although not always connected with each other, all these activities, from different points of view, draw our attention once again to the new importance assumed by collective action concerned with the defense of certain models of behavior and moral codes, rather than with the conquest of political power or the protection of economic interests. Various transformations in the private sphere and in forms of cultural production appear to have increased potential for conflicts of a symbolic nature. The variety of life experiences to which the individual has access is a result of the multiplication of group allegiances. Each of these can provide relationship and identity resources essential in turning some of the possible sources of inequality into a public debate, defining them as social problems rather than individual difficulties. As Pierre Bourdieu observes, indeed, "Each society, at each moment, elaborates a body of social problems taken to be legitimate, worthy of being debated, of being made public and sometimes officialized and, in a sense, guaranteed by the state" (1992, p. 236).

In parallel, the map of adversaries against which collective energies can, from time to time, be mobilized is equally varied: mass media, technoscientific elites, educational and social welfare institutions, entrepreneurial classes that control mass consumption, and so on. In this situation of uncertainty, instead of representing the preconditions for action concerned with economic or political goals, the definition of collective identity tends to become an autonomous problem, an object of collective action as such (although this may also apply to class conflict: Pizzorno 1978; see also Chapter 4). The same thing can be said about the search for lifestyles and ways of acting that are ethically desirable and appropriate. These needs do not result inevitably in the development of social movements.

2.3.3 Between the Global and the Local

Identities are increasingly defined within a process of accelerated cultural globalization. Globalization has produced significant cultural changes in today's world, a growing interdependence in which social actions in a given time and place are increasingly influenced by actions that occur in distant places. As Giddens suggested (1990, p. 64), globalization implies the creation and intensification of a "worldwide social relationship which links distinct localities in such a way that local happenings are shaped by events occurring miles away and vice versa." The shortening of space and time in communication processes affects the production and reproduction of goods, culture, and the tools for political regulation. Indeed, globalization has been defined as "a process (or set of processes) which embodies a transformation in the spatial organization of social relations and transactions – assessed in terms of their extensity, intensity, velocity and impact – generating transcontinental or interregional flows and networks of activity" (Held et al. 1999, p. 16).

One of the dangers perceived in globalization is the predominance of a single way of thinking, which apparently emerged from the defeat of "real socialism." The international system had been tied to a bipolar structure in which each of the two blocs represented a different ideology; the fall of the Berlin Wall, which symbolically marked the demise of the Eastern bloc, made capitalism seem the single, dominant model. In cultural terms, "modernization" processes promoted by science and the leisure industry have paved the way for what Serge Latouche (1989) called "the westernization of the world," i.e., the spread on a global scale of Western values and beliefs. Although the scenario of a single "McDonaldized" world culture (Ritzer 2000) is an exaggeration, there is an undeniable increase in cultural interactions with the exportation – albeit filtered through local culture – of Western cultural products and values (Robertson 1992). The metaphor of a "global village" stresses that we are targeted in real time by messages sent from the most faraway places. The spread of satellite TV and the internet have made instantaneous communication possible, easily crossing national boundaries.

While national and subnational identities do not fade, the impact of values from other cultures and the growth of interaction between cultures increase the number of identifications that interweave into and compete with those anchored in the territory. Globalization is not only "out there" but also "in here" (Giddens 1990, p. 22): it transforms everyday life and leads to local resistance oriented to defending cultural traditions against the intrusion of foreign ideas and global issues. The resurgence of forms of nationalism, ethnic movements, religious mobilizations, and Islamic (and other) fundamentalism(s) are in part a reaction to this type of intrusion. While cultural globalization risks causing a loss of national identity, new technologies also provide a formidable array of tools for global mobilization, easing communication between worlds once distant, with a language that defies censorship. Increased perception of issues as global also heightens people's willingness to mobilize at a transnational level. Through the presence of transnational networks of ethnocultural communities, local traditions also become delocalized and readapt to new contexts (Thompson 1995).

With some pessimism about the capacity of a new collective subject to emerge, Zygmunt Bauman has located in *liquid modernity* the cultural dimension of the social conflicts. This implies insecurity and flexibility, which make collective identities difficult to develop. While heavy/solid/condensed/systemic modernity was composed of compulsory homogeneity, liquid modernity emphasizes momentary impulses. With the end of the illusion of a *telos* (as a state of perfection to be reached), there is a deregulation and privatization of tasks and duties from collective endowments to individual management. In this view, individualism prevails over the collectivity, as community and corporations no longer offer protection by embedding the individuals in dense nets of social bonds, ensuing insecurity pushes toward the search for scapegoats. In the past, the modern state had managed fears through protection of social state institutions that constructed new webs of social bonds (Bauman 2000, p. 59) or long-term involvement in the Fordist factory; nowadays, a deregulation-cum-individualization develops fears (ibid., p. 67).

In the new context, some scholars singled out the challenges for collective identities to be difficult to develop. Individuals are seen as lukewarm toward the common good, common cause, good society (Bauman 2000, p. 36). However, this is not linked to the colonization of the lifeworld by the state, but rather by its decline, as "it is no more true that the 'public' is set on colonizing the 'private.' The opposite is the case: it is the private that colonizes the public spaces" (Bauman 2000, p. 39). The collapse of confidence is said to bring about a fading will to political commitment with endemic instability. A state-induced insecurity develops, indeed, with individualization through market flexibility and a broadening sense of relative deprivation, as flexibility precludes the possibility of existential security (Baumann 2007, p. 14).

However, anti-austerity movements seem to develop what Ernesto Laclau (2005) has defined as a populist reason. According to him, populism is a political logic: not a type of movement, but the construction of the people as a way of breaking order and reconstructing it. As neoliberalism brings about a fragmentation in the social structure, the discursive construction of the people requires new attention. The search for a populist reason, as the need for naming the self and for recognition of the self, is driven by a crisis that challenges a process of habituation, fueling processes of (new) identification. In times of crisis, a dissonance arises between expectation and reality, as a crisis suspends the *doxa*, made up of undiscussed ideas, and stimulates the elaboration of new arguments (Bourdieu 1977, p. 168). Actual protests can then be interpreted as nonconformative action using discourse and opinions to challenge habitus and *doxa*. According to empirical analyses, in fact, in today's protests the search for a naming of the self that could bring together different groups has indeed produced the spread of definitions of the self as the people, or even more, the persons or the citizens. These ideas have reflected and challenged the cultural effects of neoliberalism (della Porta 2015a).

2.4 STRUCTURAL TRANSFORMATIONS, NEW CONFLICTS, NEW CLASSES

The processes of structural change, which we discussed briefly in the preceding pages, contribute in various ways to the weakening of traditional social conflicts and their recent reemergence in new forms. It is more debatable whether it is possible to establish a global characterization of new conflicts on this basis. The transformations we have discussed – and even more so the interpretations that different scholars have provided of them – seem to point in divergent and sometimes contradictory directions.

2.4.1 Still Classes?

Several of the changes we have mentioned point at two common elements. First, there is a marked increase of activities linked to the production of knowledge and to symbolic manipulation, and the identification in the control of those activities as a major stake of conflict. The development of the administrative/service sector in fact reflects the growing relevance in the economic sphere of information-processing, compared with the transformation of natural resources. The same expansion of areas of state intervention, which leads to the multiplication of identities and of politically based interests, has made ever more essential the role of decision makers and communicators able to develop efficient syntheses between heterogeneous concerns and values.

Second, many recent transformations have produced the potential for conflicts that cut across conventional distinctions between the private and public spheres. Evidence of this includes the influence that certain styles of scientific knowledge and certain ways of organizing it have on the psychophysical well-being of the individual (for example, in the field of therapies and the health services). Alternatively, one may think of the public and collective relevance of individual consumer behavior and ways of life, which previously would have been relegated to the private sphere. Or, again, one might consider the importance of ascribed traits such as ethnicity or gender in conflicts concerning the extension and full realization of citizens' rights.

These processes point at a specific area of nonmaterial conflicts. Their stake is represented by the control of resources that produce meaning and allow actors to intervene not only on their own environment but also on the personal sphere, and above all on the link between these two levels. Rather than with economic or political power, contemporary social conflict has, according to this view, more to do with the production and circulation of information; social conditions for production and the use of scientific knowledge; and the creation of symbols and cultural models concerned with the definition of individual and collective identities. This thesis has been formulated in a number of ways and with various levels of theoretical generalization (Touraine 1981; Lash and Urry 1987; Melucci 1989, 1996; Eder 1993), although somewhat diverse conclusions have been drawn as far as the relationship between structure, conflict, and movement is concerned.

In order to try to make sense of what is undoubtedly a highly diversified debate we must first of all keep in mind that those who investigate the relationship between structure, class, and collective action sometimes move from rather different points of departure, and use the same terms in quite different ways. To begin with, we must note the difference between a "historical" and a "structural" (Eder 1995) or "analytical" (Melucci 1995) concept of class. In the first meaning, class is a historical product of capitalist society (referring in other words to the working and the capitalist class, and to the specific structural processes that produced and reinforced their identity). In the second, a class is a group of people with similar "relationships within which social resources are produced and appropriated" (Melucci 1995, p. 117). The inequalities in power and status, peculiar to postindustrial society, might well not be conducive to the reproduction of industrial class conflict, but still provide the structural roots for the emergence of new collective actors. The tension between these two different approaches has affected recent debates on the persistence of class as a factor shaping conventional political behavior, and in particular, electoral participation (e.g. Dalton et al. 1984; Dalton 1988; 2015).

A second issue among those who still recognize the relevance of structural interpretations regards the existence of a hierarchical structure of different types of conflicts, and the possibility of identifying core conflicts comparable to those which according to dominant interpretations shaped the industrial society. The most coherent attempt to identify the core conflicts of postindustrial (or "programmed") society is to be found in the work of Alain Touraine who has played an important role in the development of social movement studies. According to his path-breaking work in the 1980s, the category of social movement fulfills a fundamental task, in both defining the rules by which society functions and in determining the specific goal of sociology: "The sociology of social movements," wrote Touraine (1981, p. 30), "cannot be separated from a representation of society as a system of social forces competing for control of a cultural field." That is, the way in which each society functions reflects the struggle between two antagonistic actors who fight for control of cultural concerns that, in turn, determine the type of transforming action which a society performs upon itself (Touraine 1977, pp. 95–96). It is in relation to the concept of historicity – defined by the interweaving of a system of knowledge, a type of accumulation, and a cultural model – that different types of society can be identified, along with the social classes which accompany them.

Touraine identified four types of society, each featuring a distinctive pair of central antagonistic actors: agrarian, mercantile, industrial, and "programmed" (a term that he prefers to "postindustrial" society). A particular trait of the programmed society is the "production of symbolic goods which model or transform our representation of human nature and the external world" (Touraine 1987, p. 127; 1985). It is the control of information that constitutes the principal source of social power.

In consequence, conflicts tend to shift from the workplace to areas such as research and development, the elaboration of information, biomedical and technical sciences, and the mass media. In his view, the central actors in social conflict are no longer classes linked to industrial production but groups with opposing visions concerning the use and allocation of cognitive and symbolic resources. In contrast with Marxism, classes are not defined only in relation to the system of production (see, for example, Miliband 1989), and class action is, in fact, the "behavior of an actor guided by cultural orientations and set within social relations defined by an unequal connection with the social control of these orientations" (Touraine 1981, p. 61). As for Pierre Bourdieu, the cultural sphere is considered as the main place for the exercise of social domination. However, Touraine differed from the deterministic approach of his French colleague in that he conceives social movements as struggling to influence the cultural sphere (Girling 2004).

Mobilizations by social movements addressed, therefore, the defense of the autonomy of civil society from the attempts of public and private technocratic groups to extend their control over ever-widening areas of social life.[11] If Touraine's formulation places the analysis of conflicts and movements in the center of his general theoretical model, other scholars have still paid attention to the structural dimension, but without attempting to identify new dominant cleavages. Originally influenced by Touraine, Alberto Melucci held, however, improbable the emergence of new conflicts with a centrality comparable to that of the capital–labor conflict of the industrial society.[12] Melucci never denied the persistent importance of traditional conflicts based on inequalities of power and wealth, and of the political actors, protagonists of these conflicts. However, he identified the peculiarity of contemporary conflicts in processes of individualization which still have their roots in structural dynamics, yet of a different kind – for example, the pervasive influence of caring institutions over the self, the globalization of communications and life experiences, the growth of media systems. And he denied the possibility of reducing responses to these differentiated structural tensions to any sort of unified paradigm of collective action. The latter   itself in a variety of forms – is, rather, just one of innumerable options open to individuals struggling for an autonomous definition of their self.

2.4.2   Which Class Base for Which Social Movements?

The relationship between structural change and new conflicts has also been viewed from another perspective. A number of scholars have stressed the fact that social change has produced a new social stratum – the so-called new middle class. According to this point of view, this class is able, as a result of the resources it controls and of its position, to play a central role in new conflicts. For some time, analyses of postindustrial society have revealed, in parallel with the growth of the administrative/service sector in society, the emergence of social groups that stand out, because of their level of education, the roles they play, and their specific social location, from the traditional middle classes (Bell 1973; Gouldner 1979; Goldthorpe 1982; Lash and Urry 1987; Scott 1990). The new middle class, according to these analyses, is constituted from sectors of the population that tend to be employed in the service sector: they are highly educated, yet are not comparable with managers or traditional professionals. As a result of their technical and cultural competence and of their economic-functional position, members of the new middle class have been considered as more likely to mobilize in conflicts of the new type we have just described: that is, to fight against technocrats, public and private agencies engaged in the dissemination of information and in the construction of consensus, the military and the apparatus responsible for social control. This argument has been presented on numerous occasions in recent years, and several investigations have confirmed the persistent presence of the new middle class among sympathizers and activists of the new movements.[13]

However, it is unclear whether the link between the new middle class, new movements, and new types of conflict effectively demonstrates the existence of a specific structural base for these types of conflict. The presence *en masse* of the new middle class in protest movements could, in fact, simply reflect the traditional inclination of the intellectual middle class to participate in any type of conflict (Bagguley 1995a) given their greater confidence in their own rights and capacity to speak up and participate in political life (Bourdieu 1984). From this perspective, the reference to specific structural contradictions at the base of new conflicts somewhat loses consistency. It is, rather, the case that belonging to the middle class, on the one hand, facilitates the taking up of concerns that are generically favorable to public involvement; and on the other, puts at one's disposal individual resources and competences that can be spent in various types of political action.

In effect, comparative analysis of political participation has revealed on numerous occasions that variables of a sociodemographic type tend to explain with equal efficacy both unconventional participation (particularly widespread among movement sympathizers and activists) and conventional participation. There is, for example, a strong correlation between two factors that are usually regarded as indicators of the new middle class – youth and a high level of education – and various types of political attitudes and/or political participation (Barnes et al. 1979; Opp 1989, Chapter 7; Norris 2002, 201 ff.). Intellectuals have traditionally constituted the leadership of ethnic movements (Smith 1981). Furthermore, a comparison of political ecology and more traditional environmentalist currents showed that activists from the new middle class were present in equal measure in both sectors, in spite of the difficulty to identify conservation groups as new social movements (Diani 1995, p. 58).

Rather than on peculiar class dynamics, the undeniable relationship between membership in the new middle class and involvement in some types of protest movements might well be dependent on yet other factors. For example, it might be the outcome of the enormous rise in access to higher education, which again originated in the 1960s. More specifically, higher education might not only provide people with distinctive intellectual skills; it might also foster the growth of an egalitarian and anti-authoritarian set of values, which are overrepresented among at least some sectors of the new middle class (Rootes 1995). Alternatively, youth radicalism might be related to generational experiences, as the current members of the new middle classes have all been exposed to that particular combination of social conditions, consisting of the end of the Cold War and the spread to the middle classes of unprecedented economic prosperity (Pakulski 1995, p. 76). Or there might be lifecycle effects, as younger people's political involvement might be dependent on their biographical availability, given their more uncertain status, their still unsettled professional life, and their greater independence from family and community linkages (Piven and Cloward 1992).

Moreover, the notion of middle class risks comprising quite heterogeneous social sectors: those who work in the sector of culture and personal services and those who fulfill managerial or other technocratic functions risk remaining unclear; the sectors of the new middle class that are closer to the problems of the management of organizations (managers) and those who, instead, draw their legitimacy and their status from being controllers of professional resources, independent of specific organizational structures (professionals) (Kriesi 1993, pp. 31–32). To evaluate appropriately the importance of the new middle class in social movements, it is useful, therefore, to differentiate between its internal components. Taking inspiration from Wright (1985), who regarded classes as defined by different combinations of "assets in the means of production, organizational assets and skills or credentials," Hanspeter Kriesi identified the distinctive characteristic of the new middle class in the fact that it exercises some control over organizational resources and/or over professional skills, but does not possess the means of production (Kriesi 1993, p. 28; see also Kriesi 1989a). In particular, he suggested looking at three different sectors of the new middle class: alongside the "sociocultural specialists" are managers and those who fulfill clearly technical roles. This last group includes administrative and commercial personnel from public and private organizations, technical specialists – some highly qualified and others less so – and those working in "protective services" (the police, the army, civil protection organizations, and the like). Even the wave of anti-austerity protests have been interpreted as "middle class" phenomena. In fact, mobilizations have been presented by some observers as a manifestation of "a new middle-class politics – democratic, environmentalist – whose global import is predicted to grow" (Yörük and Yüksel 2014, p. 103).

The awareness of the various components of the new middle class and the critical evaluation of their impact on political participation, alongside that of those belonging to the traditional classes (the old middle class and the working class), help to interpret more accurately the relationship between class condition and (new) forms of participation. Analysis of environmentalist militancy (Cotgrove and Duff 1980; Jamison, Eyerman, and Cramer 1990; Dalton 1994, Chapter 5; Diani 1995) noted that those filling the highest positions in groups engaged in this kind of activity were not only highly educated and – in the broadest sense – members of the middle class, but also brought specific competences to bear on the work of the group. Analyses of the link between individual class location and political behavior have certainly brought to light a series of relevant characteristics of new forms of political participation. They have, in particular, provided important information about old and new social movement activists and sympathizers. In doing so, however, they have postulated a direct link between the structural position of individuals and collective action that is by no means clearcut. In fact, while it is possible to look at classes as aggregates of subjects who occupy analogous positions in the system of social stratification, in terms of the resources they control, the prestige they enjoy, and their social opportunities, this is not necessarily an appropriate strategy when dealing with the problem of collective action.

Alternatively, it is advisable to analyze classes as collective actors with a specific identity and self-awareness, linked to other social groups by relationships of a cooperative or conflicting nature. In this perspective, class exists only in circumstances where people mutually recognize and are recognized as part of a distinctive social group, if specific interests and solidarity between the occupants of particular social positions have been identified, and if, on this basis, specific forms of collective action are to be promoted (Thompson 1963; Tilly 1978; Touraine 1981).

Conditions favoring the return of various forms of status politics seem to have been reproduced. In these, the central role is taken by social groups brought together by certain levels of prestige and specific moral codes (Turner 1988; Eder 1993). Telling against the more structural version of the middle-class thesis, the attention paid by the middle class to its own group identity and positioning is certainly not a characteristic exclusive to recent mobilizations (Calhoun 1993). As the historical experience of the anti-alcohol movement reminds us (Gusfield 1963), the middle class has distinguished itself over time by its continual attention to moral codes, socially acceptable rules of conduct, and principles defining the "good life."

Reasons for this attitude are to be found in the historically ambiguous positioning of the middle classes between the industrial bourgeoisie and the working class. Indeed, the petite bourgeoisie came to focus on symbolic production and on the defense of its own social status as a result of its uncertain place in the class system. For similar reasons, they may have felt the need to differentiate themselves from the principal social groups, and particularly from those – the industrial proletariat, throughout the twentieth century – that most closely threatened their prestige (Turner 1994; Calhoun 1993; Eder 1993, 1995). At the same time, there are reasons to argue that substantial differences separate many recent examples of lifestyle politics from the traditional version of status politics. As Featherstone (1987) noted, reference to values and lifestyles does not necessarily characterize distinctive groups with specific identities and long-established structures. Actors involved in collective action may actually share little, apart from the common reference to a given set of values and preferences.

The relationship between new middle class and working class is not any clearer, nor has it been the subject of massive in-depth investigation. In the case of the Netherlands study by Kriesi, it seems, for example, that even belonging to the working class could facilitate mobilization in new movements, particularly as far as younger people are concerned. Thus, there would appear to be at least a partial convergence in the new movements of those social groups which were already particularly active in "historical" opposition movements: there is a certain continuity, in other words, between "old" and "new" forms of class opposition. Also in the global justice movement, a heterogeneous social base has been highlighted as an innovative feature or an enhancement by comparison to movements of the past (Andretta et al. 2003).

In sum, there is no evidence that the material and redistributive dimension has lost all significance in conflicts in which contemporary, nonworking-class movements are protagonists. For example, mobilizations for the development of collective services in urban areas and for urban renewal have certainly been determined by powerful concerns with collective and nonmaterial goods, such as those associated with the quality of life. However, they have also focused on the redistribution of material resources, placing the social groups most penalized by transformations in industrial activity and by processes of urban renewal in opposition to economic groups that were the protagonists and promoters of these processes (Castells 1977). These struggles have often seen the emergence of new alliances between working-class and community groups (Brecher and Costello 1990). Furthermore, forms of collective action have emerged based on conditions of particular unease, concerned, for example, with the struggle against "new poverties." Movements and mobilizations of homeless people have developed (Cress and Snow 1996); initiatives supporting the unemployed and marginal groups have sprung up everywhere, often in close collaboration with the voluntary sector (Bagguley 1991). In all these cases, the conflict has been concerned, once again, not only with a general notion of the quality of life, but with the allocation of material rewards among different social groups. Attention to social justice and material conditions (such as poverty) has become – as often mentioned – central in the recent wave of protest against neoliberal globalization.

2.4.3   Labor and Protest

Research on labor movements has also focused for long on its weakening, at least at the core of the capitalist world (see also Chapter 8). If the decline of strike activities could be interpreted as a sign of institutionalization of the industrial relations and depoliticization of the industrial conflicts, especially since the 1990s, the decline in union membership has been quoted as an indicator of an unavoidable crisis of the labor movement. Also in the service sector, a fragmented social base is hard to organize, especially with the growing flexibilization of the labor market and the connected increasing insecurity. And the more and more numerous unemployed and migrants were also difficult to mobilize.

   At the beginning of the new millennium, however, conflict on labor issues again seems to be on the rise, although in new forms of anti-austerity protests, as workers have organized in the South, where unions often increased their membership (Norris 2002, pp. 173 ff.) and grassroots networks linked workers transnationally (Moody 1997). New grassroots unions emerged (see below), and traditional unions started to invest more on the mobilization of the workers – for instance, the AFL-CIO started to invest as much as 30% of their budget in organizing (as opposed to the usual 5%) (Fantasia and Stepan-Norris 2004, p. 570). While labor demobilized in the private sector, in the public sector workers voiced their opposition to neoliberal reforms that cut social services (Eckstein 2001). As Piven and Cloward (2000) noticed, in the United States there has been a return to old forms of secondary action such as community boycotts, sympathy strikes, and general strikes. In France (but also in Italy and Spain) the turn of the millennium has been characterized by general strikes against pension reform, privatization of public services, cuts in public health and education. In these actions, the trade unions were joined by various movements, bridging labor issues with global justice, defense of the environment, peace, and gender equality. The claims voiced during anti-austerity protests were oriented at the defense of those rights, which had developed in the 1960s and 1970s in the first world with liberal democracies, but also in the Third World with the developmental states, or in the second world with the really existing socialism – rights to housing, health, education, job (della Porta 2017a).

The spread of a frame of global injustice has indeed been perceived as another recent tendency in the labor movement. The NAFTA free-trade agreements produced increasing transnational campaigns of Canadian, United States, and Mexican workers (Ayres 1998; Evans 2000). The dockers of Seattle, who had already taken part in a transnational strikes started by the dockers in Liverpool (Moody 1997), supported the protest against the WTO, extending their solidarity from the local to the international level (Levi and Olson 2000). In these waves of mobilization, the labor movement met other movements – environmentalist, feminist, urban, etc. (della Porta, Andretta et al. 2006). Moreover, increasing inequalities stimulated the rise of solidarity movements with marginal groups in the North (Giugni and Passy 2001), as well as protest by marginal groups themselves (Kousis and Tilly 2004).

In political economy, the analysis of the neoliberal financial crisis in the Great Recession brought about a revisitation of Karl Polanyi's double movement, which singles out a shift, in capitalist development, between social protection and free market, through the action of movements and counter-movements. Polanyi's work has been in fact referred to in order to stress similarities or differences between the first great transformation he studied and what we can call the second great transformation. Polanyi's analysis focuses attention to some specific forms that the counter-movement, as the mobilization of those who feel betrayed by changes like those produced in neoliberalism, can be expected to take. Conceiving countermovements as a reactive move, he points in fact at the ways in which these mobilizations develop as defensive and backward looking. In this perspective, he looks at the first wave of liberalism during which protections for the poor, what E.P. Thompson (1971) calls "the moral economy of bread," were taken away and this produced a rebellion not only against poverty but also against a betrayal of esteblished rights.

According to the scholars of the so-called world system approach, it was the task of antisystemic movements to resist against greedy capitalism, opposing the logic of the system. As Immanuel Wallerstein noted, 'to be antisystemic is to argue that neither liberty nor equality is possible under the existing system and that both are possible only in a transformed world' (Wallerstein 1990, p. 36). The concept of antisystemic movements builds on an analytic perspective about 'the world-system of historical capitalism' that gave rise to them, as 'class and status consciousness were the two key concepts that justified these movements' (Arrighi, Hopkins and Wallerstein 1989, p. 1). Research often noted the diminishing structural power of workers, but this is not true in newly industrialized countries as labor unrest emerges as endemic to capitalism as it wants to commodify labor. As Silver and Karatasli (2015, p. 137) remarked, "from both Marxian and Polanyian perspectives, labor unrest should be expected anytime and anywhere we find the commodification of labor: sometimes at the point of production, sometimes in political struggles over regulation of the labor market, sometimes in the form of open resistance, but at other times." In fact, two types of workers' struggles have been described: a Marx-type labor unrest by newly emerging working classes; and a Polanyi-type labor unrest, with established working classes defending their ways of life and livelihood, which are under attack (Silver 2003). These have been described also as struggles against accumulation in production versus struggles against accumulation by dispossession. Besides those on the working places, struggles also address the background conditions, that capitalist production presupposes (Fraser 2014). Integration in a world economy does not mean equal conditions – or even convergence in all countries – but rather, the division of the world into hegemonic power and dependent economy (Wallerstein 1990). Additionally, capitalism is far from stable: crises of different types (inflation and stagnation, production and distribution) emerge frequently, changing the conditions for political participation as anti-systemic movement produce adaptation in capitalism (Arrighi, Hopkins, and Wallerstein 1989).

Building on Polanyi, Burawoy singled out a sequence of three successive counter-movements: respectively, for labor rights, social rights, and human rights. While the wave of anti-austerity protests that developed between 2010 and 2014 were all reacting to a sense of political dispossession face to a separation between popular politics and power, among their characteristics was, however, a focus on domestic conditions, even if within a global consciousness. As he noted, "If these movements were globally connected, it was their national framing that drove their distinctive momentum. They may share underlying economic causes but their expression is shaped by the terms and structure of national politics" (2015, p. 16). The analysis of the relations between movements reacting to commodification or recommodification and movements reacting to ex-commodification introduces important considerations about some organizational and identity challenges for nowadays protests as a need to go global enters however in tension with the weakening of previous structures of mobilization, linked to conceptions of social protection, that each neoliberal waves brings about.

In a similar vein, David Harvey (2003) pointed instead at the capitalist logic of development and crisis, singling out different forms of accumulation, as respectively oriented to production and to dispossession – the latter reminding of the original accumulation of capital on its need to expand through special relations with noncapitalist social formations. The periodic return to accumulation by dispossession points at "the continuous role and persistence of the predatory practices of 'primitive' or 'original' accumulation within the long historical geography of capital accumulation" (Harvey 2003, p. 144). While the former is based on the exploitation of wage labor and conditions defining the social wage, the latter include the resistance to the most classic forms of primitive accumulation (especially the expulsion of peasant populations from their land, Sassen 2014), but also the withdrawal of the state from its social obligations, the destruction of culture and nature; the effects of financialization (Harvey 2005, p. 203). Accumulation by dispossession and its discontents are linked indeed to the cyclical emergence of profit making through financial speculation as an alternative to profit making through production in order to address the problems of overaccumulation. In fact, access to cheap input (in terms of land, labor and raw materials) is considered as relevant, as the widening of markets, in creating profits (Harvey 2003, p. 145). To these, Harvey adds the predation related to the credit system and financial capital, as through accumulation by dispossession, various assets are released at very low cost (Harvey 2003, p. 149).

The very logic of accumulation is expected to affect the forms of collective mobilization. As different forms of accumulation coexist – in different mix in different countries – this introduces internal tension within social movements, both progressive and otherwise. Recent movements have so appeared bifurcated between mobilizations around expanded reproduction, and mobilization around accumulation by dispossession. Different from the primitive accumulation, accumulation by dispossession brings about a withdrawal of previous achievements with a (still unfulfilled) need to search for new organizational model. As neoliberalism attacked "all forms of social solidarity that put restraints on capital accumulation" (Harvey 2005, p. 75), the forms that the social movements on the left took in the years 1945–1973, with expanded reproduction in the ascendant, emerged as inappropriate to contrast accumulation by dispossession (Harvey 2005, p. 172).

In sum,

> *Accumulation by dispossession entails a very different set of practices from accumulation through the expansion of wage labor in industry and agriculture. The latter, which dominated processes of capital accumulation in the 1950s and 1960s, gave rise to an oppositional culture (such as that embedded in trade unions and working-class political parties) that produced embedded liberalism. Dispossession, on the other hand, is fragmented and particular – a privatization here, an environmental degradation there, a financial crisis of indebtedness somewhere else. It is hard to oppose all of this specificity and particularity without appeal to universal principles. Dispossession entails the loss of rights. Hence the turn to a universalistic rhetoric of human rights, dignity, sustainable ecological practices, environmental rights, and the like, as the basis for a unified oppositional politics.*

(Harvey 2005, p. 179)

2.4.4   Movements of the Crisis?

When looking at anti-austerity protests we should consider that they developed in a situation of crisis that took different characteristics at national (and also subnational) level. The Global Justice Movement and the anti-austerity protests were both addressing neoliberal capitalism but in different moments. Research on the labor movement has often looked at waves of strikes, singling out that picks of protest are usually recorded in times of full employment when the workers are structurally stronger. Moreover, economic growth also implies higher margins for investing profits in increase in salaries and taxes to support welfare expenses. By contrast, in times of economic crisis, unemployment hinders the capacity for struggling for improved salaries and working conditions as well as the resources available for state interventions.

Strikes are therefore expected to decline and, when called for, they are more likely to be defensive than proactive (Franzosi 2004).

Also in social movement studies, a distinction has been made between movements of abundance and movements of crisis. In general, social movement studies have considered crisis as particularly unfriendly for social movements. The best that they expect was what Kerbo (1982) called long time ago movements of crisis, which he compared with the movements of abundance, as, for example, the movements from the 1960s and 1970s. In his analysis *movements of affluence* are to be found in relatively good times; they are often formed mainly by conscience members, and they are better organized and less likely to use violence (Kerbo 1982, p. 654). In contrast, *movements of crisis* are sparked by unemployment, food shortages, and dislocations, when everyday life is challenged during threatening political and social crises. Their participants are, at least in the early stages, mainly the beneficiaries of the requested changes, and protests tend to be more spontaneous, more often involving violent outbursts. In general, while movements of abundance (and opportunities) are expected to be stronger, larger, longer-lasting, pragmatic, optimistic, and more often successful, movements of crisis (and threats) are expected to be weaker, smaller, shorter, radical, pessimistic, and more often unsuccessful (della Porta 2013). In this vision, movements of crisis are conceptualized, in a way resonant of Polany, as mainly reactive types of mobilization: weakly organized, they do not have many resources for mobilization. Additionally, they would tend to be more violent and more pessimistic. They would mobilize the affected: not a large supportive constituency, but rather those who are more discontent as the unemployed who is hit in the great recession. Moreover, they have been presented as destined to fail in their attempt to resist changes.

Research on the labor movement has linked different types of mobilizations to these alternations between affluence and crisis. In fact, especially in moments of crisis, legitimacy enters in tension with profitability, so that

> *Efforts to overcome the tendency toward a crisis of legitimacy through improving the condition of the working class as a whole (rising wages, improved working conditions, social welfare provisions) can only work for short amounts of time or small segments of the working class without provoking a crisis of profitability. If the crisis of global capitalism of the 1970s was largely precipitated by a squeeze on profitability, the current global crisis of capitalism is increasingly characterized by a deep crisis of legitimacy as inequality mushrooms and growing numbers have lost access to the means to produce their own livelihood without being provided with any opportunity to make a living within the circuits of capital.*

(Silver and Karataşlı 2015, p. 140)

While comparative analyses of social movements in the European periphery show that it was exactly where the crisis was stronger that it triggered higher levels of activities with new repertoires of action as well as organizational forms and claims, and even able to achieve political success, the reflection on the different challenges for contentious actors in times of abundance versus times of crisis remains relevant (della

Porta 2017a and 2017b). As some research on labor activism has pointed at, moment of crisis can indeed trigger the creation of resources of solidarity during protests. The long strikes or the factory occupations, as the camping in the squares or the pickets of the unemployed, that characterized the anti-austerity protests, should be indeed ana- lyzed as reaction to the crisis that then creates innovative ideas and practices (della Porta 2015a). Gramsci's *organic crises,* as crises of hegemony of the ruling class, tend indeed to fuel local militancy that can then converge in campaigns and movement projects (Cox and Nielsen 2013).

Indeed, research on the protests during the Great Recession at the European peripheries singled out several differences. In particular, while Polanyi's type of coun- termovements mobilized everywhere, it has been where the socioeconomic crisis had more disruptive effects on the everyday life of the citizens that movements with more innovative characters have emerged. In particular, in countries like Iceland, Greece, and Spain, anti-austerity protests went well beyond the claims for recovering old rights, developing instead a critique of the hollowing out of social protection, but also of the way in which the welfare state had developed. The very concept of the "common good," as different from both private and public ones, pointed at the need for citizens' participation in the definition and implementation of their own rights. Also, while popular sovereignty was claimed back for citizens, there were also attempts to broaden the concept of citizenship to go well beyond the members of the nation. Including also traditional organizations, anti-austerity protest in these countries invented new collective performances which, as the protest camps, aimed at experimenting with alternative forms of democracy (della Porta 2015a; della Porta, Andretta et al. 2016).

2.5   SUMMARY

In this chapter, we have asked ourselves whether looking at the social structure and at changes in this may provide a useful key to the interpretation of collective action. We have examined a series of recent modifications to the social and political structure, and their innovative potential in relation to consolidated lines of conflict structuring. The transformation of the economic sphere – in particular, the move to a more or less advanced service and administrative sector and the decentralization of industrial pro- duction – has undermined not only the numerical consistency of the working class but also the living and working conditions which facilitated class action. Today, we face greater diversity in professional roles and interests. On the political side, the legit- imacy of the state is called into question both by the tendency toward globalization and by that toward localization, but also by a retreat of the state in the face of the market. Furthermore, the capacity of the state to create and reproduce social groups through public intervention has led to an increasing number of demands which are fragmented and increasingly difficult to mediate. New potential for conflict originates therefore in the increasingly blurred borders between the public and the private spheres, particularly from the multiplication of criteria to define rights of citizenship and the growing capacity for intervention among public and private institutions, in areas of private life such as physical and mental health. Conflicts developed around the definition of new identities with particular attention to cultural issues, lifestyles, knowledge.

Mobilizations and movements have developed in recent years around interests involving actors who can be associated in various ways with the transformations that we have just reviewed. Scholars such as Touraine have identified the central conflicts in postindustrial society in struggles for the control of symbolic production. Others have emphasized the high level of involvement of new middle-class members in new conflicts, as a result of their particular professional position and of the intellectual resources that they control. However, the flexibilization of the labor market has produced increasing poverty in the North and the South; and the attack on the welfare state by dominant neoliberal and free market economic policies has produced the return of protest on "materialistic" issues of social justice.

It is important, however, to remember that collective action does not spring automatically from structural tensions. In this respect, it is still doubtful that a new political cleavage, with the capacity to structure conflicts similar to that demonstrated by the capital–labor or the center–periphery cleavages in industrial society, has emerged, let alone been consolidated. Numerous factors determine whether this will occur. These factors include the availability of adequate organizational resources, the ability of movement leaders to produce appropriate ideological representations, and the presence of a favorable political context. The rest of our book is dedicated to the mechanisms that contribute to an explanation of the shift from structure to action.

CHAPTER 3

The Symbolic Dimension of Collective Action

On April 26, 2016, the British paper The Guardian reported on a protest that earlier that month had stormed a branch of laCaixa bank in Barcelona (Perry 2016). The action had been promoted by members of PAH (Plataforma de Afectados por la Hipoteca, or "Mortgage Victims Platform"), an organization that fought for the rights of those who had lost (or risked losing) their homes due to their inability to pay mortgages in the aftermath of the big credit crisis of 2008. Having gained worldwide notoriety when its former spokeswoman, Ada Colau, had been elected mayor of Barcelona in 2015, PAH had been conducting a massive campaign targeting not only banks but other financial operators and estate entrepreneurs that had purchased mortgages assets in order to repossess struggling homeowners' properties at a bargain price. The article then proceeded to link the events in Barcelona to initiatives that in the previous years had mobilized on basic rights for city dwellers and the use of public spaces, such as the occupation of Gezi park and Taksim square in Istanbul, the Nuits debouts protests in Place de la Republique in Paris, or the public workshops by deprived women in Dehli. It wondered if, and to what extent, the voices expressed in those actions would be listened to in the upcoming UN Habitat

Social Movements: An Introduction, Third Edition. Donatella della Porta and Mario Diani.
© 2020 John Wiley & Sons Ltd. Published 2020 by John Wiley & Sons Ltd.

Meeting, due in Quito the following fall, with the definition of a "new urban agenda" as its key theme.

Despite their media exposure, the episodes of contention mentioned in the Guardian were just illustrations of a much larger current of urban struggles. Over the last few decades, citizens have mobilized on a broad range of urban issues. As Polish sociologist Anna Domaradzka recently summarized:

> [S]ome key social conflicts nowadays concern urban issues and often center on socio-spatial rights and needs. Main areas of struggle include the growing privatization of both services and places... the gentrification processes pushing low-income groups out of upscaling neighborhoods.... and the lack of affordable housing and accessible public spaces. While a profit-oriented logic is increasingly shaping the cities, they tend to become less livable and less adapted to the residents' needs.
>
> (Domaradzka 2018, p. 608)

While growing inequalities and the resulting differential access to the opportunities offered by urban life have been central to urban mobilizations, they have often been paralleled by a quest for greater involvement of citizens in the planning and management of the urban space. Rather than focusing exclusively on redistributive issues and basic needs, urban activism has often defended the public dimension of urban life. This has not just meant opposing the increasing privatization of public spaces (as illustrated, for example, by the sale of council land to private developers in the United Kingdom), but more generally advocating a greater involvement of citizens in decision-making processes concerning their social environment (Domaradzka 2018).

Interestingly, the Guardian item was titled "Right to the City: Can This Growing Social Movement Win over City Officials?" Suggesting a connection between actions scattered in different corners of the world, the article drew on an expression, "right to the city" (henceforth, RTC), that over the last decades has been increasingly used to denote urban movements' attempts to merge concerns for urban quality of life and efforts to strengthen urban democracy into a broader, coherent political project. Originally introduced by French urban analyst Henri Lefebvre (1968) and later popularized by Marxist geographer David Harvey (2003), RTC may be defined as "both the individual liberty to access urban resources (including space, services, and infrastructure) and the ability to exercise a

collective power to reshape the processes of urbanization"
(Domaradzka 2018: 612). Across the world, the expression RTC has
been used to denote instances of local collective action addressing
urban issues (Eynaud, Juan, and Mourey 2018; Florea, Gagyi, and
Jacobsson 2018; Grazioli and Caciagli 2018; Mathivet and
Buckingham 2009; Novy and Colomb 2013; Parnell and Pieterse
2010). These were not necessarily homogeneous in terms of their
specific focus, or their proponents' ideological approach.

Still, referring to RTC has facilitated activists on multiple grounds:
it has helped them to link different, potentially contradictory local
issues into broader strategies for urban renewal; it has facilitated the
establishment of connections between experiences of collective
action in different countries and in different political phases; it has
drawn institutional actors', as well as bystander publics', attention to
urban dynamics and change as a distinctive ground for action and,
possibly reform. Of course, this has sometimes happened to the cost
of overstretching the concept, and empirical analysis suggests that
even where RTC is broadly recognized as a meaningful category, its
capacity to shape collective action at the local level is not necessarily
huge (see, e.g., Diani, Ernstson, and Jasny 2018). Even so, the evoca-
tive power of this expression and the influence it has exerted over
urban collective action across the globe should be recognized (Mayer
2009; Brenner, Marcuse, and Mayer 2012; Domaradzka 2018).

There are several points worth noting in this example. First, the fact that many
people (activists and observers alike) speak of "collective action for citizens' RTC," even
suggesting, with the *Guardian*'s editors, the existence of a "RTC movement," does not
mean that the issues they address be necessarily nor automatically part of the same,
coherent agenda. It is certainly true that the expression RTC has often been used, with
a considerable degree of success, to denote actions mobilizing people on issues ranging
from housing to urban pollution to privatization of public spaces in urban areas. However, the linking of these themes under the RTC heading has not been the result of
intrinsic properties of those issues. It has rather resulted from a process of meaning
attribution, which has emphasized the elements common to different issues and identified a symbol (RTC) that could effectively weave them together into a (quasi) coherent
narrative, to be shared by activists as well as by observers such as newspaper editors.

In other words, broad descriptions of social and political reality do not have an
independent life outside of people's efforts to characterize them as such. The fact that
one specific representation of reality somehow managed to bring under a common
heading a set of more or less disparate problems and activities does not mean that
such representation be the only plausible one. In particular, many of the themes that
RTC synthesizes in a particular way have also been addressed by global justice

activists over the last decades. Urban processes have been heavily affected by global-ization dynamics as cities competed in a new, world-scale division of labor (Sassen 1991) and global capitals identified in cities a major locus for investment, both in the North as well as in the South. Not only it is difficult to identify a RTC agenda wholly distinct from that of global justice movements between the 1990s and the 2000s (della Porta 2007): actors mobilizing on urban issues have been found to be close in variable measures to both global justice and RTC activism (Mayer 2009, 2012).

Nor did the label RCT emerge out of urban conflicts, which were necessarily new. Cities have always represented a major locus for contention, even before the advent of modern society (Castells 1983; Farro and Demirhisar 2014; Gould 1995; Nicholls and Uitermark 2017; Tilly 1986). In truth, many of the struggles often associated with RTC were already there well before the term started circulating (Domaradzka 2018, p. 610): for example, housing, health, uneven access to education, attempts by citizens to shape in some forms their urban environment had been tackled by sustained collective action innumerable times, at least as back as the nineteenth century; and the concept of "urban social movements" (Castells 1972) was coined in reference to the very same movements that in the 1960s and 1970s had inspired the articulation of the RTC idea. This is not to deny that referring to RTC has contributed to approaches to urban prob-lems that attempted to go beyond single-issue, not-in-my-backyard conceptions of urban activism. But it needs to be stated that this has been the result of a social construction, not of the spontaneous convergence of obviously coherent themes. The key message from this example is, any mobilization attempt rests on its promoters' ability to connect a set of meaningful events and issues into a coherent narrative, with which a broad and distinct constituency may identify, and to successfully challenge competing accounts of the same phenomena. It rests, in other words, on symbolic and cultural production. This draws our attention to the role of culture in collective action dynamics (Baumgarten, Daphi, and Ullrich 2014; Williams 2004). In order to explore such role properly, however, we need to be aware that for a long time the role of culture in collective action dynamics has been conceived primarily in terms of the relationship between values and action, not between interpretations and action.

3.1 CULTURE AND ACTION: THE ROLE OF VALUES

We may think of social action as driven largely by the fundamental principles with which actors identify. According to this perspective, values will influence how actors define specific goals, and identify strategies which are both efficient and morally acceptable. Moreover, values will provide the motivations necessary to sustain the costs of action. The more intense one's socialization to a particular vision of the world, the stronger the impetus to act. The characteristics of a given system of values will shape the components of action.

How is this model articulated in the case of collective action in movements? How, in other words, is it possible to describe values as the central explanatory variable in the case of actions which, by definition, call into question at least some of the (culturally legitimized) assets of power in a given society? On the one hand, we can relate collective action to lack of social integration in the system, or, alternatively, to the inability of the system to reproduce and reinforce its fundamental values. The tradition of research into movements prior to the 1960s, which largely focused on revolutionary movements of the right and the left in the first half of the century, paid great attention to interpretations of this type (Kornhauser 1959). Nowadays, according to this perspective, the emergence of grassroots, radical movements could be interpreted as evidence of the failure of society to instill free-market values among its members, most notably the younger generation. For example, schools have often been blamed by business and neoliberal politicians for their hostility to entrepreneurial culture. On the other hand, we could also interpret collective action as evidence of the emergence of trends towards social reintegration rather than disintegration; as proof, in other words, of the formation and consolidation of new value systems. For example, we could regard RTC activism as the expression of specific sets of deeply felt values. Within RTC initiatives, we find the strong influence of values related to both the historical experience of the left, fighting inequality both within and across countries and geographical areas, and to more recent aspirations to the elaboration of alternative styles and new, participatory and democratic ways of managing the urban space. One might also link the emergence of RTC activism to the gradual spread of values that prioritize self-realization over material needs (see e.g. Diakoumakos 2015 in reference to Greece).

In the last decades, the link between the emergence of new conflicts and the value dimension has been stressed with considerable force in the context of various forms of "new politics," connected with environmental issues, feminism, peace, and civil rights (Inglehart 1977; Inglehart and Welzel 2005). In the most ambitious formulation of this model, the rise of "new" political movements from the 1970s onwards is associated with more general processes of change from materialist to post-materialist values (Inglehart 1977; Inglehart and Welzel 2005). Inglehart's argument is based on two assumptions. According to what he defines as the *scarcity hypothesis* (Melucci 1989), there is a hierarchy of needs, and needs of a higher order (relating, for example, to the intellectual and personal growth of the individual) are conceivable only when those of a lower order (relating, for example, to physical survival) have been satisfied. Moreover, according to the "socialization hypothesis" (Inglehart 1990: 56), there is a continuity in adult life that leaves broadly unaltered both the fundamental principles and the order of priorities established in the formative years leading to maturity.

The experiences and lifestyles of those born in the West in the period following the Second World War, and who became adults in the 1960s or later, were very different from those of preceding generations. In particular, they enjoyed unprecedented levels of affluence, easier access to higher education, and reduced exposure to the risks of war. In Inglehart's view, this situation produced conditions which were particularly favorable to changes in needs and basic orientations. In particular, they facilitated a gradual weakening of the system of "material" values and their replacement by "postmaterial" values. The former reflect concerns relating to economic well-being and personal and collective security; the latter are oriented primarily towards the affirmation of expressive needs. They prioritize individual achievement in private, and an expansion of freedom of expression, democratic participation, and self-government in the public domain. Accordingly, these values are expected to be particularly conducive to various forms of participation in the "new social movements," given the attention that the women's or the environmental movements have paid to the connection between individual and collective goals (Melucci 1989).

The emergence of postmaterial values has been documented by an impressive amount of survey data collected in the United States and in key European countries from the beginning of the 1970s.[3] Since then, the gap between the number of people holding materialist values (i.e. in the basic formulation of the survey questionnaires, identifying "maintaining order in the nation" and "fighting rising prices" as their top policy priorities out of a list of four) and those holding postmaterialist values (i.e. assigning priority to "giving people more say in important government decisions" and "protecting freedom of speech") has narrowed substantially, with postmaterialists overcoming materialists by the start of the new millennium in most countries (Norris and Inglehart 2019, Chapter 4.1). Furthermore, the younger cohorts of the population have been shown to be consistently more sensitive to postmaterialist values than older cohorts (Norris and Inglehart 2019, Chapter 4.9).

While the postmaterialism thesis has been widely discussed since its original formulation (see della Porta and Diani 2006, pp. 68–72 for a synthesis), doubts about the relationship between movements and postmaterialism have been reinforced in recent years by two very different developments. On the one hand, the first decades of the new millennium have brought about a totally different example of the link between values and collective action. Whereas the discussion had focused on values (in particular, value change) and participatory democratic politics, the reemergence of ethnic and tribal conflicts in many areas of the world, and most particularly the spread of fundamentalism (well before September 11, 2001: Bennani-Chraïbi and Fillieule 2003; Wickham 2013), has set a dramatically different intellectual agenda. Samuel Huntington's (1993, 1996) well-known "clash of civilization" thesis and cognate arguments, suggesting a fundamental conflict between Islam and the West, have assigned values a very different role than the one implied by postmaterialist theorists. They propose a view of social movements as deeply embedded in strongly held sets of values, which represent the stake for fundamental conflicts, susceptible of orienting future relations between major areas of the world.

However, empirical tests of this thesis suggest a more complex picture: contrary to expectations, Norris and Inglehart (2002) found attitudes toward democracy to be very similar in the two camps; but they also found deep and irreconcilable differences in the definition of private lifestyles, especially in gender relations and sexual freedom. This holds true despite the substantial presence of conservative Christian values in important Western countries, most notably the United States. Norris and Inglehart's conclusion that "the central values separating Islam and the West revolve far more centrally around Eros than Demos" (2002, p. 3) brings further support to the argument of a gradual shift in priorities from "public politics" to "personal politics," and is not necessarily in contradiction with arguments about postmaterialist values in the West.

The 2010s have also seen the strengthening of political organizations and parties that advocate an agenda strongly opposed to some of the main tenets of postmaterialism. In the Western world, most impactful events like the Brexit referendum or

Donald Trump's election in 2016 have been preceded by the growth of forces that explicitly challenge the priority assigned to environmental protection over short-term economic gain through the use of traditional resources and economic practices (as exemplified by Trumps' support for coal against renewable energy sources), or try to bring back the clock on issue of gender equality, division of roles within the family, abortion, or even divorce rights and minority rights. What has been broadly framed (if possibly simplistically) as right-wing populism has achieved considerable electoral success in countries ranging from South America (most dramatically with the election of former military and openly fascist Jair Bolsonaro as Brazil president) to European countries, including recent democracies like Hungary or Poland, respectively, ruled by Orban's Fidesz party and Kascinsy's PiS), but also EU founding members like Italy with Matteo Salvini's Lega in the driving seat of a difficult coalition that also includes Beppe Grillo's Five Star Movement. In Europe, intervention in the economy and a relaunch of welfare policies in open challenge to the EU's neoliberal approach has been highly selective in terms of focus (with emphasis on traditional families) and access, restricted to the "true" nationals to the exclusion of migrants. This combination of social conservatism and (more or less mild) economic interventionism has also been explicitly linked to a new cleavage within European politics, pitching the "winners" and the "losers" of globalization processes against each other. Hanspeter Kriesi, in particular, has represented the cultural axis of the new divide in terms of "integration vs. demarcation," to emphasize the gap between social groups open to universal values and cultural pluralism, and sectors focusing instead on the strengthening of preexisting identities and value systems (Kriesi et al. 2008, 2012).

These developments represent a clear challenge to postmaterialist values. While accepting that we are facing a "cultural backlash" (Norris and Inglehart 2019), proponents of the thesis do not see them as a challenge to the theory itself. This on the ground that "far from a conservative revival, or slow-down in progressive change, the survey data confirms that the long-term trajectory of cultural evolution has continued to move Western societies in a more socially liberal direction over successive decades" (Norris and Inglehart 2019, p. 454). Norris and Inglehart (2019, Chapter 4) also add that generational differences may explain differences in support to populist parties, with younger generations more represented among supporters of what they call progressive "populist" parties like Syriza in Greece, Podemos in Spain, or Five Star in Italy (even though the latter's orientation might be reconsidered after their involvement in government with extreme right Lega). However, the link between postmaterialism and participation has also been questioned. Comparison between waves of the major surveys like European Value Survey or European Social Survey have pointed at generational effects: the generation most committed to public protest would be that of the so called baby boomers, that came of age in the 1960s, while subsequent generations would be less interested in activism. There would be no clear cohort effect, or, in other words, no general trend for younger generations, holding more postmaterialist values, to increase their involvement in protest (Grasso 2016).

This brings us to the most basic issue, one that goes beyond the details of Inglehart's thesis, namely, the relationship between values and action. If people's values can explain their fundamental sensitivity to particular questions and problems, their impact need not necessarily go beyond this level. In his study of civil rights activists in the United States in the 1960s, McAdam (1986), for instance, found that prospective activists' commitment to values of freedom and equality was a poor predictor of their actual participation. An exclusive focus on values is unlikely to generate proper insights on how values translate into action, and on why they do so in different ways in different countries. To this purpose, we need a view of social action that links the sphere of values with that of strategic and solidaristic behavior in a coherent fashion. Values are reinterpreted constantly by actors, and their impact on actual behavior is always filtered by the way actors interpret their specific context (a point, incidentally, that even theorists of value change would gladly subscribe to: Norris and Inglehart 2019, Chapters 5 and 6). Accordingly, attention must be paid both to the cognitive dimension of action, as we shall do in the following sections of this chapter, and to the relationship between action and collective identity – a theme we shall consider in the next chapter.

3.2   CULTURE AND ACTION: THE COGNITIVE PERSPECTIVE

The idea that culture, and specifically its impact on collective action, can be reduced to values has been controversial for quite some time. In particular, it has been observed that "culture influences action not by providing the ultimate values toward which action is oriented, but by shaping a repertoire or 'tool kit' of habits, skills, and styles from which people construct 'strategies of action'" (Swidler 1986, p. 273). That is to say, culture provides the cognitive apparatus that people need to orient themselves in the world. This apparatus consists of a multiplicity of cultural and ideational elements which include beliefs, ceremonies, artistic forms, and informal practices such as language, conversation, stories, daily rituals (Swidler 1986, p. 273). The content of cultural models, of which values are a key component, is of secondary importance here in relation to the vision of culture as a set of instruments that social actors use to make sense of their own life experiences.

In relation to the study of collective action, this standpoint allows us to consider problems which an analysis focusing exclusively on values would have neglected. Strong identification with certain norms and values can even represent an obstacle to actors' freedom, inasmuch as it may limit their capacity to interpret their changing contexts. As Jasper and Polletta (2019: 63) have noted

> *We are more likely to view culture as discrete meanings that can be combined in a variety of ways for a variety of strategic (and other) purposes... rather than a stable system that changes only slowly or occasionally, we now see even the reproduction of culture as an active process.*

In other words, it is always possible to interpret the experience of social movements as the unceasing production and reproduction of "cultural codes" (Melucci 1989, 1996) or as a cognitive praxis (see also Eyerman and Jamison 1991). Symbolic production is not a precondition for conflict but, rather, one of its constituent parts.

3.2.1   Interpretative Frames

Among scholars interested in symbolic aspects of collective action, the notion of the schema of interpretation, or frame, borrowed from the theoretical work of Erving Goffman (1974) has proved very influential. Frames have been defined as schemata of interpretation that enable individuals "to locate, perceive, identify and label occurrences within their life space and the world at large" (Snow et al. 1986, p. 464). A frame thus "is a general, standardized, predefined structure (in the sense that it already belongs to the receiver's knowledge of the world), which allows recognition of the world, and guides perception... allowing him/her to build defined expectations about what is to happen, that is to make sense of his/her reality" (Donati 1992, pp. 141–142; also see Johnston 2002; Johnston and Alimi 2013).

Frame analysis allows us to capture the process of meaning attribution which lies behind the explosion of any conflict. In fact, symbolic production enables us to attribute to events and behaviors, of individuals or groups, a meaning which facilitates the activation of mobilization. There are three stages to this process, corresponding to the recognition of certain occurrences as social problems, of possible strategies that would resolve these, and of motivations for acting on this knowledge. Benford and Snow (2000, pp. 615–618) define these steps as the "diagnostic, prognostic, and motivational" dimensions of framing.

Diagnostic Element

In the first place, appropriate interpretative frames allow the conversion into a social problem, potentially the object of collective action, of a phenomenon whose origins were previously attributed to natural factors, to individual responsibility, or simply deemed as unlikely candidates for being the object of sustained collective action. For example, since the early 2000s several cities of artistic and historical relevance have seen the growth of protests that identified mass tourism as one of the main responsible or the deterioration of living conditions of urban dwellers: rising rents for ordinary flats due to the spread of short-term lets such as Airbnb have elicited growing levels of contention; so have the replacement of traditional commercial outlets serving the community with those catering for the needs of the tourist crowd, or the disruption of everyday life caused by huge concentrations of (often unruly) tourists (Colomb and Novy 2017). The citizens of Barcelona in Spain, a major tourist destination, have been particularly active against mass tourism. Their campaigns have seen the involvement of left-wing nationalist parties like Candidatura d'Unitat Popular (CUP, Popular Unity Candidacy); they have also been a driving force behind the emergence in 2014 of grassroots party *Barcelona en comù* (Hughes 2018; Russo and Scarnato 2018).

The identification of one or more issues as worthy of collective action usually implies connecting them to a broader model of reference. This also applies to episodes of contention that are fairly limited in scope, or to single campaigns that take place within a delimited time frame. Recent examples of urban struggles illustrate both phenomena. For example, squatting activists in Rome managed to go beyond the limitations of a single-issue type of action. Referring to broader frames like "urban commons" or "right to the city" enabled them to develop broader platforms (Di Feliciantonio 2017; Grazioli and Caciagli 2018). Also in Italy, a network of groups tried to articulate their opposition to Expo 2015, a universal exposition held in Milan, by extending their critical discourse from the specific event to more general themes. To this purpose they referred to three broader frames: one inspired by RTC, questioning the model of development associated with mega-events; another addressing the exploitation of both humans (the workforce, minorities, etc.) and the environment taking place in the context of such events; a third exposing the cosmetic adoption of pro-environment, pro-equality rhetoric by businesses unwilling to alter the substance of their practices (Bertuzzi 2017, p. 753).

Diagnosing a problem always entails identifying the actors who are entitled to have opinions on it. This is usually a highly contentious process. Various social actors (state agencies, political parties, groups with hostile interests, media operators) try to affirm their own control of specific issues, imposing their own interpretation of these, to the detriment of representations proposed by social movements. Therefore, the latter must, in the first place, claim the legitimacy to deal with particular problems in ways compatible with their own broader orientations (Gusfield 1989; Shemtov 1999). It is through symbolic conflict that certain actors succeed in being recognized as entitled to speak in the name of certain interests and tendencies. In the case of the RTC frame, its success is reflected in the ability to identify a broad category of "urban dwellers" threatened by market forces, that brings together actors that might otherwise be reduced to a *nimby* (not-in-my-backyard) logic, focusing on specific aspects of urban decay, or be fragmented among different activist groups with specific agendas (squatting and housing, opposition to security policies, fighting inequality and deprivation, etc.). Sometimes, however, a successful frame like that of "global justice" may actually emphasize the extreme heterogeneity of the actors involved in collective action campaigns, implicitly suggesting their entitlement to speak on behalf of humankind. For example, the preparatory document of the First World Social Forum held in Porto Alegre in January 2001 stated, "Social forces from around the world have gathered here at the World Social Forum in Porto Alegre. Unions and NGOs, movements and organizations, intellectuals and artists... women and men, farmers, workers, unemployed, professionals, students, blacks and indigenous peoples, coming from the South and from the North" (http://www.communitycurrency.org/WSF.html).

It is important to remember that dominant frames always emerge from a number of alternative options, all logically plausible yet with different implications. For example, if an anticapitalist frame had been the main representation of the North–South tensions within the global justice movement, this would have rendered more difficult the involvement of moderate middle-class sectors, more focused on ethical questions. Tensions between different frames have also been identified for RTC activism: the very same idea of RTC has been articulated in different ways by activists in the North and South of the globe (Mayer 2009), with the former often prioritizing alternative lifestyles and cultural resistance by critical sectors of the new middle classes (e.g. Eynaud et al. 2018), and the latter focusing more frequently on struggles for survival by dispossessed communities (e.g. Mathivet and Buckingham 2009).

Another crucial step in the social construction of a problem consists of the identification of those responsible for the situation in which the aggrieved population finds itself. For the unemployed as well as for members of marginal groups, a powerful restraint to mobilization is the widespread belief that poverty depends on individual failure. As William Gamson noted long ago:

> [T]he heat of moral judgment is intimately related to beliefs about what acts or conditions have caused people to suffer undeserved hardship or loss. The critical dimension is the abstractness of the target... When we see impersonal, abstract forces as responsible for our suffering, we are taught to accept what cannot be changed and make the best of it... At the other extreme, if one attributes undeserved suffering to malicious or selfish acts by clearly identifiable groups, the emotional component of an injustice frame will almost certainly be there.
>
> (Gamson 1992: 32)

When looking at diagnostic practices, we also need to take into account the attempts by third parties (e.g. institutions) or by movement opponents to transform the symbolic power of movement frames, to reduce their radical potential, and possibly turn them to their own advantage. An excellent illustration of this dynamic comes from the extent to which institutional actors and even businesses and urban developers have come to use "right to the city." International organizations such as the United Nations (UN Habitat program) and UNESCO have repeatedly characterized their strategies to improve quality of urban life and access to social and cultural facilities, particularly in developing countries, in terms of RTC. In 2005, the Second World Urban Forum in Porto Alegre adopted the World Charter on the Right to the City, that summarizes under that expression a set of rights ranging from housing and work to education, health, and also participation and information (Domaradzka 2018, p. 613). The main interlocutors of this particular version of the concept are not radical, anti-systemic challengers but rather local authorities, focused on good, effective management of urban problems rather than on addressing major urban inequalities (Domaradzka 2018, p. 614). Local councils have often attempted to emphasize the cross-class nature of the issues raised by RTC activists, promoting strategies of revitalization of urban areas that emphasize the cooperation between private and public interests – for example, in the urban regeneration strategies in the UK, based on public–private partnerships (Cento Bull and Jones 2006).

Sometimes, private developers and investors have gone one step further in the reinterpretation of RTC. Usually identified as the main culprits for the privatization of the urban space, e.g. in the form of gated communities, or the creation of shopping malls or other "public" spaces with selected access, or the "requalification" (read: gentrification) of formerly lower class neighborhoods, they have developed alternative rhetorical strategies stressing "their own right to (profit from) the city... [this] hijacking of the urban movements slogans creates new challenges in terms of common narrative" (Domaradzka 2018, p. 614). Private developers have for example built on critical actors' attempts to revitalize rundown urban areas, turning them into fashionable gentrified, pseudo-"alternative" neighborhoods – as famously illustrated by the Sankt Pauli neighborhood in Hamburg (NION 2010; Novy and Colomb 2013). This reasoning can be extended much further than the RTC case, as virtually all contemporary movements address themes that can provide business opportunities. For example, in the United States large corporations have gained control of ideas generated by activists focused on issues such as breast cancer, organic food, or recycling practices. They have entered a symbolic domain previously monopolized by challengers through complex symbolic conflicts. These have often ended with corporate actors coming to "dominate fields initiated by social movements" (King and Busa 2017, p. 549).

Another strategy available to the opponents of social movements consists of denying the very foundation of their grievances. For example, the actors targeted by global justice movements challenged the negative view of globalization by emphasizing the positive consequences of the liberalization of markets. They pointed at the growth of overall income and welfare in developing countries; the statistics suggesting that the market share of developing countries is higher than before; the rise of people above the poverty level; the growth of a prosperous middle class. Apart from denying the issue, they also attempted to shift the blame to other actors: economic deprivation was framed as the product of corrupt national governments whose policies would remain disastrous unless subjected to close scrutiny from international institutions such as WTO or IMF; moreover, "no-global" protestors calling for protectionist measures were stigmatized for helping strong corporate powers in the North (both business and unions) by denying poor countries the chance to compete on the global market.

The identification of social problems and those responsible for them is, inevitably, highly selective. The highlighting of one particular problem leads to the neglect of other potential sources of protest or mobilization which do not fit the interpretation of reality adopted. For example, for a long time, the preeminence within Western society of representations of conflict according to a functional/class or national dimension has made the identification of other sources of conflict – such as gender differences – very difficult. Cultural development places actors in the position of being able to choose, from among various possible sources of frustration and revenge, those against which they should direct all their energies, not to mention their emotional identification. The process can, in this sense, be seen as a reduction of social complexity. At the same time, however, once solid interpretative frames have been established, the possibility of identifying other potential conflicts becomes limited and other ways of representing the same theme are needed. In this sense, the construction of reality, created by relatively marginal actors responsible for mobilizing movements, is inextricably linked to asymmetries of power.

Prognostic Element

The action of interpreting the world goes beyond identifying problems, however. It involves seeking solutions and hypothesizing new social patterns, new ways of regulating relationships between groups, new articulations of consensus and of the exercise of power. There is often a strong utopian dimension present in this endeavor. The symbolic elaboration of a movement is thus not necessarily limited to the selection, on the basis of the parameters of instrumental rationality, of "practical" goals in a given social and cultural context. Rather, it opens new spaces and new prospects for action, making it possible to think of aims and objectives which the dominant culture tends instead to exclude from the outset. In this sense, it is possible to conceive of movements as media through which concepts and perspectives, which might otherwise have remained marginal, are disseminated in society. Michel Foucault (1977) noted, for example, that time not only changes what is thought, but what *can* be thought, or conceived of as well. This applies to every phase of insurgency in collective action: it is, in fact, in these circumstances that spaces that were previously inconceivable unexpectedly appear, enabling action to take place (Melucci 1989, 1996).

Various prognostic elements might be present within the same movement. Once again, global justice movements provide very good illustrations of the diversity of views among their activists. Some of them had an approach that Anheier et al. (2001) defined as "rejectionist": they expressed an overall refusal of globalization as a manifestation of global capitalism. Overall, however, this was a very diverse front, consistent with the fact that opposition to capitalism has historically come from very different origins. Leftist organizations and anti-capitalist social movements may stress the exploitative practices of global free markets and call for an overthrow of capitalism. Nationalist opponents may found their opposition to capitalism on very different grounds, stressing the threat to national sovereignty by transnational powers, and thus calling for protectionist economic policies and stricter limitations to the circulation of goods and people. Religious fundamentalists may target first of all the spread of individualistic, American-dominated worldviews and lifestyles and the resulting threats to the identity and moral values of specific populations. Whatever the origins of the criticism, political intervention in the global arena by either military superpowers or the UN is to be condemned as imperialistic intervention into local affairs.

Another critical position comes from those whom Anheier et al. (2001) defined as "alternatives." Many grassroots groups, countercultural networks, groups searching for viable alternatives to dominant economic practices and lifestyles, do not aim so much to destroy capitalism as to be able to "opt out" of it; namely, to promote experiments in local sustainable economic development, projects in the area of sustainable, GM-free agriculture, alternative and socially responsible trade. From this perspective, the political element is relatively peripheral by comparison to other critical stances. Political intervention in conflicts around the world may be useful as long as it is under the control of civil-society organizations and is based exclusively on nonviolent means; for example, think of peace actions and conflict resolution initiatives in contentious areas such as Israel or the Balkans in the 1990s.

Yet another widespread attitude toward globalization, encompassing both international nongovernmental organizations (INGOs), representatives of international institutions, governments, as well as many social movements, could be characterized as "reformist" (Anheier et al. 2001). While the growing circulation of people, goods, and information across regional and national boundaries is regarded in positive terms, what comes under criticism – even fierce criticism – is the form of such processes to date. Accordingly, a whole range of measures are required to reduce the power of transnational business and financial operators and to increase the role of economic as well as political institutions in regulating flows of exchanges. Active measures to redress social injustice and inequality are in order. The more active political participation of international institutions may be accepted as long as it is explicitly aimed at enforcing human rights and protecting local civil societies in nondemocratic countries, rather than protecting Western states and business special interests.

Motivational Element

On another level, symbolic elaboration is essential in order to produce the motivation and the incentives needed for action. The unknowable outcomes and the costs associated with collective action can be overcome only if the actors are convinced (intuitively even before rationally) of the opportunity for mobilizing and of the practicability and the legitimacy of the action. It is therefore important that frames do not only address the level of social groups and of collective actors, but link the individual sphere with that of collective experience. At the same time, they must generalize a certain problem or controversy, showing the connections with other events or with the condition of other social groups; and also demonstrate the relevance of a given problem to individual life experiences (Benford and Snow 2000, p. 619). Along with the critique of dominant representations of order and of social patterns, interpretative frames must therefore produce new definitions of the foundations of collective solidarity, to transform actors' identity in a way which favors action. Gamson (1992) captured this multiplicity of dimensions when he identified three central components of the collective construction of the terms: injustice, agency, and identity frames. As motivational framing strongly connects with identity-building, we shall discuss this point in greater detail in the next chapter, when dealing with the role of identity.

3.2.2   Ideology and Master Frames

It's important to stress the difference between frames and ideology. Ideology is usually conceived as "a relatively stable and coherent set of values, beliefs, and goals associated with a movement or a broader, encompassing social entity, [...] assumed to provide the rationale for defending or challenging various social arrangements and conditions" (Snow 2004, p. 396). Although the term has remained popular over the years (Oliver and Johnston 2000; Zald 2000), it has come under growing criticism since the 1980s, for implying unrealistic levels of ideological coherence and integration, of ideological proximity among social movement participants, of correlation between ideas and behavior (see Melucci 1996 for a classic version of this critique; Snow 2004, pp. 396 ff. for a summary). The most basic critique has probably been that this notion of ideology collapses two quite different aspects of culture: values and the interpretative tools – habits, memories, prejudices, mental schemata, predispositions, common wisdom, practical knowledge, etc. – that enable people to make sense of their world (Swidler 1986).

Framing is more flexible a cultural product than ideology, at the same time more specific and more generic than the latter. It does not require a whole coherent set of integrated principles and assumptions but provides instead a key to make sense of the world. Still, and similarly to ideology, frames are also capable of delivering broad interpretations of reality. This is particularly true when one interpretation manages to impose itself as a "master frame." The expression reflects the fact that movements and conflicts do not develop in isolation but tend rather to be concentrated in particular political and historical periods (Tarrow 1989; Tilly, Tilly, and Tilly 1975). This has consequences at the level of symbolic elaboration, and the discourse of a single movement (or the organization of a movement) must be placed in relation to the general orientations of a given period. If it is possible to identify conjunctions that are particularly favorable to the development of collective action, the dominant visions of the world in that period will inform – or at least influence – the representations produced by the movements taken together.[5] Thus a restricted number of master frames (or dominant interpretative frames: Snow and Benford 1992) will emerge, to which the specific elaborations of the various organizations or movements can be reduced, more or less directly.

In the early 1970s in Italy, social movements defined conflict in terms of class struggle. At that time, various types of conflict were often interpreted and classified in the light of the Marxist model. The women's movement was first seen from the perspective of emancipation and conquest of equal opportunities rather than as an affirmation of gender differences. In the same way, representations of youth movements often connected their collective action with their social position and their precarious status. At a more directly political level, the rapid transformation of the student movement into little groups organized to resemble – or to caricature – the Leninist party can also be considered proof of Marxism's cultural domination. Models of counterculture and political proposals such as that of the environmentalists, which had little in common with representations of a class nature, were accorded little space in the development of the movements, although they were also present (Lumley 1990). It was only after the salience of dominant cleavages was drastically reduced in the 1980s that collective action was framed under different cultural models such as environmentalism (Diani 1995). Likewise, Chilean women in the years before Pinochet's 1973 coup framed their activism largely in terms of motherhood, due to the combination of social movements' heavy Marxist framing and conservative antifeminist feelings. It was only when a "return to democracy" frame, less charged in terms of class conflict, established itself in the social movement sector in the 1980s that space for new feminist frames reemerged (Noonan 1995).

In contrast, in the USA, interpretative frames linked to the role of individuals, to their rights and aspirations for personal and civic growth, acquired considerable weight after the start of the protest wave of the 1960s. The resulting cultural climate facilitated the spread of movements profoundly different from those that had developed in Italy. At a more directly political level, movements mobilized for freedom of expression (such as the Free Speech Movement), or full citizenship for African Americans, or against American involvement in Vietnam (Eyerman and Jamison 1991, p. 5;

McAdam 1988). The presence of alternative and countercultural movements was also more evident. These were not limited to strictly communitarian and other world-rejecting forms, typical of the hippy movement and various religious currents of neoorientalist derivation. They also showed some overlap with broader attempts to support practices designed to encourage inner growth and individual realization, as in the case of the human potential movement.[6]

In the early 2000s, opposition to neoliberal globalization also operated, according to some observers, as a master frame (Andretta 2003). The idea that the growing inter-dependence of economic life and the resulting reduction of barriers to the circulation of capital threaten the living conditions of the large majority of the world's population brought together farmers of the South, affected by the dominance of multinational agribusinesses and the spread of genetically modified organisms, with trade unionists of the North, who saw global liberalization and the resulting fall in corporate tax revenue as a major blow to the modern welfare state. Concerns for the obstacles posed to the free circulation of people, in stark contrast to the free circulation of goods and financial assets, for the profits globalization is often bringing to corrupted authoritarian regimes, and for the rising indifference to human rights even in Western democracies, following 9/11, all create a common ground between activists of radical libertarian movements in the West and charities working in developing countries. Since the 1990s, the indifference to environmental preservation displayed by leaders in developing countries and Western governments, particularly but not exclusively right-wing ones, have brought together Western environmentalists and the broad coalitions opposing environmental destruction and social exploitation in developing countries (Doyle 2005; Martinez-Alier et al. 2016). Of course, it remains to be seen whether the overall capacity of the frame to connect so many different experiences is also matched by a corresponding capacity to articulate issues and strategies in local contexts, a recurrent problem for activists attempting to mobilize on the global sphere (Tarrow 2005). Still, anti-neoliberal globalism seems to represent a powerful unifying symbol for many, very diverse, actors worldwide.

As the new millennium progressed, new powerful master frames, broadly (and in many ways misleadingly) referred to as "populist," have asserted themselves as a dominant interpretation of social and political conflicts (Laclau 2005; Rovira Kaltwasser et al. 2017). The most distinctive trait is a conception of social and political life based on the opposition between the "elites" and "the people." This actually takes different meanings according to different analysts. For some (Mudde 2017) the foundation of populism is moral, where the people are carriers of morality, linked to purity, authenticity, and linked to a vague sense of "community." People are seen as a homogeneous body characterized by shared history, values, and identity, which grant it moral superiority over anyone who does not conform. Others (e.g. Ostiguy 2017) question the "moral" focus of this definition, noting that populism is often indifferent to moral standards and populists are more than indulgent toward their leaders' indiscretions. Rather, populism is seen as a form of discourse stressing the opposition between "low" and "high" cultural forms: "Populism is characterized by a particular form of political relationship between political leaders and a social basis, one established and articulated through 'low' appeals which resonate and receive positive reception within particular sectors of society for social-cultural historical reasons. We define populism, in very few words, as the 'flaunting of the low.'" (Ostiguy 2017). Still others view populism as an organizational arrangement, i.e., as a top-down process through which a mass of largely unorganized people gets mobilized by leaders who establish a direct, personal relationship to their followers. Populism is primarily a vehicle to the pursuing of leaders' ambitions without any search for a coherent strategy. As a thin ideology, populism can be combined with a broad range of ideological messages that somehow qualify it (Weyland 2017).

Many of the parties and other political organizations emerged in response to the 2008 crisis on both poles of the left-right divide have been labeled, with some degree of approximation, as populists (Norris and Inglehart 2019: 7). Some of them emanated from the tradition of left-wing social movements like Syriza in Greece, which had a strong relationship to the different components of the movement that challenged the bailout policies imposed by the Trojka (Kanellopoulos et al. 2016; Seferiades 2013); Podemos in Spain, with clear links to the Indignados (Martín 2015); or the Occupy actions in the US, which however had a limited political impact (Fernández-Savater et al. 2017). Despite a more pronounced anti-elitism, progressive populists' frames built on a number of critiques of global capitalism already expressed by the global justice movements of the previous decade, and showed relative respect for the formal properties of the democratic process (e.g. Aslanidis 2018). The break with pluralist democracy has been more pronounced in the case of right wing populist parties like those who have acquired power in Poland, Hungary, or Italy in Europe, and in the USA. In part, right-wing populists try to bring under a different master frame themes that in the previous decades have mostly been acted on by progressive movements. For example, many of the urban issues usually associated with the RTC idea may also be acted on by movements and organizations on the right wing of the political spectrum. Housing issues may be the focus of mobilization attempts, advocating not so much the universalistic extension of democratic and social rights but the implementation of mechanisms of social closure, restricting access to specific sectors of the population – often the *autochtones,* on the basis of the "Italians/Germans/British first!" slogan, as the extreme right organization Casapound in Italy illustrates (Di Nunzio and Toscano 2011). Likewise, struggles against urban degradation may also take a law-and-order form, targeting social groups and categories blamed for the deterioration of living conditions (immigrants, sex workers, people on benefits, radical communities and social centers....). Again, in Italy extreme-right party the League has been a major player in the campaigns approaching issues of urban regeneration from a law and order perspective (Albertazzi, Giovannini, and Seddone 2018). Right-wing populists have also managed – far more successfully than progressive populists – to impose new master frames that break radically with the post–WWII political discourse and practice on grounds such as the division of powers between different institutional levels, or the respect of minorities. One major example is Viktor Orban's success in reframing Hungarian political identity in terms of a homogeneous, millenarian Christian tradition, threatened by EU institutions and internal liberals privileging homosexuals and immigrants/terrorists over their own people (Kováts 2018; Wilkin 2018).

3.2.3 Frame Alignment

Under what conditions are frames successful? Resonance is shaped by credibility and salience (Benford and Snow 2000, p. 619). Frames should be credible, both in their content and in their sources. Incoherent messages, or messages coming from actors with a shaky reputation, or who are unknown, are unlikely to elicit the same reception as messages from actors with an established public image.[7] Frames should also be salient, i.e. touch upon meaningful and important aspects of people's lives, and show a high "narrative fidelity" (Benford and Snow 2000). Most important, they should resonate not only with their targets, but with the broader cultural structure in which a movement develops (Williams 2004).

Successful frames emerge through a variety of ways and forms of cultural production, which would make little sense to try and systematically present here. To put it very simply, and perhaps a bit simplistically, the basic precondition for success is that processes of "frame alignment" take place between movement activists and the populations they intend to mobilize. In other words, what is necessary is a "linkage of individual and SMO interpretative orientations, such that some set of individual interests, values and beliefs and SMO activities, goals and ideology are congruent and complementary" (Snow et al. 1986, p. 464). Collective action thus becomes possible at the point at which mobilizing messages are integrated with some cultural component from the population to which they are addressed.

A major form of frame alignment is what Snow and associates call *frame bridging*. This happens when representations by movement organizers incorporate interpretations of reality produced by sectors of public opinion that might otherwise remain separated from each other. Effective frame bridging may help social movements to establish connections to potential sympathizers more powerfully and more quickly than established political actors, thus monopolizing certain themes. One example of these mechanisms comes from German anti-immigrant movement Pegida and its handling on social media like Facebook of the 2015 refugee crisis, when Germany granted access to about a million people fleeing from war ridden areas of the world. According to some analyses, members of the Christian Democratic or the Social Democratic party active on Facebook made only sparse references to refuge issues, which enabled the right-wing party Alternative fuer Deutschland to virtually monopolize – at least in the short term – social media discourse on the topic (Stier et al. 2017). While it's not surprising that an extreme right party would enjoy easier frame bridging with anti-immigrant movement sympathizers, the absence of attempts to generate counter frames focusing on other types of bridging facilitated the bridging of right-wing party and concerned citizens' frames.

Another important form of frame alignment is what Snow et al. (1986) call *frame extension*. It allows the specific concerns of a movement or organization to relate to more general goals, in contexts where the connection might not be at all evident.

This is particularly important when activists attempt to legitimize social practices that are morally contested and stigmatized by institutions and significant sectors of the population. In this context, rhetorical efforts are primarily aimed at making acceptable behaviors that are not regarded as such, rather than mobilizing a specific constituency. Activists' attempts to create new fields of activities, or reshape existing ones, provide good illustrations of these mechanisms. For example, a study that analyzed the emergence of legal cannabis markets in the United States (Dioun 2018) identified different stages of framing that pro-legalization activists had to go through in order to overcome the moral barriers against even the partial acceptance of a cannabis market. First, it was framed as a palliative for dying, relying on the acceptance of such a specific and morally commendable use (what Dioun calls a "compassionate frame"). Later on, the framing was extended to include more general references to the positive effects of cannabis on less serious conditions such as headache or insomnia (a "wellness frame"). The example shows the need for careful management of framing strategies and gradual approaches when the ultimate goal, in this particular case the establishment of a market of cannabis for recreational use, is difficult to achieve because of moral resistances among the general public, and because of legal constraints.

Analyses of social movement frames tend to emphasize the expansion of the domain covered by activists' representations. As we have seen, social movements emerge when their activists manage to assign some shared meaning to different protest events and campaigns, representing them as part of much broader collective efforts. Likewise, the evolution of single issue campaigns into full-fledged social movements relies on a similar mechanism of frame expansion. The bridging of activists' concerns with those held by some sections of the general public may also be seen as resting on some form of rhetorical expansion. Nevertheless, it has recently been suggested that specific organizations may also, on occasion, adopt opposite strategies, contracting rather than expanding their frames. For example, looking at the framing approaches used by the United Auto Workers during negotiations with automakers in 1945–1946 and 1949–1950, Lavine and co-authors identify three main types of frame contraction: "*Frame removal* occurs where movement actors cease using a frame altogether; *frame minimization* occurs when a once broadly used frame is de-emphasized; and *frame restriction* occurs when actors deliberately prevent frame growth" (Lavine, Cobb, and Roussin 2017, p. 276). In many contexts, it may be more expedient to present a more specific image of itself rather than highlighting the general nature of one's goals. For example, radical student organizations acting in conservative, repressive settings might prefer to concentrate on the more mundane elements of their activity as organizations representing students' interests rather than stressing their aspirations to promote broader social challenges.

Frame alignment broadly rests on a dynamic relationship between the development of a movement, the cultural heritage of the country in which it operates, and its institutions.[8] First, movements make reference to cultural currents that, while well rooted in a given country, are somehow overshadowed. This applies to progressive and conservative movements alike. For example, the new right in the United States has drawn inspiration largely from the authoritarian, communitarian, illiberal traditions of American society. While liberal culture was, in the 1960s and the early 1970s, able to limit the impact of the new right on public discourse, these currents have remained alive in broad sections of public opinion, and since the 1980s have resurfaced to exert a very important role in public discourse – starting with the Bush administrations and gradually growing into the far-right populism of President Donald Trump's America (Blee 2002; Oberschall 1993, p. 13; Skocpol and Williamson 2016).

Second, emerging movements draw on their own traditional heritage and on that of the broader oppositional movements in a given country, presenting them, however, from a new perspective. Western ethnonational movements of the 1960s and 1970s were often successful in linking traditional themes of peripheral nationalism, such as territory or language, which were previously perceived to be predominantly a conservative issue, with radical, anti-establishment perspectives typical of youth countercultures, or with antimilitarist and antinuclear struggles of the period. The critique of the distortion of capitalist development provided a common base for challenges to the economic subordination of "internal colonies" and for solidarity with Third-World anti-colonialist movements (Hechter 1975; Johnston 1991). Likewise, activists of no-global movements drew on several different recent traditions of collective action such as environmentalism, social justice, and internationalism, and somehow managed to integrate them, or at least to identify some shared themes that sounded plausible enough to motivate people to act (della Porta 2007).

Religion plays a very important role in social movements' framing processes. Even in advanced industrial democracies the role of religion as a source of symbols and identity is far from negligible (Braunstein, Fuist, and Williams 2017; Lichterman 2008; Norris and Inglehart 2004). Religious symbols and principles may be used to transmit mobilizing messages also to audiences that are not particularly receptive of explicitly political messages. Examples are innumerable and range from campaigns for human rights in Central America reacting to the indignation for the murders of prominent religious personalities such as Archbishop Romero in El Salvador (e.g. Nepstad 2004) to the role of Muslim anti-capitalist activists during the largely secular protest in Gezi Park, Istanbul, in 2013 (Evcimen 2017). From a very different angle, fundamentalist movements have heavily relied on religious symbols and traditions to justify their actions, including the choice of violent repertoires, and articulate their strategies. A most conspicuous recent example is the insurgent group 'Islamic State in Iraq and Syria' (ISIS), which over the 2010s has posed a major challenge to Western powers and local regimes alike in the struggle for control over the Middle East. Reference to Islam enables ISIS to define clear boundaries between believers and disbelievers, differentiating as well between "near enemies" (which included, among others, the Shia Muslim community) and "far enemies" (first and foremost among them the Western powers") who are the main responsible for the oppressed condition of the Middle East (Westphal 2018). The sharp definition of otherness provides the basis on which to justify not only the recourse to violence, but its particularly gruesome forms.

Social movements always relate to cultural elements in their society in a variety of ways, but do so with variable degrees of acceptance. Tan and Snow (2015, p. 513) identify three basic patterns: embracement, modify/reform, and rejection. The prevalence of one or the other also shapes the size and heterogeneity of the constituency that a movement can reasonably aspire to mobilize. In particular, frames rejecting dominant cultural models are most likely to engage with small, highly committed groups, and provide them with incentives to mobilize; while an approach aiming at reform, or embracing largely shared values, should facilitate the involvement of a larger constituency, yet with a more limited mobilizing capacity (see also Friedman and McAdam 1992). This tension is well illustrated by different phases and forms of African American movements. In contrast to other leaders of the African American civil rights movement in the 1960s, Martin Luther King was careful in his speeches not to emphasize the differences between blacks and whites. In fact, he tended to avoid the construction of "polemical identities." Instead, he used references to the themes and the values of the heritage of the white American elites of that period, such as the relationship between individual liberty and a sense of responsibility toward the community (McAdam 1994, p. 38). It was precisely the embracement of these broader values, rather than antagonistic values, that provided him with a base from which to argue the full legitimacy of the demands of the civil rights movement (McAdam 1994). Of course, King's approach was not shared by all activists or leaders in the 1960s civil rights movement, and certainly appears quite distant from the more confrontational perspective adopted by the Black Lives Matter (BLM) movement, that has arisen since the 2000s in response to the numerous killings of unarmed African Americans (Clayton 2018).

In different ways, all the examples of symbolic re-elaboration in the previous section remind us that collective action is both a creative manipulation of new symbols and a reaffirmation of tradition. The insurgence of a new wave of mobilization does not, in fact, represent simply a signal of innovation and change, in relation to the culture and the principles prevalent in a given period. It is also, if to a varying extent, a confirmation of the fundamental continuity of values and historic memories that have, in recent times, been neglected or forgotten (see e.g. Stamatov 2002). Reference to the past can operate both as an obstacle and as an opportunity for action. It can represent an obstacle in that long-established ways of thinking and value systems can noticeably reduce the range of options available to the actor. Too strong an identification with tradition, or, in the same way, an excessive distance between the culture of the activists and sympathizers in a movement, and the rest of society, can in certain cases reduce the efficiency of symbolic re-elaboration (Swidler 1986). It can, in particular, make the processes of realignment of interpretative frames, crucial for the success of mobilization, very difficult. On the other hand, the ability to refer to one's cultural heritage puts the cognitive and value-related resources at the disposal of actors. On the basis of these resources, it is possible to found alternative projects and an alternative political identity. In the absence of references to one's own history and to the particular nature of one's roots, an appeal to something new risks seeming inconsistent and, in the end, lacking in legitimacy (della Porta 2018a).

3.3 PROBLEMS AND RESPONSES

Given the popularity gained by the framing perspective over the years, it's not surprising that it has also been the subject of considerable discussion. A recurrent theme has been whether frames – and in particular framing skills – should be treated as a particular type of resource, subject to strategic use by skilled political entrepreneurs. Several passages in the original formulations of the framing perspective indeed suggest a view of this kind (Gamson 1992; Snow et al. 1986). The most forceful critique of this position has come from theorists who have recently brought back the study of emotions into social movement analysis. From their point of view, cultural interpretations conducive to collective action do not so much originate from cognitive processes and strategic framing as from collective processes with a strong emotional dimension. It is often explicit confrontation with anger and injustice, or direct experience of collective solidarity, rather than political entrepreneurs' skillful manipulation, that move people to collective action (Flam 2015; Goodwin et al. 2001; Jasper and Polletta 2019). At the same time, even scholars sensitive to the role of emotional dynamics recognize the functional and strategic uses of symbolic elements. As Polletta and Gardner note, "Stories can serve as a crucial resource to activists. Poignant or outrageous stories can gain support for the movements' claims. In addition, however, sometimes gaining acceptance for the story *is* winning" (Polletta and Gardner 2015, p. 534). Even acts with a very strong emotional impact like politically or religiously motivated suicides may be conceived as strategically motivated actions, intending to draw attention to a cause and send messages to its supporters and sympathizers, at a time when political opportunities seem to be close. Illustrations of this logic come from actors as diverse as Jan Palach and other critics of communist regimes in the 1960s (Zuk and Zuk 2017) and suicide bombers in the Middle East (Tosini 2010). Even repellent actions like the public executions of captives carried on by the Islamic State may be read as planned actions in support of strategic goals linked to the consolidation of new revolutionary identities (Mello 2018).

Analyses of collective action centered on the concept of interpretative frames are not exempt from *ad hoc* explanations. At any moment it is possible to uncover the existence within a given society of a multiplicity of cultural models. It is not, therefore, difficult for those studying any movement enjoying a certain success, to identify the cultural elements with which the specific interpretative frame of the movement is aligned. This poses the problem of formulating systematic hypotheses concerning the relationship between symbolic production activities and the success of attempts at mobilization set up by movement organizations. To this purpose we need to link the properties of different modes of categorization of reality to the specific nature of the movements and the conflicts which these represent. But it is essential to identify, as a preliminary step, classification criteria for interpretative frames (see Diani 1996 for examples; Eyerman and Jamison 1991).

The explanatory capacity of frames *vis-à-vis* alternative interpretations of collective action has also been controversial. For example, an exploration of conflicts on nuclear power in the 1970s and 1980s in several Western countries concluded that for all the importance of communication, it was a favorable configuration of opportunities that ultimately helped some antinuclear movements and not others to win the discursive battle (Koopmans and Duyvendak 1995). In contrast, however, an analysis of success of 15 homeless organizations in different US cities suggested that the way in which the homelessness issue was framed actually affected those organizations' chances of securing political recognition or concrete relief (Cress and Snow 1996). The same applies to a study of suffrage organizations in the United States from 1866 to 1914 (McCammon 2001; Hewitt and McCammon 2004). Of course, in evaluating these results we have to take into account the different units of analysis. While in a comparison between nations it is difficult to identify the impact of framing strategies, more fine-grained explorations of specific cases might well assign symbolic factors a greater weight. Finally, in the last decades greater attention has been paid to the way dominant discourses in a given society affect the chance of success of specific mobilizing messages. The concept of "discursive opportunities" (introduced at length in Chapter 8) has been forged to account for these dynamics (Koopmans and Statham 1999, 2010). A recent application looks at campaigns against genetically modified (GM) crops and pesticides in Argentina, Brazil, and Mexico. While discourse on pesticides is to a large extent transnational, national variations still exist. They may be explained by other elements of the "discursive opportunity structure" such as "national policy discourse, timing of political agendas, media structure and culture" (Motta 2015, p. 576).

The framing perspective on collective action has also come under fire from researchers, most interested in cultural dynamics, including some of the original proponents of the concept (Benford and Snow 2000; Mische 2003). In many instances, frames have indeed been treated as static cognitive structures; very little attention has been paid, according to critics, to the way frames are generated and evolve over time, usually in a dialogical relationship between different actors. Numerous studies have tried to address this problem by focusing on the dynamic elements of discursive practices. A major study of conflicts on abortion in the US and Germany illustrated the contentious nature and the multiple spheres involved in the processes whereby abortion issues become the object of conflicting public discourses (Ferree et al. 2002). Mische (2008) has moved one step further, illustrating how discursive and conversational dynamics not only create new representations of experience but also constitute relations between social actors. Main advocates of the frame approach have placed greater emphasis on framing practices rather than on frames *per se*, and on the processes through which frames are transformed (Snow 2004, pp. 393–396). Increasingly, narratives have been presented as a conceptual alternative to frames. The concept seems to be more conducive to account for variations in representations over time, as it denotes sequences of connected events (Polletta and Gardner 2015).

The dynamic role of cultural production has also been noted by researchers from a different background than cultural sociology, and closer to the value perspective to culture than to the frame perspective. In his broad investigation of cultural change, with prevalent but not exclusive reference to the United States, Rochon (1998) stressed its dynamic and process-oriented elements. Rather than being generated, *à la* Inglehart, by macro-structural transformations (such as growth of education or rising affluence) affecting the way individuals conceive of their own situation and life projects, value change is a critical

struggle in which multiple actors are involved. For critical values to establish themselves, the role of critical communities is essential. It is from such communities – that
may include from time to time activists, artists, intellectuals, and the like – that social
movements emerge as major agents of cultural change. The role of specific communities has received traditionally strong attention in relation to changes in urban life,
an interest which has been revived by the spread of a concept like RTC. It is therefore
appropriate to close our discussion by recalling the role played in the emergence of
specific interpretative frames by urban cultural scenes – see e.g. studies looking at
places as diverse as Berlin, Hamburg, Istanbul, or Milan (Hoyng 2014; Novy and
Colomb 2013; d'Ovidio and Cossu 2017; Turam 2015) – or by various forms of cultural
expression, including street music (Black 2014) or the visual arts (Doerr, Mattoni, and
Teune 2015).

3.4 SUMMARY

There are at least two ways of looking at the relationship between collective action
and culture. The first stresses above all the role of values. Action is thus seen to originate from the identification of social actors with certain sets of principles and concerns. Interpretations of movements in recent decades, based on these premises, have
insisted in particular on the shift from materialist values to postmaterialist values.
More recently, however, the growing relevance of fundamentalist religious movements (not only within Islam but also within Christianity) and of the populist right
has drawn analysts' attention to another, very different version of the relationship
between values and collective action.

The second approach, which we have dealt with here, underlines instead the
cognitive elements of culture. In this context, mobilization does not depend so much
on values as on how social actors assign meaning to their experience: i.e., on the
processes of interpretation of reality which identify social problems as "social" and
make collective action sound like an adequate and feasible response to a condition
perceived as unjust. Action is facilitated by "frame alignment," in other words, by the
convergence of models of interpretation of reality adopted by movement activists and
those of the population that they intend to mobilize.

Movements' cultural production implies a relationship that involves both conquering
and revitalizing aspects (or at least some aspects) of a given population's traditions. This is
at the same time an impediment and a resource for action. It is also worth noting that
explanations of collective action, centered on the concept of the "interpretative frame,"
often carry the risk of *ad hoc* explanations. One way out of this difficulty lies in linking
various types of interpretative frames developed by actors with certain perceptions of the
political opportunities provided by the environment. Recently, the framing perspective
has been criticized for its excessive dependence on cognitive elements, to the detriment of
the emotional elements of collective action. In the next chapter, which looks at mechanisms for production of identity, we shall see how the cultural and symbolic dimensions
are linked to the subjective experience of the individual.

CHAPTER 4

Collective Action and Identity

Until two years ago, I was a woman who belonged to a man. Then I met the women of the collective, and slowly I have acquired the ability to develop new and different relationships with people. Today, I feel myself to be equal in my relationship with this man and in my relationships with the women of the collective.

–Martina, member of a women's collective, Milan, Italy,
quoted in Bianchi and Mormino (1984, p. 160)

If someone asks me, "Who are you?" I'm a radical feminist... And I see radical feminism as my life's work, even though I'm spending most of my days, most of my weeks, most of my years, doing something else.

–Employee of a public interest organization, Columbus,
Ohio, USA, quoted in Whittier (1995, p. 95)

There was the miners' strike and a lot of miners' wives used to come down... And there was the American Indian from the Indian reservation... And there were delegations from South Africa. And we were just dead ordinary working-class women from the inner cities and we were talking to people who were directly involved in struggles from all over the world.

–Trisha, Greenham Common activist, UK,
quoted in Roseneil (1995, p. 149)

This [visit] gives us more confidence to continue with our struggle, for we see that we're not alone.... We hope each of you will continue forward with love, for your brothers and sisters, for communities like ours. This is the same struggle all around the world.

– Hortensia, worker and activist in Tijuana, addressing North American labor and community organizers on a visit to Mexico, quoted in Bandy and Bickam-Mendez (2003, p. 179)

We have to show ourselves in Greek society in a different way. We are not only cleaners and caregivers to the elderly. We have many talents: we can sing; one put on a photography show; another painted nicely; myself, I made an embroidery display.

– Lena, Ukrainian migrant to Greece, quoted in Christopoulou and Leontsini (2017, p. 524)

Those 18 days in prison changed my life completely. I was no longer just a girl from a small town north of Cairo. I was no longer Esraa the teacher, the girl with a few simple dreams for her future, but without any real hope that they would ever materialize...In those 18 days I found the real me... I wanted freedom for myself, but most of all, I was inspired to fight for an Egypt where every Egyptian could feel justice and freedom forever.

– Esraa, Egyptian human rights activist and blogger, quoted in Madi-Sisman (2013)

Martina was part of the Ticinese Collective, a group of women active in Milan around the end of the 1970s and the beginning of the 1980s (Bianchi and Mormino 1984). Trisha was among the women who took part in the occupation of the Greenham Common area, where cruise missiles where located in Britain between 1983 and 1991 (Roseneil 1995). Hortensia was active in Central America in the late 1990s-early 2000s in the mobilization of *Maquiladoras*, female workers in small industrial workshops (*maquilas*) producing all sort of goods for export, usually under appalling working conditions (Bandy and Bickam-Mendez 2003). Lena is a member of a migrant women's organization in Athens, Greece (Christopoulou and Leontsini 2017). Esraa played a very prominent role in the 2011 uprising that led to the fall of President Mubarak in Egypt (Madi-Sisman 2013). The anonymous quote[1] belongs to a woman who was involved in the radical feminist movement in the American city of Columbus, Ohio, between the 1970s and the early 1990s (Whittier 1995, 1997).

These women were active in very different contexts, ranging from relatively stable democracies to dictatorial regimes; the actions they participated in also varied greatly in their focus, from change in one's private life (Martina) to high risk challenges to a repressive regime (Esraa), from self-help, voluntary work prioritizing service delivery for one's group (Lena) to long term campaigns addressing broad public issues (Trisha) and basic union rights (Hortensia). And yet, for all these differences, these quotations reveal more than random commonalities. They all appear representative, in their own ways, of the relationship between collective and individual experience in social movements. In particular, they tell us about the intersection of collective involvement and personal engagement that characterizes so much collective action (Fillieule and Neveu 2019; Goodwin et al. 2001; Melucci 1989).

On the one hand, these stories are about personal change: they testify to the new sense of empowerment, and to the strengthening of the self, which originate from collective action. Fighting the cruise missiles in the context of a "women only" campaign, Trisha got access to contacts and experiences that her working-class origins would have denied her otherwise. Promoting opposition to Mubarak's regime through social media and ending up in jail as a result led Esraa to radically transform her self-image and identify with a collectivity that extended well beyond the boundaries of her previous life. For Martina, joining a self-awareness group meant transforming her private life, without developing a strong commitment to public engagement. Even in her case, however, it was the nature of collective experience that made her personal growth possible.

On the other hand, these stories are also about the continuity in one's life that a sense of collective belonging provides, the connection that people establish between different spheres of their life, as well as between different phases. For the anonymous activist from Columbus, Ohio, being a feminist provided a linkage between different types of experiences; in Trisha's and Hortensia's accounts, activism on peace or labor issues created links to a variety of other campaigns and organizations across the world. For Lena, finally, mobilizing as a migrant in a new and unwelcoming milieu required a reformulation of her and her fellows' self-representation in order to engage with their host society in a positive way.

From different angles, these stories all illustrate basic mechanisms linked to the (re)production of identity: in particular, about the relationship between personal experience, and collective action. When speaking of identity we are not referring to an autonomous object, nor to a property of social actors; we mean, rather, the process by which social actors recognize themselves – and are recognized by other actors – as part of broader collectivities, and develop emotional attachments to them (Melucci 1996; Pizzorno 1978; Polletta and Jasper 2001). These "collectivities" need not be defined in reference to specific social traits such as class, gender, ethnicity, sexual orientation, or the like, nor in reference to specific organizations (although they often get defined in those terms). Collective identities may also be based on shared orientations, values, attitudes, worldviews, and lifestyles, as well as on shared experiences of action (e.g., individuals may feel close to people holding similar postmaterialist views, or similarly approving of direct action, without expressing any strong sense of class, ethnic, or gender proximity). At times, identities may be exclusive, and rule out other possible forms of identification (as in the case of religious sects expressing a wholesale rejection of the mundane world). Other times (actually, most of the time), however, they may be inclusive and multiple, as individuals may feel close to several types of collectivities at the same time.

Building or reproducing identities is an important component of the processes through which individuals give meaning to their own experiences and to their transformations over time. Through the production, maintenance, and revitalization of identities, individuals define and redefine individual projects, and possibilities for action open and close. The individual stories we just reported show us precisely that "identities are often personal and political projects in which we participate" (Calhoun 1994a, p. 28). At the same time, the construction of identity and the rediscovery of one's self cannot be reduced simply to psychological mechanisms; they are social processes that imply interactions and negotiations on meaning with a plurality of actors. Consistently with what has long been asserted by both sociological (Jasper and McGarry 2015; Melucci 1996; Pizzorno 1978; Touraine 1981) and sociopsychological (Stott, Drury, and Reicher 2017; Stryker, Owens, and White 2000) perspectives on collective action, we regard identity as neither a thing one can own, nor a property of actors, but as the process through which individual and/or collective actors, in interaction with other social actors, attribute a specific meaning to their traits, their life occurrences, and the systems of social relations in which they are embedded (Flesher Fominaya 2019; for recent surveys of this line of inquiry see Ghaziani, Taylor, and Stone 2016).

In the following pages we discuss some characteristics of identity construction. We show, first, that identity production is an essential component of collective action, through the identification of actors involved in conflict, the facilitation of trusting relationships among them, and the establishment of meaningful connections between events that took place at different periods in time. We also note, however, that social identification is simultaneously static and dynamic. Reference to identity also facilitates collective action because it evokes the continuity and the solidity of allegiances over time. However, identity is also open to constant redefinitions. Links postulated by social actors with certain historical experiences and with certain groups appear, in fact, always to be contingent. They are the fruit of symbolic reinterpretations of the world that are inevitably selective and partial. Moreover, identities are forged and adapted in the course of conflict, and their boundaries can be modified quite drastically in the process. As a result, in spite of their relative stability, even feelings of identification can be – and in fact are – subject to recurring modifications (Flesher Fominaya 2010, 2019; Jasper and McGarry 2015; Maddison and Partridge 2014; Nakano 2013).

Linked to the above is the presence of multiple identities – or, in other words, individuals' feelings of belonging to several different collectives, sometimes defined in reference to very diverse criteria. It is true, as we just noted, that identity operates as an organizing principle in relation to individual and collective experience: for example, it helps actors to identify their allies and their adversaries. At the same time, however, the definition of lines of solidarity and of opposition is often anything but clear: the rise of feminist movements has created, for example, new lines of identification that have often revealed themselves to be in contrast with those that preceded them (for example, those of class). Rather than uprooting these older lines of identity, new identities coexist with them, generating tensions among actors' different self-representations,[2] or between activists who identify with the same movement yet belong to different generations (Baumgarten 2017; Chironi 2019; Whittier 1995, 1997). Although the very concept of collective identity may imply some degree of homogeneity among the actors sharing some identification, such homogeneity is at best partial, as actors who are similar on some traits/attitudes/experiences usually differ substantially on other dimensions (Daphi 2017; Flesher Fominaya 2010; Melucci 1984). One should also note, though, that multiple identities need not necessarily be in a tense relation to each other.

Recognizing the dynamic nature of identity draws our attention to the multiple practices through which identity is constituted and constantly re-elaborated. In section 4.3, we explore the multiple symbolic levels and the multiple settings in which social actors elaborate shared (if partial and contingent) definitions of themselves in relation to both their personal stories and their social environment. It is indeed important to look at the "co-determinants of identification: situations, circumstances, and actors' motives" (Eidson et al. 2017: 340). This also includes paying attention to how political and institutional processes may affect identity construction.

4.1   IDENTITY AS A CONDITION AND A PROCESS

Identity should not be regarded simply as a precondition for collective action. It is certainly true that social actors' identities in a given period guide their subsequent conduct. Action occurs, in fact, when actors develop the ability to define themselves, other social actors, and the "enjeu" (stake) of their mutual relationship (Touraine 1981). At the same time, however, identity is not an immutable characteristic, preexisting action. On the contrary, it is through action that certain feelings of belonging come to be either reinforced or weakened. In other words, the evolution of collective action produces and encourages continuous redefinitions of identity (Bernstein 1997; Flesher Fominaya 2010; McGarry and Jasper 2015; see e.g. Melucci 1996).

Let us look more closely at the mechanisms by which action constitutes identity. This happens, first, through the definition of boundaries between actors engaged in a conflict. In contrast to macrostructural approaches to the analysis of social conflicts, the sociology of action has drawn attention to the problematic nature of the structure–action nexus, stressing that conflict cannot be explained exclusively in the light of structural relationships and the contrasting interests that these have determined. It originates, rather, in the interaction between structural tensions and the emergence of a collective actor that defines itself and its adversaries on the basis of certain values and/or interests (Touraine 1981). Collective action cannot occur in the absence of a "we" characterized by common traits and a specific solidarity. Equally indispensable is the identification of the "other" defined as responsible for the actor's condition and against which the mobilization is called. The construction of identity therefore implies both a positive definition of those participating in a certain group, and a negative identification of those who are not only excluded but actively opposed (Melucci 1996; Touraine 1981). It also includes a relationship with those who find themselves in a neutral position. The process of identity building has often been compared to the writing of a dramaturgical piece. It has been suggested that movement identities come to life to the extent that they are able to identify "protagonists, antagonists, and audiences" in a given conflict or campaign (Hunt, Benford, and Snow 1994). Along similar lines, others have stressed the substantial "character work" through which movement actors attempt not only to identify actors playing positive and negative roles in a given struggle, but also to raise emotional responses to them (Jasper, Young, and Zuern 2018).

In the second place, the production of identities corresponds to the emergence of new networks of relationships of trust among movement actors, operating within complex social environments. Those relationships guarantee movements a range of opportunities (see Chapter 5). They are the basis for the development of informal communication networks, interaction, and, when necessary, mutual support. They seem to be an essential replacement for the scarcity of organizational resources; furthermore, information circulates rapidly via interpersonal networks, compensating at least in part for limited access to the media; trust between those who identify with the same political and cultural endeavor enables those concerned to address with greater efficacy the costs and the risks linked to repression; finally, identifying themselves – and being identified – as part of a movement also means being able to count on help and solidarity from its activists (Gerlach 1971; Juris 2008; Osa 2003).

The presence of feelings of identity and of collective solidarity makes it easier to face the risks and uncertainties related to collective action. In the case of the workers' movement, close proximity of workplaces and living spaces facilitated the activation and the reproduction of solidarity (see Chapter 2). Socialist subcultures constructed "areas of equalities" where participants recognized themselves as equal, and felt they belonged in a common destiny (Pizzorno 1993). In postindustrial society, however, direct social relationships founded on territorial proximity have become weaker. While this has not necessarily meant the disappearance of community relations, on the whole, systems of social relations are more distantly connected than they were in the past to a defined territorial space. Their borders extend now to encompass entire national and supranational communities (Aunio and Staggenborg 2011; Castells 2012). As a result, while locality is still an important source of identity, in relative terms collective solidarity is less dependent on direct, face-to-face interactions than was the case. The shift from premodernity to modernity and the emergence of public opinion integrated via the printed word (the "communities of print and association" described by Sidney Tarrow 1998) had already facilitated the development of identities disconnected from specific localities. But these trends have undergone a further acceleration with the expansion of the media system and the electronic revolution (Bennett and Segerberg 2013; Walgrave, Bennett, Van, et al. 2011; Wellman 2001).

To identify with a movement also entails feelings of solidarity toward people to whom one is not usually linked by direct personal contacts, but with whom one nonetheless shares aspirations and values. Activists and movement sympathizers are aware of participating in realities that are much vaster and more complex than those of which they have direct experience. It is in reference to this wider community that the actor draws motivation and encouragement to action, even when the field of concrete opportunities seems limited and there is a strong sense of isolation. It is, of course, an open issue as to the extent to which the spread of computer mediated communication may facilitate the diffusion of identities disentangled from references to any specific time and space (see Chapter 5, section 5.4).

4.2   IDENTITY AND TIME

Collective identity also connects and assigns some common meaning to experiences of collective action dislocated over time and space. At times this takes the form of linking together events associated with a specific struggle in order to show the continuity of the effort behind the current instances of collective action. Let us look, for example, at the "Call of the European Social Movements," issued before the European Social Forum in Florence in November 2002:

> We have come together from the social and citizens movements from all the regions of Europe, East and West, North and South. We have come together through a long process: the demonstrations of Amsterdam, Seattle, Prague, Nice, Genoa, Brussels, Barcelona, the big mobilizations against the neoliberalism as well as the general strikes for the defense of social rights and all the mobilizations against war, show the will to build another Europe. At the global level we recognize the Charter of Principles of WSF and the call of social movements of Porto Alegre.

> (cited in Andretta 2003)

Here, occurrences that took place at different points in time are brought together as the background of the 2002 meeting, to show continuity between them. Likewise, there is an obvious attempt to connect across space mobilizations taking place in all corners of Europe, and to relate them as well to recent developments of collective action on a global scale.

Linking events in multiple localities with specific traditions and memories from the past is not always easy. After all, the Social Forum activists of 2002 were referring to events that had occurred over a limited time span. But this is not always the case, and sometimes activists' attempts to develop broader identities, encompassing actions from multiple localities, may conflict with the peculiar history of a specific country. A recent analysis of protest activities in Romania in 2011 and following years illustrates this point. Promoters of student protests of 2011 and 2013, anti-government mobilizations of 2012, or environmental actions from 2013 tried to stress their connections to the Indignados and Occupy campaigns of 2011. Yet, their approaches were also heavily influenced by the recent history of their country, and in particular by the legacy of the anti-communist protest of the late 1980s (Abăseacă 2018).

We should also note that references to previous waves of activism often exceed the personal memory of activists. For example, references to the Carnation Revolution, which toppled the dictatorship in Portugal in April 1974, played a role in building the identity of groups active in the anti-austerity movement of the 2000s. This was not a matter of simple personal transmission, as most of the anti-austerity activists had not lived through the 1970s revolution. Rather, it was part of larger, complex processes of memory building, concerning the way the memory of those events were re-elaborated in contemporary Portuguese society (Baumgarten 2017). More in general, legacies and memories of important critical junctures such as the transition to democracy have been found to affect social movements at later stages in Southern Europe as well as in Eastern Europe, or in the North Africa (della Porta 2017a; della Porta, Andretta et al. 2018).

Securing continuity over time is also important because social movements characteristically alternate between "visible" and "latent" phases (Melucci 1996). In the former, the public dimension of action prevails, in the form of demonstrations, public initiatives, media interventions, and so on, with high levels of cooperation and interaction among the various mobilized actors. In the latter, action within the organizations and cultural production dominate. Contacts between organizations and militant groups are, on the whole, limited to interpersonal, informal relationships, or to inter-organizational relationships that do not generally produce the capacity for mass mobilization. In these cases, collective solidarity and the sense of belonging to a cause are not as obvious as they are in periods of intense mobilization. Identity is nurtured by the hidden actions of a limited number of actors. And it is precisely the ability of these small groups to reproduce certain representations and models of solidarity over time that creates the conditions for the revival of collective action and allows those concerned to trace the origins of new waves of public action to preceding mobilizations. An illustration of this process comes women's organizations in Spain under Francisco Franco's regime, that lasted from the mid-1930s to 1975. Despite the inability to take a visible, public role, not only those organizations managed to keep action on women's issues alive: they also succeeded to transmit ideas and practices coming from movements that had been active before the advent of dictatorship to the new waves of militancy that followed its demise (Valiente 2015).

The linking function of identity does not operate only on the level of collective representations and socially widespread perceptions of certain social phenomena. It also relates the latter to individual experience. In constructing their own identity, individuals attribute coherence and meaning to the various phases of their own public and private history. This is often reflected in their life histories and biographies, i.e., the "[i]ndividual constellations of cultural meanings, personalities, sense of self, derived from biographical experiences" (Jasper 1997, p. 44). Long-lasting militant careers develop with a constant commitment to a cause, even if articulated in different ways at different times. It is true that any wave of mobilization attracts to social movements people with no previous experience of collective action – at least for biographical reasons. Still, continuity in militancy – the fact that those who have already participated in the past are more likely to become active once again than those who have never done so – has been confirmed by a large number of studies (Fillieule and Neveu 2019; McAdam 1988; Vestergren, Drury, and Chiriac 2017). The "1968 generation," for example, has remobilized in various waves of protest, from environmentalism to global justice (Passerini 1996; della Porta 2018a).

Speaking of continuity over time does not necessarily mean assuming that identity persists, let alone that it is fixed. Reference to the past is, in fact, always selective. "Continuity" in this case means rather the active re-elaboration of elements of one's own biography and their reorganization in a new context. In this way, it becomes possible to keep together personal and collective occurrences which might otherwise appear to be incompatible and contradictory. As an example, let us look at a case of radical collective action that would seem to presuppose a drastic personal transformation at the moment of mobilization – that of terrorism. Biographies of Italian terrorists of the 1970s (della Porta 1990) show that they had in several cases moved from militancy in Catholic organizations to armed struggle. In this case, there was clearly a marked break in forms of action and political programs. Nevertheless, there were also elements of coherence in these histories that seem, on the surface, to be so lacking in continuity. One of these was the aspiration to construct social relationships that went beyond the inequalities and the distortions of the present. Also common to both biographical phases was a conception of collective action as the proclamation of absolute truths and the concrete testimony of one's own ideal (and ideological) principles, no matter how distorted.

On the other hand, the outset of each new experience of collective action inevitably means also breaking with the past to some degree. In some cases, the decision to engage in collective action, or join an organization or a project, which is clearly different from what individuals have done up to that point, results in a radical personal transformation. In these cases, people experience genuine conversions, which often mean breaking with their previous social bonds. The transformation of identity can be much more profound in these cases. It will affect not only the political leanings of individuals and their levels of involvement in collective action, but also global life choices and even the organization of everyday life.

The same phenomena are often found among those who join religious movements (Everton 2015; Smilde 2005; Snow, Zurcher, and Ekland-Olson 1980). Conversion to a cult or a sect often implies a more or less radical transformation of one's identity and loyalties, and this is deeper the more demanding membership criteria in the new group are. For example, joining a group like Hare Krishna implies the acceptance of a highly ritualized lifestyle in which everything has to be in accordance with the sect's precepts (Rochford 1985). Furthermore, the history of conflicts typical of industrial society documents the force of "traditional" political identities and the often exclusive and sectarian nature of collective action. In the century of great ideologies, abandoning political and/or class positions – that is, giving up a certain system of social relationships and of affective identifications in order to adopt another – was always costly. A good example of this is provided in the segmentation of Northern Ireland along religious lines (one could also think of the Israeli–Palestinian conflict for another obvious illustration of this pattern). In Northern Ireland, religious identities have provided criteria for the organization of social relations at all levels, including community and family linkages. Ties cutting across sectarian barriers have been difficult to build. Attempts have been made over the last decades by different types of organizations, from environmentalist to women's, to develop new intercultural forms of political participation, yet with variable degrees of success, even after the Good Friday agreement of 1998 (Cinalli 2003; Hughes, Campbell, and Jenkins 2011; Muir 2011).

4.3 MULTIPLE IDENTITIES

In modern society, social movements have often been represented as "characters" with a specific ability to act and also, accordingly, with a coherent and integrated identity. Over the last few decades, however, increasing attention has been given to the systems of relationships in which actors are involved (a major contribution coming from Italian theorist Alberto Melucci: 1996). In turn, this has enabled us to recognize the multiplicity of identities and allegiances that characterize militants and movement groups. If identity is, first, a social process and not a static property, then the feelings of belonging among groups and collectives are, to a significant extent, fluid. In fact, identity does not always presuppose a strong "collective we." Identifying with a movement does not necessarily mean sharing a systematic and coherent vision of the world, nor does it prevent similar feelings being directed to other groups and movements as well. Forms of allegiance that are not particularly intense or exclusive can, in certain contexts, guarantee continuity of collective action (Ackland and O'Neil 2011; for empirical illustrations, Diani 1995; Elliott, Earl, and Maher 2017; Melucci 1989).

An excessive insistence on the role of identity as a source of coherence may actually lead to neglecting the importance of forms of multiple identity (Calhoun 1994a). It is certainly possible that in some historical conjunctures, a dominant identity integrate all the others, generating a hierarchical structure. Continental European political systems in the twentieth century, in which major political cleavages were consolidated, came closer to a hierarchical model – or, in Georg Simmel's (1955) terms, a "concentric circle" – in which identification with a political party matched in a fairly coherent way identification with other social organizations such as unions, cultural and leisure time clubs, cooperatives, etc., thus generating specific "political subcultures" (see e.g. Lijphart 1969; Rokkan 1970). Even allowing for the accuracy of the accounts provided by the political subcultures model, however, in the last few decades, most analysts have suggested identities to have a polycentric rather than a hierarchical structure. People's involvement with multiple groups and organizations may combine in variable forms and generate specific identities that are somehow unique. At the individual level, one's identity ultimately depends on the particular intersection of a number of group allegiances in this person. This does not mean that there be no regularities at all, as identities can be seen as "networks of overlapping roles based on generic affiliations" (Light 2015): recent discussions of movement identities from the point of view of "intersectionality" point in this direction (Maddison e Partridge 2014; Okechukwu 2014).

In order to mobilize constituencies with multiple affiliations, movement activists need to perform some kind of "identity bridging" (Elliott et al. 2017). In other words, we need to explore how different group identities may be reconciled and kept together under broader headings. This is far from simple, as collective identities expressed by different movements or different movement organizations may prove incompatible, or at best difficult to integrate. The rise of feminism has revealed the persistent subordination of women within workers' movement organizations or in many of the "new movements" themselves. In this way, they have shown the deep contradictions in actors' identities that, nevertheless, can generally be explained with reference to the same area of "progressive" movements. Often times, gender identities have failed to overcome the barriers posed by other lines of differentiation, such as race – as reflected for example in the tensions between white and Aboriginal feminists in Australia (Maddison and Partridge 2014). Racial differences have actually been repeatedly identified as major obstacles to the construction of broader identities. This has been documented in a variety of situations, ranging from the difficult coexistence of deprived, black local communities and mainly white environmental organizations in South Africa (Waldman 2007) to the role of progressive whites in political and cultural movements focused on blacks in the United States (McCorkel and Rodriquez 2009).

While the relations between whites and non-whites is usually embedded in deep inequalities and asymmetries of power, tensions have also affected movements that in principle have excellent reasons to conduct joint mobilizations, such as those standing for minority rights. At one level, minorities face several common problems and experience very similar conditions, from racism to social exclusion, which may provide the basis for a shared sense of belongingness; at another level, however, different groups may be rooted in very different cultures and historical experiences, which may be difficult to reconcile. In the United Kingdom, for example, relations between Muslim and Hindu groups are often complicated by a legacy of hostility in their countries of origin, which does not facilitate the growth of a common, easy-to-mobilize identity (Diani and Pilati 2011). In the United States, building a panethnic movement identity that brought together different Asian American organizations has required considerable work on the part of activists, in order to find a common ground between groups that may differ even markedly not only in terms of ethnicity but also of class. How to manage what have been called "interlocking identities" (Nakano 2013) has proved a major task.

Interestingly, tensions between different identities and expectations may also regularly be found among actors that claim to identify with the same collectivity, be it a specific organization, or a specific social movement. Even within specific organizations that apparently share the same ideological position one can find different interpretation of such positions, that may often lead to internal fractures. For example, an exploration of dynamics within groups mobilizing in support of asylum seekers in Ireland identified divisions running at times between radical and reformist positions, other times between reformist and nonreformist, conservative stances (Moran 2017). More generally, we need to recognize that the motivations and expectations behind individuals participating in social movements are, in fact, much richer and more diversified than the public images of those movements, as produced by their leaders, would suggest. By taking part in the life of a movement, people also seek answers to their own specific aspirations and concerns. Even the identity of a single group can therefore be seen as a meeting point for histories, personal needs, and heterogeneous representations. For example, the analysis of the experience of the Ticinese Collective conducted by Melucci and his collaborators in the early 1980s led to the identification of two basic tensions in the way in which feminist practice was perceived (Bianchi and Mormino 1984). The first distinguished between action aimed at society beyond the movement and that which was inwardly directed, toward practices of personal change in small groups; the second between action that was purely affective and solidaristic, and action that aimed to value women's competences and professional qualities. At the same time, the same dichotomies offered a useful key to identifying the main tensions in the identity of the Milanese feminist movement taken as a whole. There were, in fact, consciousness-raising groups, or lesbian groups that were virtually unconcerned with public action and concentrated on the affective-solidaristic side of action. On the other hand, writers' groups and those concerned with reflection on intellectual issues from a women's perspective associated a low level of external intervention with their goal of calling attention to women's intellectual and professional capacities. Among the groups concerned with external intervention, some placed a high value on the solidaristic element, such as feminist collectives in squatter communes; others were concerned with consolidating women's presence in both the economic and the cultural sphere (Bianchi and Mormino 1984, p. 147). Almost four decades later, an investigation of the Non Una Di Meno, a feminist network fighting violence from men against women in Italy, found comparable heterogeneity between activists operating under the same label. Differences across generation groups on key issues like the attitude to sex work and surrogate motherhood proved particularly salient (Chironi 2019).

Both specific organizations and broader movement sectors, comprising of multiple groups and associations, may thus be seen as arenas for struggles over the definition of collective identities. What is cursorily termed "movement identity" is, in reality, largely a contingent product of negotiations between collective images produced by various actors and various organizations. On the one hand, organizations aim to affirm their own specific formulation of their collective identity as the global identity of the movement. On the other hand, the reinforcement of an organizational identity allows, at the same time, for differentiation from the rest of the movement (Taylor 1989). Therefore, one identifies with an organization not only to feel part of a wider collective effort but also in order to be a particular, autonomous, distinctive component of such an effort. In this way it becomes possible to anchor identity to organizational forms, which are more structured and solid than those constituted by networks of informal relationships among the various components of a movement. The persistent relevance of identification with specific organizations has actually led some analysts to question the rationale of speaking of "collective identity" in reference to whole movements. Clare Saunders (2008, 2013) has been most vocal in arguing that, contrary to dominant wisdom, the building of strong collective identities may be actually damaging to the cohesion of a social movement. This is due to the fact that identities and solidarities ultimately develop in reference to specific organizational units with a relatively clear profile, rather than to more vague entities like movement sectors, which in turn may pitch one organization against another and lead to factionalism. One does not have to buy Saunders' argument entirely to recognize the importance of the tensions between identification with specific organizations, and with larger entities like a movement (we further elaborate on this in Chapter 6).

An additional element of complication lies in the fact that movement identities can also be shared by individuals, detached from every organizational allegiance. It is indeed possible to feel part of a movement without identifying with any specific organization and even express an explicit dissent towards the notion of organization in general. In particularly effervescent conditions, simply to participate in meetings and demonstrations gives the sensation of being able to count on the definition of strategies and on goals, even without having passed through the filter of specific organizations. In fact, when identification mechanisms tend to shift mainly toward specific organized actors, this is an indicator of a movement demise. One of the characteristic traits of the wave of working-class protests that crossed Italy between 1968 and 1972 was the modification of the relationship between militancy in specific trade-union organizations and militancy in the workers' movement in its broad sense (Pizzorno et al. 1978). New forms of representation were introduced in factories (factory councils). They offered ample opportunities for participation even to those who were not enrolled in any of the traditional unions. The push toward trade-union unity and to overcome preexisting group allegiances was also strong in those years. Group allegiances came to dominate once more only when mobilization was in decline and movement identity was weak (Pizzorno 1978; also see, in reference to US working class activism, Fantasia 1989).

The importance of personal identification with a movement, not mediated by ties to any organization, and of highly personalized ways of acting collectively, has been repeatedly emphasized in social movement research, for example by analysts contrasting the new social movements of the 1970s and 1980s with working class or nationalist movements of the past (e.g. Melucci 1996). One implication of this shift toward more individualized styles of activism is the growing importance of public meetings, in which individuals can play significant roles, over organizations as the crucial loci where identity is generated. Both the mobilizations opposing capitalist globalization in the early 2000s and the Indignados and Occupy campaigns in the following decade illustrate these dynamics (Flesher Fominaya 2010; Moore 2017). For some, organizations' "failure" to build solid identities and secure activists' loyalties might actually result in stronger identification with broader, if more vaguely defined, entities like movements (Flesher Fominaya 2010, somehow complementing Saunders' points). These analyses strongly resonate with the argument that in increasingly individualized societies, in which computer mediated communication gives easy access to multiple public spheres, also protest is becoming increasingly individualized and less dependent on the mediating role of organizations. The more radical version of this thesis is probably due to Lance Bennett and Alexandra Segerberg (2011, 2013,

2015), who have proposed to replace the concept of "collective action" with that of "connective action" to identify the new forms of grassroots participation. In their view, while the model of action based on group identities, which characterized among others the "new social movements" from the 1970s and 1980s, still exists, mobilizations in the new millennium depend more on the personal identification with a variety of causes that individuals combine in different ways depending on their specific orientations (also see Castells 2012; Monterde et al. 2015).

4.4   HOW IS IDENTITY GENERATED AND REPRODUCED?

4.4.1   Self- and Hetero-Definitions of Identity

If identity is a social process rather than a property of social actors, then feelings of belongingness and solidarity in relation to a certain group, the recognition of elements of continuity and discontinuity in the history of individuals, and the identification of one's own adversaries, may all be subject to recurring re-elaboration. Identity emerges from processes of self-identification and external recognition. Actors' self-representations are, in fact, continuously confronted with images which institutions, sympathetic and hostile social groups, public opinion, and the media produce of them (Diani and Pilati 2011; Holland, Fox, and Daro 2008; Longard 2013; Melucci 1996).

Identity building presupposes the development of specific narratives on the part of movement activists, and their ability to challenge the alternative narratives put forward by their opponents (Daphi 2017; Hancock 2016; Polletta and Gardner 2015). These stories reflect at the same time an aspiration to differentiate oneself from the rest of the world and to be recognized by it. A collective actor cannot exist without reference to experiences, symbols, and myths that can form the basis of its individuality. At the same time, however, symbolic production cannot count solely on self-legitimacy. It is necessary for certain representations of self to find recognition in the image that other actors have of the subject. Movements do indeed struggle for the recognition of their identity. It is only in the context of mutual recognition among actors that conflict and, more generally, social relationships can exist (Pizzorno 2008; Simmel 1955; Touraine 1981). Without this, self-affirmed identity on the part of a group will inevitably lead to its marginalization and its reduction to a deviant phenomenon.

The story of movements is therefore also the story of their efforts to impose certain images of themselves, and to counter attempts by dominant groups to denigrate their aspirations. Sometimes, such aspirations imply claims to be recognized as different. A major example comes from the conflicts related to the construction of the modern nation-state. The development of vast, highly centralized political units led to an emphasis on cultural homogenization, through the affirmation of one "national" language and one "national" culture. Assimilationist policies often followed from this, in view of the multicultural nature of the territories coming under the dominion of new state formations. Cultural traditions different from those of the social groups, promoting the construction of the new nation-states, were stigmatized as relics of the past. For example, the narratives that supported the construction of the French national identity led to the marginalization of the Provençal and Breton cultures. These were represented as mere residues of a backward, premodern society, whose survival represented an unwelcome obstacle to the spread of the positive values of progress of which the French state made itself the bearer (Beer 1980; Greenfield 1992).

The power to impose negative and stigmatized definitions of the identity of other groups constitutes, in fact, a fundamental mechanism of social domination. Especially at the early stages of mobilization, social movement activists are routinely described by powerholders as depraved, morally weak, corrupted people, unable to adapt to society's basic values. This applies to the early nineteenth-century's reactionaries facing massive social change (Tilly 1984a: 1) as well as to the establishment's attempts to delegitimize protestors following the clashes during the 2001 anti-G8 mobilization in Genoa. In the period between August 2001 and November 2002, when the European Social Forum took place peacefully in Florence, the Italian government and sympathetic media waged a massive campaign portraying the movement as an unruly bunch, and invoking severe restrictions on rights to demonstrate. A great effort had to be put into counter-framing activity by movement activists (Andretta et al. 2002).

Social movements challenging forms of domination deeply embedded in cultural practices, lifestyles, mental habits, and inbred stereotypes offer a particularly fitting illustration of these dynamics. Stigmatization from the outside often ends up blocking the development of a strong autonomous identity and limiting the possibilities for collective action. This is very clear, for instance, in the case of gay and lesbian movements (Armstrong 2002; Bernstein 1997; Valocchi 2009). In all cases, challenging negative stereotyping is a major component of movements' cultural production. A most blatant example is the stereotyping of women as uninterested in the public and political dimensions of social life, inclined towards the private sphere, most particularly family life, and as lacking the rational abilities that are held to be essential in order to act in the public sphere (Ferree and Mueller 2004, p. 596).

Another rhetorical strategy for movements consists of stressing not so much the value of diversity, but their proximity to the mainstream, "normal" population and its fundamental principles and lifestyles. This has been particularly relevant in the case of the populist movements of the recent decades. Their particular definition of identity relies precisely on a representation of themselves as the representatives of the "real," "ordinary" people, threatened by a cosmopolitan elite detached from any historical tradition and national loyalty. Such elite, which according to populists often includes sections of the "new social movements" of the 1970s and 1980s, is portrayed as incapable of empathy with the "person in the street." While the debate on the specific, defining features of populism is open (see e.g. Mudde 2017; Ostiguy 2017; Weyland 2017), the claim to the people as a homogeneous category has enabled sectors of society threatened by globalization processes to develop some sense of commonality, as well as identify some shared targets (Kriesi and Pappas 2015), thus generating an embryonic collective identity. For example, activists of right-wing English Defence League, established in 2009, seem to have built their identity on claims of "victimhood" (Oaten 2014). This rests on portraying the ordinary English citizen as a threatened category, and identifying the culprits in both an indifferent establishment and the uncontrolled immigration of hostile alien groups, most notably, Muslim people.

A crucial aspect of identity building concerns the relationship between "objective" elements in the experiences of individuals and collectivities, and the activists' agency in creating specific representations of themselves. In other words, is identity building primarily a process of discovery of actors' "nature," rooted in historical experience or in structural factors, a nature that had previously been hidden due to manipulation by dominant groups? Or is identity ultimately a social construction without objective foundation of any sort? As it often happens, the answer lies somewhere in between. Structural factors such as race, gender, or class are still regarded as influential on the way people think of themselves and provide a justification to their acting collectively, especially outside the affluent North (Elbert and Pérez 2018; Kenny 2005; Okechukwu 2014); different phases of capitalist development have also been linked to the development of identities, including some, like homosexual ones, that are often considered detached from socioeconomic dynamics (Valocchi 2009, 2017). It has also been argued that activists in the same movement elaborate their identities in different ways, depending on their class location. One exploration of activists mobilized on issues of social justice, democracy, and equality found for example that middle-class activists tended to define their activism as a career, working-class activists rather thought of it as a calling, while low-income activists regarded their activism as a way of life, with little distinction between their private and activist lives (Valocchi 2012).

At the same time, it is widely accepted that identity be ultimately a social construction. Even students of nationalist movements, arguably the most explicitly rooted in historical experience, are skeptical of essentialist views of identity. Differences run in the historical foundations of the symbols and myths used to fabricate modern national identities. Some argue that modern national identities draw upon events, institutions, myths, and narrations that precede by a long time the existence of the nation-state (Smith 1986). Others object that large parts of the myths on which these are based do not have any historical foundation, and that one should rather talk of "invention of tradition" (for a classic formulation: Hobsbawm and Ranger 1983).

Even where identity appeals to the history of the group and to its territorial and cultural roots, symbolic re-elaboration is always present. Studies of collective memory have shown that actors reappropriate social experiences and history, manipulating them and transforming them creatively, forging new myths and new institutions (Swidler and Arditi 1994: 308–10; Franzosi 2004) as it emerged, e.g., in the fiftieth anniversary of the 1968 movement (Porta 2018a). In fact, it is not necessary to attribute "objective" foundations to identity in order to recognize its continuity over time. A national sense of belonging, for example, is not reproduced solely at times of great patriotic fervor, or in reference to major historical legacies. On the contrary, its revitalization over time also depends – perhaps most importantly of all – on preconscious practices and on the persistence of mental forms and consolidated lifestyles (Billig 1995). But if this is the case, then it becomes important to look at the forms through which identity is developed and sustained, beyond intellectual and doctrinal production.

4.4.2   Production of Identity: Symbols, Practices, and Rituals

It would be dangerous to hazard a complete classification of forms of identity production, but it is nevertheless possible to identify some of its basic manifestations.[10] The
identity of a movement is, first, reinforced by reference to models of behavior that define
in various ways the specificity of its activists in relation to their adversaries. In adopting
certain styles of behavior or certain rituals, movement militants directly express their
difference (whether from "ordinary" people or, in the case of populist movements, from
the elites). Think, for example, of the Black Block and the Tute Bianche (literally, "white
overalls") in the global justice movement (Andretta et al. 2002). Activists also refer to a
series of objects, associated in various ways with their experience. Among these are a
series of identifiers that enable supporters of a particular cause to be instantly recognizable: for example, the smiling sun of antinuclear protesters, or particular styles of
clothing such as the Palestinian keffiyeh or traditional Tibetan clothes, or the tattoos
and shaven heads of right-wing movements (Blee 2007; Yangzom 2016); characters who
have played an important role in the action of a movement or in the development of its
ideology, such as Martin Luther King and Malcom X in the 1960s black mobilizations in
the United States, Ronald Laing and Franco Basaglia in the radical mental health movements in the 1970s and 1980s (Crossley 1999); artifacts, including books or visual documents that help people to reconstruct the history of the movement and its origins in
time, or to identify its stakes, such as Rachel Carson's *Silent Spring* (1962) or Naomi
Klein's *No Logo* (1999). The body itself has been identified as a distinct source of identity, e.g. in the case of the Slow Food movement (Hayes-Conroy and Martin 2010).
Events or places of a particular symbolic significance also provide important sources of
identification. Examples include the Seattle anti-WTO demonstrations in 1999 (Smith
2001), the killing of Carlo Giuliani during the anti-G8 demonstrations in Genoa in 2001
(Andretta et al. 2002), the Tiananmen square massacre of 1989 in Beijing (Calhoun
1994b), or the events in Tahrir Square in Cairo in 2011 (Bayat 2012a). These elements
are merged into stories or narratives (Polletta and Gardner 2015; Somers 1994; Zamponi
2018), which circulate among members of a movement, reflecting their vision of the
world and reinforcing solidarity.

Combining these elements sometimes produces identities that are difficult to
associate strongly with any specific social trait or historical experience. For example,
it has been observed that in societies characterized by multiple cultures and traditions, as in the United States, conditions exist for the development of forms of
"symbolic ethnicity" (Gans 1979). These forms of identification have no foundation in
the historic and cultural heritage of a given group, but mix together symbols and references deriving from diverse social groups to form a new synthesis. Collective identities such as Rastafarianism are a case in point: they are founded only partly on
specific cultural models and religious allegiances; they are also the product of choices
made by individuals who come from a range of backgrounds but derive feelings of
belonging and incentives for action through reference to a particular culture. It is
therefore possible to be a "Rasta" without having historical roots in this group
(Kuumba and Ajanaku 1998).

Models of behavior, objects, and narratives are often merged in specific ritual forms. The ritual component fulfills an important role in movement practice, and above all in the production of identities. In general, rituals represent forms of symbolic expression by which communications concerning social relationships are passed on, in stylized and dramatized ways (Kertzer 1988). These consist, in particular, of procedures that are more or less codified, through which a vision of the world is communicated, a basic historical experience is reproduced, a symbolic code overthrown. They contribute to the reinforcement of identity and of collective feelings of belonging; and at the same time, they enable movement actors to give free rein to their emotions (Goodwin et al. 2001).

Demonstrations and more generally public events promoted by movements facilitate the activation of emotional attachment to a collectivity, which, in turn, contributes to the emergence and consolidation of collective identity. One recent example of such mechanism of identity formation may be found in the Migrant Trail, an annual protest event staged along the US–Mexico borderlands to protest migrant deaths (Russo 2014). Gatherings or marches that mark particularly significant events in the history of opposition movements or their constituency often take a pronounced ritual character (Kertzer 1996). By demonstrating on May 1st or March 8th, workers' and women's movements remind themselves and society at large of their roots, thus revitalizing their identity. On a more modest scale, protest movements across the world have promoted demonstrations on the anniversaries of crucial events in their development, from the assassinations of Black American leaders Martin Luther King and Malcolm X, to the Chernobyl nuclear accident, to the Milan bombings, which, in 1969, marked the beginning of a particularly dramatic period in Italy's life. In all these cases, remembrances of the past operate as "collective memory anchoring" (Gongaware 2010), and contribute to maintain a sense of movement continuity. Rituals remain important even in those cases where movements have succeeded in gaining power. The French revolutionary government celebrated the advent of "new man" in ceremonies at the Champs de Mars; the Italian Fascist regime, for its part, stressed its continuity with Italy's glorious past by celebrating the anniversary of the foundation of Rome (Berezin 2001; Hunt 1984).

Ritual practices cannot, however, be reduced simply to public demonstrations of a celebratory nature. All protest events promoted by movements have a ritual dimension, which often assumes a powerfully dramatic and spectacular quality. The forms that demonstrations take, the type of slogans shouted, the banners or placards waved, even the conduct of marshal bodies, are all elements that, potentially, render the practice of a movement distinctive. Opponents of nuclear energy have often acted out, in the course of their demonstrations, the catastrophic consequences of an atomic explosion. Similarly, women's, ethnonationalist, and youth movements have included theatrical-type performances in their repertoire of collective action, alongside political demonstrations (see also Chapter 7). Through rituals, traditional symbolic codes are overturned and the rules that habitually determine appropriate social behavior are denied. For example, by recounting in public their experiences of sexual abuse, many American women have transformed episodes, which might otherwise have produced only feelings of shame and personal isolation, into a source of pride (Taylor and Whittier 1995). Similarly, the Occupy Wall Street recounted, in public, their own personal experiences with the injustice produced by the "1 percent" as a testimony of identification with the "99 percent" (della Porta 2015a; Gerbaudo 2012).

Identities are often created and reproduced in specific social and/or communitarian settings. Especially in authoritarian regimes, community solidarities facilitate the emergence of a collective identity, which would not be possible in reference to broader categories like class or national citizenship. This has been for example the case of China, where land-related protests on behalf of farmers' rights have been based on kinship networks and the revitalization of villages collective identities (He and Xue 2014). Communities of practice and taste have also frequently provided the setting for the emergence of collective action identities. Over 30 years ago, Melucci (1984) identified in cultural activities, the patronage of specific cafes, bookshops, meditation centers, etc. the basis for various forms of identity politics and the development of "movement areas" in Milan. The concepts of subculture and counter-culture have often been used to characterize sectors of the population sharing similar cultural orientations (see also chapter 3), yet with varying degrees of hostility and open challenges to cultural power and dominant lifestyles (Goh 2018; e.g. the gay and lesbian scene: Rupp and Taylor 2003). Some have spoken of "social movement scenes" to stress the association of these sub- and counter-cultures to specific physical space, normally city neighborhoods (also see Crossley 2015; Haunss and Leach 2009; Roman Etxebarrieta 2018). Still others (Kaplan and Lööw 2002) have used the concept of "cultic milieu" to characterize the collection of organized labor and environmentalist groups, anarchists and progressive Christians, gay and lesbian organizations, and Catholics involved in the global justice campaigns and stress analogies to the cultural underground of the 1960s. In more recent times, the impact of the 2008 financial crisis over living conditions of huge sectors of the population in Western democracies has resulted in the spread of communitarian and cooperative forms of collective action and new types of identities (Arampatzi 2017; Arampatzi and Nicholls 2012; Loukakis et al. 2018).

The spread of the Internet and computer-mediated-communication has obviously broadened the notion of community and the perception of its boundaries. In Chapter 6, we will discuss how online communities may represent a particular way of coordinating collective action. Here we limit ourselves to a few references to the complexity of the process of identity building in the virtual sphere. It has been repeatedly suggested that online interactions and discussions may contribute to the building of a sense of collectivity and to its politicization (Alberici and Milesi 2016). This seems to operate in two main ways (Milan 2015). First, social media facilitate actors' identification and mutual recognition as part of a larger collectivity: the easier interaction, the possibility of becoming aware of the existence of many people with similar views to your own, the immediate access to information on ongoing events all contribute to people's ability to connect themselves and what they are doing to a larger set of actors and activities/episodes. Second, social media enable individuals to act as such on a virtual public sphere that is much more accessible, courtesy of the technological element, for people lacking any roots in specific organizations. Social media create the conditions for people acting publicly as individuals rather than as members of organizations. Some have stretched the argument to the point of suggesting that identification with specific collectivities be no longer required for the development of collective action – Bennett and Segerberg (2013) speak of a move from "collective action," based on collective identity, to "connective action," mobilizing connected individuals. Others have been more skeptical about the opportunity to dismiss the role of both organizations and collective identity (among them Diani 2011, 2015, p. 9; see Priante et al. 2018 for a synthesis of the debate on these and related issues).

4.4.3   Identity and the Political Process

For political movements, the construction of identity is often conditioned by variables of a strictly political nature. The criteria by which social groups identify themselves and are identified externally echo characteristics of the political system and of the political culture of a given country. It seems that the development of collective identity can be explained by reference to a reformulated version of the well-known argument that forms of policy making determine forms of political action, and not vice versa (Lowi 1971). Social actors, in fact, tend to structure their action and establish alliances in different ways on different policy issues, with large interest groups dominating distributive policies and more pluralistic networks characterizing regulatory policies. Other peculiarities of policy areas have also been singled out for their impact on the structure of contention. For example, the emergence in the United States of a specific identity linking Asian Americans, and the development of "pan-ethnic collective action" (Okamoto 2003, 2010) at that level, have been put down to the fact that, in crucial areas such as those of immigration policy and the rights of minority groups, public agencies tended to treat ethnic groups as homogeneous. This despite their seeing each other as profoundly different, such as the Vietnamese or the Koreans. In this case, the adoption of a certain political/administrative criterion has produced interests and identities that enable different groups to act collectively on a number of issues (Omi and Winant 1994).

On another level, actors' identities are also defined in the context of dominant political divisions/cleavages in a given society. Movements develop in political systems that already have a structure: they try to modify it and to activate processes of political realignment (Bartolini and Mair 1990; Dalton 2018; Tilly 1978). When established political identities are salient, i.e. still capable of shaping political behavior and solidarities (Kriesi et al. 1995, p. 1), emerging social movements have to produce identities that are sufficiently specific to provide the foundations for the diversity of the movement in relation to its adversaries; but at the same time, sufficiently close to traditional collective identities in order to make it possible for movement actors to communicate with those who continue to recognize themselves in consolidated identities. Under those conditions, opportunities for genuinely "new" movements, i.e. movements cutting across established cleavages, will be relatively limited (Diani

2000a). For example, the emergence of a relatively integrated environmental movement in Italy was only possible in the 1980s, when the salience of the left-right cleavage started to decline. Its strength in the previous decade had actually prevented the early examples of anti-nuclear struggles to be the subject of mobilizations that genuinely cut across the main political divisions of the time (Diani 1995, p. 2). In a very different context, and up to the present, the strength of the multiple ethnic and religious cleavages that structure political life in Lebanon prevents movements that mobilize on nonsectarian issues (e.g., sexuality, or the struggle between privatization and public goods) to achieve public visibility and ultimately to consolidate a specific identity (Nagle 2013). In order to develop campaigns that cut across established cleavages, substantial identity bridging work is needed. Organizations working for peace from both sides of a protracted conflict provide a neat illustration of the difficulties associated with this practice. Organizations operating in stressful conditions, such as Israeli–Palestinian peace movement groups, cannot only relying on storytelling in the building of shared collective identities. To the contrary, "visible confirmatory actions" are essential steps toward the creation of mutual trust in such contexts (Gawerc 2016).

On top of institutional arrangements and salience of cleavages, interactions with authorities may represent another important source of identity. It has long been noticed how "encounters with unjust authority" (Gamson, Fireman, and Rytina 1982) may facilitate the consolidation of both motivations to act and hostility toward powerholders and their representatives (see also Chapter 8). For example, accounts of Italian terrorists of the 1970s often mentioned mistreatment by police or by the judiciary as one of the driving forces behind their radicalization (Catanzaro and Manconi 1995; della Porta 1990). In much broader – and milder – terms, we can view interactions with state agents who do not behave according to expectations or political representatives who fail to recognize people's genuine needs as facilitators of the development of political identity. An example of this mechanism comes from an analysis of how the identities of local residents, participating in an antiroad protest in England in 1993–1994, evolved during the conflict (Drury, Reicher, and Stott 2003). The role of the police in supporting the bailiffs in the eviction of protestors from the area seems to have contributed to enlarge participants' feelings of identification from the boundaries of the local communities towards a global social movement. Likewise, an investigation of the relation between everyday life and protest in 1990s Argentina showed that the transformation of an unemployed, divorced woman with no tradition of political interest whatsoever into a prominent community organizer depended in no small measure on the sense of outrage that she experienced at her interactions with two types of "unjust authorities": "political authority," in the form of the local governor, who portrayed hungry protestors as a mob; and "social authority," in the shape of a fellow male protestor who reproduced gender stereotypes by dismissing the role of women in the struggle (Auyero 2004).

Another, comparatively less explored yet very important dimension of identity building is the one that takes place when the authority confronted is not merely unjust but repressive – sometimes a totalitarian regime. In those cases, the conditions of identity work are clearly different from those that activists face in more open settings.

While identity building, as we have seen, relies heavily on public displays, such displays are impossible, or at least extremely risky and problematic, under heavily repressive conditions. A study of the identity work of Jewish resistance fighters in Nazi-occupied Warsaw highlighted the "dissonant" nature of the construction of Jewishness in such setting (Einwohner 2006). Although resistance under such harsh conditions required strong emotional work, and therefore also an "amplification" of identity mechanism, the levels of repression and the need to operate hidden from public scrutiny demanded instead a suppression of emotion.

Religious institutions have often provided a favorable setting for the production of identity under repressive conditions. Opposition to the communist regime in Poland heavily relied on religious symbols and practices to reinforce identity and commitment to the cause (Osa 2003). Religious celebrations provided the context for the production and spread of nationalist interpretative frames in the Baltic republics at the time of their enforced association with the Soviet Union. The Catalan and Basque churches played a similar role during Franco's dictatorship in Spain (Johnston 1991). The legitimization of religious rituals creates opportunities for collective gatherings, and therefore for the strengthening and the diffusion of alternative messages, in repressive regimes. The funeral of the Abbot of Montserrat monastery, a well-known Catalan nationalist and opponent of the Franco regime, in 1968, represented an opportunity for different sectors of Catalan opposition to get together and reinforce their collective solidarity (Johnston 1991: 156–58). Mosques and religious institutions have also played an important role in supporting opposition to secular autocratic regimes in the Middle East. Religious functions in Reza Pahlevi's Iran not only supported the emergence of opposition cultures in that country, but also ensured that these cultures developed a marked theocratic character, paving the way for the advent of the ayatollahs' regime (Moaddel 2002). Decades later, mosques also provided a meeting point and opportunities to coordinate to dissenters in the region, eventually contributing to the 2011 uprisings (Clark 2004; Hoffman and Jamal 2014; Wickham 2002). The specific characteristics of the religious spaces that are used by social movement activists are then reflected in the evolution of those movements – with, for instance, a most relevant impact of the Catholic Church on the evolution of Solidarity in Poland during and after the transition to democracy (della Porta 2015a; 2017a).

4.5 SUMMARY

Identity construction is an essential component of collective action. It enables actors engaged in conflict to see themselves as people linked by interests, values, common histories – or else as divided by these same factors. Although identity feelings are frequently elaborated in reference to specific social traits such as class, gender, territory, or ethnicity, the process of collective identity does not necessarily imply homogeneity of the actors sharing that identity, or their identification with a distinct social group. Nor are feelings of belonging always mutually exclusive. On the contrary, actors frequently identify with heterogeneous collectives who are not always compatible among themselves on fundamental issues. To reconstruct the tensions through the different versions of identity of a movement, and how these versions are negotiated, represents, according to some scholars, a central problem for the analysis of collective action.

Identity plays an important role in the explanation of collective action even for those who see in collective action a peculiar form of rational behavior. Those who perceive in collective identity certain criteria for evaluating, in the medium and long terms, the costs and benefits of action, are numerous. However, those who hold that this use of the concept of identity cannot be proposed are equally numerous. Because of its strongly emotive and affective components, as well as its controversial and constructed nature, it is difficult to associate identity with behavior of a strategic type. Identity develops and is renegotiated via various processes. These include conflicts between auto- and hetero-definitions of reality; various forms of symbolic production, collective practices, and rituals. It is important, furthermore, to bear in mind the characteristics of the political process, that can influence definitions of identity.

CHAPTER 5

Individuals, Networks, and Participation

Viale Sarca is a long, fairly anonymous road on the Milanese periphery, lined with tenements that mostly used to host workers of the Pirelli factory nearby. In the late 1990s, urban renewal brought new intellectual glamour to the area, following the location, on the former Pirelli estate, of the campus of the second state university of Milan. Developers were nowhere to be seen, however, in 1985, when Mario Diani traveled there to meet Antonio, a local environmental and political activist. Mario was researching the Milanese environmental movement and Antonio's name had been passed to him as the contact person for a grassroots political ecology group operating in the area. The offspring of southern Italian farmers turned industrial workers who migrated to Milan in the 1950s, Antonio had followed a fairly common path of political socialization: exposed to trade unionism and communist party politics in his teens, he had become involved with radical left group Lotta Continua (Continuous Struggle) in the 1970s and had later developed an interest in the link between social deprivation and environmental degradation. He was also an active member of a local Green List that was forming at the time. In order to promote campaigning on environmental issues in the highly polluted northern Milanese periphery, he had drawn upon the contacts developed

Social Movements: An Introduction, Third Edition. Donatella della Porta and Mario Diani.
© 2020 John Wiley & Sons Ltd. Published 2020 by John Wiley & Sons Ltd.

during his previous militancy. The core activists in his new environmental group all shared a past of activism in the same local branch of Lotta Continua. Acquaintances and contacts developed over the years had also proved useful with the promotion of specific actions: Antonio had collaborated with a range of local organizations across the broad spectrum of the New and the Old Left, including local branches of parties and unions, cultural and cooperative associations.

Now let's fast backward to the 1940s to meet a far less pleasant character, SS officer Odilo Globocnik. A committed Nazi since his youth and a former Gauleiter of Vienna following the annexation of Austria by Germany in 1938, Globocnik was appointed by Himmler in 1939 as SS and Police Leader in the Lublin District in Poland. In that role he was responsible, among other criminal acts, for the liquidation of the Warsaw and other ghettoes in the country, and the creation of a number of extermination camps (Perz 2015). Altogether he was associated with the death of about 1.5 million people in the camps he supervised, among them Sobibor, Majdanek, and Treblinka. In his undertakings he could rely on the assistance of a "committed staff," consisting mostly of fellow Austrians. The main reason for their joint recruitment was not, however, their national origin but rather the fact that they had all been part with Globocnik of the same networks back in the early 1930s when Nazi organizations were illegal in Austria. As historian Bertrand Perz put it, "These were not just anymen, but a group of perpetrators with very close personal and ideological ties" (Perz 2015, p. 400).

And finally, let's jump back to contemporary times and to decent people, the migrant women, mostly from the Balkans and the former Soviet Union, that account for large part of the informal economy of domestic and personal care in Greece: already in 2001, they were estimated to account for 45% of the workforce in that sector in the country (Christopoulou and Leontsini 2017, p. 514). Still, their capacity to gain visibility in public life, particularly in Athens, was limited: while the creation of a Migrants' Forum in 2002 had enabled many ethnic organizations and leaders to play some role and strengthen the position of their communities in urban dynamics, these were largely male-dominated affairs. Female domestic and *care workers, in contrast, remained largely invisible (Christopoulou and Leontsini 2017, p. 515). Gradually, however, connections between immigrants have developed, partially on the margins of the Migrants' Forum, partially through largely personal connections. This has led to the creation of specific associations, defined on variable criteria (sometimes national, sometimes linguistic). Most important, however, has been the emergence of a web of connections that cuts across different associations, sometimes via umbrella organizations, most frequently through informal interpersonal networks. Such connections support activities that are often closer to mutual support and community care than to standard political advocacy (Christopoulou and Leontsini 2017).*

These stories deal with very diverse examples of collective action. In terms of substance, there is very little indeed in common between a 1980s activists from the Italian new left, a Nazi mass murderer, and contemporary immigrant women in Athens. And, one could reasonably question our speaking of "collective action" in reference to participation in a highly bureaucratic apparatus like the Third Reich SS. Yet, even the closest collaborators of SS-Brigadeführer Globocnik came to occupy that position not so much by virtue of formal bureaucratic procedures but because of the informal connections they had developed to each other during their militancy in the Austrian Nazi party in the preceding years. In one way or the other, and despite moving from very different premises, these stories all illustrate the main themes of this chapter, namely, the dynamic nature of the relationship between networks and participation, and the duality of the link between individuals and organizational activities. First of all, social networks affect participation in collective action, while in turn participation shapes networks, reinforcing preexisting ones or creating new ones. Social networks may increase individual chances to become involved, and strengthen activists' attempts to further the appeal of their causes: when Antonio decided to start a local environmental action group, he successfully tried and convinced his former comrades in Lotta Continua to join him in the new enterprise. That they not only quickly got involved with the environmental issues but agreed to support the particular agenda Antonio was proposing, depended in no small measure on the mutual trust, sense of companionship, solidarity, and the shared understandings and worldviews that had been forged and developed through their long-term acquaintance in Lotta Continua. From this perspective, therefore, previous social networks facilitated the development of new forms of collective action at later stages. For all the immense substantive differences and the more formalized nature of the process, channeled through the bureaucratic structures of the SS, also Globocnik relied on previous networks to constitute a group of trusted assistants that could assist him in his murderous deeds. Fighting liberal democracy in 1930s Vienna provided them with a mutual bond that proved instrumental in their subsequent evolution into senior members of the Nazi machine (Perz 2015).

At the same time, social networks are not only a facilitator but also a product of collective action: while people often become involved in a specific movement or campaign through their previous links, their very participation also forges new links, which in turn affect subsequent developments in their activist careers, and indeed in their lives at large (Livesay 2002). Let us look at Antonio's involvement with Lotta Continua from this angle: the members of his local branch had been recruited to New Left radicalism via a range of ties, developed in school and peer groups, in political organizations (e.g., youth branches of traditional left parties) as well as in other associations (e.g., church-related ones). Participation in Lotta Continua was therefore as much the product of previous networks (including previous forms of participation) as it was the source of networks that people like Antonio could draw upon at later stages.

Another important mechanism is highlighted by our stories, namely, the duality of individuals and organizations: our uniqueness as individuals is determined by the particular combination of our group memberships; at the same time, by being members of different groups, we create linkages between them (Simmel 1955; Breiger 1974). Looking at people's membership in associations and organizations, and at their participation in social and cultural activities close to social movement milieus, we can derive important information about their involvement in collective action. Antonio is a case in point. His identity as a "political man" was determined by the intersection of militancy in a grassroots ecology group and in a left-wing local Green List; on this ground, he differed markedly from other environmental activists, who combined environmentalism with membership in mainstream, moderate recreational, or cultural associations. At the same time, though, by being active in a local political ecology group and in a New Left party, and by participating occasionally in other local groups, Antonio somehow linked them all; he provided a channel of communication which proved useful for promoting joint initiatives, and also facilitated the growth of mutual trust and solidarity between the different groups. The stories of migrant women in Athens also point at the role of individuals in connecting groups and organizations: coming from different countries, and/or belonging to different linguistic or religious groups, they may have been members of different associations. Yet, by meeting informally in urban spaces during their leisure time, or in activities on issues of general interest for migrant people, they created a web of interpersonal connections and mutual trust that was the basis for broader solidarities. They contributed, in other words, to linking communities that would have been otherwise kept apart by their origins and cultural differences.

To sum up, the relationship between individuals and the networks in which they are embedded is crucial not only for the involvement of people in collective action, but also for the sustenance of action over time, and for the particular form that the coordination of action among a multiplicity of groups and organizations may take. In the next section, we ask whether being linked to people who already participate may facilitate individuals' decisions to devote time and energy to collective action. We map the origins of this question, as well as the criticisms that a response based on the role of networks has attracted. Behind these questions lurks a much broader debate on the relationship between structure and action. Over the past decade, this discussion has attracted many contributions from scholars with a specific interest in collective action. Although we cannot address that debate here (Crossley 2011; for summaries of the discussion: Mische 2011), we nevertheless have to be aware of the broader theoretical context in which our specific research interests are located.

Later in the chapter, we move to the other side of the individual–networks relationship, that is, the contribution that individuals give to the making of social movements out of the multiplicity of groups, associations, and concerned individuals involved in collective action on certain broad issues. Although some organizations require exclusive commitments, most do not. We explore these processes of network-building and mutual understanding, made possible by individuals' multiple memberships in various types of informal groups and more formal associations. In doing so, we connect our discussion – once again, mostly implicitly – to the broader debate on the role of social networks as a source of individual as well as collective opportunities (Coleman 1990; Edwards, Foley, and Diani 2001; Prakash and Selle 2004; Putnam 2000). From that particular angle, networks facilitating involvement in social movement activities may be regarded as one particular version of "social capital" (Diani 1997).

However, individuals do not create connections solely through organizational memberships, but also through their participation in various types of social and cultural activities (music festivals, communities of taste, reading groups, alternative cafes, cinemas, theaters, etc.). By doing so, they reproduce specific subcultural or countercultural milieus that offer both opportunities for protest activities and for the maintenance and transformation of critical orientations even when protest is not vibrant (Melucci 1996). The final part of the chapter deals with this issue; it also addresses in that context the question of whether the diffusion of computer-mediated communication may alter the conditions under which alternative critical communities and cultural settings are reproduced, and people are recruited. The literature on the role of networks and virtual and real communities in the "network society" (Castells 1996, 2012; Gonzalez-Bailon 2017; Loader and Mercea 2011; Van de Donk et al. 2004) provides the broader context for this discussion.

5.1 NETWORKS AND PARTICIPATION

One solidly established fact in social movement research is the frequency with which people involved in collective action are connected to other activists either through personal ties or joint involvement in activities. In one of the first explorations of the importance of personal networks for recruitment processes, Snow, Zurcher, and Ekland-Olson (1980) showed social networks to account for the adhesion of a large share (60–90%) of members of various religious and political organizations. Diani and Lodi (1988) found that 78% of environmental activists in Milan in the 1980s had been recruited through personal contacts developed either in private settings (family, personal friendship circles, colleagues) or in the context of other associational activities. Far more recently, Passy and Monsch (2014) found network ties to have played a role for the recruitment of between 76% and 38% of members of three Swiss organizations working on transnational issues like the environ-ment, development, or migration. On a larger scale, data on participants in the Greek anti-austerity protests of the early 2000s (Rudig and Karyotis 2013) suggest that over 80% of the protesters (estimated to be one third of the reek population) had previous experi-ences of activism, often in unions or left-wing parties.

Embeddedness in social networks not only matters for recruitment; it also works as an antidote to leaving, and as a support to continued participation. For example, members of voluntary associations in America, whose social ties are mostly to other organization members, are more likely to remain committed to those organizations than are those who instead have a greater share of connections to nonmembers (McPherson, Popielarz, and Drobnic 1992). A study of dropouts from Swedish tem-perance organizations also discovered substantial positive and negative bandwagon effects, as people tended both to join and leave in clusters, and to be affected more heavily by their closest links (Sandell 1999; see also Sandell and Stern 1998; Tindall 2004). Being embedded in a specific subculture certainly facilitates the acquisition of its dominant cultural traits, including the predisposition to protest (Perez 2018).

What are the mechanisms behind the empirical correlation between previous involvement in networks and participation? Networks actually perform different functions. At one level, they facilitate the spread of information and opportunities for participation among people that may be interested in a cause, but would other-wise be unable to identify proper channels of participation; at another level, they affect the probability that people be socialized to specific values and develop an interest in specific causes through the influence exerted on them by their personal connections; still at another level, contact and comparison with people in one's circle may generate the social pressure that not only helps people to join but also provides them with the motivation to continue acting over time even when the costs of action are rising (Passy 2003; Passy and Monsch 2014; Tindall 2015). These functions often – although not always – occur through mechanisms of "bloc recruitment" (Oberschall 1973): cells, branches, or simply significant groups of members of exist-ing organizations are recruited as a whole to a new movement, or contribute to the start of new campaigns. This applied to Antonio's case, where the local branch of Lotta Continua was instrumental to the foundation of a Green List in the North Milan area; it also applied to Globocnik's efforts to create a cohesive group support-ing his murderous activities (Perz 2015).

The relevance of such functions may change, depending on whether we are looking at recruitment rather than at the strengthening of commitment and the extension of militancy over long periods of time. It also depends on the type of action we are looking at, or on the variable public exposure of different organizations. For example, among the organizations studied by Passy and Monsch (2014), Greenpeace was the least reliant on personal networks when recruiting members. This is not sur-prising, given Greenpeace's massive use of advertising techniques, its professional-ized approach to activism, that reduces the cost of action for ordinary fee-paying members, and its public visibility. All that may well facilitate individual decisions to join independently of pressures exerted through personal networks.

On the other hand, networks seem particularly important for adhesion to high-risk activities. Available evidence suggests that the more costly and dangerous the collective action, the stronger and more numerous the ties required for individuals to participate. A study of recruitment to the civil rights project Freedom Summer, aimed at increasing blacks' participation in politics in the southern states of the United States in the 1960s, showed that joining was not correlated with individual attitudes but rather with three factors: the number of organizations individuals were members of, especially the political ones; the amount of previous experiences of collective action; the links to other people who were also involved with the campaign (McAdam 1986). In her study of a similarly risky, though very different, type of activism, della Porta (1988) found that involvement in terrorist left-wing groups in Italy was facilitated by strong interpersonal linkages, many to close friends or kin. Participation in Nazi organizations in the 1930s, that we have seen to be a predictor of later commitment to the Nazi extermination machine during WWII (Perz 2015), was in turn facilitated by strong embeddedness in the broader networks connecting right-wing, nationalistic, and paramilitary organizations in the turbulent years that had followed defeat in the First World War (Anheier 2003). Far more recently, the fact that opposition to Hassad's highly repressive regime in Syria took off in the "peripheral" Dar'a region has been imputed to the province's dense social networks involving clans, labor migration, cross-border movements, and crime. These complex multiple networks "effectively connected individuals of different origins and strata in an otherwise prohibitive authoritarian context" (Leenders 2012: 419). Strong ties to friends and acquaintances have also been found to increase the chance of joining radical Islamist organizations (Ahmad 2014).

Looking at the role of networks improves our understanding of collective action dynamics from different angles. On the one hand, recognizing the impact of social networks on both individual participation and overall levels of activism among a given population provides the foundations for a critique of structural-deterministic approaches to collective action. According to such perspectives, one could explain individual involvement with the presence of certain skills (e.g., levels of education or political experience), or to account for the overall mobilization capacity of a given social group in the light of its properties. For example, the diminished levels of mobilization by the working class in Western democracies could be imputed to its contraction and its overall reduced centrality in the economic process. In contrast, many students of social movements nowadays associate collective action with catnets, i.e., with the co-presence in a given population of cat(egorical traits) and net(work)s. Sharing certain class locations, gender, nationality, or religious beliefs certainly provides the elements on the basis of which recognition and identity-building may take place. But it is through the channels of communication and exchange, constituted by social networks, that the mobilization of resources and the emergence of collective actors become possible (Tilly 1978).

Paying attention to networks in facilitating recruitment and sustaining participation in collective action has also enabled scholars to challenge views of protest and countercultural behavior as unruly and deviant. Still in the early 1970s, established academic wisdom regarded individual involvement in social movements as the result of a "mix of personal pathology and social disorganization" (McAdam 2003, p. 281). At the micro level, collective action was explained by the marginal location of the individuals involved in protest activity, and the lack of integration in their social milieu; at the macro level, by the disruption of routine social arrangements, brought about by radical processes of change and modernization (Buechler 2011, p. 6; Kornhauser 1959). Admittedly, those interpretations had some empirical foundation: for example, even the study that in many ways drew first analysts' attention to the role of networks suggested that joining religious sects, deeply hostile to the secular world, such as Hare Krishna, was often the preserve of people with personal difficulties and lacking extended relational resources (Snow, Zurcher, and Ekland-Olson 1980). These extreme cases, however, do not challenge the general finding that people participating in collective action are more, and not less, likely to rely on extensive relational capital. Not only that: the relevance of these findings is not restricted to recruitment to social movements proper. Similar dynamics may be found in organizations with no explicit political goals, and/or reluctant to include protest and direct action among their tactical options, such as charities and volunteer groups (Wilson 2000); the same seems to apply to established interest representation groups such as unions (Dixon and Roscigno 2003).

Looking at networks also enables us to question the separation of protest and routinized politics. Mass society theory posited a fundamental opposition between protest politics and democratic politics (Buechler 2011, p. 6; Kornhauser 1959). It also assumed that associations would discourage radical collective action because of their capacity to integrate elites and ordinary citizens, socialize their members to the rules of the game, give them a sense of political efficacy, and provide them with primary attachments and a more satisfactory life. These tenets were challenged by scholars who claimed that grassroots, contentious collective action was ultimately just "politics by other means." From this perspective, social movements were merely one of the options that challengers could draw on to pursue their policy outcomes and their quest for membership in the polity (Tilly 1978). In contrast to accounts of participation in social movements as dysfunctional behavior, social movement activists and sympathizers were portrayed as rich in both cognitive resources and entrepreneurial and political skills (McCarthy and Zald 1987; Oberschall 1973). Most important to us, as the studies mentioned above remind us, activists were also found to be rich in relational resources, i.e., well integrated in their communities, and strongly involved in a broad range of organizations, from political ones to voluntary associations and community groups. The development of cross-national surveys analyzing individual participation has largely backed this argument with reference to both institutional politics and protest politics, as participation in the two is strongly correlated (Dalton 2008; Norris 2002).

5.2   DO NETWORKS ALWAYS MATTER?

The role of networks in recruitment processes has been questioned from different angles. On logical grounds, the network thesis would be inconsistent with the fact that those most inclined to action are young people, biographically available because their original family ties no longer bind them as they used to, and new family and professional ties are still developing. Most fundamentally, the network thesis would also be largely tautological, given the spread of ties across groups and individuals: "lateral integration, however fragile, is ubiquitous, thus making opportunities for protest ubiquitous" (Piven and Cloward 1992, p. 311). Rather than highlighting exclusively those cases in which ties are found to be predictors of involvement, analysts should also look at those cases when networks are present yet participation does not result.

It has also been suggested that focusing on networks diverts attention away from the really crucial process for mobilization, namely the transmission of cognitive cultural messages (Jasper and Poulsen 1995). Although this may happen through networks, it may also take place through other channels such as the media. Campaigners may have to resort to "moral shocks" with strong emotional impact in order to recruit strangers that they cannot access via personal networks. This may be particularly the case for movements who try to bring new issues onto the political agenda, and/or whose leaders do not have a significant political background:

> The use of condensing symbols without social networks may mean that a movement is more likely to employ extreme moralistic appeals that demonize its opponents. It may be more likely to rely on professional or highly motivated bands to do much of its work, as with animal rights activists who break into labs. In contrast... movement organizers [who] can tap into an active subculture of politically involved citizens... can rely on earlier framing activity... They have correspondingly less need of moral shocks administered to the public.

> (Jasper and Poulsen 1993, p. 508)

Sustained involvement in collective action may also be facilitated by the participation, not necessarily planned or anticipated, in events that turn out to have a powerful emotional impact – sometimes on entire collectivities, other times, on specific individuals (Goodwin et al. 2001; Turner and Killian 1987). In his analysis of grassroots protests by dispossessed social groups in Argentina, Javier Auyero (2004) illustrated the mechanisms through which a woman with no interest in politics nor ties to political activists turned into a community leader in a small Argentinian town in less than a week, following her occasional involvement in a blockade, promoted by local residents to complain about joblessness and hardship in the region. Given her background, a network explanation for such developments seems implausible. That this happened was due in much larger measure to the interplay of several expressions of outrage: at a judiciary system that was failing her in her struggle to secure help for her kids' upbringing from her estranged husband; at local politicians attempting to manipulate local people's protests to pursue their own political ends; at the provincial governor's framing of hungry people's collective action as criminal behavior; not to mention dismissive attitudes by male fellow protestors (Auyero 2004).

Empirically, a number of studies of specific protest campaigns over the years have shown participation to depend on a number of factors in addition to, and sometimes in opposition to, social networks. Social-psychological studies have often pointed at the role of ideological stances and levels of identification with a movement as predictors of actual participation (Cameron and Nickerson 2009; Saab, Harb, and Moughalian 2017). A sense of political efficacy has also been found to correlate with inclination to participate (Saab et al. 2017), as well as interest in specific issues (Grasso and Giugni 2016), or the quality of mediated messages to which prospective activists are exposed (Ketelaars 2017). Even studies that still found evidence supporting the role of networks in recruitment and participation have highlighted variations in the relevance of those factors. For example, a replication of McAdam's study of Freedom Summer that looked at participants and dropouts in the Nicaragua Exchange Brigade in the 1980s failed to confirm the original findings (Nepstad and Smith 1999). In that case, ties to people directly involved were the most powerful predictor of participation, but the number of prospective participants' ties to other organizations did not matter. However, the relationship was reversed for people who joined after the organization's third year in existence, with the number of organizational links being important and ties to actual participants no longer helping. Younger participants in the anti-austerity campaigns of the 2010s also seem to have been influenced by embeddedness in previous organizational networks less than activists from previous generations (Grasso and Giugni 2016, 2018; Rudig and Karyotis 2013).

The combination of criticism and mixed findings has prompted analysts of social networks to substantially qualify their points. It is now widely recognized that, when looking at the relationship between networks and participation, it is important to specify its terms. More sophisticated multilevel models have been developed: some have specified the interplay of networks and motivations by looking explicitly at participants and nonparticipants in specific campaigns (e.g. van Laer 2017); others have pointed at the variable contribution that networks may give to participation, depending on the type of action.

Questions such as "What networks actually explain what?" and "Under what conditions do specific networks become relevant?" have become crucial. In their search for solid answers, some have looked at the type of actions and organizations. Passy (2003; see also Passy and Monsch 2014) showed how these functions took different forms depending on the traits of the organization trying to recruit, and its visibility in the public space. For example, the social connection function (establishing a tie between prospective participants and organizations) seemed more important for adhesion to organizations that are not very visible in the public space, like the Third World solidarity group Bern Declaration, than for organizations with a strong public presence, like the Swiss branch of WWF.[1] Along similar lines, a comparison of individual acts of altruism like blood giving with participation in voluntary associations and protest activities found that while romantic relations facilitated participation in any form of action, others were more specific (Beyerlein and Bergstrand 2016). It is therefore useful to try and summarize some of the main facts that researchers have identified over the years.

We have already seen (section 5.1) that radical activism often needs dense supporting networks. At the other extreme, participation in organizational activities that are not very demanding might not necessarily require the backing of strong social networks. For example, adhesion to cultural associations that promote practices fairly close to market activities (e.g., individual meditation, alternative health practices like yoga, etc.) may easily occur even though people's decisions to get involved are not supported by specific social networks (Stark and Bainbridge 1980). Even public interest groups, like those active in the environmental movement, may rely on networks to a variable extent, depending on their levels of moderation and institutionalization. For example, Diani and Lodi (1988) found that recruitment to organizations in the more established conservation sector depended more on private networks than recruitment to more critical groups, which largely took place through ties developed in previous experiences of collective action. They explained this difference by suggesting that exclusively private ties (i.e., ties developed in contexts detached from collective action milieus) may be enough to facilitate adhesion to organizations that have widely accepted policy goals (for example, supporting a local group campaigning to create new green spaces in the neighborhood). In contrast, joining organizations with some radical stances, like political ecology ones, may require people to overcome higher barriers. Accordingly, this may be easier if people are linked to acquaintances met during specific experiences of collective action rather than in more generic settings like one's neighborhood. However, adhesion to very demanding forms of collective action may also occur without networks playing a major role. As we have seen in the case of world-rejecting religious sects, who require of their members a total break with their previous lifestyles and habits, involvement may be easier for isolated individuals than for people who are well embedded in social networks. In all likelihood, network links would exert some kind of cross-pressure, thus discouraging prospective adepts from joining (Snow et al. 1980).

Increasingly, researchers have recognized that people are involved in multiple ties, and that while some may facilitate participation, others may discourage it (Kitts 2000). Taking this possibility into account, McAdam and Paulsen (1993) tried to determine what dimensions of social ties are most important, and how different types of ties shape decisions to participate. Their conclusions substantially qualified earlier arguments (including their own: McAdam 1986) on the link between participation and former organizational memberships. As such, embeddedness in organizational links did not predict activism, nor did strong ties to people who already volunteered. Instead, what mattered most was a strong commitment to a particular identity, reinforced by ties to participants, whether of an organizational or private type. Having been a member of, say, left-wing groups in the past did not represent a predictor of participation in Freedom Summer unless it was coupled with a strong, subjective identification with that milieu.

Being directly linked – mostly via organizational ties – to people who already participate may thus not be an essential precondition for recruitment. Lack of direct ties may be overcome if prospective participants are embedded in organizational networks compatible with the campaign/organization they are considering joining

(Kriesi 1988; McAdam and Fernandez 1990; McAdam and Paulsen 1993). However, we can also think of the reverse situation, with people mobilizing through contacts developed in contexts not directly associated with participation, but that nonetheless create opportunities for people with similar presuppositions to meet and eventually develop joint action. Research on adhesion to two action committees campaigning against low-flying military jets in two German villages (Ohlemacher 1996) showed that recruitment attempts were far more successful for the committee whose members were mostly part of neutral organizations in their village rather than of explicitly political ones. Membership in apparently innocuous organizations such as parent–teacher associations or sport clubs enabled members of the committee to reach, and gain the trust of, a broader range of people than they could have had they been members of organizations with a more clear-cut political identity. Similar mechanisms may also influence involvement in non-protest actions. For example, membership in religious congregations, and the resulting ties to fellow members, may enable people to engage in a variety of activities in the community, but without any bearing on levels of involvement in the congregational activities. Congregations offer individuals the opportunity to form close links of friendship and support, but the resulting social capital may exert its effects mainly beyond the boundaries of the congregation (Becker and Dhingra 2001).

Other times, it is the position one occupies within a network that matters, rather than the mere fact of being involved in some kind of network. In one of their explorations of participation in Freedom Summer, Fernandez and McAdam (1989) looked at individual centrality in the network, which consisted of all the activists who had applied to take part in the campaign in Madison, Wisconsin. Joint memberships in social organizations of all sorts represented the links between individuals. Those who were more central in that network (i.e., who were either linked to a higher number of prospective participants, and/or were connected to people who were also central in that network) were more likely to go through the training process undeterred, and eventually to join the campaign. In that case, involvement in networks did not count as much as one's location within them.

The context in which mobilization attempts take place is also very important, as local conditions affect how social networks operate. Kriesi (1988) studied recruitment to the 1985 People's Petition campaign, which collected signatures against the deployment of SS20 cruise missiles in the Netherlands. In areas where countercultural milieus were weak, people already had to be members of local political organizations in order to mobilize in the campaign; where countercultural milieus were strong, and the overall attitudes toward collective action were in general more favorable, there was less need for links to members of specific political organizations to encourage adhesion: more people were recruited through personal friendship networks or even in other forms not based on network links at all (e.g. self-applications: Kriesi 1988, p. 58). Strong countercultural milieus seemed to have an autonomous capacity to motivate people, which in turn made specific organizational connections less necessary. Along similar lines, McAdam and Fernandez (1990) found that recruitment to the Freedom Summer campaign depended more strongly on membership in organizational networks on a campus with a weak tradition of activism like Madison, Wisconsin, than on a campus with a strong tradition of alternative politics like Berkeley. However, some recent comparative explorations suggest that it is the resources and opportunities offered by urban environments to have the greatest impact over chances of participation, rather than the mere presence of previous ties. At times this may reflect primarily the resources linked to the relative affluence experienced by urban middle classes (Schoene 2017). Other times, urban neighborhoods may facilitate action by the most dispossessed sectors of the population, that rely on the connections developed in the streets of metropolitan cities (Bayat 2012b).

Special attention needs to be paid to the role of interpersonal social networks in supporting collective action within repressive regimes. In those cases, the involvement of dissenters into activist networks has often occurred through connections developed in settings that could appear as neutral and ultimately not harmful to rulers. Examples include the activities of theaters in the Velvet Revolution that toppled the communist regime in Czechoslovakia in 1989 (Glenn 1999), the role of mosques and bazaars as meeting points for the opponents to Reza Pahlevi's regime in 1970s Iran (Ashraf 1988), or the culinary societies in Franco's Spain (Hess 2007). Although their mobilizing role is also massive in democratic regimes (Coddou 2017; McAdam 1988), churches have been particularly important in nondemocratic situations, also due to their high moral status and the particular respect they may command. In cases where repression also targets churches, like contemporary China, at least in the sense of banning any form of proselytizing, recruitment has taken primarily the form of interpersonal ties (Qi 2017; Vala and O'Brien 2007).

5.3 INDIVIDUALS AND ORGANIZATIONS

As the stories of Milanese left-wing activists and Athenian migrant women, with which we opened this chapter, illustrate well, the importance of social networks for collective action in movements goes beyond their support of individual activism. On the contrary, by participating in the life of a movement activists create new channels of communication between the groups and organizations active within it, and society at large. For example, environmental activist are also frequently members of organizations with other primary goals such as community groups or cultural associations; they may as well have extended personal ties to political representatives or government agencies. These multiple, encompassing social networks increase their capacity to act (Stoddart and Tindall 2010). At the same time, while multiple interpersonal connections increase the capacity of movement groups to establish alliances with, and recruit members from, various social milieus, ties between the members of specific organizations may become particularly dense. In some cases (for example, sectarian groups), the density of such ties may stretch to the point of preventing connections to other social settings. Let us look, in turn, at the role of interpersonal ties in exclusive and inclusive organizations.

5.3.1 Exclusive Affiliations

In some cases, participation implies committing to specific organizations. Exclusive organizations demand a long novitiate, rigid discipline, and a high level of commitment, intruding upon every aspect of their members' lives (Curtis and Zurcher 1974; Zald and Ash 1966). In general, the greater the degree to which an organization is founded on symbolic incentives – either ideological or solidaristic – the more exclusive it will be. The most obvious illustrations of this pattern include self-referential communities or sects whose main characteristics are closure in the face of the outside world, a totalitarian structure, incompatibility with other forms of collective engagement, and the view – among themselves – that adherents are the repositories of truth (Wallis 1977). Though they are not necessarily residential communities, the lifestyle of these groups is markedly separate. Interaction with other groups is usually limited, while the tendency to concentrate on activities internal to the group is very strong. Organizations active in neo-religious or neo-communitarian movements often easily fall into this category; but political fundamentalist and radical organizations are not dissimilar (Anheier 2003; Blee 2002).

In these settings, the single adherent/activist inhabits a world in which relationships and norms are highly structured: this leads to a radical transformation of personality. The prevalence of sectarian organizations within a movement sector produces networks that are highly, if not completely, fragmented. The only significant level of interaction is among adherents to a specific organization. In some cases (for example, those sects that can count on numerous local groups, such as the Jehovah's Witnesses, but also political organizations with a strong territorial presence) these contacts can also develop over a wide geographical area. However, contacts rarely extend beyond the confines of the single organization. The "movement network" consists, therefore, of a series of cliques; that is to say, groups of actors – members of a given organization – who are strongly linked to each other and barely or not at all with adherents to other groups.

5.3.2 Multiple Affiliations

In most cases, however, participation takes place in inclusive organizations that allow multiple memberships and have no aspiration to monopolize their members' commitment. Already in the early 1970s, individual activists were regarded as interorganizational links, and thus as basic structural features of movement "organizational fields" (Curtis and Zurcher 1973; see also Chapter 6). Many empirical investigations have followed, adding details to the broad picture. Diani and Lodi (1988) have documented multiple commitments in Italian environmentalism, with 28% of activists being involved in several other environmental organizations, and the same percentage active in both environmental and other political or social groups. A study of Dutch environmentalism in the late 1980s found 43% of core activists to have personal links to other movement activists (25% in Italy according to Diani and Lodi 1988), and 67% to be connected to other new social movement participants (Kriesi 1993, p. 186).

Patterns of multiple participation seem to be affected by organizational features. An investigation of members of voluntary US associations found that bigger organizations not only were able to secure their members' commitment for a longer time but could also rely on more ties to other groups, generated by their members' overlapping affiliations (McPherson 1983). However, other data (e.g. Diani 1995, p. 113) suggest a more ambiguous relationship between an organization's size and its members' propensity to engage in multiple activities.

Multiple affiliations play an important role in integrating different areas of a movement. To belong to the same movement organizations (just as, more generally, to organizations of other types) facilitates personal contact and the development of informal networks which, in turn, encourage individual participation and the mobilization of resources. Personal contacts are also instrumental in linking organizations to each other. Similarly to economic organizations (Mizruchi 1996), political organizations are often connected by the fact that they share certain activists; or else by personal relationships and friendships among their members and leaders.

A pioneering study of movement activism in the Greater Vancouver area (Carroll and Ratner 1996) exemplifies these processes well. By looking at the joint affiliations of over 200 activists in seven social movements (labor, urban/antipoverty, gay/lesbian, feminism, environmentalism, peace, aboriginal) they were able to document not only the extent of overlapping memberships, but their patterning. Among Vancouver activists, only 27% were active in a single organization, whereas 28% collaborated with multiple organizations within the same movement, and 45% with multiple organizations in several movements (Carroll and Ratner 1996, p. 605). Activists in peace and urban/antipoverty movements were the most inclined toward multiple memberships (67% and 71% were involved in multiple organizations in multiple movements), while gay/lesbian, feminist, environmentalist, and aboriginal activists seemed to be the least so (34%, 32%, 39%, and 42% of them, respectively, were actually committed to a single organization). Overlapping memberships constituted a core bloc of labor, peace, and urban/antipoverty organizations. Feminist and environmental organizations were linked to this bloc through their connections to labor and peace movements (1996, pp. 605–606). While this specific pattern of linkages need not be taken as the norm, and it may well vary substantially in different periods and localities, the Vancouver study well illustrates the potential returns of a network approach to the study of movement sectors.

Data on people who demonstrated against the Iraq war on February 15, 2003, in eight Western countries (Walgrave and Rucht 2010) likewise indicate the extent of multiple memberships among activists. Of the demonstrators who were members of peace organizations before February 15, 53% were also active in other organizations mobilizing on transnational issues such as Third World development or migrants' rights; 45% in social, cultural, or religious organizations; 35% in classic interest representations organizations such as parties and unions; and 32% in environmental or women's organizations. Among first-time peace protestors, rates of involvement fell drastically, though they remained far from negligible (11%, 29%, 15%, and 13%, respectively, in the four categories we just mentioned: Diani 2009).

Overlapping memberships contribute to social movement activity in a variety of ways. In many ways, one could say that they do for movement organizations what interpersonal networks do for individual activists. First, they facilitate the circulation of information and therefore the speed of the decision-making process. This is essential, inasmuch as the speed of mobilization compensates at least in part for the lack of organizational resources over which movements have control. In the absence of formal coordination among organizations, mobilization becomes possible through informal links among activists (Carroll and Ratner 1996, p. 611). Persons working across organizations also facilitate the development of shared representations of conflicts. Among Vancouver activists there were different ways of framing the conflicts, one based on a political-economy perspective, another based on an identity perspective, and a third based on a liberal perspective. The distribution of these frames varied depending on activists' commitment to overlapping memberships: those who acted as linkages between different movements and organizations were disproportionately close to a political-economy frame, whereas adopters of an identity frame were more inclined to concentrate on individual organizations (Carroll and Ratner 1996, p. 611).

Another important function of multiple memberships lies in their contribution to the growth of mutual trust. Whether it is a question of economic activities or of political mobilization, committing resources to a joint initiative involving other actors is always, to some extent, risky. In each case, the route to mobilization requires actors to conduct some exploration of their environment, in search of trustworthy allies (Diani 1995, p. 1). This process is much simpler if there are ongoing links between the central activists of the various organizations concerned. This does not mean that other alliances are not possible, or even more frequent. But the relative cost of forging these other alliances will usually be higher, inasmuch as contacts between the different groups are not "routinized" through interpersonal connections.

The hypothesis that cooperation among organizations is more likely where personal contacts exist among their leaders has been supported by a few studies, dedicated both to movements and to political organizations in the wider sense. In both cases it has become clear that the leaders of organizations who work or campaign together tend to be linked by shared experiences that precede the formation of the coalition itself. The denser the relationships among the leaders and the activists of various movement organizations, the higher the chances of cooperation among them (Diani 2003; Galaskiewicz 1985, p. 293; Simpson 2015). There is no reason to think that the impact of networks that predate the emergence of a particular movement is limited to individual decisions to participate; rather, they also influence opportunities for cooperation among organizations.

Finally, looking at activists' multiple affiliations can constitute a useful way of comparing the structure of particular movements in different periods, and of tracing its modifications over time. A pioneering study of the organizational affiliations of 202 key figures in the women's movements of the state of New York between 1840 and 1914 reconstructed the structure of the interorganizational networks in three different historical phases, identifying the central organizations for each phase (Rosenthal et al. 1985). A phase of powerful activism between 1840 and the end of the 1860s saw numerous overlaps between participation in women's organizations and in antislavery or temperance organizations. The following phase, until the end of 1880, saw a reduction in conflict, and in contrast to the previous phase was characterized by the disappearance of many organizations and by the difficulty of revitalizing organizations of national importance. Between 1880 and 1914, there was a revival of campaigns for universal suffrage.

The configuration of networks seems to have depended significantly on the characteristics of the environment in which the movements were operating and on the availability of resources for mobilization. In local networks, where resources were usually limited, the integration and density of relationships were higher. As it was essential to use available resources to best effect, there was little space for factionalism and core activists distributed their multiple memberships fairly evenly across the board of local women's organizations. In contrast, organizations with national structures, that were therefore able to count on greater organizational resources, could be more tempted to accentuate their rivalries and ideological distinctions. As a result, the networks created by multiple memberships were more fragmented and consisted of different subgroups (or cliques) barely connected to each other.

Another exploration of the same data (Rosenthal et al. 1997) looked at multiple memberships in women's organizations in four different milieus (three local communities, plus one network of women active at state level in New York) between 1840 and 1920. They highlighted the different roles played by national and local women's organizations (e.g., in terms of their different relationship to other radical movements); the division of labor between few multi-issue organizations and the multiplicity of groups operating on a smaller scale and in semi-isolation; the limited contacts between suffrage organizations and charitable ones.

While most studies of the duality of individuals and groups focus on rank-and-file activists, we can also apply this perspective to relationships between movement leaders, eventually extending the analysis to the ties involving members of other sectors of the elites. Data about the overlapping memberships linking core activists of the German peace movement of the 1980s to members of other political groups documented the strong integration of the movement leadership with churches, trade unions, university, media, and other established social and political organizations (Schmitt-Beck 1989; see also Schou 1997; Stoddart and Tindall 2010). On the other hand, movement activists who are well connected to external actors may also increase the centrality of their own organizations in their specific movement networks. For example, the centrality and influence in the environmental network of transnational environmental movement organizations in the 1990s were found to depend in no small measure on the extent of their members' informal ties to key officials of UN agencies or other international governmental organizations (Caniglia 2001).

5.4   INDIVIDUAL PARTICIPATION, MOVEMENT SUBCULTURES, AND VIRTUAL NETWORKS

Individual participation in a movement's life is by no means restricted to membership in specific (mainly political) organizations. By going places, being connected to several groups or associations, patronizing specific venues, cafes, or bookshops, individuals create and reproduce dense webs of informal exchanges. As a result, informal social networks constitute subcultural oppositional dynamics. These help to keep collective identities alive even when open challenges to authority may not be taking place (when, in Melucci's [1989, 1996] words, movements are going through phases of "latency"). In this sense, networks provide the structure of social movement "free spaces" (Polletta 1999), i.e., areas of social interaction in which holders of specific worldviews reinforce mutual solidarity and experiment with alternative lifestyles (Creasap 2012; see also Haunss and Leach 2009).

Taking part in the life of several organizations and coming into contact with their activists and supporters, individuals construct a series of unique social relationships. In these, the political dimension of action intersects and overlaps with the private dimension, to generate the foundations of a specific form of subculture. In a movement network, individuals pursue goals that are not only concerned with political ends but also and often more significantly with personal self-realization. Even individuals who are not members of any specific organization may come together from time to time for specific initiatives and activities organized by cultural operators, service structures, and so on. Affiliation to a particular movement area can therefore be seen as a strictly personal choice, which brings with it a low level of identification with movement organizations. Similarly, the adoption by movement activists of alternative symbolic codes does not automatically create a homogeneous identity, nor does it provide the legitimacy for rigid organizational structures. Some degree of shared identity certainly characterizes a movement understood in its entirety, but this is then articulated with extreme variability and flexibility by different actors (Melucci 1984).

Different versions of these models can be found in the movements that have emerged since the 1960s. In the 1980s, Melucci and associates (Melucci 1984) documented how in Milan, the end of a Leninist model of politics, based on mass, "revolutionary" organizations with a rigid structure had given way to a style of movement participation that was largely individualistic and saw people's involvement in several types of cultural and political activities, from consciousness-raising groups to single-issue campaigns. Some radical, direct-action sectors, critical of neoliberal globalization, have also reflected this model over the last decades (Juris 2008; Wall 1999). These sectors express a radical indifference, if not hostility, to the role of organizations as promoters and/or coordinators of collective action. For people involved in these networks, political activism is first and foremost a matter of lifestyle, the expression of deeply felt cultural and political orientations rather than adhesion to any specific political project and the organizations that could support it.

In these cases, participation in a movement life most of the time consists of involvement in cultural and/or social activities – music concerts, dramatic performances, happenings, always with a critical edge and an element of symbolic and/or political challenge to some kind of authority – rather than of public demonstrations. The latter are far from absent, and some may be massive and with a great public impact – think of the demonstrations taking place in the context of G8 or WTO meetings (della Porta, Andretta et al. 2006; Smith 2001), but also of the anti-capitalist riots that shattered the City of London on June 18, 1999. But demonstrations are not the most important activity, nor are they associated with the idea of formal organization. When pooling resources is required, this tends to take the form of "affinity groups" (Bennett 2005; McDonald 2002) that form to pursue a specific goal (stop a new road, save a tree, mount a boycott to the local branch of a global brand) and disband within a short period of time.

The street parties promoted by the Reclaim the Streets network in the late 1990s in the United Kingdom provided opportunities for radical challenges to dominant ideas of urban space that were public yet did not rely on any organizational structure, depending instead on the dense subcultural networks of the participants (Seel, Paterson, and Doherty 2000). While it might be simplistic to conclude from these examples that a radical transformation of collective action has actually taken place, it is certainly important to recognize the presence of these forms alongside others in which organizations and organizational identities still play a major role (see e.g. Diani 2015).

The debate on the role of subcultural and countercultural activities within contemporary social movements has become even livelier since the 1990s, with the spread of computer-mediated communication (henceforth, CMC). Questions whether organizations still have a role in grassroots mobilization, whether dense face-to-face community networks are still necessary to support collective action, whether identity bonds still need some kind of shared direct experience and/or "real" interaction to develop, have all been made more acute by technological developments. There is widespread agreement – and there has been for a few decades – that CMC has drastically reduced the costs of promoting action and coordinating the sympathizers of a cause. It has been long recognized that CMC is a powerful facilitator of activism through technical support to interest group activity, "the maintenance of dispersed face-to-face networks," whether for geographic reasons or for the nature of their activities, and the development of cultural and "socio-spatial enclaves" (Calhoun 1998, pp. 383–385). The communities of experts cum activists mobilizing on a global scale on communication rights and internet regulation illustrate the former case (Padovani and Calabrese 2014; Pavan 2012); networks of critical hackers like Anonymous, attempting to disrupt the operation of national and supernational institutions, the latter (Dobusch and Schoeneborn 2015; Uitermark 2017). Extreme right groups have also been documented to use massively CMC to develop transnational ties and largely increase their influence (Caiani and Parenti 2016). Other studies, however, have suggested the new media arena not to be necessarily the most obvious recruitment ground for radical groups (see e.g. Andersson 2018 on the Swedish radical left).

The extent of the impact of the internet over patterns of collective action at large has been more widely debated. Since the early phases of the "internet revolution," some analysts have announced the emergence of radical new forms of action, made possible by the new technologies (Castells 1996, also see 2012). One particularly influential argument has suggested a shift from *collective action,* based on the notion of collective identity, to *connective action.* In the latter, individuals would not have to rely on collective identifications – nor on specific organizational structures – to mobilize; their use of CMC would facilitate their combining their personalized interests in different causes (Bennett and Segerberg 2013). Given the breadth of these claims, it's no surprise that they have met with variable degrees of caution.

The contribution of CMC to the creation of new types of identities, able to generate the same mechanisms of commitment as those developed in traditional communities, has been particularly disputed. Critics have noted that most instances of personal interaction in electronic discussion groups actually miss some of the requirements usually associated with the concept of social relations (Cerulo 1997; Cerulo and Ruane 1998). Participants in those lists often hide their personal identity, participate occasionally, are not tied by any sort of committed relationship, and are mostly involved in dyadic or at most triadic interactions. For skeptics, this seems unlikely to generate the levels of trust and mutual commitment that past research suggests is required of participants in costly and potentially disruptive collective action (Calhoun 1998, p. 380; Diani 2000b; Tilly 2004a, p. 5). For others, however, the internet creates a specific set of interactions rather than being the mere interface of "real" social life. In that context, recourse to hidden identities, anonymity, etc. may represent in its own right a specific way to challenge power and destabilize it (McDonald 2015).

Empirical evidence on the type of ties established by CMC has been mixed. Some studies of social movements as online communities have stressed the power of CMC in reproducing movement identities by keeping alive the connections between multiple actors and bridging different protest communities (Ackland and O'Neil 2011; Walgrave, Bennett, Van Laer, et al. 2011). At the same time, examples of community networks have long suggested that virtual networks operate at their best when they are backed by real social linkages in specifically localized communities, while their capacity to create brand new ones is uncertain (e.g. Hampton and Wellman 2003). As for transnational networks, again, while CMC contributes to the efficient coordination of global campaigns, it often connects people (an international activist elite) who also know each other and meet in person on the occasion of meetings and other events, rather than ordinary "virtual citizens" (Keck and Sikkink 1998; Lahusen 2004; Pavan 2012). It has also been repeatedly suggested that, far from democratizing access to protest activities, CMC actually reproduces existing social divisions. Available data on access to the internet and other forms of digital communication suggest access to be strongly affected by class position and the attached resources such as skills or time (Schradie 2018).

The debate on the role of CMC in the Arab revolts of 2011 (for a synthesis: Diani 2011) well illustrates the more general term of the discussion regarding the capacity of CMC to facilitate activists and organizations by reinforcing existing links, or to create new types of alternative communities from scratch. Some analysts emphasized the role of the Internet in helping dissenters to coordinate in a repressive environment, and securing protestors in Cairo or Tunis the support of international public opinion (Castells 2012; Lotan et al. 2011). Others took a very different line, one media critic arguing for example that "By fixating on technologies and the few youth that actively use them, we ignore a much more powerful narrative – the story of how synergies are created between classes to mobilize as a network without depending on social media. In Egypt, these networks may include family connections, neighborhoods, mosques, and historical institutions, such as the previously banned Muslim Brotherhood. New technologies hardly erode or overwhelm these classic models of communication and information sharing" (Srinivasan 2011). While recognizing the undeniable impact of the internet, still other analysts pointed at the variable role that CMC played among different social groups and in different settings (Howard and Hussain 2013; Khamis and Vaughn 2011; Zhuo, Wellman, and Ju 2011). As this discussion suggests, care is required when assessing the impact of new technologies over recruitment and participatory processes.

5.5   SUMMARY

In this chapter, we have illustrated some aspects of the impact on recruitment and participation processes and on the overall structure of social movements, of the networks in which social movement activists are embedded. First, we have showed that individuals often become involved in collective action through their personal connections to people already involved. Those connections help them overcome the innumerable obstacles and dilemmas that people usually face when considering whether to become active on a certain cause. Not only that: the amount and type of individual networks also affect the chances of people remaining active for a long time, or instead reducing their commitment, or cutting it altogether, after brief spells. In reaction to criticisms of the role of networks in individual mobilization, researchers have qualified their arguments by exploring what types of networks are more likely to affect what types of collective action, and how the relationship between the two may change under different social and political circumstances.

We have also paid attention to the fact that individuals not only become active in a movement through their previous connections but also create new connections by the very fact of being involved in multiple forms of activism and associations. From this perspective, individual activists operate as bridges between different organizational milieus, linking, for example, social movement organizations to established political actors or institutions, or organizations mobilized for different causes. By doing so, they affect the overall structure of social movement "industries" (McCarthy and Zald 1987) or "families" (della Porta and Rucht 1995). At the same time, though, ties resulting from overlapping memberships are not always restricted to organizations; individual movement activists are also frequently involved in countercultural or subcultural practices. This may take the form of real-life experiences, through personal participation in specific activities, but also develop through involvement in virtual communities, such as those made possible by the diffusion of computer-mediated communication.

CHAPTER 6

Organizations and Organizing within Social Movements

The 2010s have seen a variety of protest activities developing in both the affluent North and the global South, sometimes with deep political consequences. The year 2011 was particularly hectic in that regard, so much so that Time magazine identified "the protester" as its "person of the year" (http://content.time.com/time/person-of-the-year/2011). In Spain, the Indignados movement started a wave of protest against the establishment and political elites that was matched by similar initiatives across the world, from the Occupy actions in the USA to the occupation of Gezi Park in Istanbul, fighting urban development plans, from the Greek anti-austerity Aganaktisménon (Indignados) movement to the revolts in North Africa that toppled the Tunisian and Egyptian dictatorships, and shook several others in the Middle East. For all their differences, those episodes of contention displayed some common elements, or better, presented some features that attracted the attention of observers. The first one was the massive recourse to the internet as a major channel for promoting initiatives and communicating with the rest of the world. The second was the widespread suspicion of, and indeed open hostility to, organizational forms that evoked any hierarchy and/or bureaucracy. This usually included organizations close to the traditional left, such as trade unions or left-leaning political parties.

Social Movements: An Introduction, Third Edition. Donatella della Porta and Mario Diani.
© 2020 John Wiley & Sons Ltd. Published 2020 by John Wiley & Sons Ltd.

The third element was the use of the public space: the most visible activities of protesters took place in specific areas that took a strong symbolic relevance and reflected participants' intention of claiming back control on the public sphere: Puerta del Sol in Madrid and Plaça de Catalunya in Barcelona for the Indignados, Syntagma Square in Athens for the Aganaktisménon, Zuccotti Park for the Occupy New York, Tahrir Square in Cairo or Taksim Square in Istanbul.

Looking primarily at the Arab revolts, but also commenting on the Spanish Indignados, sociologist Manuel Castells built on these two features in his exploration of new forms of collective action. Writing in the aftermath of those events, he went as far as claiming that they heralded the emergence of a new kind of social movement, the "networked social movement" (Castells 2012). In such movements, the coordinating roles hitherto taken up by more or less bureaucratic organizations would be replaced by two different yet related mechanisms: computer mediated communication (CMC), enabling actors to engage sympathizers and observers on any geographical scale, coupled with direct participation in specific locations. Referring to the endless meetings and workshops that took place in the squares mentioned above, as well as in innumerable other locations, some have identified meeting arenas as a new organizational model through which collective action may be coordinated, alongside formal organizations, networks, and institutions (Haug 2013). More recently, the gilets jaunes (yellow vests) protests that have swamped France since November 2018 have also heavily focused on the occupation of public spaces. Although their most prominent actions have taken the form of conventional demonstrations in major cities, one distinctive feature has been the innumerable pickets that have taken place at roundabouts along all French major roads. Another one has been their dependence on an informal network structure, consisting of weak ties, often conducted through the internet, between different local chapters that might differ widely in their main goals, tactics, and worldviews, with variable levels of identification with the right and the left of the political spectrum. At the time of writing (Spring 2019), while maintaining some mobilizing capacity, the gilets jaunes seemed to struggle to identify common themes, and to merge into a coherent platform the broad range of anti-elites grievances they were voicing in their specific actions (Leca 2018).

Regardless, or perhaps because, of their huge heterogeneity, the collective actions of the 2010s have revitalized a number of broad theoretical debates. The one addressed in this chapter concerns the ways in which collective action is organized. In order to develop, collective action needs some degree of coordination and continuity, as well as actors' capacity to identify themselves as part of a specific collectivity. Such roles have historically been, and continue to be, performed by organizations. For all their differences, organizations like Amnesty International or Oxfam in the transnational public sphere, Greenpeace or WWF in the environmental field, Hamas or the Muslim Brotherhood in the Middle East, all enable people interested in certain causes to participate in action in a coordinated way; they provide them with incentives and motivations to act; they offer contexts in which to try and live up to one's own ideals. Organizations also provide continuity to action. This happens not only because they have the resources to keep action going even when individual citizens' commitment to the cause may be fading; it also happens because they represent and reproduce specific identities over time, in a manner that individuals usually struggle to achieve. Of course, in the mid-term this may also turn into a force of conservatism, as organizations may end up prioritizing their own reproduction over the pursuit of specific goals, and may struggle to adapt to changing conditions; still, it is difficult to deny that some degree of organization is essential for movements to grow and consolidate.

However, the protest campaigns of the last decades, and in particular the support that new technologies have given to protesters, have raised questions about the emergence of new ways of organizing collective action, and in particular whether formal organizations, or even groups with lower levels of formalization, should still be seen as a major player in collective action processes; or whether, alternatively, the new informal connections made possible by communication technology would inevitably replace the ties created by associations, that have characterized modern social movements (Tarrow 2011, p. 3). Of course, the empirical validity of claims about the death of organizational forms may be disputed, even in the cases mentioned above: it is difficult to ignore the role of a formal organization like the Muslim Brotherhhood in the evolution of contention in Egypt (Monier and Ranko 2013), or the emergence of new organizations, including a party like Podemos (Chironi and Fittipaldi 2017), from the Indignados movement; nor should we forget that most instances of collective action are promoted by variable combinations of informal groups and formal organizations, from organizations championing minority and migrants' rights in Europe (Eggert 2014; Eggert and Pilati 2014) to groups fighting social and environmental degradation in Cape Town (Diani et al. 2018), to name just a few examples. In fairness, even theorists of the impact of ICT on collective action readily acknowledge that in empirical terms, internet-mediated ties are just one of the forms through which action is coordinated, alongside more conventional organizations (Bennett and Segerberg 2013). In practice, most social movements can still be seen as the outcomes of "hundreds of groups and organizations – many of them short-lived, spatially scattered, and lacking direct communication, a single organization, and a common leadership – episodically take part in many different kinds of local collective action" (Oberschall 1980, pp. 45–46).

While they have largely agreed on the fact that some level of organization is necessary for collective action to develop, analysts have approached the issue from very different angles: "Scholars of social movements have long understood the relevance of organization to understanding the course and character of movement activity, but they have rarely agreed about the forms, functions, and consequences of organization with respect to social movements" (Snow et al. 2019, p. 8). The most obvious illustration of these difficulties have been attempts to define "social movement organizations" (SMOs). Some analysts have challenged the very notion that organizations active in social movements carry any specificity vis à vis other types of political organizations such as public interest groups. Accordingly, they have used terms such as "interest organizations" to denote organizations promoting collective interests in the public arena (Burstein 1998).

Even those who have used the concept of SMO, however, have shown considerable ambiguity in its definition. Some have pointed at differences in the main sources of power and legitimacy, suggesting SMOs to depend primarily on their mobilizing capacity, while parties and interest groups would rely in the first place on electoral votes and influence (Rucht 1995). It should be noted, however, that such differentiation does not necessarily imply distinct organizational forms. Protest can be – indeed, it is routinely – mobilized by actors with a very diverse organizational profile. The original proponents of the concept defined the SMO as a "complex, or formal, organization that identifies its goals with the preferences of a social movement or countermovement and attempts to implement those goals" (McCarthy and Zald 1987, p. 20 [1977]), a conception that only fits highly structured and formal organizations. Conversely, another definition sees SMOs as "associations of persons making idealistic and moralistic claims about how human personal or group life ought be organized that, *at the time of their claims making*, are marginal to or excluded from mainstream society" (Lofland 1996, pp. 2–3), but that hardly seems applicable to organizations such as Greenpeace, Amnesty International, or the like, whose constituency comes primarily from the middle classes. And again, little is said about the organizational properties that should differentiate SMOs from other political organizations. Still other analysts have identified the distinctive organizational model of social movements in invisible, interpersonal networks that would keep together on a largely informal basis people sharing the same critical orientations. (see in particular Melucci 1996; see also Juris 2008; Taylor 1989).

> *Facing this complex situation, the most common (and apparently sensible) answer has been everything holds: ... social movement activity is organized in some fashion or another. Clearly there are different forms of organization (e.g., single SMO vs. multiple, networked SMOs) and degrees of organization (e.g., tightly coupled vs. loosely coupled), and ... differences in the consequences of different forms and degrees of organization.... But to note such differences is not grounds for dismissing the significance of organization to social movements.*

> (Snow et al. 2019, p. 8)

As sensible as this statement may sound, it misses the fact that by "organization" we can mean at least two quite different sets of processes: on the one hand we may refer to a specific set of actors with identifiable boundaries that operate in a coordinated way in the pursuit of specific goals, with a specific capacity of agency; on the other, we may refer to the mechanisms through which social actors operating in a distinct subsystem coordinate their behavior, regardless of whether they are associated with any specific, recognizable entity (be this a bureaucracy or a highly informal group). Any type of collectivity, from a local community to an online community, from a professional group to a nation, requires indeed some (variable) degree of coordination. Most of the times such coordination is not formalized, or if it so, it is only partially, as the capacity to act as a single agent may be extremely limited (nations, for example, operate as coherent agents only in the rhetoric of nationalist leaders and activists).

Organization theorists have increasingly recognized the difference between these different meaning of the term *organization*. On the one hand, we have classic formal organizations, the focus of organization theory. They represent a form of coordination based on relatively clear criteria in relation to (1) the identification of members (who is a member and who is not); (2) the definition of hierarchical positions (who is responsible for what and subordinate/superordinate to whom); (3) the rules that guide the behavior of organization members; (4) the arrangements in place and the subjects responsible for monitoring members' conduct; and (5) sanctioning inappropriate actions or styles of behavior. Organization theorists Göran Ahrne and Nils Brunsson (2011) called this model a *decided order*. They also noted, however, that "organization" – i.e., various degrees of coordination of human behavior – may also exist when not all the traits of the "decided order" are present. In those cases, various forms of "partial order" emerge. In the attempt to preserve the distinctiveness of organizations as a particular way of coordinating human behavior, focusing on decision making processes, while overcoming rigid dichotomies between organization and other forms of coordination such as networks or institutions, organizational analysts have suggested what is both a terminological and conceptual shift. They have proposed, in particular, moving the focus from "organizations" to "organizing" (Ahrne and Brunsson 2011; Ahrne, Brunsson, and Seidl 2016) or "organizationality" (Dobusch and Schoeneborn 2015), i.e., to the set of mechanisms and infrastructures that enable coordination in the absence of formalized bureaucracies (Ahrne and Brunsson 2011; Ahrne et al. 2016; Den Hond et al. 2015; Dobusch and Schoeneborn 2015; Haug 2013). Such processes may not display all the defining properties of organizations, yet perform some of their functions in a way that still generates some level of coordination and identity.

Recognizing the multiplicity of specific organizational forms promoting collective action also requires recognizing the differences between the two meanings of "organization" identified above. In that light, as we shall illustrate, some of the recurring discussions in the field lose significance, as it is perfectly possible to identify, within a specific social movement, different organizational models at play. The structure of this chapter reflects the conceptual tension between "organizations" and "organizing." We shall look first at different types of organizations that are closest to the "decided order" model, albeit with quite a range of variation. Then we'll shift our focus to organizing. We'll introduce the concept of "mode of coordination" as a tool to map different ways in which organizations and activists interact with each other. We'll suggest that within complex collective action fields, forms of coordination emerge out of the repeated interactions between different and independent actors. Next, we'll ask to what extent the spread of new technologies has been altering patterns of coordination of collective action. Finally, we'll explore some basic mechanisms of organizational change, looking at both changes in specific organizations and in the structure of broader fields.

6.1 ORGANIZATIONS WITHIN SOCIAL MOVEMENTS

Despite social movements being routinely perceived as the result of the initiatives of multiple actors, we need to remember that a substantive share of collective action, including of the radical type, is actually promoted by specific groups or associations. The specific organizational forms that they take may range from the extremely hierarchical and formalized, such as twentieth century mass parties, to the extremely decentralized and informal, such as alternative communes or grassroots groups. Here we'll differentiate in particular between professional, mass participatory, and grassroots organizations.

6.1.1 Professional Protest Organizations

These organizations are probably the closest to Ahrne and Brunsson's (2011) "decided order" model. According to McCarthy and Zald, a professional social movement organization is characterized by four characteristics:

1. Leadership devotes full time to the movement. A large proportion of resources originate "outside the aggrieved group that the movement claims to represent."
2. Membership is small or nonexistent, based on a paper membership. Membership is more than allowing a name to be added to membership rolls.
3. There is an attempt to convey the image of "speaking for a constituency."
4. The organization tries to affect policy toward that same constituency (McCarthy and Zald 1987, p. 375 [1973]).

Ordinary members have little power and "have no serious role in organizational policymaking short of withholding membership dues. The professional staff largely determines the positions the organization takes upon issues" (McCarthy and Zald 1987, p. 378).

However, professional SMOs do not necessarily address themselves to their "natural" constituents, i.e., those groups (whether dispossessed like the unemployed or the homeless, or fairly well-off like in many new middle-class mobilizations) whose interests they promote, the way a normal pressure group would. Rather, they have a "conscience constituency" composed of those who believe in the cause they support. Their leaders are entrepreneurs whose "impact results from their skills at manipulating images of relevance and support through the communication media" (McCarthy and Zald 1987, p. 374). They rely more on their reputation for technical expertise on specific matters than on mass mobilization (McCarthy and Zald 1987, pp. 29 and 379).

The advantages associated with professional organizations have long been identified. Back in the 1970s, in his classic comparative analysis of US citizens' organizations, Gamson (1990 [1975])) found that challengers were more likely to win when they possessed a well-structured organization. Formal organizations would appear better placed to mobilize "because they facilitate mass participation, tactical innovations, and rapid decision-making" (Morris 1984, p. 285). Structured organizations are also more likely to survive beyond a wave of protest to favor mobilization in succeeding waves (McCarthy and Zald 1977). Professional organizers often spread mass defiance rather than dampening it, and "professionalization of leadership and the formalization of movement organizations are not necessarily incompatible with grass-roots protest" (Dee 2018; Staggenborg 1991, pp. 154–155). Moreover, long-term survival is favored by the presence of motives for and methods of action that are already legitimated (Clemens and Minkoff 2004).

However, there are also problems. While professional organizations can generate a constant flow of funding, they are bound by the wishes of their benefactors. "The growth and maintenance of organizations whose formal goals are aimed at helping one population but who depend on a different population for funding are ultimately more dependent upon the latter than the former" (McCarthy and Zald 1987: 371). Patrons provide important resources, but they are usually available only for groups with low-level claims and consensual legitimacy – the disabled rather than the unemployed, for example (Walker 1991). Similar consequences (see Lahusen 2004) may result from growing collaboration with authorities:

> *The establishment of a working relation with the authorities also has ambivalent implications for the development of the SMO: On the one hand, public recognition, access to decision-making procedures and public subsidies may provide crucial resources and represent important successes for the SMO; on the other hand, the integration into the established system of interest intermediation may impose limits on the mobilization capacity of the SMO and alienate important parts of its constituency, with the consequence of weakening it in the long run.*
>
> (Kriesi 1996, pp. 155–156)

Echoing Robert Michels's analysis of the bureaucratization of socialist parties, Piven and Cloward developed in their classic *Poor People's Movements* (1977) a most explicit critique of the role of formal organizations in hampering goal attainment in protest movements of the dispossessed. Investment in building a permanent mass organization was seen as a waste of scarce resources. Moreover, such organizations tended to reduce the only resource available to the poor: mass defiance. It is certainly true that even professional bureaucratic organizations may promote radical challenges and defiance, and engage in various forms of vicarious activism on behalf of a fee-paying passive membership (see, e.g., Greenpeace: Diani and Donati 1999). But organizations focused entirely on fundraising and the attraction of financial resources are likely sooner or later to face problems with their capacity to mobilize people. All in all, according to critics, professionalization might lead to defeat by taming protest (Piven and Cloward 1977).

6.1.2   Transnational Social Movement Organizations

It's interesting to note how the terms of a conversation that were set in the 1970s re-emerge periodically in the debate. In the last couple of decades, the focus has been on the so-called *transnational social movement organizations* (TSMOs). Jackie Smith defined TSMOs as "international nongovernmental organizations engaged in explicit attempts to [change] some elements of the social structure and/or reward distribution of society" (Smith 1999, p. 591). According to the *Yearbook of International Organizations,* TSMOs have grown from 110 in 1953 to almost 1800 in 2013 (Smith et al. 2018). Among them, a small number (sometimes referred to as "the Big Ten") stand out because of their numerous national chapters, membership in the millions, and strong levels of bureaucratization. These include the likes of Amnesty International, Greenpeace, Friends of the Earth, WWF-World Wide Fund for Nature, or Oxfam. These organizations display many traits of the professional organization, even though participation is encouraged – if largely in the form of voluntary work and contributions to specific projects, rather than in decision-making processes, and with low levels of investment in the building of internal solidarity.

The acronym TSMO suggests that big organizations operating on a transnational scale with variable yet significant contributions from professionals may still be regarded as part of social movements. At the same time, the growth of professional organizations has also been seen as a sign of the transformation of social movement organizations into NGOs (nongovernmental organizations), focused on policy making and service delivery usually renouncing any confrontational angle. However, any generalized conclusion in that regard would be unfounded. Close examination of changes that take place in specific organizational fields suggest a more complex picture, and do not sustain the idea that the emergence of NGOs be necessarily an indication of a transformation of a social movement sector. For example, the evolution of the set of organizations, devoted to peace-building in conflict ridden Croatia since the 1990s to present times, suggests different paths leading to the emergence and consolidation of NGOs attempting social change, not all of which had origins in the confrontational social movement sector (Heideman 2017). The Croatian case also suggests that challenges to powerholders do not necessarily take the form of explicit confrontations and may be effectively conducted through largely formalized organizations. All this points at the multiple nuances of professionalization processes within voluntary organizations (Heideman 2017).

6.2   PARTICIPATORY MOVEMENT ORGANIZATIONS

Different organizational types can be grouped under this broader model. In particular, we differentiate between mass protest organizations and grassroots groups. They meet only partially (sometimes, very partially) the "decided order" parameters.

6.2.1   Mass Protest Organizations

This model combines attention to participatory democracy with certain levels of formalization of the organizational structure. In the social movements of the 1970s, many political organizations like the communist K-Gruppen in Germany, the New Left parties in Italy, the Trotskysts in France, had adopted fairly rigid and hierarchical organizational structures, close to the model of the Leninist party (Lumley 1990; della Porta 1995). Gradually, however, this model fell out of favor for its excessive emphasis on the professional revolutionary role, and its indifference to grassroots democracy. With the crisis of the 1970s protest movements, alternative forms of organization developed, as exemplified by the emergence of Green parties. These were formed for the most part during the 1980s campaigns on environmental issues, and nuclear energy in particular, although they never were the official political representatives of the environmental movement (Richardson and Rootes 1995). In seeking to defend nature, these parties also sought to apply the "think globally, act locally" principle to their organizations. The Greens rejected, initially at least, any structured organizational power, just as they rejected centralizing technologies. They developed a ritual of direct democracy by introducing consensual decision-making, rotation of chair roles, and so on.

The model of open assemblies and always revocable delegates did not survive long, however. Participatory democracy may often reduce the decision-making efficiency of assemblies and lead to very long periods of confusion and incertitude. Particularly after they entered first regional and then national parliaments, the Greens began to develop stable organizational structures, with membership cards, representative rather than direct democracy within the party, and a stable leadership. Public funding of the parties created a constant and generous flow of finance that was used to develop a professional political class, set up newspapers and supportive associations. The Green parties' structure thus became formal and centralized. Participation moved toward excluding membership of other organizations, and ideological incentives began to predominate. Over the last decades we have witnessed repeated examples of this pattern (see e.g. della Porta, Fernandez et al. 2017). A major instance comes from the Spanish Indignados movement and its imitators across the globe in the 2010s. They started off with a strong emphasis on grassroots participation and democratic decision making, but over time evolved into more complex organizational models. In Spain, for example, while both the *Podemos* party or local electoral cartels like *Barcelona en comù* kept an emphasis on direct democracy, they still combined it with some degree of bureaucratization and centralization (Chironi and Fittipaldi 2017; Kioupkiolis 2016; Martín 2015).

It is not difficult to identify the processes behind these recurrent switches. They not only have to do with the oligarchic tendencies to be found in any sort of organization, but also with problems associated with the model of participatory organizational democracy. In fairness, the concrete realization of the organizational principles of grassroots democracy has never been a simple matter. Many activists have complained of the *de facto* oligarchies that tend to form and impose their will when collective decision making becomes difficult. An organized minority can win out in an assembly by wearing down the majority, and forcing them to give up and leave after hours of strenuous discussion. In a few extreme cases, physical force has been used by some groups to occupy important decision-making positions such as the chair of meetings. Even without reaching those excesses, the risks of a "tyranny of emotions," whereby the most committed activists profit from the lack of formal procedures and secure control of decision-making processes, have been pointed out in reference to several movements of the recent and not-so-recent past (Flesher Fominaya 2015; Polletta 2002).

6.2.2 Grassroots Organizations

In contrast to the mass protest model, the grassroots model combines strong participatory orientations with low levels of formal structuration. The existence of organizations of this kind depends on their members' willingness to participate in their activities. Such participation may be encouraged through different combinations of ideological and solidaristic incentives. Oftentimes, this is related to locality. For example, the local groups that opposed road building in many corners of Britain in the 1990s (Seel et al. 2000) could not rely on a strong ideological profile given the heterogeneity of their participants, and instead emphasized shared concerns in specific issues; so do the single issue citizens' committees that characterize so much political activity in contemporary democracies (della Porta and Fabbri 2016; della Porta and Piazza 2008) or the residents' associations promoting collective action in deprived urban areas across the globe (Alexander 2010; Diani et al. 2018; Domaradzka and Wijkstrom 2016; Lichterman 1995). Other times, shared critical attitudes play a stronger and more explicit role in motivating participation, as in the semiformal direct action groups that developed in the context of growing opposition to neoliberal globalization (Juris 2008), in the local independent women's collectives that marked the spread of feminist movements in the 1970s and 1980s (Whittier 1995), or in the different groups involved in the Piqueteros mobilizations in Argentina from the late 1990s (Rossi 2017).

There are innumerable examples of grassroots organizations that have been successful in the pursuit of their goals, such as local environmental groups (Juris 2008) across the globe in both democratic and authoritarian polities (Rootes 2003; Rootes and Brulle 2013; Temper et al. 2018). At the same time, depending so heavily on their members' voluntary participation, grassroots organizations' capacity to act with continuity over time is obviously limited. Many of them actually see an alternation of phases of activism and latency, comparable to those identified in reference to earlier movements (Melucci 1996; Taylor 1989). Sometimes, informal groups operate as "intermittent structures," i.e., "organizations or organizational units that are deployed and then "folded up" until their period of activity arrives again" (Etzioni 1975, p. 444; quoted in Lindgren 1987). "Intermittent social movement organizations" (Lindgren 1987), that resurface each time their issues of concern become salient political topics again, remind us that permanent stable structures are not necessarily a requirement for success.

Grassroots organizations may also face problems if they rely too heavily on ideology to secure their members' cohesion and commitment. Ideological incentives are an important surrogate for the lack of material resources, but their use increases the rigidity of the organizational model because transformations have to be incorporated into the normative order of the group. Moreover, organizations employing symbolic incentives will run a greater risk of internal conflict (McCarthy and Zald 1977). Especially for grassroots groups with very critical views of mainstream society, closure to the external world helps the formation of identity but also reduces the capacity to handle reality and identify reasons for failure.

6.3   FROM ORGANIZATIONS TO ORGANIZING: MODES OF COORDINATION OF COLLECTIVE ACTION

Ahrne and Brunsson's (2011) concept of "partial orders" has been mostly applied to organizational forms that do not fully correspond to the bureaucratic model but can still be identified as distinct agents in a relatively clear way. For example, an umbrella organization coordinating various groups and associations may not coincide with a bureaucracy *strictu sensu*: it coordinates actors with distinct, specific identities, it has a more limited set of rules, and exerts a more limited control on its members than a standard organization. However, it still represents a model of coordination that shows some agentic capacity. Likewise, a neighbourhood action group may be loose in terms of formal rules but still display a capacity to act as a unit or sanction the misbehaviour of its members. While neither umbrella organizations nor neighbourhood informal groups are full-fledged bureaucracies, they are still close to specific actors.

However, we may also apply similar concepts to those used by Ahrne and Brunsson to explore the relations between groups and organizations that operate in the same broad organizational field. As classically defined by DiMaggio and Powell (1983, pp. 64–65), a field consists of "organizations that, in the aggregate, represent a recognized area of institutional life." More specifically, collective action fields comprise of all voluntary groups and associations engaged in the promotion of collective action and the production of collective goods (Diani 2015, p. 2). Sometimes, those organizations manage to work together with some continuity, develop some mutual trust, and/or come to share some specific identity. They come closer, to some extent, to some kind of "emerging social order" as theorized by Ahrne and his co/authors (Ahrne et al. 2016, p. 95).

In order to capture some of the variation in the ways actors relate to each other within fields, Diani (2013, 2015) has proposed a typology of "modes of coordination" of collective action. They are defined by different combinations of network multiplexity. In particular, Diani shows how modes of coordination are formed by the different properties of the relational patterns in which two essential mechanisms of collective action, *resource allocation* and *boundary definition*, are embedded. Sometimes, decisions about the allocation of personal and organizational resources are taken mostly within specific groups or organizations, with little negotiation with other actors in the same field. People decide whether to commit (or to continue to be committed) to a specific organization; organizations concentrate on their own specific campaigns. Other times, a considerable amount of energy may be devoted to the building of collaborative relations with other groups, resources may flow through dense exchanges between different actors in a field, and even individual activists may participate in initiatives promoted by a multiplicity of groups.

The definition of boundaries, i.e., of criteria that assign social actors to different groups and categories, represents another essential dimension of collective action (Tilly 2005, p. 8; Wang, Piazza, and Soule 2018), and indeed social action at large (Abbott 1995; White 2008). Boundaries mirror processes of identity building, establishing connections across time and space, e.g. within different phases of personal biographies, between generations, or between events occurring simultaneously in different locations. Analogously to what we noticed for resource allocation, "boundaries" within organizational fields may largely coincide with those of distinct groups or associations, focused on strengthening their own separate identity. They may also, however, be more encompassing and involve multiple actors. Through the joint forging and/or the circulation of symbols, the expression of emotions, or the sharing of militancy and friendship with people across a field, actors may develop a sense of belonging to a broader collective that goes beyond the confines of any specific group or organization. Rather than implying the replacement of an organizational identity with a group identity, it is reasonable to expect a variable tension between the two levels of identification (Melucci 1996; Diani 2015).

The variable intensity of the network exchanges within a field, related to resource allocation and boundary definition, enables us to identify four basic modes of coordination: *the social movement, coalitional, subcultural/communitarian* and *organizational* modes (see Figure 6.1). These modes represent ideal types; any specific episode or any field of collective action is likely to display different combinations of these modes. Nevertheless, it is useful to distinguish between them analytically, given that they represent quite distinct relational and cultural patterns (i.e., network structures and identity processes), which, in turn, enable and constrain different kinds of action. If organizations interested in a given issue or cause decide to work primarily on their own agenda, without engaging in sustained collaborations with other groups, and focus on the definition of their own specific identity, then they operate following what may be called an "organizational" mode of coordination. It does not matter in that regard whether they are closer to a bureaucratic or a participatory model, as long as they tend to act without developing systematic ties to other actors in the field. However, the very same groups and associations may also relate to each other through other "modes of coordination." Let us explore them one at a time.

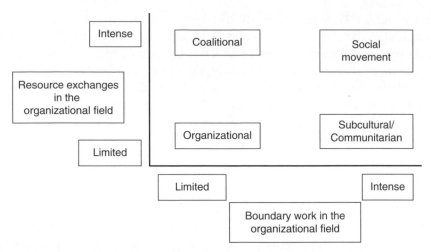

FIGURE 6.1 Modes of coordination of collective action (Adapted from Diani 2012; Reprinted with permission from Cambridge University Press. © 2012).

The "social movement" mode of coordination is the opposite of the organizational mode. It is defined by the intersection of *dense networks of informal inter-organizational exchanges* and processes of *boundary definition* that operate at the level of broad collectivities rather than specific groups/organizations. Coordination takes place through dense interpersonal networks, multiple affiliations, and symbolic production. The terms of inter-organizational collaboration are informal, and need to be renegotiated each time a new issue/opportunity/threat emerges. In other words, each collective action event can be regarded as the product of a specific negotiation about the forms and the content of resource allocation. At the same time, movement networks are not pure instrumental channels for the circulation of resources. Rather, they represent cognitive structures that also enable the circulation of ideas and meanings (Melucci 1996; for some heterogeneous empirical illustrations see Edwards 2014; Fishman 2014).

Precisely because of the strong symbolic dimension of movement networks, boundary definition processes play a key role in shaping collective action. Social movements have no formal boundaries and no formally defined criteria for inclusion or exclusion. Instead, the boundaries of a movement are defined by processes of mutual recognition whereby social actors recognize different elements as part of the same collective experience and identify some criteria that differentiate them from the rest (Diani 2015; Melucci 1996; Mische 2008). Accordingly, organizations do not belong in a movement because of their traits, but because they define themselves as part of that movement, and are perceived as such by significant others. Also, while inter-organizational exchanges are subject to constant negotiation, the establishing of new alliances is easier if there are routines and recurrent practices that also reflect in particular identities and definitions of boundaries. Processes of boundary definition are also essential as they enable actors to link separate protest events or campaigns into larger collective efforts. For example, a recent analysis of protest in Barcelona neighborhoods suggests that even local informal groups, tackling some specific aspects of the urban crisis, actually create through their activism the foundations for larger platforms and broader campaigns (Blanco and León 2017).

Processes of boundary definition within movements may be sustained by different kinds of practices. Symbolic production plays a very important role. People active in different groups or associations may come to share a sense of commonality and solidarity because they share values or beliefs, a common understanding of the environment in which they operate, or similar lifestyles and tastes (see Chapter 4 on these dynamics). At the same time, solidarity between groups may also originate from the embeddedness of their members in the same social milieus through their multiple affiliations, their personal connections, and their participation in other groups' activities (as shown in Chapter 5). If the activists of two groups with different specific agendas are nonetheless involved in the initiatives of both, or have personal relationships with at least some of the members of the other group, then this may be taken as an indicator of a deeper link: specific primary goals may differ, yet those groups will be embedded in a broader web of relations that somehow defines a broader, encompassing boundary than the one defined by the confines of each group or association (for illustrations see Carroll and Ratner 1996; Diani 2015; Shepard 2016; Simpson 2015).

It is important to recognize both the analogies and the differences between a social movement mode of coordination and what has become known in organization theory as "network organization" (Gulati and Gargiulo 1999; Podolny and Page 1998; Powell 1990). In contrast to classic formal organizations, which are based on the vertical integration of multiple units, the "network organization" model points at another way of coordinating activities, based on the independence of the single components, horizontal integration, flexibility in goals and strategies, and multiple levels of interaction with the possibility of communitarian elements. Most frequently associated with the novel forms of production introduced by firms like Benetton or IBM (Castells 1996, ch. 3), the "network organization" model can also be detected among groups promoting collective action.

Network organizational models are useful to coordinate efforts around specific campaigns or policy issues, in which many different activists and organizations have a stake. They do so while being neither dependent on the organizations that originally set them up, nor able to exert a leadership role beyond the boundaries of their specific domain. Many network organizations are inherently temporary – they do not survive the specific mobilization or campaign they are supposed to coordinate; however, some of them may convert into full-fledged organizations, increasingly independent from their original founders, and with a distinct identity. Mobilizations on a transnational scale provide many illustrations of this pattern. They include the *Rainforest Action Network* (https: //www.ran.org), that campaigns to protect the rainforest and targets financial actors backing destructive projects; the *People's Global Action* network (http: // peoplesglobalaction.org), that connects hundreds of grassroots organizations worldwide, or the *Climate Action Network* (http: //www.climatenetwork.org). Back in the 1990s, the Alliance for Sustainable Jobs and the Environment played a visible public role in the 1999 Seattle anti-WTO demonstrations in bringing together environmentalists, working-class activists, and local community organizers (Bircham and

Charlton 2001, pp. 271–289; Heery, Williams, and Abbott 2012; on cross class coalitions, also see Rose 2000). The Social Forum model inspired by the experience of the World Social Forum in Porto Alegre is another important example of network organization coordinating innumerable groups scattered across space (see e.g. Byrd and Jasny 2010; Saunders 2014).

The network organization model represents a style of coordinating resources that is in many ways intermediate between an "organizational" and a "social movement" mode of coordination. Network organizations tend to have some rules that regulate the allocation of resources, and an identity that is more sharply defined than the identity of whole movements such as the global justice movement of the 2000s, the Indignados of the 2010s, or the environmental movement. They share with the social movement mode of coordination the fact of coordinating groups and organizations that maintain their specific identity while also being part of a larger unit. But they have a more distinct identity than larger movements, and are more clearly identifiable (for example, one can contact and interact directly with the Climate Action Network, but cannot do the same with the "environmental movement" as such). In that regard, they are closer to an "organizational" mode of coordination.

Social movement action on a large scale has always been organized in network forms. Examples may be found throughout the history of modern contention, from nineteenth-century working class (Ansell 1997) and women's organizations (Edwards 2014; Rosenthal et al. 1985) to environmental or women's movements (Assoudeh and Salazar 2017; Di Gregorio 2012; Diani 1995) to mention just a few. Recently, however, the spread of mobilizations on a global scale has made the role of networks particularly visible. Increasingly, we see examples of coalitions that involve both transnational actors and networks and local actors on issues such as environmental protection, deprivation, or human rights; thus, expanding the range of forms of transnational contention (Ariemma and Burnside-Lawry 2016; Moghadam 2000; Smith et al. 2018). However, it is important to remember that coalitions are not necessarily movements.

Multiplexity sets apart the social movement mode of coordination from another pattern that is often equated with them, namely, the "coalitional" mode. While it is very difficult to think of social movements without thinking of coalitions, the opposite does not necessarily apply (see, e.g., Tarrow 2005, pp. 164–165). This does not mean, of course, that ad hoc coalitions, focusing on specific issues, may not evolve into broader social movements, addressing with relative continuity broader sets of issues. For example, many coalitions formed to address specific environmental problems have followed that pattern over the last decades (Fagan and Jehlicka 2003; Rootes 2003; Rootes and Brulle 2013). Nor should we forget that many of the mechanisms considered behind the start of a successful coalition are similar to those that support social movement dynamics, such as preexisting social ties between prospective members, conducive organizational structures, some shared ideology, culture, and identity, a favourable institutional environment, and adequate resources (see also van Dyke and McCammon 2010; Van Dyke and Amos 2017). At the same time, coalitions may be driven in principle by purely instrumental motives, requiring no broader definitions of boundaries that outlive specific campaigns. In other words, coalitions may develop and achieve their goals even if participants' loyalties remain firmly within the boundaries of specific organizations. A lot of single-issue, local protest of the reactive type is best conceived as an instance of coalitional action rather than as a "social movement." Even much broader campaigns, however, may be more appropriately framed as coalitions, or at least treated as the product of multiple modes of coordination. For instance, the demonstrations that challenged the imminent war against Iraq in February 2003 seemed to combine modes of coordination close, on the one hand, to peace movements; on the other, to ad hoc anti-governmental coalitions, bringing together people and organizations with highly diverse agendas (Walgrave and Rucht 2010; see also Heaney and Rojas 2015).

Finally, we need to consider a range of situations in which collective action develops not because of the coordinating role of groups or associations, but because of the actions undertaken by committed individuals. In the language of modes of coordination, this prefigures a situation in which inter-organizational linkages are sparse, yet feelings of identification with some broad collectivity are widespread, and are embedded in shared practices and mutual affiliations by individual activists. Diani has called this a "subcultural/communitarian" mode of coordination (2013, 2015). Several factors might account for the lack of dense inter-organizational networks. Sometimes this may depend on repression, as alliance building may be discouraged by the high costs associated with public action in a repressive regime. In these cases, activists promote collective action primarily through the interpersonal connections developed through their involvement in apparently neutral forms of social organization. In post–WWII Eastern European communist regimes, dissenters' activities often occurred under the cover provided by cultural organizations like theatres or literary circles (e.g. Glenn 1999; Osa 2003). Under Francisco Franco's fascist regime that ruled Spain between 1936 and 1975, churches often provided a meeting place for opponents in the regions with a distinct historical and cultural tradition such as Catalonia or the Basque country (e.g. Johnston 1991). Likewise, the mosques or the bazaar have often been singled out as the places in which opposition to autocratic regimes of the MENA region flourished (Ashraf 1988; Parsa 2013). At the same time, the mobilization of deprived social groups in the Arab revolts of 2011 has been associated at least partially with the web of social ties people develop in everyday life in urban neighbourhoods (Bayat 2012a). Interestingly, the role of community connections in urban areas has also been singled out as an important driver of mobilization for social groups located in democratic systems, but short in organizational resources, such as migrants or squatters (see e.g. López 2017).

In other cases, the absence of dense interorganizational networks may be due not so much to regime repression but to activists' rejection of bureaucratic forms of organization. Many "new social movement" activists of the 1980s or 1990s, or global justice activists of the 2000s, were embedded in extensive informal, interpersonal networks rather than in specific formal organizations (Juris 2008; e.g. Taylor and Whittier 1992). More recently, the Occupy campaigns of 2011 relied on exchanges between activists that developed in different relational arenas – urban spaces, virtual electronic spaces, and intellectual spaces – in which the mediating role of organizations was largely absent (Moore 2017).

The concept of "subcultural/communitarian mode of coordination" seems particularly effective at capturing patterns of collective action on cultural issues. As we saw in Chapter 1, analysts of *new social movements* stressed that contemporary collective action does not necessarily target state authorities, nor aims primarily at political power, but, rather, focuses on challenging patterns of cultural domination by introducing new, different forms of knowledge, and/or experimenting with alternative lifestyles (e.g. Melucci 1996). For example, the emergence of new academic fields in the United States such as women's studies or Asian American studies may be seen as the result of collective action conducted by communities of like-minded individuals rather than as the direct outcome of mobilizations conducted by specific organizations (Arthur 2009).

Epistemic communities of activists combining specific knowledge with political commitments have also been singled out as a main drive behind attempts to strengthen communication rights world-wide, e.g. on the governance of the internet (Pavan 2012). The interpersonal connections between people sharing specific values or lifestyles represent another basis for coordinating collective action without relying necessarily on the mediating role of organizations. Lesbian, gay, bisexual, and transgender (LGBT) communities have often been identified as a major example of community-based collective action (Armstrong 2002; Ghaziani 2014). However, instances of collective action coordinated through "subcultural/communitarian" forms may be found across a variety of situations, from critical cyclists (Williams 2018b) to atheists (Simmons 2018) to soccer fans (Perasović and Mustapić 2018).

6.4   DO WE STILL NEED ORGANIZATIONS? COMMUNICATION TECHNOLOGY AND COLLECTIVE ACTION

Singling out subcultural/communitarian dynamics as a distinctive mode of coordination provides us with a nice introduction to the big question regarding the impact of new information and communication technologies (henceforth, ICT) on the organizing of collective action. Recently, Ahrne and Brunsson's discussion of organizing has been reframed in terms of communication processes, and their impact on three fundamental dimensions of *organizationality*: "interconnected instances of decision-making .... attributed to a collective entity or actor .... through speech acts that aim to delineate what the entity or actor is or does ('identity claims')" (Dobusch and Schoeneborn 2015: 1006). As the example of the Anonymous hacker community suggests, symbolic production may enable even very loose collectivities to develop some capacity to act in a coordinated way (Dobusch and Schoeneborn 2015).

The attention paid by organization theorists to communicative practices and the role of new technologies parallels in many ways Bennett and Segerberg's (2013) thesis that we would be moving from "collective" to "connective" action. The former is defined by "strong leadership, brokered coalitions between formal organizations, and action frames that draw on ideological or group (class, race, gender, nationality) identity" (Bennet and Segerberg 2013, p. 2). In contrast, "connective action uses broadly inclusive, easily personalized action frames as a basis for technology-assisted networking" (ibidem). According to Bennett and Segerberg (2013, p. 5), "connective action" better captures some distinctive features of contemporary society. One is the quest for personalized forms of action, as many people "often prefer more direct ways of acting politically than voting or becoming members of formal organizations." Another trait of connective action is the shift from collective action frames to personal (easy-to-personalize) action frames. "Sometimes those frames are created by organizations offering easy personal access to events or actions being promoted by organizationally enabled networks. Sometimes [they] .... Emerge directly from crowds, and, in some cases, they "go viral" and become embraced as the common frame for action" (2013, p. 6). And finally, connective action is based on digital forms of organization as technology-enabled networks may become dynamic organizations in their own right.... seemingly disjointed crowd-enabled connective action networks may achieve coherent organizational form in the sense that they develop capacities for (a) resource allocation and provision, (b) responsiveness to short term external events such as police actions or the success or failure of protest actions, and (c) long-term adaptive responses such as resource seeking in the long tails of dying or transitioning networks (2013, pp. 8–9).

Bennett and Segerberg don't dismiss traditional organizations entirely but rather point at three different kinds of action:

> *organizationally brokered collective action [focusing on] ....resource-intensive mobilization and formalized (leadership based, professionally organized) relations with followers, with the aim of cultivating commonly defined emotional commitments to the cause..... organizationally enabled connective action .... [based on] loosely tied networks of organizations sponsoring multiple actions and causes around a general set of issues in which followers are invited to personalize their engagement (more or less) on their own terms.... crowd-enabled* **connective** *action [consisting of] dense, fine-grained networks of individuals in which digital media platforms are the most visible and integrative organizational mechanisms.*
>
> (Bennett and Segerberg 2013, p. 13)

This third model is actually the one that is closest to the subcultural/communitarian model outlined in the previous section.

Bennett and Segerberg's approach is just one among those arguing that the pervasive influence of ICT requires a radical restructuring of social movement research agendas. While in earlier assessment of the relation between ICT and action the focus was often on relatively specific aspects such as patterns of digital protest (Earl 2010; Earl and Kimport 2011), there is growing awareness of the need to broaden our understanding of the multiple implications of ICT for collective action (Earl and Garrett 2017). Some analysts have spoken of a technology-media-movement complex (TMMC) in order to stress that new technologies may define a new field for collective action (Flesher Fominaya and Gillan 2017). In order to make sense of such field and its boundaries, we need to take into account different dimensions of the relationship between ICT and action, such as the tension between ICT as a pragmatic tool and as the source of specific identities, and that between the emancipatory power of ICT and its role of reproducing existing inequalities.

At the same time, when addressing the multiple facets of the impact of ICT on social movements it is also important to recognize the deep roots of the link between communication and collective action. Technological change has always influenced the organizational structure of social movements as well as their tactics. Sidney Tarrow famously characterized the modern social movements that developed since the eighteenth century as "communities of print and association" (Tarrow 2011, p. 3). He also noted how the expansion of both printed and electronic means of communication had permitted an "externalization" of certain costs: if organizations were previously required to be highly structured to get a message across, today a lightweight one may be adequate, provided it can rely on the support of some kind of media. Even what are now regarded as "traditional media," such as the press, have often played an independent role in the promotion of collective action. For example, they hugely contributed to the success of the so-called "White March," that took place in Brussels in 1996 to voice people's anger at the authorities' handling of the Dutroux pedophilia case (Walgrave and Massens 2000). Pre-internet communication technologies have also helped citizens to get together on specific issues and short-term campaigns. For example, mobile phone communications between private citizens were credited with the success of the demonstrations that in January 2001 forced Philippine President Joseph Estrada to resign (Tilly 2004a, p. 5).

The question is, of course, whether the advent of the internet has brought about a qualitative major, rather than incremental, change in the way communication shapes action. Initially, observers emphasized in particular its practical contribution to a better coordination of protest activities. As an authoritative, nonacademic source like the Canadian Security Intelligence Service put it in the aftermath of the 1999 Seattle protests against WTO: "The internet will continue to have a large role in the success or failure of antiglobalization protests and demonstrations. Groups will use the internet to identify and publicize targets, solicit and encourage support, organize and communicate information and instructions, recruit, raise funds, and as a means of promoting their various individual and collective aims" (quoted in Van Aelst and Walgrave 2004: 121).

The first decades of the new millennium have amply vindicated the Canadian police's predictions. The global justice initiatives of the early 2000s showed how the links between the websites of different organizations provided an easy way to spread information beyond email (Van Aelst and Walgrave 2004). It seems reasonable to suggest that the major no-global initiatives of the late 1990s and early 2000s were made possible by the internet, even though, as Seattle demonstrates, it was the combination of local grassroots organizing and web-based information diffusion that did the trick (Bennett 2004; Van Aelst and Walgrave 2004. See also Seattle activists' accounts on www.wtohistory.org).

The contribution of ICT was not limited to expanding the capacity to act of already solid organizations such as Greenpeace or Oxfam; to the contrary, ICT also brought together networks of activists with very informal organizational structures, if any, like the independent information network Indymedia. Its first site was born during the 1999 Seattle campaign, and then spread to form other networks, including the European Counter Network that connected anarchists and autonomists and *centri sociali* (Wright 2004). Over the years, analysts' attention has increasingly focused on the multiple ways in which ICT enables collective action by facilitating interpersonal connections rather than interorganizational ones (Gonzalez-Bailon 2017; Gonzalez-Bailon and Wang 2016). It has been suggested that ICT hugely contributes to the creation of connections between like-minded people that are not located in the same region. Such connections are particularly useful when the focus of the action are highly technical issues that require specific technical competence and are not easily translated into mass participation. One example is the campaigns on "communication rights" that address issues such as the global regulation of the internet (Padovani and Calabrese 2014; Pavan 2012). Campaigns on cultural issues that may attract wide interest from individual members of the public but not necessarily from organizations may also hugely profit from ICT, as the UK-originated Stand Against Modern Football campaign illustrates (Hill, Canniford, and Millward 2018). The impact of ICT has also been highlighted on campaigns such as the one that brought down President Hosni Mubarak in Egypt in 2011. Some accounts portrayed it primarily as the outcome of innumerable interactions between protesters, made possible by tools like Twitter (for a more cautious view: Brym et al. 2014; Lotan et al. 2011).

While there are few doubts that ICT matters for the coordination of collective action, it is not always clear how it does so. Let us look at some of the issues that are still open. The first refers to the contribution of ICT to strengthening the protesters' position in their interactions with state apparatuses, most notably the repressive ones. The combination of media such as mobile phones and internet access has enabled protesters to expose state repression – e.g. in the form of violent behavior by the police – and/or to document situations of deprivation or of violation of basic rights in a much more effective way than before (see e.g. Castells 2012; Hermida and Hernández-Santaolalla 2018; Suh, Vasi, and Chang 2017). Acting primarily on the online sphere has also been argued to reduce activists' exposure to repression, particularly in authoritarian regimes, but not exclusively to them, as the case of Anonymous illustrates (e.g. Massa 2017). At the same time, both approaches are susceptible to counter-responses by state authorities and opponents. Activists' attempts to spread information about their actions and/or opponents' misbehavior may be diluted by the diffusion of fake news over the same media, again a practice that long precedes the advent of the internet by the way (e.g. Cunningham 2003; Tan 2018). And, police forces may develop effective tools to search the internet, thus ending up identifying whole networks of activists in a much easier way than if connections between them had to be dug out via investigations on the field (see Diani 2011 for a summary of this debate in relation to the Arab Spring).

Similarly debatable is the question whether ICT contributes to social movements' internal democracy. The suggestion that it might facilitate horizontal coordination, the sharing of ideas, and democratic deliberation following open debates has been popular since the early 2000s, particularly among analysts of global justice movements and of Occupy/Indignados mobilizations. The reliance of those movements on "affinity groups" (i.e., self-organized and self-governing groups based on a commonality of values and interests) heralded for some a radical overturning of traditional bureaucratic models of political organizing (McDonald 2002), to which ICT tools could contribute significantly (Castells 2012). At the same time, the tension between the aspiration to include everybody in participatory decision making and the need to take quick decisions and operate in an effective way has long been highlighted, well before the advent of the internet (see e.g. Gamson 1990 [1975]).

A number of studies have identified difficulties to implement a genuinely participatory style of participation via the new media. For example, while student activists in the UK in 2010/2011 relied heavily on ICT to organize their protests, the use of social media did not necessarily result in greater grassroots participation: "towards the end of the cycle, activists were found to be using social media – via 'secret' Facebook groups – in ways that reinforced emerging group hierarchies, arguably contradicting their initial commitment to open-access networks and participatory democracy" (Hensby 2016, p. 466). Even an extremely informal network like Anonymous, where participants drastically reject hierarchy and leadership, has seen the periodical emergence of dominant groups from the apparently unstructured interactions between its activists (Uitermark 2017). One should also notice that informed participation via internet requires a significant amount of personal resources, and therefore does not necessarily translate into opportunities for more inclusive and balanced styles of participation (Milan and Hintz 2013). On the other hand, the foundation of the divide that most analysts identify between a small core of very active online participants and a mass of passive users has also been questioned. We might want to pay closer attention to the different ways through which people participate in online communities, rather than focusing on frequency of interaction and centrality in the exchanges (Fuster Morell 2010).

Still another widely debated question has been whether ICT may help creating collective identities that somehow bind people together in relatively stable ways. As we noticed in Chapter 4, collective identity implies not only the sharing of some beliefs, condition, or interest. It also implies actors' ability to recognize each other as part of a collectivity with some sense of continuity, and mutual solidarity between its members. When the role of ICT became an issue widely debated among analysts of collective action, critics questioned that interactions that occurred purely in the online realm might create the mechanisms of trust and mutual commitment, associated with identity mechanisms (see e.g. Diani 2000b). Over the last couple of decades, skeptics have been challenged on a number of grounds. Some have raised doubts about the very solidity of the concept of *collective identity*. Introducing the concept of *connective action,* Bennett and Segerberg (2013) have, for example, suggested that the advent of ICT contributes to the emergence of forms of public action that no longer depend on people feeling part of larger collectivities with some stability (classes, ethnic or national groups, ideological fronts, etc.). Protest activities are rather the domain of individuals converging together on different causes in coalitions that vary over time, depending on people's individual priorities and aspi-rations. Without embarking on such broad debates, several contributions have sug-gested that interactions on the web may actually contribute to the emergence of specific identities. This seems to work particularly well for lifestyle movements: for example, the web of ICT-mediated links between those who participate in the activ-ities of the so-called Slow Food movement (more a subculture/community, in the language of modes of coordination) points at the coexistence of material and idea-tional exchanges, which help to strengthen a specific identity among people involved (Hendrikx et al. 2017).

Other studies have pointed at the role of the internet in creating and reinforcing not only practical exchanges, but also and primarily symbolic, identitarian connec-tions between actors scattered across vast territories. Examples include organizations promoting social forums across the globe as part of the global justice movement(s) (Vicari 2014), the solidarity links that were reinforced among the Turkish and Kurd-ish diaspora in Europe following the 2011 campaign at Gezi Park (Giglou, Ogan, and d'Haenens 2018), or transnational extreme right networks (Caiani and Parenti 2016). It would be a mistake, however, to stick to a rigid opposition between online and offline networks as if they represented two distinct domains. Regardless of the emphasis they assign to the role of ICT in collective action dynamics, most analysts recognize the interdependence of the interactions that take place on the internet with those that happen offline. Recent studies focused on processes of boundary definition point for example at the role of connected cores of activists with a specific local basis even when the focus of action is clearly not restricted to a specific area, as in the case of the campaign against immigrant deportations in the US (for a broader argument see also Ashuri and Bar-Ilan 2016; van Haperen, Nicholls, and Uitermark 2018). And, an analysis of support for radical movement goals and tactics, conducted in Hong Kong at the time of the 2014 Umbrella movement, suggests that radicalization did not depend entirely on exposure to online messages and influences. Rather, in that case at least, the development of a radical identity was facilitated by the interaction between the use of alternative online media and direct, offline participation in the movement activities (Lee 2018). Along similar lines, a study of the tweets posted during the mobi-lizations following an infamous gang-rape incident in South Delhi, India, in Decem-ber 2012 found strong analogies between online and offline emotional patterns (Ahmed, Cho, and Jaidka 2017).

6.5 HOW DOES ORGANIZING WITHIN SOCIAL MOVEMENTS CHANGE?

The distinction between "organization" and "organizing" also informs our under-standing of the ways in which patterns of coordination change over time. We can dif-ferentiate, in other words, between transformations occurring in the profile of specific groups or associations, participating in a movement; and transformations in the way multiple groups interact within larger collective action fields.

6.5.1   Changes within Specific Groups or Associations

Just as the organizational characteristics of social movements vary, there is no single model accounting for organizational changes. A Weberian approach, focusing primarily on bureaucratization, initially dominated in the sociology of social movements as in other areas. Michels' "iron law of oligarchy," which states that in order to survive as an organization a political party increasingly pays attention to adapting to its environment rather than to its original goals of social change, was also held broadly valid for social movements (Breines 1980; Rucht 1999). Institutionalization used to be considered a natural evolution for social movement organizations. Recurrent lifecycles were identified in the histories of a number of movements. Drawing on the experience of the West European new social movements of the 1980s, Kriesi (1996) described for example the internal structuration of organizations operating within movements along similar lines, as varying in degrees of (1) formalization, with the introduction of formal membership criteria, written rules, fixed procedures, formal leadership, and a fixed structure of offices; (2) professionalization, understood as the presence of paid staff who pursue a career inside the organization; (3) internal differentiation, involving a functional division of labor and the creation of territorial units; and (4) integration, through mechanisms of horizontal and/or vertical coordination.

However, organizational change within social movements does not always follow the path from the informal to the bureaucratic, from the participatory to the professional. In the first place, many social movements have displayed since the very beginning a combination of highly informal and pretty formalized, bureaucratic groups: for example, the US civil rights movement in the 1950s and 1960s included fairly bureaucratic organizations like the *National Association for the Advancement of Colored People* (NAACP), founded in 1909 (McAdam 1982); and the campaigns against the memoranda imposed on Greece by the "Troika" (the European Commission, the European Central Bank, and the International Monetary Fund) saw a central, if somehow contested, role for large bureaucracies like the Trade Unions (Diani and Kousis 2014; Rudig and Karyotis 2013; Vogiatzoglou 2018). On the other hand, many organizations established during phases of rising collective action do not survive for a significant time spell (Minkoff 1995, p. 3). Some dissolve because their aims have been achieved, as in the case of network organizations coordinating specific campaigns. Others because of internal factionalism, the inability to link core activists' and leaders' agendas to the needs of their broader constituencies, or strategic and tactical disagreements. These tend to become more acute at times of de-mobilization, when groups struggle to attract new members and reproduce their capacity to act (della Porta and Tarrow 1987). But it is also possible for organizations to suffer from internal dynamics even when external conditions seem to be favorable. This happened, for example, to the South African Anti-Privatisation Forum (APF), that collapsed at a time of intensifying collective action in the country, having been a major player throughout the first decade of the 2000s (Runciman 2015).

Moderation of an organization's aims is not, of course, the only possible development even for those organizations that actually do survive in the long term.

Some case studies suggest that institutionalization does not necessarily imply the dismissal of radical strategies within movement organizations (see, for example, Dee 2018). Other social movement organizations dismiss institutionalization altogether and actually become more radical as time progresses. Their aims become more ambitious, the forms of action adopted less conventional, and they become increasingly isolated from the outside world. One outcome of 1968, although certainly not the only one, nor the most important, was the formation of clandestine organizations that grew out of the student movement in Italy and Germany and adopted increasingly radical forms of action, including in some cases murdering political opponents. Although they were eventually defeated, they represent a tragic and extreme illustration of how reacting to a hostile environment can bring about an increasing closure of channels of communication with the outside world (della Porta 1995).

The direction taken by a social movement, therefore, may be that of moderation, but equally that of radicalization; of greater formalization, but also of progressive destructuration; of greater contact with the surrounding environment, or of sectarian "implosion." One must not forget that changes in specific organizations do not necessarily all take the same direction: the institutionalization of one organization can go along with the radicalization of another, and the overall profile of a social movement sector may remain relatively stable over time as a result. For example, an analysis of changes in environmental organizations in the 1990s showed that trends toward institutionalization and professionalization went along with the emergence of new grassroots radical actors, and that established organizations played a key role in environmental movements since the rise of environmental mobilization in the late 1980s (Diani and Donati 1999).

6.5.2   Changes in the Structure of Fields

While specific groups or associations may change their profile over time (although, as we have seen, not necessarily toward greater institutionalization and moderation), patterns of organizing may also change within organizational fields. In other words, "organizational change" may also mean a transformation in the modes of coordination that connect groups and associations active on a given cause to each other, and not just a change in the traits of specific actors. This implies shifting our attention to the structure of collective action fields (see, e.g., Stevenson and Crossley 2014).

First of all, the emergence of social movements may be read as a transformation in relational patterns. While the rise of new waves of contention brings about new organizations and possibly new organizational models (Minkoff 1995; e.g. Tarrow 1989), we may also look at the emergence of a social movement as the emergence – or strengthening – of connections between actors that previously operated mainly independently from each other, privileging organizational logics of action or at best engaging in *ad hoc* instrumental coalitions. In the language of modes of coordination, the emergence of a movement implies the building of new, or the revitalizing of previously dormant, boundaries *and* the construction of stronger ties between actors that before did not feel part of the same collective project. We might even argue that the *newness* of a movement ultimately rests on its capacity to build boundaries and sustained collaborations that cut across the established cleavages of a given society (Diani 2000a). For example, environmentalism developed through the development of sustained collaborations between heterogeneous actors, some of whom holding different stances on traditional left-right divides (Diani 1995; Rootes 2003). In this perspective, and consistently with research on network governance (Jones, Hesterly, and Borgatti 1997, p. 927), changes in network composition through a relaxation or tightening of the boundaries and criteria for inclusion become a central issue for research; so do the conditions for alliance building within fields (van Dyke and McCammon 2010; Zietsma et al. 2017).

An interesting illustration of how a focus on modes of coordination may contribute to our understanding of the evolution of contention over time comes from the systematic mapping of social protest in Argentina from 1989–2003 (Schuster et al. 2006). The application of protest event methods to a dataset of over 5,000 events identified major changes in actors and patterns of contention over 15 years. The capacity of a restricted group of union or party organizations to promote and coordinate collective action was at least partially replaced by a number of coalitions focusing on issues that were at the same time more differentiated and more specific, if still broad (Schuster et al. 2006). Translated into the language of modes of coordination, we might have been witnessing in Argentina over the 1990s a shift in the relative weight of organizational vs. coalitional modes, in parallel with the emergence of new civil society actors. We could also wonder to what extent the emergence of spontaneous forms of popular protest as those represented by *piqueteros* and neighborhood action groups reflected communitarian modes of coordination, or modes closer to a social movement model (Auyero 2007; Delamata 2004). In the former case, the cohesion and coordination of collective action would be secured through the solidarities and the social ties provided by embeddedness in local communities, rather than by interorganizational exchanges; in the latter, we would be witnessing the capacity of grassroots groups to set up broader alliance patterns (see also Gastón 2018).

We may also use the conceptual lens of modes of coordination to chart the weakening of social movement processes within collective action fields. From that perspective, the focus moves from changes in the properties of specific actors to changes in the system of interaction. In relational terms, the demise of a social movement mode of coordination implies that resource exchanges become less dense, and identities and boundaries come to be defined primarily in relation to specific organizations rather than to broader collectivities like movements or subcultures. We have, in other words, the prevalence of an "organizational" mode of coordination. It is worth noting that this pattern of relational change may be detected in fields in which actors are getting increasingly "institutionalized" as well as in a context of radicalization. It matters less, in other words, whether the specific organizations active in a field are primarily of the public interest group kind, or, at the opposite, closer to radical sects; or whether we are looking instead at fields accommodating organizations with different profiles and strategies. The key aspect of the process is that each organization is basically acting on its own, instead of being connected to other players in the same field. This applies regardless of the substantive properties of the actors involved. For example, in the case of environmentalism, a transformation from a social movement to an organizational mode of coordination would often determine a situation in which each organization becomes – or at least competes with others to become – "owner" of a specific sub-issue and focuses on securing its specific niche, from energy to animal rights to traffic, with lower levels of identification and alliance-building with similar organizations (see e.g. Diani and Forno 2003). But a similar pattern of fragmentation of previous ties of cooperation and solidarity could also be found in situations in which competition between radical organizations is pushing them toward the adoption of increasingly violent repertoires (della Porta 1995; della Porta and Tarrow 1987).

6.6 SUMMARY

The organizations engaged in social movements have often been described as loosely structured, decentralized, and prone to engage in contentious political challenges or countercultural practices. However, research has shown that, in reality, a plurality of organizational models coexist within any social movement. Organizations differ, sometimes to a very high degree, in their response to dilemmas such as whether focusing on the mobilization of people or other types of resources, adopting some kind of formal hierarchy or a totally informal structure, targeting their efforts at opponents or also providing services and opportunities to their own constituents. Apart from recognizing different organizational types, we have also stressed the importance of differentiating between *organization,* meant as a bounded set of actors operating according to distinct rules, and *organizing,* meant as the principles that enable coordination between social actors. Referring to organizing has allowed us to emphasize that, when talking of the organization of collective action, we need to refer to the ways in which multiple actors connect to each other in complex network patterns. In order to identify some basic patterns we have introduced the concept of mode of coordination. Starting from "organizational" modes of coordination, we have introduced a few basic models, out of many more that could be identified: the professional social movement organization and the participatory movement organization (more specifically, two versions of it, the mass organization and the grassroots organization, that differ in levels of bureaucratization). We have then contrasted this mode of coordination to a social movement one, implying multiple relations between a plurality of actors. We have also argued that a lot of collective action gets coordinated through still other modes, that we have labeled *coalitional* and *subcultural/communitarian.*

The next step has been discussing how the coordination of collective action might have been affected by contemporary communication technologies, suggesting in particular that ICT might contribute to the spread of subcultural/communitarian modes. In the last section we have looked at changes in organizational forms, once again differentiating between organizations and organizing. In relation to the former, we have showed that the evolution of social movement organizations is not unidirectional: some organizations become institutionalized, turning themselves into moderate bureaucracies, while others may become more radical, or turn into sects. Finally, we have suggested that the concept of *mode of coordination* may help us to trace the evolution of the complex patterns of relations that occur between groups and associations in collective action fields, thus adding another dimension to our understanding of organizational change.

CHAPTER 7

Eventful Protests

The anti-austerity protests of the years 2010s have been defined as a catalyzer of an aggregation process involving groups and organizations active in countries all over the world: blue-collar workers and farm workers, consumers and environmentalists, churches and feminists, pacifists and human-rights associations. In fact, already during the Global Justice Movement at the beginning of the millennium, heterogeneous and initially loosely connected groups had mobilized together, mainly against international organizations, using different strategies: from lobbying to marches, from boycotts to petitions, from strikes to netstrikes. In Seattle and afterwards, demonstrators from many countries challenged the legitimacy of the decisions of some international governmental organizations and sought to hinder their plans. Also against austerity, protestors sought to influence policy makers and public opinion in various ways.

During those protests, the development of a "new spirit" has been noted in the occupied squares which represented the space for the formation of new subjectivity, based on a recomposition of former cleavages and the emergence of new identifications. These spaces have been defined, in fact, as spaces of becoming, with "the spontaneous coming together in a moment of 'irruption'" (Karakayalí and Yaka 2014, p. 118). In this sense, "Recomposition is also connected to the emergence of new subjectivities and social practices, and eventually to the emergence of new norms as well" (Karakayalí and Yaka 2014, pp. 118–119). In particular, in Turkey, the protests around the Gezi Park were often read as producing and reproducing the conditions for their own existence.

Social diversity brought about the need to invent new categories for the definition of the self. The focus on "becoming" emerged through practices that stress the importance of encounters – often celebrating the diversity of people in the various squares. So, "in the intermixing of bodies, signs, objects, voices, stories, and emotions, Gezi solidarity renewed existing ties and spawned new intimacies and affections, giving its participants a 'belonging in becoming,'" as "Amid the temporary absence of the state within the barricaded Gezi zone, heterogeneity of visibilities and voices collectively exist, gaining radical and transformative potentials [...] namely, a queer becoming in togetherness that transgressed self-castigating sensations of anxiety and fear in the face of state violence" (Zengin 2013). Engaging in the very definition of their identities, social movements express a claim to exist that comes even before the claim of recognition. Regarding the Gezi mobilization, Gambetti (2013) stated, "One reason why the state resented the mobilizations was because they embodied the constative 'we exist.'" The "collective thereness" (Butler 2014) of bodies refusing to be disposed of was a manifestation of endurance, but also a demand for existing as part of a larger totality. Frequently heard were statements like "This has never happened before; what is happening here is amazing" (della Porta and Atak 2017). As Avramopoulou (2013) noted, "If anything, the Gezi resistance made it possible to get many voices attuned to the passionate attachment of claiming 'to be present, to exist' (as in the slogans chanted in the streets)."

In these intense times, emotions were strongly felt. Excitement was recalled at the observation of the unexpected: "Everyone was excited and hopeful about the unexpected gathering of millions from multifarious segments of society – soccer fans, feminists, LGBTQs, socialists, Kemalists, environmentalists, Kurds [...] – in the Gezi protests. The forum's atmosphere was cordial: no harsh debates, no confrontations whatsoever" (Bozcalı and Yoltar 2013). An element of surprise was emphasized, as extraordinary time implied "the suspension, sometimes spontaneous, sometimes deliberate, of an awareness of the vulnerability of individual bodies in order to cross that threshold of fear, or, as specified by yet another memorable graffiti printed across the pavement steps that leads to the entrance of the park, to cross the remaining steps to the threshold of fear" (Parla 2013).

The assessment of living in exceptional moments brings about the breaking of routines, leaving hope for what was once considered impossible. Protesters experience "everyday chance encounters and have the chance to experience a different kind of knowledge going beyond the mere experience of effects. The reason for this is that in the rebellious practice of commoning, people encounter the very causes of their own capacity to act, their 'trans-individual' condition, the fact that everything and everyone is enchained in a 'causal community'" (Karakayalí and Yaka 2014, p. 132). In action, citizens indeed changed their identification.

Democracy thus developed in the streets. Remaining with the Turkish example,

> The Gezi spirit became an historical opportunity by which people creatively engaged in the very definition of democracy. They became active residents of their city by claiming their right to the city as the most basic of their democratic rights. They became politicized global citizens by forging links of solidarity and inspiration with other urban movements around the world. They became conscious bearers of their Ottoman past and their republican present, demanding a change to a brighter future that is at the same time cosmopolitan and democratic. This was to be a democracy beyond its limited definition as the rule of the elected people. It was to be an inclusionary democracy where people engaged in how they were to be ruled, and had a say on what their cities would look like.
>
> (Örs 2014, p. 8)

As we shall see in section 7.1, a characteristic of protest is its capacity to mobilize public opinion through unorthodox forms of action and so put pressure on decision makers. The brief outline given above of anti-austerity protest describes a series of different actions, which, taken together, form a repertoire of collective action. Section 7.2 will present tactics very different in terms of their radicalism and the "logic" driving them. For social movement actors, choices concerning the forms of action to adopt are important but difficult decisions, involving strategic calculations but also considerations of values and culture. In fact, as we shall see in section 7.3, the necessity to simultaneously address different types of public creates a number of tactical dilemmas. In addition, choices are influenced both by internal variables and by interactions with other actors. Protests spread in time and space through cyclical dynamics. Cross-national diffusion is discussed in section 7.4. In this process, eventful protests acquire an important role (section 7.5).

7.1   DEFINING PROTEST

In Gezi, as in other anti-austerity protests, activists marched and arranged blockades; there were concerts and vigils, dancing and fasting. People occupied real and virtual spaces. What do all these actions have in common? In the first place, they are forms of protest (i.e. nonroutinized ways of affecting political, social, and cultural processes). In fact, "social movements employ methods of persuasion and coercion that are, more often than not, novel, unorthodox, dramatic, and of questionable legitimacy" (Wilson 1973, p. 227). Protests are "sites of contestation in which bodies, symbols, identities, practices, and discourses are used to pursue or prevent changes in institutionalized power relations" (Taylor and van Dyke 2004, p. 268).

According to the principles of representative democracy, the decisions of a government can be challenged immediately by the parliamentary opposition or punished subsequently by the voting choices of citizens in elections. Aside from military intervention, the channels for exerting pressure on a foreign government include bilateral diplomacy or negotiations in one of the many international government organizations (IGOs). However, particularly since the 1970s, increasing numbers of citizens have come to affirm the legitimacy of other forms of pressure on governments. When faced with laws or decisions considered to be unjust these citizens adopt forms of action that challenge established norms. Especially from the 1960s on, a "new set of political activities has been added to the citizens' political repertoire" (Barnes et al. 1979, p. 149). In fact, researchers added a long list of new and unconventional forms of political participation – including signing petitions, lawful demonstration, boycotts, withholding of rent or tax, occupations, sit-ins, blocking traffic, and wildcat strikes – to the more traditional ones, such as following politics in the newspapers, discussing politics with others, working for political parties or their candidates, attending political meetings, contacting public officials, or persuading friends and acquaintances to vote in particular ways. These newer forms have become increasingly legitimized: "In advanced industrial societies direct political action techniques do not in fact bear the stigma of deviancy. Nor are they seen as antisystem-directed orientation" (Barnes et al. 1979, p. 157).

This expansion of the repertoire of political participation appeared to be a "lasting characteristic of democratic mass publics" (Barnes et al. 1979, p. 524). Indeed, more than two decades later, Pippa Norris (2002, p. 221) observed, on the bases of World Value Surveys polls, that "There are many reasons to believe that the shift from traditional interest groups to new social movements has influenced the agencies, repertoires, and targets of political participation ... The analysis of protest politics shows that many of these forms of activity, such as petitions, demonstrations, and consumer boycott, are fairly pervasive and have become increasingly popular during recent decades. Protest politics is on the rise as a channel of political expression and mobilization." According to Norris's data (2002, p. 197), in "older democracies" 60.7% of the population have signed a petition, 19.1% have attended a demonstration, and 17.1% have joined in boycotts. In a pooled set of established democracy, according to International Social Survey Program, the level of political participation in 2014 remained similar to the one registered 10 years earlier (Dalton 2017, pp. 30–32).

An important characteristic of protest is the use of indirect channels to influence decision-makers. As Michael Lipsky (1965) noted a long time ago, protest is a political resource of the powerless. The events that shook the United States in the 1960s – from the "Freedom Summer" campaign to register black voters in the Southern states, launched by civil rights activists in 1964, to the "March on Washington" in support of ethnic minority civil rights – all had something in common: "They were engaged in by relatively powerless groups; and they depended for success not upon direct utilization of power, but upon activating other groups to enter the political arena. Because protest is successful to the extent that other parties are activated to political involvement, it is one of the few strategies in which even politically impoverished groups can aspire to engage" (Lipsky 1965, p. 1). Protest, then, sets in motion a process of indirect persuasion mediated by mass media and powerful actors. Powerless actors must mobilize the support of more powerful groups. In fact, protest mobilizes a variety of actors. Those directly interested in political decisions comprise a protest constituency. From this constituency a leadership emerges to lead action and maintain external relations. The mass media spread their message, addressing in the first instance the reference public of the decision-makers. The latter are the true targets of protest. In order to succeed, protest must produce positive stimuli, winning the sympathies of those who have more resources to invest in the arenas where decisions are taken. While collective action by groups who already possess power can be aimed directly at decision makers, the powerless must seek to involve those who have the possibility of influencing them. In addition, the influence exerted by social movements can be either positive, creating sympathy for their cause, or negative, threatening (for example) to create disorder. This is why the characteristics of the mass media, and of channels of communication in general, are particularly relevant for social movements: their capacity to address public opinion is indeed a crucial component of their action.

Social movements certainly do not use protest alone and they do not have a monopoly on protest. Other actors, such as political parties or pressure groups, also make use of protest action and occasionally make alliances with social movements for particular campaigns. However, protest (particularly at its most innovative and radical) has been considered a form of action typical of social movements because, unlike political parties and pressure groups, they have fewer channels through which to access decision makers. Forms of action are particularly important for them since social movements are "often remembered more for the methods of persuasion adopted by them than for their objectives" (Wilson 1973, p. 226).

The marches, boycotts, occupations, and other forms of action used during anti-austerity campaigns have something else in common. They are all part of a modern repertoire of collective action, defined as the "whole set of means [a group] has for making claims of different types on different individuals" (Tilly 1986, p. 2). As Alimi (2015, p. 413) summarized:

> In cases where movements face a fairly responsive political environment to their claims, repertoires may include lobbying, press conferences, litigation, but also demonstrations, street rallies, vigils, and human chain marches. These latter repertoires are meant not only to display to authorities determination, solidarity, size and scope of supporters the movement has, but also to strengthen the leverage of political allies. During election campaigns, most notably, movement repertoires may include setting up political action committees to support candidates, presenting their own candidates, engaging in bloc voting, or employing bolder repertoires like harassing politicians .... But there are other repertoires that aim to influence authorities in a more indirect manner, expressing claims embedded in conflicts that transcend the political (in the narrow, institutional sense of the term) and revolve around cultural, societal, moral, and personal conflict domains and issues. Symbolic issues that are often linked with issues of identity (individual and collective linked), consciousness, and solidarity characterize much of the work of movements like LGBT, religious, women, environmental, consumerism, and lifestyle. Identity deployment and presentation through unconventional, unique clothing and hairstyle, consumption and consumerism – all are repertoires that challenge institutional, cultural codes and practices. ... These repertoires are part of individual activists' daily practices of resistance, but they can also accompany more collective representations, as when demonstrations are peppered with theatrical tactics, such as wearing costumes and putting on street shows.

Charles Tilly has made an important contribution to the study of collective action by identifying the differences in types of contentious action in particular historical periods. Protest was certainly not unheard of prior to the formation of the nation-state: peasants burnt down mills in protest against increases in the price of bread; subjects dressed up in order to mock their superiors; funerals could be turned into the occasion for denunciations of injustice. The tactics adopted by protestors varied from the utilization of irreverent symbols and music (as in charivari) to field invasions and grain seizures. However, they all had two characteristics in common:

> Broadly speaking, the repertoire of the mid-seventeenth to the mid-nineteenth century had a parochial scope: it addressed local actors or the local representatives of national actors. It also relied heavily on patronage – appealing to immediately available power holders to convey grievances or settle disputes, temporarily acting in the place of unworthy or inactive power holders only to abandon power after the action.

(Tilly 1986, pp. 391–392)

The forms taken by collective action began to change in the nineteenth century when the old parochial and patronage-dependent repertoire was replaced by one that was national ("though available for local issues and enemies, it lends itself easily to coordination among many localities") and autonomous ("instead of staying in the shadow of existing power holders and adapting routines sanctioned by them, people using the new repertoire tend to initiate their own statements of grievances and demands" – Tilly 1986, pp. 391–392), involving actions such as strikes, electoral rallies, public meetings, petitions, marches, insurrection, and the invasion of legislative bodies. In the past, assemblies converged on the private residences of the crowd's enemies, whereas today the preferred targets are the seats and symbols of national public power (Tilly 1986, pp. 392–393). The older repertoire tended to use the same type of action as the authorities, either in the form of caricature or temporary substitution; the new one invented autonomous forms. People used to participate in the traditional repertoire of collective action as members of preconstituted communities, whereas they do so as representatives of particular interests in the modern repertoire. The old repertoire took advantage of official celebrations or occasions; the new involves the deliberate organization of assemblies and occasions for action. This transformation in the form of protest followed from the creation of the nation-state, the development of capitalism, and the emergence of modern means of communication. As Tilly (1986, pp. 395–396) put it:

> As capitalism advanced, national states became more powerful and centralized local affairs and nearby patrons mattered less to the fates of ordinary people. Increasingly, holders of large capitals and national power made the decisions that affected them. As a result, seizure of grain, collective invasions of fields and the like became ineffective, irrelevant, obsolete. In response to the shifts of power and capital, ordinary people invented and adopted new forms of action, creating the electoral campaign, the public meeting, the social movement, and the other elements of the newer repertoire.

The new repertoire responded therefore to a new situation in which politics was increasingly national in character, the role of communities diminished and organized association spread, particularly among the laboring classes (Tilly 1984b, p. 309). There is another characteristic typical of the modern repertoire besides its national scale and autonomous character: its modular quality, i.e. the possibility of being used by a variety of actors to achieve a variety of objectives. In traditional societies the repertoire was specific, direct, and rigid, as noted by Sidney Tarrow: "In a society divided into orders, isolated by poor communication and lack of literacy and organized into corporate and communal groups, it was rare to find forms of collective action distinct from the conflicts that gave rise to them" (Tarrow 1994, p. 35). The consolidation of the nation-state, the expansion of the means of communication (whether roads or newspapers), and the growth of private associations favored instead the development of a new, general, flexible, and indirect repertoire. This in its turn facilitated the diffusion of protest and the mobilization of new and diverse groups within the population.

According to Tilly and Tarrow, the modern repertoire that emerged with the French Revolution has changed little since. Boycotts, barricades, petitions, and demonstrations are all still present (and indeed probably dominant) in the panorama of protest. However, if we look back at the example that opened this chapter, a number of new elements can be identified – elements that can be explained by transformations in the very characteristics held to be essential for the emergence of the modern repertoire. First, capitalism developed from nation-state-based industries to multinational corporations. Second, while the nation-state has certainly not disappeared, it is now flanked by sub- and supranational entities possessing increasing powers (see Chapters 2 and 9 in the present volume). Mobilizations such as the one in Gezi Parks, are transnational in nature. Third, new media such as television, but especially more recently fax, mobile phones, and the internet, have transformed the ambitions and communication capacity of social movements. In particular, the internet is exploited for online mobilization and acts of dissent: the term *electronic advocacy* refers to "the use of high technology to influence the decision-making process, or to the use of technology in an effort to support policy-change efforts" (Hick and McNutt 2002, p. 8). Also, in part thanks to the internet, transnational campaigns have grown longer, less centrally controlled, more difficult to turn on and off, and forever mutable in terms of networks and goals (Bennett 2003a). Additionally, old repertoires can emerge again in times of intense struggles, such as in the labor conflicts in Italy in the 1970s but also in anti-austerity protests in Argentina or Spain (della Porta 2016; Favretto and Itcaina 2016; Flescher-Fominaya 2016).

7.2   THE LOGICS AND FORMS OF PROTEST

The citizens and organizations opposing austerity policies did so in a variety of ways. First, the forms of action were more or less radical in nature, ranging from more conventional petitioning to more disruptive blockades, and including a number of episodes of violence. Opinion poll research has traditionally ordered forms of participation on a single continuum from least to most extreme, singling out various thresholds:

> *The first threshold indicates the transition from conventional to unconventional politics. Signing petitions and participating in lawful demonstrations are unorthodox political activities but still within the bounds of accepted democratic norms. The second threshold represents the shift to direct action techniques, such as boycotts. A third level of political activities involves illegal, but nonviolent, acts. Unofficial strikes or a peaceful occupation of a building typify this step. Finally, a fourth threshold includes violent activities such as personal injury or physical damage.*
>
> (Dalton 1988, p. 65)

Second, although the forms of action adopted concentrated to a large extent on the political system, it should be noted that movements also made use (to differing degrees) of cultural strategies aimed at changing value systems. While political strategies seek, above all, to change external realities, cultural strategies seek an interior transformation. As already noted, some social movements are directed primarily to value systems, while others concentrate on the political system (for example, Rucht 1994). Moreover, movements themselves alternate between phases of greater politicization and retreat into countercultural activity (Melucci 1984; on Italy, della Porta 1996a). In addition, both cultural and political strategies are also characterized by varying degrees of extremeness, ranging from moderate subcultural evolution to radical countercultural challenge in the first case and from negotiation to confrontation in the second (Rucht 1990).

However, as we shall seek to demonstrate more fully in what follows, forms of action can also be distinguished according to the logic, or *modus operandi*, which the activists assign them.

7.2.1   The Logic of Numbers

The logic of numbers, to which James DeNardo referred in *Power in Numbers* (1985), underlies numerous forms of protest. Since "there always seems to be power in numbers" (1985, p. 35), a movement's destiny depends to a great extent on the number of its supporters. As DeNardo notes:

> *The size of the dissidents' demonstrations affects the regime both directly and indirectly. Naturally the disruption of daily routines increases with numbers, and the regime's ability to control crowds inevitably suffers as they grow larger. In addition to the immediate disruption they cause, demonstrations by their size also give the regime an indication of how much support the dissidents enjoy.*
>
> (1985, p. 36)

Just as political parties attempt to increase the number of electors who support them and pressure groups seek to maximize the number of their adherents, social movements should seek to mobilize the greatest number of demonstrators possible.

From this point of view, protest stands in for elections. The logic behind it is, to a certain extent, the same as that behind representative democracy: implementation of the majority's decisions. Protest serves to draw the attention of elected representatives to the fact that, at least on certain issues, the majority in the country is not the same as the majority in parliament. Thus, the fear of losing electoral support should push the people's representatives into changing their position, realigning themselves with the country "at large."

Marches are one of the main tactics designed to demonstrate the numerical strength behind protest. The Seattle demonstration started a new wave of "politics on the street" with large marches that had seemed just a memory of the past. Large demonstrations are organized during countersummits, defined as arenas of "international-level initiatives during official summits and on the same issues but from a critical standpoint, heightening awareness through protest and information with or without contacts with the official version" (Pianta 2002, p. 35). Millions of people joined the international day of protest against the Iraq war on February 15, 2003 (della Porta and Diani 2004a; Waalgrave and Rucht 2010). Large protest marches targeted austerity measures in Iceland, Spain, Greece, Italy, Portugal, and million marches called for justice in Tunisia and Egypt (della Porta, Andretta et al. 2016; della Porta 2017a).

Petitions (as well as referendums) are also used to demonstrate the numerical strength of support for movements. In the 1980s, petitions and demands for referendums were presented in all of the countries affected by the deployment of cruise and Pershing missiles. Millions of signatures were collected in Italy, the Netherlands, Germany, and the United States. In the 1990s, the campaign led by Jubilee 2000 collected 24 million signatures under a petition asking to drop the debt of the poorest countries (Anheier and Themundo 2002). The use of petitions has been facilitated by the internet: transnational campaigns against multinational corporations such as De Beers, Microsoft, Monsanto, Nike, etc., run especially via online petitions, with the collection of signatures via mailing lists and websites. Referendums called from below opposed the privatization of water supply in Italy as well as in Bolivia, while in Iceland a petition against the payout over Icesave collapse was signed by a quarter of the Icelandese population (della Porta, O'Connor et al. 2017; Cernison 2019).

Netstriking also follows a "logic of numbers," and is another form of online protest that has proliferated in recent years among radical organizations as a "virtual practice for real conflicts" (according to the association StranoNetwork: see Freschi 2000, p. 104; della Porta and Mosca 2005). A netstrike is "comparable to a physical procession that occupies a road to make it inaccessible" (www.net-strike.it). Netstriking consists of a large number of people connecting simultaneously to the same domain at a prearranged time, in order to jam a site considered a symbolic target, and to make it impossible for other users to reach it. The mobilization and its motivation are normally communicated in advance to the owner of the site targeted by the protestors. When a netstrike is in progress online protestors activate a channel of communication (generally, a chat-line or a mailing-list) in order to coordinate their protest action. Netstriking can accompany nonvirtual protest that ideally links offline and online environments – for instance, a netstrike was promoted against the WTO website during the protests in Seattle (Jordan 2002).

Through the logic of numbers an attempt is made to influence public opinion, the final repository of political power. Given that demonstrators are also voters, it is assumed that their representatives will change their position rather than risk not being reelected. However, it would be naive to assume that the opinions of elected representatives simply follow those of the general public on every occasion. First, voting is structured by a whole series of questions and depends on a balance between different motivations. It is far from certain that individuals will abandon their traditional electoral choice on the basis of a preference on a particular issue, even when they agree with the movement on that issue. Movement activists have, therefore, not only to increase support, but also to produce strong preferences in favor of their claims. Second, protest campaigns have a limited duration and, as a result, their political influence is less direct. Indeed, "the problem with all movement alliances, but especially those with the parties, is how to keep commitment firm once the persuasive sounds of the marching thousands have become a distant echo" (Rochon 1988, p. 174). Third, even mass events – such as online petitions, campaigns, and netstrikes – are often ignored by those they target (Rucht 2003a), their impact on observers depending on how much they capture the attention of the mass media (Gurak and Logie 2003, p. 26). Fourth, as the anti-austerity protests signaled, power is shifting toward decision makers that are less and less accountable to public opinion and citizens–electors (see Chapter 8). Thus, it would be extremely dangerous for social movements to depend solely on such a logic; a logic that does not in any case fully reflect their own concept of democracy, which emphasizes participation, not majority vote (see Chapter 9). We can add, however, that beyond externally oriented strategic considerations, the logic of numbers also plays an important symbolic function for the movement activists themselves. Large demonstrations empower participants by spreading the feelings of belonging to a large community of equals.

7.2.2 The Logic of Damage

The logic of inflicting material damage, in a *modus operandi* analogous to war, must be considered alongside the logic of numbers. This logic is reflected, in its most extreme form, by political violence. Urban bread riots in Latin America as well as in Africa had dramatically contested free-trade policies, and the austerity measures connected with them, demanded by the International Monetary Fund, and asked for "work, bread, justice and liberty" (Walton and Seddon 1994).

In protest events, violence has both symbolic and instrumental aims. Violence is part of broader repertoires of action, often justified as a symbolic refusal of an oppressive system, but it is also used, as in the anti-austerity riots, to win specific battles, or to obtain media attention. In social movement studies, a processual approach has moved attention from individual predispositions or root causes toward relational dynamics. As Bosi and Malthaner wrote:

> *Actors not only shift back and forth between violent and nonviolent forms of action, but also use them in various combinations. In other words, violence is not an entirely exceptional form of political action, but has to be examined in the context of other nonviolent and "routine" forms of political action. Thereby, the decision to use violent means or not is not only the result of available repertoires of action, but is shaped by the groups' goals and identity orientation and, particularly, responds to changing environments and actions of their opponents and/or allies. ... Violence emerges as a result of relational dynamics that evolve as sequences of interaction in which mutual responses and adaptations contribute to the gradual escalation of violence. Such interactions are considered to be the result – and part – of temporal sequences of events and causal dynamics bounded together through their connection to the state – that is, through claims that implicate the state and through reactions by the state.*

> (Bosi and Malthaner 2015, pp. 440–441)

Also research on civil war addressed various dilemma in the use of a logic of damage. Social movement studies pointed at the importance of organizations through their capacity to socialize and control their members. In particular, "groups with strong institutions (as indicated by the ability to distribute financial resources across the organization without significant corruption, for example) implement commander preferences, while those with weak ones implement those of combatants (which evolve during war)" (Wood 2015, p. 455). Guerrilla groups with a political wing are more likely to exhibit restraint in their use of violence (Stanton 2013). Gutiérrez Sanín and Wood (2014, p. 215) also stressed the importance of the group ideology, which they define as "a more or less systematic set of ideas that includes the identification of a referent group (a class, ethnic, or other social group), an enunciation of the grievances or challenges that the group confronts, the identification of objectives on behalf of that group (political change – or defense against its threat), and a (perhaps vaguely defined) program of action." Relational factors are important as well, as violence escalate in the interaction with the state but also with rivals and competitors:

> Patterns of violence may diffuse directly (without the mediation of institutions stressed earlier), as combatants imitate or learn enemy or rival repertoires. The emergence of revolutionary movements may reflect characteristics of the state, not just the armed organization). Second, whether or not a fledgling rebel organization develops the coherence necessary to pose a sustained challenge to the state depends on its social embeddedness – the type and extent of its social networks – before) and during the conflict.

(Wood 2015, p. 456)

Riots have been defined as a specific form of oppositional collective behavior. Urban riots staged by excluded ethnic minorities as well as exclusionary riots against ethnic minorities have usually aimed at specific concessions, and rioters usually practiced much more self-restraint than is often admitted (Hobsbawm 1952; Bergmann 2002).As Kotronaki and Seferiades (2012, p. 158) noted, "One common, emblematic property of all riots – apparently at odds with the long history incubating them – is the unexpected, convulsive nature of their outburst." To this "explosiveness," Waddington (2015, p. 423) added "the inescapable fact that rioting typically involves intensely distasteful and violent courses of behavior, including violence towards the police (and occasionally members of the public), and the often gleeful and celebratory destruction or theft of property... Such activities are inevitably condemned by politicians and the mass media as self-defeating, irrational, and wantonly criminal." Based on an understanding of the crowd as "homogeneous, unthinking, amoral, and prone to manipulation" (Waddington 2008), pathologizing riots as "criminal" or "irrational" underestimate the importance of the social and political contexts in which the riot occurs and the relational dynamics with other actors (Waddington and King 2005). According to Waddington's (1992) Flashpoints Model, preexisting grievance triggered by shared experience of inequality, and/or discrimination, as well as the deterioration of the relations between police and specific community relations, are important factors in the development of the incidents. Often, mass-media and politicians demonize and criminalize some groups, calling for repression. The habit of protest and resistance by the community involved also play an important role.

Riots are often triggered by "the incidence of an extraordinary, non-normalized event of coercive violence... which upsets both standard conceptions of injustice as well as entrenched notions of how to cope with a 'bleak future'" (Kotronaki and Seferiades 2012, p. 158). These events produce outrage, also unleashing a process of "cognitive liberation" in which grievances are risen up. The triggering event represents a "rupture" in the rioter's habitus, inducing a "moment of critical reflection" in which the chronically troublesome issues that have become almost subconsciously submerged as "natural" parts of the everyday lives of particular sections of society suddenly become salient and contentious (Akram 2014, p. 13). As Waddington summarized:

> It is this capability of the triggering incident to enhance the salience of grievances related to the prevailing socio-political context that helps to explain the characteristic behaviors and emotions of any given riot. Instances of aggression, looting, and vandalism invariably exhibit patterns of selectivity and restraint that are directly related to important contextual factors, while the frequently reported sensations of "liberation," "joy," and "potency" commonly experienced by rioters stem from the collective feeling of having "turned the tables" on a repressive police force, having forced themselves to be heard by an otherwise unsympathetic and unyielding political system, and having temporarily reassumed some degree of control over their lives.
>
> (2015, p. 426)

Using violence has, however, many limitations and constraints. In the first place, violent action may cause an escalation in repression and alienate sympathizers. Violence polarizes the conflict, transforming "relations between challengers and authorities from a confused, many-sided game into a bipolar one in which people are forced to choose sides, allies defect, bystanders retreat and the state's repressive apparatus swings into action" (Tarrow 1994, p. 104). Although it is true that a lack of resources may encourage the use of more extreme tactics, "this impulse is constrained ... by the erosion of support occasioned by repression and moral backlash. The crucial question, therefore, is whether the government's additional responsiveness to violent protest will provide sufficient compensation for the movement's smaller size" (DeNardo 1985, p. 219). While direct action has on occasion been associated with substantive successes, it has also been noted that violent action often leads to an escalation in conflict. In a democratic regime the state holds a monopoly on the legitimate use of force and most challenges to that monopoly are doomed to fail, transforming political conflict into a military confrontation in which the state has by far the greater firepower (della Porta 1995).

Leaving aside violence, a certain amount of material disruption is present in many forms of protest. The action taken by social movements is often inherently disruptive in the sense that it obstructs the normal course of events by threatening disorder (Tarrow 1994, p. 103). Their challenge to the elites accentuates uncertainty and by so doing produces tangible, and on occasion material, losses. Some protest strategies stress economic damage. Typical is the labor strike, oriented to suspend production, and therefore reduce the profits of the factory owners. By striking, workers halt production and inflict damage on their employer; this economic cost should lead a rational employer to reach agreement with the workforce. More extreme forms of action such as wildcat or rolling strikes and industrial sabotage are sometimes used to increase pressure on the employer by exacerbating the economic cost.

The logic that underlies the industrial strike is difficult to translate into nonindustrial contention. In these cases the opposing party is less easily identified, and disruption tends to work through the trouble it causes to third parties not directly responsible for public decisions and who may turn against the protestors as a result. Strikes in public services are, indeed, particularly delicate to manage as their immediate victims are the citizen-users. Thus, one of the principal dilemmas of protest lies in the often contradictory requirements of threatening disorder on the one hand, while on the other seeking to avoid stigmatization by public opinion. Indeed, unions in the service industries are themselves becoming more cautious about using the strike weapon, knowing that they risk losing public support rather than undermining the legitimacy of government decisions.

Boycotts (a tactic that became very popular in the global justice movement) also aim at reducing the sales, and therefore the profits, of targeted firms. The underlying logic of many movement campaigns is "naming and shaming" that, especially when conducted against multinationals, aims at making public opinion aware of especially glaring cases of ignoring human rights by spreading detailed information about them, and often asking people to punish the companies involved by boycotting their products. Consumer *boycott* is "the rejection of a product with the purpose of limiting a corporation's profit margin, influencing its stock market value, damaging its reputation, or more broadly mobilizing public awareness about a matter concerning the politics of products. Social movements mobilize boycott actions" (Micheletti and Stolle 2015, p. 479). The boycott, producing direct damage to the targeted economic enterprises, adapt to a situation in which multinational companies have growing power (according to the activists, even more power than many nation-states). The boycott of specific multinational companies follows this logic, also exploiting the importance of a clean image for firms that rely more on their logo than on the quality of their products. A similar tactic is used by online activists who mock international organizations by building fake websites in order to attract users looking for the official websites or create websites with similar names.

Also based on a logic of damage are distributed denial of service attacks – a main tool used by Anonymous to spread a political message (Barnard-Wills 2011). Anonymous represents an evolution in digital activist tactics (Ravetto-Biagioli 2013), operating at the intersection of trolling and political reaction against institutional practices perceived as limiting free speech – "I came for the lulz but stayed for the outrage," stated an Anon (Coleman 2011, p. 3). Its digital sit-ins (DoS – denial of service attacks) are "the cyberspace equivalent of a protest march that blocks access to a factory. ... Much like a sit-in at a lunch counter or government office, a DoS attack disrupts the public face of a target to draw attention to its actions and provoke a response" (Jarvis 2014, p. 338). Anonymous mobilizes for free access to information (Deseriis 2013, p. 34). Actions are often addressed against the websites and communication infrastructure of organizations that are accused of limiting access to information and information technologies. They have been in fact compared with the action of textile workers and weavers who, in the nineteenth century, destroyed weaving machinery as a form of protest against the use of new machinery to reduce workers' rights:

> While the Luddites destroyed the hardware of wide knitting frames, shearing frames, gig mills, and power looms, the hackers and activists affiliated with Anonymous hack passwords and firewalls, protected databases, and Internet filtering software. ... Such operations have both a political and an economic function. On a political level, they express an organized response of Internet users against all forms of restriction on the free circulation of information. Furthermore, by taking off-line symbolic targets such as the official websites of state institutions and hacking security firms, they expose the vulnerability of the corporate and state apparatus of control. On an economic level, such actions have the effect of devaluing classified information, proprietary data, and technologies.
>
> (Deseriis 2013, p. 34)

These forms of protest, although not as stigmatized as the violent ones are, have some shortcomings. For instance, the boycott is very much dependent on mass-media coverage in order to be effective in producing a "loss of face" (Vegh 2003; Gamson 2004, p. 258). Moreover, they have to be managed carefully in order to limit the risk of negative effects on the workers of boycotted firms or countries. Moreover, when practiced by individual citizens, unconnected to each other, boycotting may become solipsistic, and "a poor way to sustain a sense of injustice and indignation" (Jasper 1997, p. 265).

7.2.3   The Logic of Bearing Witness

Forms of protest that might be defined as based on a logic of bearing witness have developed alongside those based on the logic of numbers or the logic of inflicting damage, particularly since the 1970s. Such action is not designed to convince the public or decision makers that the protestors constitute a majority or a threat. Rather, it seeks to demonstrate a strong commitment to an objective deemed vital for humanity's future. This logic is perhaps most in accord with the concept of participatory democracy that is widespread among social movement activists (see Chapter 9). The right to influence decision-making processes comes from neither formal investiture nor intrinsic power but from force of commitment. In actions of this kind, activists are willing to run personal risks to demonstrate their convictions and reinforce the moral message being conveyed by their protest.

Bearing witness is expressed, in the first instance, through participation in actions that involve serious personal risks or cost. Civil disobedience, knowingly breaking what are considered to be unjust laws, rests on this logic. Typical actions of this type of repertoire have been the destruction of fields of genetically modified maize by the Confédération Paysanne, Greenpeace raids against whaling boats, the blockages of nuclear sites, but also episodes of passive resistance to police intervention. While attempting to penetrate "red zones" during countersummits, demonstrators in Prague, Gothenburg, and Genoa were perfecting what in Great Britain is called "pushing and shoving," namely the shoulder-to-shoulder pressing that police and strikers do in picket lines. Symbolic provocation is also crucial in the revival of civil disobedience in demonstrations against globalization. Part of the global justice movement, the Disobedients stage conflicts by covering their bodies with protective materials and using plastic shields to protect themselves against police batons, but they proceed with their hands up in the air as a sign of nonaggression. These techniques of civil disobedience have been adapted in the anti-austerity protests – for instance, in the days of action organized by Blockupy against the European Central Bank in Frankfurt, Germany. In many such actions, the risk of arrest testifies to the conviction that something had to be done about a decision considered profoundly unjust, even if this involved running very serious costs indeed.

A further characteristic of action based on the logic of bearing witness is its sensitivity to alternative values and culture. Conferences, journals, concerts, and documentaries have the task of educating the public to a different understanding of the world. Although in the majority of cases contemporary social movements seek to bring about political transformations, they share the conviction that reform cannot come from above. Changes in individual consciousness must accompany the transformation of political structures. This logic is especially visible in the consumer activism that indeed "challenges our sense that money and morality cannot be mixed" (Micheletti 2003, p. 3). Presenting consumption as a potentially political act, ethical consumerism stresses the central role of individuals in taking responsibility for the common goods in their everyday life. Boycotts of bad products, but also *buy*cotts of fair ones (environmentally friendly and solidaristic) as well as socially responsible investments are ways not only of resocializing wrongdoers and changing business activities, but also of practicing certain values (Follesdal 2004). As Micheletti (2003, p. 150) stresses, political consumerism defends a normative stance; "virtues should be embedded in market transactions. Democratic political consumerism is a virtue practicing activity." Moreover, it is a form of action that resonates with an individualized culture (Stolle and Hooghe 2004, p. 273), as "cosmopolitan citizens in global societies process their political choices increasingly in terms of how those choices affect their own lifestyles" (Bennett 2004a, p. 102). In sum, while consumer choice has long been a tool for activism (as, for example, in the anti-slavery movement in the 1700s), it has spread recently based on the belief that "these and other identified multi-leveled and complex problems (e.g., overfishing, deforestation, and climate change) might be dealt with and perhaps even solved if consumers globally are mobilized to put economic pressure on corporations and other institutions" (Micheletti and Stolle 2015, p. 479).

Political consumerism is defined as consumers' use of the market as an arena for politics in order to change institutional or market practices found to be ethically, environmentally, or politically objectionable. When people mobilize politically in the market and use their economic means to attempt to influence political matters they function as "citizen-consumers" applying citizen responsibility to private market transactions (Micheletti and Stolle 2015). As boycotts have shortcomings – damaging the workers and citizens of some firms or country – *buycotts* spread as an alternative, as deliberate choice of certain products over others. To spread political consumerism choices, consumer-oriented social movements often resort to culture jamming or adbusting, by changing the meaning of corporate advertising through artistic skills or through street performances. Lifestyle commitments imply committing one's lifestyle to some political principles, such as, voluntary simplicity, vegetarianism, veganism. As Micheletti and Stolle (2015, p. 481) observed, "These efforts can be said to form movements that not only promote new consumer lifestyles but also, implicitly if not explicitly, newer worldviews that challenge present-day political, social, economic, and cultural thinking and structures. They thereby affect diverse arenas of social life and, in so doing, create new solidarity networks."

The capacity of directly transmitting their message is a characteristic of forms of action that rely most heavily on the logic of bearing witness. Because they oppose the idea that the ends justify the means, contemporary social movements have sought forms of action that reflect the objective to be obtained as closely as possible. The attention paid to the immediate impact of symbols seeks to facilitate the diffusion of the social movement message in a situation where the media tends to report superficially: "If the message is embedded in the activity, then a report of the activity makes people think about the issue as well" (Rochon 1988, p. 120). "Guerrilla theater" and other uses of drama "embody preferred frames in the symbolism they used – in effect performing the frame through costume, props, puppets, and other visual images" (Gamson 2004, p. 253). The logic of bearing witness also leads to an accentuation of the emotional intensity of participation.

Volunteering is also a form of bearing witness, even if in a milder way. In this perspective, Anheier and Scherer noted:

For a long time, the research agendas for civil society, volunteering, and social movements have developed in parallel, and remained largely unconnected. Typically, seminal work on social movements rarely references seminal work on volunteering and civic engagement, and vice versa. This is at first surprising given the overlap in subject matter; but it is also understandable since all three fields have made great efforts to develop an interdisciplinary approach to highlight different aspects of social reality. Only more recently has a growing body of academic work emerged and begun to integrate these distinct literatures.

(2015, p. 494)

In particular, while volunteering has been mainly associated with engagements in *nonpolitical* forms in, e.g., as charities, neighborhood groups, fraternal organizations, sport or music groups, some of these groups also seek social change, so politicizing some issues. Also, beside service provision, voluntary work socialize to democratic practice, so that voluntarism often implies inherently political acts (Eliasoph 2013).

Bearing witness is also the basis of nonviolent techniques. In particular, civil resistance is shaped by Mohandas K. Gandhi's conclusion that oppression is most effectively countered with nonviolent means of struggle – in particular, *Satyagraha* ("clinging to the truth") as a spiritually inspired form of resistance. Civil resistance can be defined as "a form of contentious politics that eschews violent repertoires in favor of nonviolent ones. Unarmed mobilization can be employed against virtually any type of adversary, although the state usually features as the principal antagonist in most episodes of civil resistance" (Ritter 2015a, 468). It is "a technique of action by which the population can restrict and sever the sources of power of their rulers or other oppressors and mobilize their own power potential into effective power" (Sharp 2005, p. 39). Civil resistance is "neither passive nor conflict evading: civil resisters eschew violence, but they do not eschew conflict. Indeed, nonviolent resistance is intended precisely to be used in, or even to instigate, conflict situations" (Ritter 2015a, p. 469).

Nonviolent resistance has been considered as particularly effective. According to Erica Chenoweth and Maria Stephan (2011), who studied over 300 violent and nonviolent campaigns oriented to regime change, the end of foreign occupation, or secession, nonviolent resistance is "nearly twice as likely to achieve full or partial success as their violent counterparts" (Chenoweth and Stephan 2011, p. 7). In fact, civil resistance "facilitates the active participation of many more people than violent campaigns, thereby broadening the base of resistance and raising the costs to opponents of maintaining the status quo" (Chenoweth and Stephan 2011, pp. 10–11).

The success of nonviolent resistance is, however, linked to some specific political pre-conditions, such as available allies, characteristics of the armed force, and international contexts (Schock 2005; Sharon Erickson Nepstad 2011). Daniel Ritter (2015a; 2015b) suggests:

> *Authoritarian regimes that are well integrated into the Western political system of trade, aid, and military collaboration may eventually find themselves constrained by their rhetorical embrace of Western values, such as democracy and human rights when challenged nonviolently by domestic opposition coalitions. Trapped by its discursive, albeit hypocritical, espousal of democratic values, Western-aligned regimes cannot resort to repression without risking the external, and indirectly internal, support on which it depends. As a result they vacillate, which allows the revolutionary movement to grow until it becomes nearly impossible to control.*

(2015a, p. 471)

7.2.4 Prefiguration and Movements

Protest has a prefigurative character, enacting the future social relations social movements want to construct. As described in the incipit, the protest camps, as temporarily occupied spaces, assumed a central role in anti-austerity protests. Those who protested in Tahrir, Kasbah, Sol, Syntagma, or Zuccotti have not just criticized existing representative democracy as deeply corrupted, but also experimented with different models of democracy. In part, conceptions and practices of democracy were inspired by the participatory and deliberative models of previous citizens' mobilizations. In part, however, they also innovated on them, in a process of collective learning from detected weaknesses of those models in the past, and adaptation to new endogenous and exogenous challenges. In the protest wave mentioned in the incipit, the *acampada* – at the same time repertoire of protest and organizational form – represented a major democratic experiment, adopted and adapted from one context to the next.

If the social forums had been the democratic invention of the global justice movement of the previous decade, the *acampadas* represented in part an updating of those, but in part also a development oriented to overcome their perceived failures. Conceptions of participation from below, cherished by the progressive social movements, are in fact combined with a special attention to the creation of egalitarian and inclusive public spheres. With an emphasis on consensus, the *acampadas* refused associations privileging the participation of the persons – the citizens, the members of the community. From the relational point of view, whereas the social forum process was oriented to networking, the *acampadas* follow a more aggregative logic (Juris 2012). From the cognitive point of view, while the forum aimed at building political alternatives, the *acampadas* were more prefigurative.

Transparency, equality, and inclusivity are cherished as the camps are set in open-air space in order to enforce the public and transparent nature of the process. Meeting in public spaces also points at the inclusiveness of the process, and the refusal of delegates represents a further emphasis upon equality. With the occupation of the public squares, the Indignados movements stressed the open and transparent nature of their democratic model, as the very essence of parks and squares is public. Not only are Tahrir, Kasba, Puerta del Sol, and Syntagma open-air spaces, but they were also most important points of encounters for the citizens. Keeping the main site of protest in the open, the movements also put a special emphasis on the inclusivity of the process, aiming at involving the entire agora. Not only parties and unions, but also associations of different types were indeed unwelcome. The camps, in open air, enact a reclaiming of public spaces by the citizens. So, in Egypt, in a society characterized by gated communities for the rich and slums for the masses of poor, the encounters at Tahrir but also the painting of murals represented a reappropriation of public space, especially after 30 years of emergency law had prevented gatherings (Winegard 2012). The heterogeneity of the participants was mentioned with pride – 'people of different backgrounds, of different classes, just sitting together talking' (Gerbaudo 2012, p. 69).

In the camps, direct, unmediated democracy was often called for through the creation of spaces for "the people," or the "citizens." In Spain, Greece, or the United States, the assemblies took a central role for the elaboration of strategic and tactical decisions for the movement: from the creation of a general program, either specific claims or at least statements of intent, but even more for the everyday management of the camps (Nez 2011a). General assemblies often broke down into committees, which then reconvened within it, the spokes of the various commissions referring to the general assemblies. Commissions on topics such as communication, mutual respect, infrastructure, laws, and action coordinated working groups that worked through consensus. Liaison persons had to keep contacts between the various subgroups. Thousands of propositions were thus put forward and, in part, approved by consensus: on politics, economy, ecology, and education. On the model of the one in Puerta del Sol, all general assemblies in Madrid neighbourhoods operated as spaces that had to be "transparent, horizontal, where all persons can participate in an equal way" (Nez 2012, p. 84). In the United States as in Spain, "each camp quickly developed a few core institutions: if it was any size, at least there would be a free kitchen, medical tent, library, media/communication center where activists would cluster together with laptops, and information center for visitors and new arrivals" (Graeber 2012, 240). Inclusion, absolute and of all, is a main principle of the assemblies.

A main democratic formula, coming from the global justice movement but further elaborated in the anti-austerity protests, is the consensual method. While in previous movements direct democracy through consensus had been experimented with in spokes-councils, during the *acampadas* it was applied to the general assemblies, involving often hundreds of thousands of people. A consensual, horizontal decision-making process developed based on the continuous formation of small groups, which then reconvened in the larger assembly. According to David Graeber, "The process towards creative thinking is really the essence of the thing" (Graeber 2012, p. 23). Deliberation through consensus is in fact seen as an instrument against bureaucratization, but also against the routinization of the assembly and a way to build a community. While the global justice movement developed upon parties, with puppets and a carnival-like atmosphere, it was noted that "OWS, in contrast, is not a party, it's a community" (Graeber 2012, p. 240).

Democracy in the square was in fact defined as first of all inclusive and respectful of people's experiences. As Graeber (2012, p. 211) noted about OWS:

> *anyone who feels they have something relevant to say about a proposal ought to have their perspectives carefully considered. Everyone who has strong concerns or objections should have those concerns or objections taken into account and, if possible, addressed in the final form of the proposal. Anyone who feels a proposal violates a fundamental principle shared by the group should have the opportunity to veto ("block") the proposal.*

So, after someone made a proposal, the facilitator, after asking for clarifying questions, started to look for consensus. This process foresaw friendly amendments, temperature checks, hand signals (Graeber 2012, pp. 214–215). Consensus was thus assigned a deep meaning as capable of developing a truly collective thought, as very different from the sum of individual ideas.

In the *acampadas*, the aim was often stated as building a community through the prefiguration of different relations describing Occupy Boston, and citing an activist who talked about the "small slice of utopia we are creating," Juris (2012, 268) singled out some tactical, incubating, and infrastructural roles of the occupied free spaces: among the first were attracting media attention and inspiring participation; among the second, "providing a space for grassroots participatory democracy; ritual and community building, strategizing and action planning, public education and prefiguring alternative worlds that embody movement visions"; among the third, networking and coordination.

A similar prefigurative functioning has been noted in a form of action such as occupation. Widespread in various movements (from the labor movement with factory occupation to the student movements with the occupation of school and universities), occupation has been particularly relevant in the urban movements in the form of squatting – that is, the "appropriation of abandoned spaces... a partial attack on the unjust distribution of urban goods, but it is also a grassroots political intervention at the core of urban politics" (Martìnez 2013, p. 871). Miguel Martìnez says that squatters defy the "rules of the urban growth machine" for their own sake as well as to promote citizens' protests. Squattings nurture "a persistent *autonomous* and *radical* urban movement with a pragmatic orientation, although some institutional bonds and constraints can also play a significant role in its expansion" (Martìnez 2013, p. 870).

In several European cities, previously vacant buildings have been occupied for residential purposes, within a movement for housing rights, involving precarious workers, the unemployed, students, and different groups of migrants so developing "an effective form of welfare from below" (Mudu 2014, p. 158). In connection with them, occupied social centers have grown since the 1970s as "liberated spaces":

> *The properties are empty and disused large buildings, not previously used for housing (such as former factories, schools, theatres, cinemas, etc.), which are occupied by groups of radical/antagonist left-wing activists. Their aim is to self-manage political, social, and countercultural activities, practicing participatory and non-hierarchical modes of political and social relationships opposed to the logic of market, capitalism, and to public authorities. From these "liberated spaces," the occupants/activists often launch radical/antagonist political and social protest campaigns, addressed outside the squatted places towards the neighborhood where are located, the city, and the urban fabric, and the society at large. In fact, social centers cannot be considered only physical spaces, but also collective actors of the radical/antagonist left.*
>
> (Andretta, Piazza and Subirats 2015, pp. 208–209)

7.3   STRATEGIC OPTIONS AND PROTEST REPERTOIRES

Forms of protest, then, are extreme to different degrees and, most importantly, follow different types of logic. How and why is one form of protest chosen rather than another? A first answer can be sought in the complexity and multiplicity of the objectives protest is meant to achieve. Lipsky notes that "protest leaders must nurture and sustain an organization comprised of people with whom they may or may not share common values. They must articulate goals and choose strategies so as to maximize their public exposure through communications media. They must maximize the impact of third parties in the political conflict. Finally, they must try to maximize chances of success among those capable of granting goals" (Lipsky 1965, p. 163). As Rochon (1988, p. 109, emphasis added) observes in connection with the peace movement, "the ideal movement strategy is one that is *convincing* with respect to political authorities, *legitimate* with respect to potential supporters, *rewarding* with respect to those already active in the movement, and *novel* in the eyes of the mass media. These are not entirely compatible demands."

First, given that every action has an attached cost but can also be a benefit in and of itself (Hirschman 1982), it is important for social movements to find tactics that are also suitable for realizing internal aims. Many forms of protest "have profound effects on the group spirit of their participants," since "in the end, there is nothing as productive of solidarity as the experience of merging group purposes with the activities of everyday life" (Rochon 1998, p. 115). Protest action has an important internal function: creating that sense of collective identity that is a condition for action toward a common goal (Pizzorno 1993). In fact, "movement strategists are fully aware that at least some of their tactics must widen the pool of activists and develop 'solidarities,' rather than 'merely' having an impact on politicians" (Rochon 1998, p. 159). For the labor movement, strikes had more than a simply instrumental function (Fantasia 1989), and this is also true of occupations for the student movement (Ortoleva 1988), both reinforcing a sense of identity. Solidarity is born out of shared risks on the barricades: "As they faced off against hostile troops or national guardsmen, the defenders of a barricade came to know each other as comrades, developed a division of labor of fighters, builders and suppliers, and formed social networks that would bring their survivors together in future confrontations" (Tarrow 1994, p. 44). According to participants, one of the main benefits of the many transnational countersummits has been increasing mutual knowledge and understanding (Pianta 2001). In particular, the United Nations-sponsored intergovernmental summits on women's issues, environment, and poverty served as arenas for networking, frame-bridging, and protest training (for a review, Smith 2004, p. 322). Nonviolent direct action strengthens the feeling of belonging; "a community that is formed in the process of struggle is a very precious thing, and fulfills a lot of needs that are not met in daily life" (Epstein 1991, p. 8).

However, actions that strengthen internal solidarity do not always serve to create support outside the movement. Note that if protest leaders must favor more radical action in order to maintain rank-and-file support, these are precisely the kinds of action that risk alienating potential allies. Protest leaders must avoid action that is too extreme if they are to win over their target groups within the public, but in doing so they run the risk of losing the confidence of their protest constituency. Opinion polls have shown that the more peaceful and institutional a course of unconventional political action is (petitioning, for example) the greater the level of public approval. Approval falls where the action taken is direct, even if nonviolent, and is minimal where violent action is concerned (Barnes et al. 1979). If the protest on global justice sensitized the public opinion to the goals of the activists, their forms of protest were often criticized as too radical (della Porta, Andretta et al. 2006). Especially in relation to sympathetic governments, radical tactics risk being counterproductive (Cress and Snow 2000, pp. 1097–1098).

Similar problems develop in the relations between activists and the media, as the latter play an important role in determining the resonance given to, and therefore the effectiveness of, protest. Even though it is debatable to what extent protest events are first of all "newspaper demonstrations," i.e. oriented mainly on media coverage (Neveu 1999, p. 28 ff.), media are indeed the most obvious shaper of public sensitivity (Jasper 1997, p. 286). The success of protest action is undoubtedly related to the amount of media attention it receives, and this also affects the character of social movement organizations (Gitlin 1980).

As research on protest coverage has demonstrated (McCarthy, McPhail, and Smith 1996), in order to obtain media coverage, action must involve a great many people, utilize radical tactics, or be particularly innovative. It should be remembered that it is the content of the message transmitted as well as the quantity of publicity received that is important for a social movement. Journalists can be particularly demanding regarding protests. On the one hand, they demand "news," and therefore novelty; on the other, they tend to conform to accepted standards of "good taste" (see also Chapter 8). Though their obligation to the wider community may lead many journalists to sympathize with certain demands, they tend, nonetheless, to condemn extreme forms of action. On the other hand, more moderate action, although it might garner greater support, is rarely newsworthy. Thus, "Conformity to standards of news worthiness in political style, and knowledge of the prejudices and desires of the individuals who determine media coverage in political skills, represent crucial determinants of leadership effectiveness" (Lipsky 1965, p. 170). Successful movements are often those that are able to develop controversies in such a way that they are more newsworthy by using symbols and images that capture attention – "the secret of movement access to the media is to engage in colorful protest" (Rochon 1998, p. 180).

Beyond visibility, social movements have the problem of having their messages spread by media often more interested in scandals than information:

> One difficulty for political movements is that the media generally present images of their protest without any elaboration of the substantive issues involved. Demonstrations are described as large or small, well-behaved or unruly, a cross section of the populace or composed of fringe elements. But the issues that brought

the protestors together are presented in terms of one-line slogans, if at all. The problem is not so much one of political bias as it is a matter of the exacting criteria used by the media to determine what is newsworthy. Size, novelty, and militancy are newsworthy. Critical policy perspectives are not.

(Rochon 1988, p. 102)

In conclusion, for the most part social movements use forms of action that can be described as disruptive, seeking to influence elites through a demonstration of both force of numbers and activists' determination to succeed. At the same time, however, protest is concerned with building support. It must be innovative or newsworthy enough to echo in the mass media and, consequently, reach the wider public that social movements (as "active minorities") are seeking to convince of the justice and urgency of their cause. Forms of protest must therefore adapt as the occasion requires to the needs of potentially conflicting objectives, such as threatening elites and winning over the public (through the intervention of a third actor, the media, which has an agenda of its own).

In order to overcome these limitations, social movement organizations indeed try to hone their communicative skills and pay careful attention to communication campaigns, press conferences, and, especially, carefully written dossiers (for instance, on ecological associations, see della Porta and Diani 2004b). Moreover, movements develop their own media: labor movements had dailies and publishers; more recent movements have developed their own radio stations as well as websites (see Chapter 8).

The leaders of social movement organizations find themselves faced with a series of strategic dilemmas in choosing the form that protest should take. Any form of action needs to cover a plurality of sometimes contradictory objectives. In addition, strategic options are limited by a series of factors internal as well as external to protest itself. Material resources constrain strategic choices, but repertoires are not just instruments: they belong to, and represent, a movement culture, and are therefore linked to the activists' values. The aims, in this sense, do not fully justify the means, and much of the debate inside social movements about issues of repertoires does not only address their efficacy but also their meaning and symbolic value. Indeed, stressing the euphoria and pleasure involved in protest, James Jasper (1997, p. 237) observes that "tactics represent important routines, emotionally and morally salient in these people's lives."

The repertoire of action is finite, constrained in both time and space. The "technology" of protest evolves slowly, limited by the traditions handed down from one generation of activists to the next, and crystallized in institutions. The public march is a good example: although, as we saw, there have been changes in the rituals, it is still one of the principal forms of protest in the campaign against neoliberal globalization. Having developed out of the practice of electoral banqueting, the technique was slowly perfected and institutionalized by the elaboration of rituals and structures such as the closing rally and the stewarding of marches (Favre 1990).

Repertoires are the byproduct of everyday experiences: for instance, the barricades derived from the tradition of using chains in order to block access to neighborhoods at night or in moments of turmoil. As Traugott (1995, p. 47) writes of the "Day of the Barricades," a people's revolt against the French king Henri III, "The great innovation of 12 May 1588 was to fortify the line of demarcation represented by the chains and to use the barriers thus created to impede the movements of King Henri III's Royal Guards." The success of those first barricades contributed to keeping that form of action alive for more than four centuries.

Thus, repertoires are handed down, reproduced over time, because they are what people know how to do when they want to protest. The forms of action used in one protest campaign tend to be recycled in subsequent ones. The anti-Vietnam War movement in the United States adopted tactics that had earlier been used by civil rights campaigners. The youth movement in mid-1970s Italy inherited (in a radicalized form) the modes of protest used by the student movement of the late 1960s (della Porta 1995). The global justice movement mixed forms of nonviolent direct action developed by the peace movements with the large marches and petitions strategies coming from the nineteenth-century repertoire (Whittier 2004, p. 539).

In addition, the choice of tactics symbolically expresses proximity to previous movements. The adaptation of older forms of action legitimizes protest by referring to myths and heroes of the past, since "the use of standard protest forms also evokes past political movements whose struggles have long since been vindicated as just" (Rochon 1988, p. 110). For instance, protestors against the World Bank meeting in Washington in 2001 wore gas masks in order to refer to a history of police repression (Whittier 2004, p. 540). In the anti-austerity protests, demonstrators organized camps in symbolically relevant spaces (della Porta 2015a). Memory of previous protest is embedded in space and rituals (della Porta, Andretta et al. 2018) – a typical example is the importance of 1968 for future student protests (della Porta 2018a; Zamponi 2018).

Such references to the past are a constraint on social movements as well as a resource. In any given period, knowledge concerning "what is to be done" to protest against a decision by those holding power is limited, and this limits collective action: "The existing repertoire constrains collective action; far from the image we sometimes hold of mindless crowds, people tend to act within known limits, to innovate at the margins of the existing forms, and to miss many opportunities available to them in principle" (Tilly 1986, p. 390). Rooted in the shared countercultures, repertoires contain the options considered practicable, while excluding others: "These varieties of action constitute a repertoirc in something like the theatrical or musical sense of the word; but the repertoire in question resembles that of commedia dell'arte or jazz more than that of a strictly classical ensemble," Tilly wrote. "People know the general rules of performance more or less well and vary the performance to meet the purpose at hand" (Tilly 1986, p. 390).

These limitations on the range of protest forms are only part of the story: although some forms of action can be adapted to more than one situation, many others cannot. They divide, among other, along social-group lines: prisoners climb onto the roofs of jails; soldiers refuse rations; students organize "alternative" courses; the unemployed occupy a factory and start working. One of the most common forms of collective action taken today, the strike, was until recently considered a tactic adapted almost exclusively to the working class. In fact, repertoires depend to a great extent on the cultural and material resources available to particular groups. The most militant styles of action will be most widespread among those groups that face particular difficulty in obtaining material rewards and for whom symbolic gratification acts as a substitute. Moreover, the particular subcultures to which movements refer contribute to the creation of distinctive repertoires. Religious organizations, for example, employ and modify rituals typical of their faith. The peace movement is nonviolent because the use of violence is too close a reminder of the militarism they wish to condemn. Hackers look for forms of online protest that express their specific concerns about having free access to information (in particular, free software) and rights to privacy (Castells 2001, ch. 2; Jordan 2002). Finally, repertoires change from state to state: it is more common to build barricades in France than in Switzerland; on the other hand, direct democracy is resorted to more frequently in Switzerland than in France (Kriesi et al. 1995).

While the weight of tradition must be acknowledged, there is also innovation in protest as in other forms of action: "Contenders experiment constantly with new forms in the search for tactical advantage, but do so in small ways, at the edge of well-established actions. Few innovations endure beyond a single cluster of events; they endure chiefly when associated with a substantial new advantage for one or more actors" (Tilly 1986, p. 7). Forms of action initially restricted to particular actors (and condemned by others) become generalized: white-collar workers go on strike; shopkeepers block the streets. New tactics are constantly being created in order to meet media criteria of "newsworthiness." Particularly in phases when collective action is on the rise, given forms of action spread from one social group to another, and often from one country to another. The student movement brought sit-ins across the ocean to Europe. In the wake of a massive wave of labor mobilization in Italy in the late 1960s, the use of striking quickly became widespread among many different sections of the population. The global justice movement and later anti-austerity movements also adopted a series of protest forms that had originated in other traditions: vigils from religious groups, civil disobedience from the women's movement, and so on.

It should be added that socialization in protest tactics is not a matter of blind reflex but a critical learning process. Social movements are producers of knowledge, among others, on how to organize and protest (della Porta and Pavan 2017). Thus, not all forms of action carry over from one period to the next, one social group to another, or from one country to another. It is, above all, those considered successful or particularly well adapted to a movement's context or culture that are most easily transferred from one movement to the next (Soule 2004, p. 302). Protest forms that have proved unsuccessful have far less probability of surviving.

Beside success, however, different generations can develop different tastes for specific forms of action (Jasper 1997, p. 250). Interestingly enough, the ritual of marches has changed to adapt to modern (or "postmodern") times: from those intended to show unity and organization to more theatrical forms, emphasizing a colorful expression of diversity and subjectivity (Rucht 2003b). In recent demonstrations of the global justice movements and in anti-austerity protests, the younger cohorts of activists have transformed the images of marches with their more playful and spontaneous outlook.

Repertoires also emerge, and are transformed, in the course of physical and symbolic interactions. Changes take place in encounters with the authorities, in a series of reciprocal adjustments. Political violence, for example, is rarely adopted overnight or consciously. Rather, repeated clashes with police and political adversaries gradually, and almost imperceptibly, heighten extremism, leading to a justification for ever more violent forms of action. In Italy during the 1970s, extremist tactics emerged in the course of an escalation of the use of force during marches and demonstrations (della Porta 1995). The interventions of the police and *carabinieri* became increasingly determined, while extreme left and right groups clashed with ever more lethal weapons: stones, Molotov cocktails, tools, and eventually guns. Radicalization develops in a spiral of negative and unforeseen feedback. Those involved (particularly the police and demonstrators) interact, causing escalation through a series of vicious circles. In these situations, participants react according to their own worldview, gambling that the outcome will be as they expected. Their choices, however, are often based on erroneous calculations.

This circle of action and reaction becomes a routine until a more or less casual event (such as an accidental killing of a demonstrator or a police officer during low-intensity clashes) produces a qualitative leap in the level of violence (Neidhardt 1981). Violence does indeed have a relational component – deriving from interchanges between people – as interpersonal processes "promote, inhibit or channel collective violence and connect it with nonviolent politics" (Tilly 2003, p. 20). Protest does not always develop toward violence, however: waves of contention might follow different paths (Koopmans 2004, p. 29). A learning process on the part of both movement activists and the police defused the forms of conflict that had characterized the 1970s.

There is a further dimension (to be dealt with at greater length in the next chapter) that affects the strategic choices made by social movements. Lipsky noted that protest must be in a position to mobilize potential allies and influences elites. It is normal that the greater the possibility of widening their range of alliances, the greater the attention social movements will pay to the preferences of potential supporters. For the global justice movement, the support of many well-known and respected NGOs as well as prominent individuals both attracted media attention and often discouraged coercive intervention on the part of the police (Andretta, della Porta, Mosca, and Reiter 2002 and 2003).

7.4   PROTEST SPREADING IN TIME AND SPACE

The strategic choices made by social movements evolve over time and are the result of interaction between a number of different actors.

7.4.1   Cycles of Protest, Protest Waves, and Protest Campaigns

A concept, particularly useful for analyzing evolution over time, is the protest cycle. Though varying in dimension and duration, protest cycles have had a number of common characteristics in recent history:

> *a phase of heightened conflict and contention across the social system that includes: a rapid diffusion of collective action from more mobilized to less mobilized sectors; a quickened pace of innovation in the forms of contention; new or transformed collective action frames; a combination of organized and unorganized participation; and sequences of intensified interactions between challengers and authorities which can end in reform, repression and sometimes revolution.*

> (Tarrow 1994, p. 153)

If some scholars criticize the use of the concept of a cycle as seeming to imply a regular, "periodically recurrent sequence of phenomena" (Koopmans 2004, p. 21), they nevertheless confirm the unequal distribution of contention over time: "periods of relative quiet alternate with waves of intense mobilization that encompass large sections of societies, and quite often affect many societies simultaneously" (Koopmans 2004, p. 21).

Waves of protest are composed of interrelated campaigns – i.e. a series of interactions connected to each other from the thematic point of view and oriented towards a common aim (della Porta and Rucht 2002a and 2002b). Examples of campaigns are protests on abortion rights in the women's movements, or against the deployment of cruise and Pershing II missiles in the peace movement, or for "dropping the debt" of less-developed countries in the global justice movement. The global justice movement has indeed adopted the campaign as a formula that is particularly effective in linking heterogeneous social movements and movement organizations.

The concepts of cycles, waves, or campaigns all attempt to describe and explain periods of intensified protest. As in cultures and the economies, there is indeed a recurrent dynamic of ebb and flow in collective mobilization. In particular, by demonstrating the vulnerability of the authorities, the first movements to emerge lower the cost of collective action for other actors. In addition, the victories they obtain undermine the previous order of things, provoking countermobilization. Repeatedly, spin-off movements contributed to the mobilization of other groups, inventing new forms of action, enlarging the protest claims, and winning some concessions, but also pushing elites and countermovements to form law-and-order coalitions (della Porta 1998a). Mobilization develops in time,

> *from institutional conflict to enthusiastic peak to ultimate collapse. After gaining national attention and state response, they reached peaks of conflict that were marked by the presence of movement organizers who tried to diffuse the*

insurgencies to a broader public. As participation was channeled into organiza-
tions, the movements, or part of them, took a more political logic – engaging in
implicit bargaining with authorities. In each case, as the cycle wound down, the
initiative shifted to elites and parties.

(Tarrow 1994, p. 168)

This pattern has consequences for the repertoires of collective action. In the initial stages of protest, the most disruptive tactics are often to the fore. New actors invent new tactics as emerging collective identities require radical action (Pizzorno 1978). As the cycle of protest continues, the reaction of the authorities produces simultaneous processes of radicalization and institutionalization. Evolution in protest tactics, therefore, accompanies changes in the external environment:

When disruptive forms are first employed, they frighten antagonists with their
potential cost, shock onlookers, and worry elites concerned with public order.
But newspapers gradually begin to give less and less space to protests that would
have merited banner headlines when they first appeared on the streets. Repeating
the same form of collective action over and over reduces uncertainty and is
greeted with a smile or a yawn. Participants, at first enthused and invigorated by
their solidarity and ability to challenge authorities, become jaded or disillu-
sioned. The authorities, instead of calling out the troops or allowing the police to
wade into a crowd, infiltrate dissenting groups and separate leaders from fol-
lowers. Routinization follows hard upon disruption.

(Tarrow 1994, p. 118)

The analysis of protest cycles is particularly useful for an understanding of the development of political violence, frequently one (though not the only nor the most important) of protest's outcomes. In fact, the forms of violence used tend to vary according to the stage of the cycle. At the outset of protest, violent action is usually limited in its presence, small in scope, and unplanned. Typically, violence in these phases is an unforeseen result of direct action such as sit-ins or occupations. As protest develops, violent forms of action initially spread more slowly than nonviolent ones. They frequently take the form of clashes between demonstrators and police or counter-demonstrators. Starting out as occasional, such episodes, nonetheless, tend to be repeated and take on a ritual quality. During this process small groups begin to specialize in increasingly extreme tactics, build up an armory for such action, and occasionally go underground. The very presence of these groups accelerates the exodus of moderates from the movement, contributing to a demobilization that only the most violent groups escape (at least temporarily). The final stages of the cycle thus see both a process of institutionalization and a growing number of violent actions.

A glance at the development of the global justice movement would confirm at least some of these dynamics. The incubatory stages of mobilization were characterized by activity that concentrated prevalently on information campaigns and lobbying, with only a handful of symbolic demonstrations carried out by small activist networks. The movement extended beyond its initial base during this phase, mobilizing groups involved in earlier movements (the women's movement and the environmental movement, but also the labor movement) or in political parties and religious associations. Each of these actors contributed particular forms of action to a common repertoire: the feminist groups brought the practices of civil disobedience they had honed in the campaign to legalize abortion; the religious associations brought with them the gospels; the environmentalists the practice of nonviolent occupation they had previously used against nuclear power-station sites; the parties of the left mobilized a mass following and offered channels of communication with public institutions. Although the heterogeneity of the various constituencies involved inevitably led to disagreements over what forms of action should be adopted, this diversity enriched rather than hindered the movement's capacity for mobilization during its expansionary phase. After their initial indecision, governments reacted by ordering police intervention, particularly to suppress the attempts at blocking the sites of international summits. While remaining on the whole peaceful, nonviolent civil disobedience escalated on some occasions, above all when police reacted in a muscular fashion to attacks by fringe anarchist groups (della Porta, Peterson and Reiter 2006).

Each cycle broadens the repertoire of collective action. This was as true of the Warsaw Pact countries in the years around 1989 as it had been of the waves of protest that swept Europe and the United States in the 1930s and the 1960s. It is indeed especially at the peak of a wave of mobilization that citizens develop new forms of collective action. Sidney Tarrow notes: "The factory occupations that marked the French 1936 strikes were similar to the sit-down strikes of Flint and Akron; while the university occupations of Berlin, Turin and Paris in 1968 linked students to their American homologues." He continues: "As for Solidarity, its most striking feature would prove to be the roundtable discussions between Solidarity leaders and the government that foreshadowed the forms of negotiations that swept Eastern Europe in 1989" (Tarrow 1994, p. 167–168). The acampadas of the anti-austerity protests – which came to be known as Occupy – are a case in point.

7.4.2   The Cross-National Diffusion of Protest

Particularly relevant in the process of strategic adaptation is cross-national diffusion. More and more, ideas about forms of action (as well as ideology and organizational repertoires) travel cross-nationally. Like scientific or technological innovations, social movement ideas set in motion processes of diffusion: "Protest makers do not have to reinvent the wheel at each place and in each conflict ... They often find inspiration elsewhere in the ideas and tactics espoused and practiced by other activists" (McAdam and Rucht 1993, p. 58). Ideas concerning organizational structure, strategies of action, or definitions of the world "travel" from movement to movement, sector to sector, city to city, center to periphery, and, on occasion, periphery to center. Diffusion can be either direct or indirect depending on whether it comes about through unmediated contacts between movement members or is mediated by the mass media (Kriesi et al. 1995, p. 185). In addition, diffusion can come about through either unconscious or conscious imitation. In the past it has been claimed that collective behavior spread through "circular reactions," the responses of each individual reproducing the stimuli coming from his neighbor (Blumer 1951, p. 170), without much attempt by individual participants to evaluate the situation and rationally respond to it. However, since the 1970s it has been recognized that the "interpretative interactions," based on a conscious evaluation of the situations, underlying more institutional forms of political participation are also present in protest. More "interpretative" processes such as identification and imitation are also present alongside mechanisms such as suggestibility and circular reaction (Turner and Killian 1987). The greater awareness of the actors involved should favor, although it cannot automatically ensure, the success of mobilization.

Cross-national diffusion is not new. The student movement in the 1960s, the feminist movement in the 1970s, and the peace movement and the ecological movement in the 1980s are all examples of what have been called "global" movements, developing contemporaneously throughout the world and displaying significant similarities in different countries. Going further back in time, the revolutions of 1848 and the antislavery movement were collective phenomena that grew to cover more than one continent. However, it is also true that the process of diffusion does not involve all movements equally, nor is the exchange always symmetrical.

First, it is more likely that diffusion will take place between countries that are close together geographically as interactions tend to be strongest between neighboring countries. Geographical proximity is not always important, however. History also counts as it is more likely that diffusion will take place between movements from countries with a history of past interaction. Besides direct interaction itself, the "cultural understanding that social entities belong to a common social category [also] constructs a tie between them" (Strand and Meyer 1993, p. 490). Similarities in social and political structure must also be taken into account. Finally, the status of the "transmitting" country also has a certain importance. In fact, although there are exceptions, in the social movement sector as in others, moving from center to periphery, from the "first" to the developing world, brings a reduction in influence.

All of the characteristics just mentioned influence both the direct diffusion through personal interaction emphasized by the traditional literature, and the indirect diffusion by way of the media noted in more recent studies (Strand and Meyer 1993). As far as direct interaction is concerned, geographical proximity, historical interaction, and structural similarities all tend to be reflected in visions and norms that facilitate direct contacts between the activists of parallel movements. Unmediated exchanges are rendered more probable by the existence of cross-border associations, cultural exchange programs, linguistic knowledge, or even a common language.

The various levels of proximity discussed above also favor the development of more formal contacts and organized channels of communication. Relations will become more formal after personal contacts have permitted initial exchanges to take place and as the movements become increasingly structured. Diffusion of ideas can then take place through the translation of movement documents, the organization of international conferences, the creation of computer-mediated networks, and so on. It has been noted that in the 1960s, the process of diffusion between student movements was initiated through personal contacts, but that "once established, this identification enabled diffusion to take place via a variety of nonrelational channels. These channels included television, newspapers, and writings of both a scholarly and a radical nature" (McAdam and Rucht 1993, p. 71). Countersummits and supranational social forums are indeed praised by activists, especially as occasions for exchanging ideas and networking (Pianta 2002).

Geographical and cultural proximity is also important in producing functional equivalence, similarity in the situation of the "transmitting" and "adopting" movements being a factor in facilitating this process of diffusion. Furthermore, the same elements facilitate the social construction of that similarity, the definition of their situation as similar to that of the transmitter on the part of adopters (Strand and Meyer 1993). Regardless of actual similarities, the subjective perception of common circumstances leads to an idea being considered relevant and adopted. The passage of ideas from the American student movement (the transmitter) to its German counterpart (the adopter) was facilitated by the similarities in the definition of the collective identities of the two groups (McAdam and Rucht 1993). Similarly, appeal to global identities facilitates cross-national campaigns against neoliberal globalization (della Porta, Andretta et al. 2006).

The traditions of particular movements also help to explain a greater or lesser propensity to exchange information and to "copy" each other at the international level. Despite appeals to internationalism, for example, the conviction that their destinies were more closely linked to those of capitalists in their own country than they were to workers in other countries appears to have prevailed in national labor movements for a long time. Environmentalist groups, on the other hand, have always been conscious of the difficulties in providing national solutions to environmental problems, which spread from country to country by way of polluted rivers and air. The rich and various repertoire of action of the global justice movement is indeed the product of enhanced occasions for transnational encounters.

Recent protests across the world also maintained a transnational stance, but national governments and policies seem to be the first target. Even though the financial crisis the movements react to is one and global, its timing and dynamics varied across countries. Protests followed the geography of the emergence of the economic crisis, which hit with different strength and in different times national economies. Even if protests kept a strong link to their national context, there is no doubt that since the end of 2010 mobilizations flourished in a number of countries that shared some characteristics at the level of both protest visions and protest practices (della Porta and Mattoni 2014).

Despite a substantial focus on the national level of mobilization, processes of diffusion were at work in the recent wave of protest. Research, indeed, has already singled out numerous examples of cross-national diffusion of frames and repertoires of action from one country to the next. Both direct, face-to-face contacts and mediated ones have contributed to bridge the protest in various parts of the world. Direct forms of diffusion seemed to have been more relevant within some geopolitical areas: Egyptian activists learned from Tunisians, thanks also to some direct conflicts. Spanish Indignados were in direct contacts with Greek activists, and also very relevant in steering the Occupying movement (Romanos 2014). Across more distant areas, various means of communication helped a quick information exchange and mutual learning, especially between social movement cultures that shared some common roots (Roos and Oikonomakis 2014). In some occasions, global protests took place that certainly had a transnational dimension. For instance, in October 15, 2011, a Global Day of Action launched by the Spanish Indignados produced demonstrations worldwide: protest events were registered in 951 cities in 82 countries. The forms of transnational brokerage in the newest social movements emerged as, if not weaker, at least different: they indeed seem more grassroots, less embedded in formal social movement organizations, and resting more on connections through social networking sites, participatory web platforms, and to some extent micro-blogging spheres.

7.5 EVENTFUL PROTEST

In a recent essay on Tilly's contribution to research on repertoires of protest, Tarrow (2008, p. 226) described his initial work as moved by a "structuralist persuasion." Tilly (2008, p. 2) himself commented that "in those distant days," "method meant statistical analysis," and explanation "ignores transformative processes." Even if focusing on normal, everyday events, in later work Tilly stressed more and more eventful histories over event-counting. Explaining the evolution of repertoires of protest, he moreover added to external circumstances (among which regime and opportunity structures), also the history of contentious politics itself (Tilly 2008). In a similar vein, concepts such as transformative events or "eventful protest" have been coined to stress the effects of protest on the social movements and the activists themselves. Protest events tend in fact to fuel mechanisms of social change: during protests, organizational networks develop; frames are bridged; personal links foster reciprocal trust. Especially during some protest events, collective experiences develop through the interactions of different individual and collective actors, which with different roles and aims take part in them (della Porta 2008).

In his work on the history of the French labor movement in the eighteenth and nineteenth centuries, William H. Sewell (1996) defined the concept of *eventful temporality*. Differently from teleological temporality, that explains events on the basis of abstract trans-historical processes "from less to more" (urbanization, industrialization, etc.), and from "experimental temporality," comparing different historical paths (revolution versus non-revolution, democracy versus non-democracy), "*Eventful temporality* recognizes the power of events in history" (Sewell 1996, p. 262). According to Sewell, events are a "relatively rare subclass of happenings that *significantly transform structure*"; an eventful conception of temporality is "one that takes into account the transformation of structures by events" (Sewell 1996,

p. 268). Events have transformative effects in so far as they "transform structures largely by constituting and empowering new groups of actors or by re-empowering existing groups in new ways" (Sewell 1996, p. 271). Some protest events put in motion social processes that "are inherently contingent, discontinuous and open ended" (Sewell 1996, p. 272).

With reference to eventful temporality, the concept of *transformative events* has been developed to single out events with a high symbolic (and not only) impact. As McAdam and Sewell observed:

> *No narrative account of a social movement or revolution can leave out events (...). But the study of social movements or revolutions – at least as normally carried out by sociologists or political scientists – has rarely paid analytic attention to the contingent features and causal significance of particular contentious events such as these.*

> (2001, p. 101)

The two scholars therefore called for analysis of the ways in which events "become turning points in structural change, concentrated moments of political and cultural creativity when the logic of historical development is reconfigured by human action but by no means abolished" (McAdam and Sewell 2001, p. 102).

Moments of concentrated transformations have been singled out especially in those highly visible events that end up symbolizing entire social movements – such as the taking of the Bastille for the French Revolution or the Montgomery bus boycott for the US civil rights movement. It is particularly during protest cycles that some events (e.g. the contestation of the Iran shah in Berlin in 1967, or the Battle of Valle Giulia in Rome in 1968) remain impressed in the memory of the activists as emotionally charged events, but also represent important turning points in the evolution of the organizational structures and strategies of the movements (della Porta 2018a; Zamponi 2018). The history of each movement and of contentious politics in each country always includes some particularly eventful protests.

In the conception of *eventful protest*, della Porta (2008) puts the focus on the internal dynamics and transformative capacity of protest, looking however at a broader range of events than those included under the label of transformative event. Her assumption is that protests have cognitive, affective, and relational impacts on the very movements that carry them out. Through protest events, new tactics are experimented with, signals about the possibility of collective action are sent (Morris 2000), feelings of solidarity are created, organizational networks are consolidated, and sometimes public outrage at repression is developed (Hess and Martin 2006). Protest is, therefore, in part at least, a byproduct of protest itself, as conflicts do produce social capital, collective identity, and knowledge, that is then used to mount collective mobilization. What makes protest *eventful* are *cognitive* mechanisms, with protest as an arena of debate; *relational* mechanisms, that brings about protest networks; and *emotional* mechanisms, through the development of feelings of solidarity "in action" (della Porta 2013; della Porta 2015a). Although protest is used every day by the most varied people, it is still a type of event that tends to produce effects, not only on the public authorities or public opinion but also (possibly mainly) on the movement actors themselves. These effects are all the more visible in some specific forms of protest that require long preparatory processes, in which different groups come together (e.g. transnational campaigns), stress the relevance of communication (e.g. social forums), and are particularly intense from the emotional point of view (e.g. symbolic and physical struggles around the occupied sites). These kinds of protest are especially eventful, as they have a very relevant cognitive, relational and emotional impact on participants and beyond participants. Long-lasting events (such as the protest camps of the anti-austerity movement), inclusive communicative arenas, and free-spaces are forms of protest that seem particularly apt to create relational, cognitive and emotional effects on protestors. The transnational character of recent protest, as well as the internal heterogeneity of recent waves of mobilization (with "movement of movements" as its self-definition), have added values to the relevance of those relational, cognitive, and affective mechanisms that make protest eventful.

7.6 SUMMARY

This chapter has been dedicated to the analysis of the principal forms of action adopted by social movements; in other words, to forms of protest. Protest has been defined as nonroutinized action in which indirect channels of influence are opened through the activity of a series of collective actors. Although protest forms are so widespread that it would be difficult to define them as unconventional, it is still true that protest goes beyond the routinized forms of participation in representative democracy. It has been said that the tactics used by social movements form repertoires with specific characteristics. In particular, a repertoire of national, autonomous, and modular forms of protest has developed since the nineteenth century. More recent transformations in both the distribution of power at national and international level and in the structure of mass communications are reflected in the development of new forms of protest such as countersummits and transnational boycotts, as well as in internet protest actions. In distinguishing in this chapter between the various forms of protest, the fact that different logics of action were simultaneously present in each repertoire was stressed: the logic of numbers, which seeks to display the strength of support for a movement; the logic of material damage, based on the capacity to interrupt everyday routine; and the logic of bearing witness, which seeks to demonstrate the emotional commitment of protestors.

Social movement leaders face a series of strategic dilemmas in choosing one or another form of action, because each sends messages to different publics with different demands: the movement activists who seek to reinforce internal solidarity; the media, in search of "news"; potential allies, who prefer more moderate forms of action; and, finally, decision makers, who seek partners whom they can trust. However, repertoires of actions are not just instruments of protest but also reflect the activists' values. Historical traditions fostered through institutions and socialization limit the range of options that can be considered, but forms of protest travel from one movement to the other and from one country to the other, with frequent innovation and learning processes. Additionally, repertoires are produced via relational mechanisms, during interactions between various (movement and nonmovement) actors. Series of cyclical dynamics create a succession of waves and cycles in protest, and radicalization and institutionalization in the forms of action adopted. Protest are eventful also in the sense that they produce new relations, frames and repertoires in the protest arenas.

CHAPTER 8

Political Opportunities for Social Movements

In Latin America, a wave of left-wing electoral victories started with the election of Hugo Chávez in Venezuela in 1998, continuing with those of socialist Ricardo Lago in 2000 in Chile; of Workers" Party leader Lula da Silva in 2002 in Brazil; left Peronist Néstor Kirchner in 2003 in Argentina; Tabarè Vasquez of Broad Front in 2004 in Uruguay, MAS" Morales in 2005 in Bolivia, and Rafael Correa in 2006 in Ecuador (Levitsky and Roberts 2011a). Long-term causes for these victories included massive waves of protest against increasing inequality and severe poverty, notwithstanding growth, with particularly devastating effects during the economic crisis of 1998–2002. In this process, movement parties were formed and alliances between movements and parties intensified.

While all of these leaders and their parties had in common the promise to reduce extremely high levels of inequality, there were notable differences between the institutionalized left-wing parties in countries such as Brazil, Chile, and Uruguay and the so-called populist left of Chávez in Venezuela, with Argentina, Bolivia, and Ecuador in between. The societal resistance to austerity policies found, in fact, different forms of expression in the different Latin American countries: from social movement protests – using forms such as strikes and demonstrations, but also riots, highway

Social Movements: An Introduction, Third Edition. Donatella della Porta and Mario Diani.
© 2020 John Wiley & Sons Ltd. Published 2020 by John Wiley & Sons Ltd.

blockages, and occupations of land or public buildings – to electoral ones, either through support to the left-wing opposition or
through the emergence of new parties on the left. The different
forms of resistance were influenced by the political alignments as
well as the institutional outcomes of neoliberalism. In particular,
the countries that saw the most explosive patterns of social protest (especially Venezuela, Argentina, Bolivia, and Ecuador) were
characterized by bait-and-switch market reform that had the
effects of de-aligning the party systems, triggering reactive
sequences, which went from partial decomposition of the party
system to the rise of new parties. In fact, "The political expression
of societal resistance was quite different where conservatives
imposed market reforms over staunch leftist opposition and critical junctures left in place party systems that were both institutionalized and programmatically aligned – the outcome of contested
liberalism. Under contested liberalism, societal resistance could be
channelled toward established parties of the left, thus weakening
anti-systemic forms of social or electoral protest. This outcome
moderated the reactive sequences of the aftermath period, which
largely consisted of the progressive electoral strengthening of
these institutionalized leftist or center-left parties" (Roberts 2015,
pp. 61–62). Whilst in Brazil, Chile, and Uruguay, it was the center
right that pushed for neoliberalism, with center-left parties
remaining in opposition (with Peronist groups switching in power
in Argentina), in Venezuela, Bolivia, and Ecuador there was
instead a mass protest against the neoliberal process seen as
embraced by all established parties, and these protests triggered
the emergence of new parties when they destabilized the existing
party system.

   The interactions between movements and left-wing parties then
influenced their paths to power and the policy orientations of the
latter when in government. While Venezuela moved toward the
most statist policy, Argentina, Bolivia, and Ecuador adopted hetero-
dox policies and Uruguay, Chile, and Brazil tended toward neoliberalism even if in a rather social-democratic form, with adoption of
some redistributive social policies (Pribble and Huber 2011). In
parallel, promotion of citizens" participation and plebiscitarian
appeals to direct popular majority have been especially present in

Bolivia, Ecuador, and Venezuela, with only Chávez pushing for more radical democracy, while Brazil and Uruguay moved toward corporatist relations with interest groups. Once in power, left-wing parties became in general more and more divided on the role of participatory democracy, with overall a fading of initial radical democratic principles, substituted by "revamped versions of societal corporativism" (Goldfrank 2011, p. 163), as well as difficulty in addressing the new challenges in terms of citizenship rights, in particular, on security and identity issues (Yashar 2011).

In general, while the older left parties tended to abandon state interventionist policies, the emerging left-wing movements grew at a time of widespread discontent with neoliberal policies (Madrid 2009). In Brazil, Chile, and Uruguay, Marxist parties – which had been strongly repressed under dictatorship, were founded before the democratization but had institutionalized afterwords, with control of various societal organizations, and access to government through routine alternation – tended to maintain a liberal democratic orientation and programmatic moderation. Differently, an outsider path characterizes parties that emerged after democratization that did not consider the democratic regime as an effect of their struggles, and mobilized against the entire party system. Quickly achieving power in the collapse of the party system, they aimed at a plebiscitarian refoundation (Levitsky and Roberts 2011b).

When looking at recent developments in Latin America, Bolivia emerges as the case in which a proper movement party developed. At the origins of the Movement for Socialism (Movimiento al Socialismo – MAS), "there was little difference between the coca growers'/campesinos movement and the party – the latter was merely the political instrument of the former" (Van Cott 2008, p. 103). Not only did MAS, as a new party, emerge from within social movements, but social movements also remained influent even after the party achieved power. In fact, Morales' leadership was rooted in social movements that had promoted participatory organizational models. In particular, a strong social movement on indigenous rights as well as a large potential community have been considered as important preconditions for MAS" rise. With Bolivia having the highest proportion of indigenous people in Latin America

(62 per cent), the emergence of the MAS was triggered by social movements that were able to overcome the traditional conflicts between the more politicized Aymara in the highlands and the Quechua in the lowlands. Since the mid-1980s, the weakening of the left-wing parties that had traditionally defended indigenous rights, face to austerity, provided the indigenous movements with experienced leaders as well as inclusive frames. Beginning in the mid-1990s, networking was strengthened in the organization of massive Marches for Sovereignty and Dignity, while in the same period the constitutional process catalysed the attention of the indigenous organization.

In particular, the formation of the MAS came out of the very strong movement of coca growers (cocaleros), which mobilized against the eradication policies required by the United States, and the capacity of its leaders – especially Evo Morales – to bridge anti-neoliberal and ethnic calls. Coca growers were in fact particularly successful in Bolivia, in both organizing and developing a dynamic formation of collective identity that addressed the specific challenge of defending a questionable good. This was facilitated by deep-rooted acceptance of coca use in Bolivia, where its criminalization, under pressure from the United States, happened later than in other countries. As the economic crisis, especially after the collapse of mining, made Bolivia more and more dependent on coca – also spreading corruption – miners relocated as coca growers, bringing new resources of militancy to their already rooted union. Low state repression in the 1980s as well as the tradition of structured relations between the peasants and the state under the left-wing military regime also facilitated mobilization, as the coca growers bridged their identity as peasants producing coca with a syndicalist identity, pushing for a politicization of ethnic identities (Ochoa 2014). In a 2002 MAS document, titled "Our ideological principle," reference is in fact made to the failure of internal colonialism and of the left, championing the potential of indigenous culture (Ochoa 2014). In its evolution, MAS was then able to rely upon broader networks of social movements, in the countryside but also in the cities (Anria 2018; della Porta 2020).

As this short account on Latin America recent political developments indicates, social movements interact with political systems, that they influence and are influenced by. As noted in earlier chapters, ideology, repertoires, and structures constitute material and cultural resources for action, which vary from country to country. In attempting to select the most influential of the many determinants of collective action, quite a number of comparative analyses of social movements have concentrated on political variables. It has already been noted that the activities of social movements are in part expressive; in part instrumental; in part directed at their own members; in part designed to transform the external environment. In their protest activities, however, social movements are eminently political.

What follows will seek to identify the main characteristics of the political system and suggest some reflections on the way in which they influence particular character- istics of social movements. As was noted in the introductory chapter, the concept of political opportunity structure has become central to interpretations of interaction between institutional and noninstitutional actors. A problem in the research on political opportunities is a lack of clarity concerning the explanandum as political characteristics have been investigated in order to explain a large number of movement characteristics, ranging from social movement mobilization (Eisinger 1973), to the emergence of the protest cycle (Tarrow 1983), the relationship between allies" atti- tudes and movement behavior (della Porta and Rucht 1995), and the predominance of either confrontational or assimilative protest strategies (Kitschelt 1986, pp. 67–68). Few attempts have been made, however, to address the question of which variables in the complex set of political opportunities, explain which (of the numerous) character- istics of social movements. In what follows, we shall try to single out the specific effects of specific opportunities on emergence of movements, levels of mobilization, protest repertoires, and chances of success. Additionally, political opportunities have been seen as a set of structures conditioning collective action, diverting attention from the dynamic interactions of various actors within long lasting processes, with several players acting within complex fields of action. Social movements interact with other societal actors, that work sometimes as opponents and sometimes as supporters. Indeed, as already noted, among the first definitions of the political opportunity struc- ture were those looking at changes that could cause sudden ruptures in the system. Attention has therefore concentrated on aspects such as electoral instability or elite divisions (see, e.g., Piven and Cloward 1977; Tarrow 1989).

Social movements move in a multi-organizational field, interacting with a variety of other actors. They find both allies and opponents within the public administration, the party system, interest groups, and civil society. During a cycle of protest, social movement organizations, political parties, interest groups, and voluntary associations frequently enter into relations of conflict or cooperation on both specific issues and the more general one concerning the right to protest. Many actors, including institu- tional actors, become involved in protest campaigns on particular demands such as peace or abortion, but coalitions also form on the issue of "law and order" on the one side, and "civil rights" on the other (della Porta 1998a).

In fact, institutional factors are mediated by two intervening sets of variables: the alliance structure and the opposition structure. Considering the field of action within which social movements move, the alliance structure can be defined as composed by those political actors who support them; the opposition structure as composed by those political actors who are against them (della Porta and Rucht 1995). Alliances provide resources and political opportunities for challengers; opposition erodes them. Institutional actors (such as political parties and interest groups) and other social movements can be found on both sides. The configuration of power – that is, the distribution of power among the various actors operating within the party or interest group system – will influence the result of the conflicts (Kriesi 1989b). While it is elections that determine whether the party allies or opponents of a social movement will be in power, the attitudes of the various actors mentioned above are influenced by other factors.

Reviewing research and theorization on the political context for protests, this chapter begins with an analysis of institutional opportunities (8.1) as well as prevailing strategies (8.2), turning then to role of opponents (with particular attention to the policing of protest) and allies (especially within the party system) (8.3 and 8.4, respectively). As we shall stress, political opportunities are far from structural, in the sense of both immutable and "given": not only are their effects filtered through the activists' perceptions, as opportunities are appropriated by movement activists, but moreover they interact with discursive opportunities (8.5).

8.1   POLITICAL INSTITUTIONS AND SOCIAL MOVEMENTS

Largely embedded in nation-states, political institutions at various levels are targets and arenas of social movements. As Mark Beissinger (2015, p. 595) recently noted:

> *Of the variety of large-scale structural influences on contentious collective action, the state is often considered among the most consequential. The reasons are multiple and fundamental. Given their defining claim to supremacy in binding rule making within the territories under their authority, states naturally become arenas within which collective action flows. No other authority is made to bear such direct responsibility for the conditions under which we live, nor is thought to possess such means for altering those conditions.*

This is in fact true not only of the more politically oriented movements, but also of those aiming at cultural changes. If states are target of resistance, they are also main arenas for contentious politics. Given their coercive power but also interstitial power (as capacity to penetrate everyday life), state shape their societies:

> *The repressive, material, and regulatory capacities of states and how these are wielded are widely considered among the most important factors shaping mobilization. But states also have more subtle means for influencing collective action*

through their control over public imaginations. Through their enormous powers to socialize, normalize, and mobilize affect, states can define and constrain how individuals understand themselves and pursue their interests, shaping collective action in constitutive ways.

(Beissinger 2015, p. 596)

Of course, the capacity of states to exercise power within and outside of their border varies enormously and so do the political regimes that define the procedures to access state power (Munk 2001, p. 123). While movements are certainly relevant also in authoritarian regimes, social movement studies have mainly focused on democracies. In particular, Alexis de Tocqueville's famous contrast between the "weak" American government and the 'strong" French government is usually an implicit or explicit starting point for analyses that links institutional factors and social movement development (Kriesi 2004, p. 71). Postulating an opposition between state and civil society, Tocqueville considered that a system in which the state was weak and civil society strong (the United States) would face a constant but peaceful flux of protest from below. Where the state was strong and civil society weak (France), episodic and violent revolt would result instead.

Sidney Tarrow (1994, pp. 62–65) has convincingly criticized this hypothesis, claiming that Tocqueville's analysis was partial even in respect of the historical situation to which the author referred. Not only does the US Civil War raise doubts about the capacity of a "weak" state to integrate conflicting interests, but also recent studies of the French Revolution have demonstrated the existence of a very robust civil society in that country. In both countries, the state and the rights of its citizens grew in steps: conscription mobilized citizens as soldiers, stimulating new demands; the unified fiscal system created a single target for protest; conflict within the elites pushed the various parties involved to appeal to public opinion, extending the franchise; the means of communication built by the state were also used by challengers; new forms of aggregation and expression were legitimized by elections; and the creation of new administrative units led to the creation of new collective identities (Tarrow 2015).

If Tocqueville appears to have exaggerated the characteristics of both France and the United States in order to construct a dichotomy between the "good" and the "bad" state, the idea that the strength or weakness of states influence social movement strategies remains central to the literature on collective action in general and on revolutions in particular. This approach, "*à la* Tocqueville," has frequently been linked to the assumption that a large number of points of access to the political system are an indication of openness. As Hanspeter Kriesi (2015, pp. 668–669) noted, following political scientist Arend Lijphart's (1999) distinction between majoritarian and consensus democracies, a main criterion for classification of institutional opportunities is the concentration of political power:

Majoritarian democracies concentrate political power, while consensus democracies divide it. Lijphart's scheme uses two dimensions for summarizing how power is divided – the "executive–parties" dimension and the "federalism–centralism" dimension. For our purposes, his "executive–parties" dimension is more important. It is characterized by five aspects: the number of parties (two-party systems vs multiparty systems), the electoral system (majority and plurality methods vs proportional representation), the concentration of power in the cabinet (single party vs coalition governments), the executive–legislative relations (dominance by the executive vs balance between the two), and interest group arrangements (pluralism vs corporatism). The dimension mixes formal, institutional, and informal power arrangements, but the resulting pattern in a given country is ultimately driven by the electoral system.

Many case studies that use categories that refer to the power of the state focus on the central executive. In general, an institutional system has been considered more open (and less repressive) the more political decisions are dispersed. The prevalent belief is that the greater the number of actors who share political power (the greater therefore the institutional checks and balances), the greater the chance that social movements gain access to the system. However, while a weak executive may ease access to the decision-making process, it will have less capacity of implementing policies to meet social movement demands. Hypotheses concerning the effects of institutional variables on the evolution of social movements cover three main areas: territorial decentralization of power, functional dispersal of power, and the extent of power in the hands of the state (Kitschelt 1986, pp. 61–64; Rucht 1994, pp. 303–312; Kriesi 1995).

As for territorial decentralization, a basic suggestion is that the more power is distributed to the periphery (local or regional government, states within a federal structure), the greater the possibility for individual movements to access the decision-making process. The nearer an administrative unit is to ordinary citizens, the easier it will be to gain access. Thus, all else being equal, the greater the degree of power passed from the national government to the regions, from the regions to the cities, from the cities to local neighborhoods, the greater the sensitivity of the political system to pressure from below. Following the same logic, federal states are considered more open than centralist ones (see, for example, Kitschelt 1986; Kriesi 1995; Giugni 1996). In fact, decentralization of power to regional and local bodies often increases the opportunities for social movements mobilizing at the local level. As research in, for instance, Italy and France indicates (see, respectively, della Porta and Andretta 2002; della Porta 2004c; della Porta and Pianta 2008), citizens' committees protesting against the construction of infrastructure for high-speed trains or hazardous waste significantly increase their chances of victory when they can ally themselves with influential local administrators. The same was true for the massive movements against the privatization of water supply in Bolivia (Anria 2018).

As far as the functional separation of powers is concerned, the institutional system can be broadly considered more open the greater the division of tasks between legislature, executive, and judiciary. Moreover, looking at each of these powers separately, the greater the autonomy of individual actors the more numerous will be the channels of access to the system. In the first place, the parliamentary arena has been considered more open the greater the number of seats assigned by proportional representation, so increasing the possibilities for access by a variety of actors (see, e.g., Amenta and Young 1999). From the general proposition that a higher number of autonomous actors equals greater openness of the system, it follows that, as far as the characteristics of the executive are concerned, the possibilities for access will be fewer in a presidential system than in a parliamentary one because there are fewer decision-makers. In the arena of government, it can generally be expected that elite attitudes to challengers will depend on whether the government is homogeneous or a coalition. The more fragmented the government or the greater the number of parties that compose it, the easier it will be to find allies, although the chances of actually implementing policies will be fewer. Cultural variables such as traditions of loyalty to the leadership or personalistic divisions within parties and the prevalence of individualistic or collective mediation of consensus also influence government stability and compactness. The openness of the system to pressure from below should also increase in proportion to the power of elected organs.

The characteristics of the public bureaucracy also influence social movements. Kriesi et al. (1995, p. 31) note that "the greater the amount of resources at its disposal, and the greater the degree of its coherence, internal coordination and professionalization, the stronger it will be. Lack of resources, structural fragmentation, lack of internal coordination and of professionalization, multiply the points of access and make the administration dependent on its private interlocutors in the system of interest-intermediation." A further element of relevance for the functional distribution of power is the autonomy and powers of the judiciary. A strong judicial power can intervene in both legislative and executive functions, as when the Constitutional Court or the magistracy become involved in legal controversies between social movements, their adversary, and state institutions. The greater the independence of the judiciary, the greater the possibility of access for social movements.

The last matter to be dealt with concerns the overall amount of power in the hands of the state, as compared with other actors such as pressure groups, political parties, the media, and ordinary citizens. For example, returning to public administration, the possibility of outside intervention varies a great deal from state to state. In general, where public administration is rooted in Roman law, which rejects external contacts, there tends to be greater resistance to pressure from noninstitutional actors (not simply social movements but political parties also). The Anglo-Saxon model of public administration, on the other hand, with more numerous channels of access for noninstitutional actors, tends to be more open. In this respect, the institutional structure of political opportunity will be more open (and the state weaker) where citizens maintain the possibility of intervening with the legislature and executive independently of mediation through political parties, interest groups, or bureaucrats. The greater the degree of citizens' participation through referendums for the proposition or abrogation of particular measures and the procedures for appealing against the decisions of the public administration, the more open the system.

Since the 1990s, the general trends in the evolution of political institutions has been somehow contradictory in terms of the openness/closedness of political opportunities. Devolution at the subnational levels and a growing autonomy of the judiciary have certainly increased access to public decision making. However, the shift of competencies from legislative assemblies to administrations has made decision-making processes less transparent and decision makers less accountable to the electorate. The neoliberal trend in capitalism in the 1990s significantly reduced the space for political intervention. The privatization of public services and the deregulation of the labor market have in fact limited the possibilities for citizens and workers to exert pressure via political channels. The Bolivian case cited in the incipit, but also more in general the revival of the left in Latin America, build, however, on the capacity of social movements and parties to mobilize grievances around extreme and increasing inequality and to channel social mobilization into the party system (Roberts 2015; della Porta, Fernandez et al. 2017).

More importantly, movements face a shift in the locus of power from the national to the supranational level (see also Chapter 2), with increased power wielded by a number of international organizations – especially financial organizations (WB, IMF, WTO) but also macroregional organizations (first and foremost the EU). International governmental organizations have facilitated economic globalization, through policies liberalizing trade and the movement of capital, while attempting to govern processes that cannot be addressed exclusively at the national level. In this sense, globalization has not just weakened the power of politics over economics, but has also generated transnational conflicts on the policies of international institutions, producing different results depending on the organization and field of intervention involved. In particular, opposition has arisen to the neoliberalist policies of the so-called international financial institutions that wield strong coercive power through the threat of economic sanctions and conditionalities on international credit. More generally, parallel to the acquisition of power by these largely nonrepresentative, nontransparent bodies, criticism has centered on their manifest deficit of democracy, in particular in terms of electoral accountability.

The financial crisis of the years 2000s has further increased these trends, fueling a democratic crisis, which can be defined as a crisis of responsibility as political institutions gave away their competences and, with them, the potential to protect citizens" rights (della Porta 2015a). In the European Union, it was addressed through the imposition of policy choices from electorally unaccountable institutions. In fact, while formally still in charge of policy making, national governments have lost the capacity to choose among alternative options and are instead forced to implement unpopular austerity measures. The imposition of conditionality in exchange for loans weakened national democracy and sovereignty as, while national governments formally maintain the competence to impose extremely unpopular measures, de facto their sovereignty is denied by the lending institutions. In what Fritz Scharpf (2011) defined as a "pre-emption of democracy", "In countries like Greece and Ireland in particular, anything resembling democracy will be effectively suspended for many years as national governments of whatever political colour, forced to behave responsibly as defined by international markets and organizations, will have to impose strict austerity on their societies, at the price of becoming increasingly unresponsive to their citizens"

(Streeck 2011, p. 184). Also, with a rather explicit scorn for representative institutions, neoliberal policies have been imposed by a closed, self-sustained and unchecked class of decision makers with monetarist assumptions that has been empowered during the crisis. The governance of the European Monetary Union is increasingly devolved to economically oriented actors such as the Council for Economic and Financial Affairs or the European Central Bank, all of which are oriented by a monetarist paradigm calling for labour market deregulation and cuts in pensions and health care (de la Porte and Heins 2015). The European Union has constrained the democratic dialectics between government and opposition, often imposing – in some cases formally, through conditioned lending, in some case informally, through various forms of pressure – on parties in government and in the opposition to support those policies. Finally, fiscal autonomy, and with it national sovereignty, have been dramatically reduced through new EU instruments to impose fiscal probity with strong spillover (restrictive) effects on social policies (Heins and de la Porte 2015).

But what are the effects of all these institutional properties on the characteristics of social movements? In the first place, opinion polls as well as cross-national comparative analyses of specific movements (for instance, the antiwar movement in 2003) indicate that the existence of protests cannot be easily explained by institutional variables such as the degree of functional or territorial distribution of power (Waalgrave and Rucht 2010; della Porta 2004b and 2005a). Second, depending on whether a movement has allies within the central executive power, the openness of the institutional system appears to have ambivalent effects on the possibilities of success for social movements. To begin with, it has frequently been observed that in decentralized states challengers can rely on a variety of actors to penetrate the system. However, decentralization of power does not always work in social movements' favor: "multiple points of access is a two-edged sword ..., as multiple points of access also means multiple points of veto" (Amenta and Caren 2004, p. 472).

Dispersal of power increases the chances of access not just for social movements but also for all political actors, including movement's opponents. It can happen that a movement's allies find themselves in government at national level and take decisions favorable to that movement, only to find these decisions blocked by either decentralized bodies governed by other political forces or by other arms of the state such as the courts. Even the use of referendums can favor the opponents of social movements as well as the movements themselves. Similarly, the public bureaucracy can be influenced by political parties and pressure groups as well as by social movements; the mirror image of this is that a strong and independent bureaucracy increases the autonomous points of access to the decision-making process for social movements but also for other collective actors. In the Latin American cases we cited, presidential systems were certainly more difficult to penetrate by challengers; they increased however the capacity of movements near presidents to implement their programs of deep policy changes. Institutional variables may have a stronger influence on the strategies adopted by social movements, however. In a more interactive perspective, the institutional context influences which strategies are more effective, but not if and when a movement will be successful: "as political circumstances become more difficult, more assertive or bolder collective action is required to produce collective benefits" (Amenta and Caren 2004, p. 473). As will become clear in what follows, as far as the relative moderation of repertoires is concerned, institutional openness must be combined with inclusive political culture (itself naturally codified, at least partly, in legislation).

8.2   PREVAILING INSTITUTIONAL STRATEGIES

Social movements are permeated by the political culture of the systems in which they develop. The strategies adopted by collective actors are influenced by the mutable and flexible spirit of the time – the Zeitgeist – which echoes developments within the economic cycle (della Porta 2015a), and also by certain relatively stable characteristics of national political cultures (Kitschelt 1985, pp. 302–303). In general, research indicated that the more egalitarian, liberal, and inclusive the political culture, the less antagonistic and confrontational the opposition. Taking further the analysis of those aspects of political culture relevant to interaction between social movements and institutions, Hanspeter Kriesi has emphasized the importance of prevailing strategies, which he defines, following Scharpf (1984, p. 260), as "an overall understanding, among those who exercise effective power, of a set of precise premises integrating world-views, goals and means." Referring in particular to the procedures used by members of a system when dealing with *challengers,* he claims that "national strategies set the informal and formal rules of the game for the conflict between new social movements and their adversaries" (1989a: 295). Countries with a strategy of exclusion (that is, repression of conflict) will tend to have an ideologically homogeneous governing coalition and polarization of conflict with opponents. Where there is a strategy of inclusion (co-optation of emergent demands), on the other hand, governments will be ideologically heterogeneous and open toward external actors.

A country's democratic history also influences its prevailing strategies toward challengers. Past authoritarianism often reemerges in times of turmoil. Young democracies tend to fear political protest, and also have police forces that remain steeped in the authoritarian values of the preceding regime (Flam 1994b, p. 348; on Italy, see Reiter 1998; della Porta and Reiter 2004a and 2004b). In fact, it has been argued that in each country new social movements have "inherited" consequences from the reactions reserved originally for the labor movement. In Mediterranean Europe, France, and Germany, absolutism and the late introduction of universal suffrage led to a divided and radicalized labor movement. In the smaller, open-market countries, in Great Britain and in Scandinavia, on the other hand, where there was no experience of absolutism and universal suffrage was introduced early, inclusive strategies produced a united and moderate labor movement. As a comparative study of American, British, and German unions showed:

> *state repression of the rights of workers to combine in the labor market appears to have had three related consequences for unions. First and most obviously, repression politicized unions because it compelled them to try to change the rules*

of the game ... A second consequence of repression is that, if sufficiently severe, it could reduce differences among workers originating in their contrasting capacity to form effective unions ... Finally, ... repression politicized unions in an additional and more subtle way, by giving the initiative within the labor movement to political parties.

(Marks 1989, pp. 14–15, passim)

These (self-reproducing) prevailing strategies influenced the way in which the conflict between labor and capital was played out, leading to exclusion in certain cases and integration in others (Kriesi 1989b). Initially elaborated in response to trade unionism, these strategies developed their own self-perpetuating logic through political socialization and interaction: "Once the relationship between the union and party-political wings of the labor movement had been molded, it was difficult to break" (Marks 1989, p. 175). The tendency of national strategies to live on beyond the conditions that gave rise to them helps to explain the reactions to new social movements. Institutional systems characterized by inclusion are more open to new challengers, just as they had been to the old ones; systems with exclusionary strategies, in contrast, continue to be hostile to newly emerging claims. In fact, the difference in elite attitudes to challengers appears to be linked to prevailing conceptions of relations with challengers. The elites in these countries tend to recognize the legitimacy of interests lying outside the party system, knowing that the movement of today may be the interest group of tomorrow. In other countries, France, for example, an exclusionary attitude has prevailed.

As comparative analyses have shown, critical junctures, such as the transition to democracy, have long-lasting effects. So, for instance, some path-breaking research on the Iberian peninsula, based on a comparison of Spain as a case of participated pact and Portugal as a case of eventful democratization, has shown how the path of transition influences the interactions between power holders and protestors in the ensuing regime, in particular with regard to democratic practice, defined as "the way in which actors within a democracy understand and make use of opportunities for political action and influence, and interact with other participants in the polity" (Fishman 2013, p. 5). This refers to emerging institutions, but also to implicit cultures that define norms; so action affects the recognition of civil society voices. Cultural processes working in times of flux have an impact on future practices by reconfiguring fundamental elements of national identities and the public rituals that affirm them: the carnation revolution in Portugal produced inclusive strategies toward social movements, while the opposite happened after elites pact in Spain.

What, then, can be explained by this set of variables? First, what was said concerning institutional openness also applies here, at least in part. While strategies of accommodation and inclusion may favor social movement access to the system, they will do the same for its opponents too. In an inclusive system, governments hostile to social movement claims can be forced to compromise; on the other hand, a government inclined to be friendly might also be constrained to follow a more moderate policy than they would otherwise.

The relative predominance of either a strategy of inclusion or a strategy of exclusion may also have contradictory effects on levels of mobilization. On the one hand, the anticipated costs of mobilization will be lower in traditionally inclusive countries; on the other hand, the advantage expected from protest would be smaller, since inclusive countries tend to value consensus. Although exclusionary strategy heightens the costs of collective action, it also renders it in a certain way more necessary. The other side of the coin is that accommodatory strategies lessen the costs of action but also the costs of inaction. So, for instance, the opposition to austerity policies took more disruptive forms in Spain, with the spreading of protest camps, than in Portugal, where it was rather channeled within participatory institutional channels (della Porta, Andretta et al. 2016).

The link between prevailing strategies and repertoires of action seems stronger: repertoires of protest are more conventional in traditionally inclusive countries. A comparison of political repression in nineteenth-century Europe, for example, suggested that "those countries that were consistently the most repressive, brutal, and obstinate in dealing with the consequences of modernization and developing working-class dissidence reaped the harvest by producing opposition that was just as rigid, brutal, and obstinate" (Goldstein 1983, p. 340). In general, the most radical ideologies and strategies developed in countries characterized by low parliamentarization and the political isolation of the labor movement (Bartolini 2000, pp. 565–566). On the other hand, institutionalization of collective bargaining contributed to depoliticize conflicts on social inequality by constraining them within industrial relations. In fact, "repression stimulated working-class radicalism; whilst political relaxation and a structure of free collective bargaining encourages reformism" (Geary 1981, p. 179). However, individual participation in protest action, including the most extreme forms, on occasions turns out to be relatively high in traditionally inclusive countries and, vice versa, low in countries with a tradition of exclusion.

While acknowledging a certain influence of past experiences on social movement strategies, it should be remembered that a country's "traditions" are hardly set in stone. The nineteenth-century French elites, for example, were considered open to change, while their German counterparts were hostile to any and every reform:

Where a national bourgeoisie is weak or tied to an existing and authoritarian state, as in Russia before the First World War, or countries in which the middle class increasingly abandons liberal values and comes to support a semi-authoritarian political system, as was to some extent the case in Imperial Germany and prewar Spain, there the prospect of working-class liberalism appears to be weaker, while political radicalism on the part of labor becomes more marked. Conversely, the Republican traditions of at least some sections of the French bourgeoisie and the buoyant liberalism of the British middle class enabled a fair proportion of the workers to remain in the liberal camp.

(Geary 1989, pp. 2–3)

The picture changes in the second half of the twentieth century, however. In fact, after the Second World War, the collapse of Nazism and the Allied Occupation led to a rethinking of past repressive traditions in Germany and the adoption of inclusive strategies toward the labor movement. In France, on the other hand, the absence of such a historical rupture allowed strategies of exclusion to be maintained until at least the 1960s. Similarly, it has also been noted that past elite behavior is not enough to explain recourse to repressive strategies in relation to the antinuclear movement (Flam 1994b, p. 345). In conclusion, while national strategies do have a certain influence on the repertoires of action adopted by social movements, they are not sufficient to explain the strategic choices they make. In the first place, they are not equally long-lived in every country. Second, they do not have the same effects on all movements. Third, they appear to affect some movement strategies and not others.

8.3 SOCIAL MOVEMENTS' OPPONENTS

The effects of established institutions as well as historically rooted national strategies are then filtered through social and political actors that operate within complex fields. As Jan Willem Duyvendak and James Jasper (Jasper and Duyvendak 2015; Duyvendak and Jasper 2015) suggested, various players interact in complex arenas. In looking at them, social movement studies focused in particular on countermovements and state apparatuses, mainly the police.

8.3.1 Noninstitutional Opponents

When looking at the opponents of social movements, we can start observing that they can be either institutional or noninstitutional actors. Traditionally, the labor movements has organized against factories' owners that have tried to constrain workers' right to form associations to represent them, to strike, to negotiate collective contracts. Nowadays, there is in fact a growing industry of consultants that are hired by corporations to reduce the workers' rights or resist their expansion (Luce 2014). Often movements' opponents do organize collectively. So, for instance, environmental movements meet the organized resistance of business organizations representing specific economic interests in, for instance, construction projects that are considered as environmentally unfriendly (della Porta and Piazza 2008). Peace movement and civil right movements find fierce adversaries in arms producers. Besides business interests, also religious or conservative movements often mobilize to resist social and political gains by women, homosexuals, ethnic minorities, or the poor. Especially since the years 2010s, so called "anti-gender" movements have developed claiming a restriction of the rights of women, lesbians, gays, transsexuals – calling for reversing laws in the policy areas such as reproduction but also education (Kuhar and Paternotte 2017).

Given these developments, research pointed at the increase of corporate political activity as well as of "private politics," through which firms directly address civil society (Soule 2009; Baron 2010). Targeted by social movements through a repertoires adapted to the marketplace (Balsiger 2014a), firms "equipped themselves with specialized units dealing with risk management, corporate social responsibility (CSR), or public affairs, with the purpose of observing a company's "contentious" environment and developing strategies to respond to demands from civil society" (Balsiger 2015, p. 653). Firms' repertoires to respond to protest include communication strategies of "reputation management" and counter-campaigns, alongside "quiet politics" by the lobbying of members of governments, legislations, administrations (Werner 2012; Culpepper 2010):

> *Management scholars have repeatedly pointed out that firms have started to engage in activities that have traditionally been regarded as core government activities: public health, education, social security, or the protection of human rights. This "new political role" of corporations is interpreted as the result of regulatory gaps that emerge due to increased globalization of markets and the limited reach of states and international regulation.*
>
> (Balsiger 2015, p. 654)

Private politics increases as firms prefer to self-regulate rather than to give in to public regulation, but also as activists realize they have no success when calling for state intervention (Balsiger 2014b).

For movements directed at markets and firms, the *industry opportunity structure* represents the set of economic, organizational, cultural, and commodity-related factors that enhance or constrain movements in their interactions with corporate targets (Schurman 2004, p. 251). As Soule and King (2015, p. 697) summarized:

> *Key dimensions of the industry opportunity structure include the relationships among actors in the industry's organizational field and the nature of the goods or services produced by the industry, which, to the extent that these can be harmful, may offer more opportunities for activism than do others.*

Similarly, *corporate opportunity structures* and *corporate mediation* affect the development of social movements (King 2008a, 2008b; Dauvergne and LeBaron 2014). Opportunities includes concentration, regulation, characteristics of CEO, of corporate board and board of governors, firms' reputation, status and visibility. Organizational size, dominant competitive position, and having high status or a positive reputation increases the attractivity of some corporations as targets of protest (King 2008b; Lenox and Eesley 2009; McAteer and Pulver 2009). Visible targets attract in fact more media attention (King 2011), which then increases the reputation risks (King 2008b; McDonnell and King 2013). Also, specific corporate cultures make some firms more receptive to pressure in order to protect their image (Vasi and King 2012).

The term *countermovements* has been coined in relation to those opponents that, in particular for their reliance of "street politics" have been assimilated to social movements. Countermovements have been said to arise in reaction to the successes obtained by social movements, and the two then develop in symbiotic dependence during the course of mobilization. While the use of the term to define right-wing movements is not convincing – as all types of movements do at times act reactively, countering the moves by other action – the movements-countermovements dynamics appear indeed important to address. In general, the relationship between movements and countermovements has been defined as one of loosely coupled conflicts, in which the two sides rarely come together face to face (Zald and Useem 1987; cf. also Lo 1982), but they are nevertheless influenced by the action of movements that oppose their claims. As Rapoport (1960) stressed, the type of relations between social movements and countermovements can indeed vary: they might resemble debate to the extent that they are based on an attempt to persuade opponents and the authorities, and games to the extent they are based on rational calculations of costs and benefits. Sometimes, as was the case in Italy in the 1970s, their interaction resembles far more a battle in which the objective is to annihilate the enemy. Interactions between movements and countermovements lead to a strong sense of conflict and the prevalence of a Manichean view of politics (della Porta 1995). At the same time, the two tend to imitate each other, reciprocally adapting particular tactics and the choice of arenas in which to act (see, for example, Meyer and Staggenborg 1996). This has been noted, for instance, about the "anti-gender" movements that, even if sponsored by powerful institutions, have framed themselves as defending a victimized minority against a culture of death. Also from the point of view of the organizational structures and repertoire of action, there have been attempts to emulate what were perceived to be winning strategies being used by their adversaries (Kuhar and Paternotte 2017), The presence of nonviolent countermovements chiefly affects the chances of success for social movements; the presence of violent countermovements, on the other hand, leads to radicalization of their repertoires of action. Recently, the concept of backlash has been used to define conservative, often radical right with some support in religious circles, movements that mobilized against gender rights (della Porta 2020).

As for the institutional opponents, it must be stated at the outset that the state cannot be identified merely as an enemy of social movements. Rather, the state is 'simultaneously target, sponsor, and antagonist for social movements as well as the organizer of the political system and the arbiter of victory" (Jenkins and Klandermans 1995, p. 3). However, state agencies may be either allies or opponents: Government agencies can support or oppose movement claims, since some of the agencies might believe in movement goals and others hold opposing beliefs. These agencies can offer important resources to their respective sides. Not all public agencies are aligned, however, and, as the chapter that follows makes clear, many of them become arenas for transactions between different collective actors, social movements among them.

8.3.2   The Policing of Protest

An important aspect of the state's response to protest is the policing of protest, or police handling of protest events – more neutral terms for what protestors usually refer to as *repression* and the state as *law and order* (della Porta 1995, 1996b; Earl,

Soule, and McCarthy 2003). Protest policing is a particularly relevant issue for understanding the relationship between social movements and the state. According to Lipsky (1970, p. 1):

> *The study of the ways police interact with other citizens is of primary importance for anyone concerned with public policy and the just resolution of contemporary urban conflict. Police may be conceived as 'street-level bureaucrats" who "represent" government to people. And at the same time as they implement government policies, police forces also help define the terms of urban conflict by their actions. The influence of police on political attitudes and developments is fundamental because of the unique role of law enforcement agencies in enforcing and reinforcing the norms of the system.*

One can add that, in their turn, protest waves have had important effects on police organizations (see, e.g., Morgan 1987; Reiner 1998). In fact, the various styles of police intervention have received some attention in the sociological literature. Gary T. Marx (1979), working from a phenomenological perspective, distinguished acts of repression according to their purpose: creating an unfavorable image of opponents; gathering information; restricting the flow of resources for movements; discouraging activists; fueling internal conflicts within the leadership and between groups; sabotaging specific actions. Charles Tilly (1978, pp. 106–115) classified political regimes according to the degree of repression or "facilitation" they manifest toward different collective actors and actions. Police actions can vary in terms of force used (brutal or soft), extent of conduct regarded as illegitimate (ranging between repression and tolerance), strategies for controlling various actors (generalized or selective), police respect for the law (illegal or legal), moment when police act (preemptive or reactive), degree of communication with demonstrators (confrontation or consensus), capacity to adjust to emerging situations (rigid or flexible), degree of formalization of rules of the game (formal or informal), degree of training (professional or improvised) (della Porta and Reiter 1998, p. 4).

Research has picked out three main strategic levels for protest control, favored differently by the police in various historical periods (della Porta and Reiter 1998): coercive strategies, i.e. use of weapons and physical force to control or disperse demonstrations; persuasive strategies, meaning all attempts to control protest through prior contacts with activists and organizers; informative strategies, consisting in widespread information-gathering as a preventive feature in protest control; and the targeted collection of information, including use of modern audiovisual technologies, to identify law-breakers without having to intervene directly.

It has been noted that the combination of these dimensions tends to define two different, internally consistent models for controlling public order. The *escalated-force model* gives low priority to the right to demonstrate, innovative forms of protest are poorly tolerated, communication between police and demonstrators is reduced to essentials, and there is frequent use of coercive means or even illegal methods (such as *agents provocateurs*). The *negotiated control model*, by contrast, sees the right to demonstrate peacefully as a priority; even disruptive forms of protest are tolerated, communication between demonstrators and police is considered basic to peaceful conduct of protest, and coercive means are avoided as far as possible, emphasizing selectivity of operations (McPhail, Schweingruber, and McCarthy 1998, pp. 51–54; della Porta and Fillieule 2004). To these dimensions one might add the type of information strategy police forces employ in controlling protest, with a distinction between generalized control on all demonstrators and control focusing on those possibly guilty of an offense.

In Western democracies, a radical transformation in strategies for controlling public order and associated operational practices and techniques, from the escalated-force model to negotiated control, was noted, particularly following the protest wave that culminated in the late 1960s. While the widespread conception of rights to demonstrate one's dissent has tended to become more permissive, intervention strategies have moved away from the coercive model until then predominant. During the 1970s and 1980s, though with pauses and temporary reversals, we may note a trend toward growing tolerance for minor breaches of the law. Among changes apparent in strategies for controlling public order has been a reduction in the use of force, greater emphasis on *dialogue,* and the investment of large resources in gathering information (della Porta and Reiter 1998). These strategies, officially called de-escalation (or also prevention), are based on a number of specific pathways and assumptions. Before protest events, demonstrator representatives and the police have to meet and negotiate in detail on routes and conduct to be observed during demonstrations (including the more or less symbolic violations permitted to demonstrators), charges are never to be made against peaceful groups, agreements reached with demonstration leaders are never to be broken, and lines of communication between them and the police must be kept open throughout the demonstration. The police must first and foremost guarantee the right to demonstrate peacefully; violent groups must be separated from the rest of the march and stopped without endangering the security of the peaceful demonstrators (Fillieule 1993; della Porta 1998b).

What was seen by many as the consolidated "post-68" standard, no longer subject to debate, has proved however fragile when faced with the new challenge of transnational protests. The Genoa G8 countersummit reignited an almost forgotten debate on the fundamental rights of citizens and the question of how much power the state is allowed to use in protecting the rule of law (Andretta, della Porta, Mosca, and Reiter 2003, ch. 4). So, negotiated strategies were not consistently implemented in the control of transnational protests, where priority has been often given to security concerns (della Porta, Peterson, and Reiter 2006).

Later on, responses to terrorist attacks included a sharpening of the laws on public order and increasing police power that have been deployed against austerity protests. As Peterson and Wahlstrom (2015, p. 636) noted:

Since 9/11 2001 the US-defined "war on terror" has dramatically extended the geopolitical scope of the governance of dissent to the global scale and with this extension clouded the traditional distinction between domestic threat and foreign threats. In response to terrorist actions or the threat of terrorist actions numerous democracies across the globe enacted anti-terrorist acts, such as the Patriot Act in the United States and the Prevention of Terrorism Act in India, which have radically expanded the repressive powers of the federal government thereby infringing on civil rights of assembly and protest. Post-9/11 has witnessed an unparalleled international cooperation and intelligence sharing between police authorities and security services and private corporate intelligence agencies in this new situation for the governance of dissent.

In particular, surveillance has developed, given new technological opportunities but also following political choices. The massive collection of information is oriented toward preemption, with security services targeting entire communities considered as at risk of radicalization – especially Muslims, through a "religious profiling," which in effect risks criminalizing Muslims per se. It has been even suggested that, in country as the United States, restrictions on police spying on oppositional groups have triggered a privatization of spying (Mitchell and Staeheli 2005). In fact, in democratic as in authoritarian regimes, state institutions have shown "increased concern with defining and shaping 'appropriate' individual and community conduct, regulation and control" (Raco 2003, p. 78; see also Earl 2011). Additionally, the control of more and more transnational protests brought about a growing coordination of police units from different countries, with also increasing processes of militarization of public order, even in countries, such as Great Britain, once considered as best examples of *citizens' policing*. This militarization, including equipment, training, organization and strategies, has been tested in the fight against organized crime, but also street crimes and football hooliganism, migrating then to the control of protest.

Various explanations have been suggested for the choice of policing strategies. Quantitative research, often based upon broad cross-national comparisons, has singled out some causal determinants of police styles, for example, in terms of violation of human rights, misconducts etc. (Davenport 1995). Ethnographic research and case studies have for their part illuminated the motivations for the different police styles in dealing with different social and political groups (e.g. P.A.J. Waddington 1994; D. Waddington 1992).

The forms state power takes have a clear impact on the policing of protest. If repression is much more brutal in authoritarian than in democratic regimes (e.g Sheptycky 2005; Uysal 2005), even authoritarian regimes vary in the forms of protest they are ready to tolerate, as well as in the forms in which they police the opposition. Moreover, variations do also exist in democratic regimes, with some countries considered as traditionally more inclusive, others more exclusive (della Porta 1995). In both types of regime, the police strategies in addressing the demonstrations reflect some more general characteristics of state power. In this sense, it is to be expected that the change in the balance of state powers related with the various transformations mentioned above has an impact on the styles of protest policing. In particular, the wave of transnational protests that marked the turn of the millennium as well as the massive anti-austerity protests seem indeed to have challenged some well-established police strategies and structures (e.g. della Porta, Peterson, and Reiter 2006).

Neoliberal development affected some broader trends in policing. Even if in a selective way and with frequent inversions, the policing of protest in democratic regimes has been characterized by some trends toward a growing publicization, nation-alization, and demilitarization. First of all, the tasks of policing is at the core of the definition of a Weberian state power that claims the monopoly of force. Second, pro-cess of state building brought about the assumption by the central state of the control of public order. Even if the degree of centralization in the police structures clearly var-ies, and local police bodies often keep specific profiles and styles (see, e.g. Kriesi and Wisler 1998 on Switzerland and Winter 1998 on Germany), there has been however a progressive orientation of protest and its policing toward the national level. Third, here as well with cross-country differences, there has been also a progressive transfer of public order control from the military to the police. So, especially since the 1980s, research on the policing of protest in European democracies and the United States has singled out a reduction of strategies of control based on an escalation of force, with low priority given to the right to demonstrate, and an increase in mistrust of a negotiated control, with a broader recognition of the right to demonstrate (McPhail, Schweingruber, and McCarthy 1998, pp. 51–54; della Porta and Fillieule 2004).

If we look at the evolution of the policing of protest nowadays, these trends seem to have met some (more or less brisk) reversal. Although public order policing had never been exclusively under public control (see, e.g., private policing on university campuses or in the factories, but also the use of organized crime to intimidate union-ists and protestors), the privatization and semi-privatization of spaces such as shopping malls as well as the outsourcing of police functions to private companies (e.g. in the airports but also universities) has recently increased and made more visible the role of private police bodies in the control of protest. Private police has been tradi-tionally used to repress the labor movement, in the United States as in Italy (Earl 2004; della Porta and Reiter 2004a and 2004b), but it had then declined, gaining new strength with the rise of a global corporate security sector (Singer 2004). In fact, "Par-ticularly in conjunction with extraction industries operating in weak states, private security corporations have been contracted to quell protest" (Peterson and Wahlstrom 2015, p. 637) – by global corporations but also by weak national governments. While penal law had focused on punishment of crime, an arsenal of new provisions allow for broad control over entire communities, considered as dangerous.

As for the effects of protest policing, changes in the repressive capabilities of regimes are an important factor in explaining the emergence of social movements. In France, Russia, and China, social revolution broke out when political crisis weakened state control and repressive power (Skocpol 1979). Likewise, an inability to maintain social control facilitated the rise of the civil rights movement in the United States (McAdam 1982). And in Italy, the protest cycle of the late 1960s first emerged as a more tolerant style of policing was developing (della Porta 1995).

As far as levels of mobilization are concerned, the harshest styles of protest policing ought to increase the risk of collective action and diminish the disposition of actors to take part. In Turkey, the emergency laws that followed the attempted *coup d'etat* have been successful in repressing the activists that had so massively mobilized during the Gezi Park event in 2013. However, it should be added that many forms of repression, particularly when they are considered illegitimate, create a sense of injustice that increases the perceived risk of inaction, as it happened in particular during the Arab Spring, especially in Egypt as Mubarak's brutal policing of the protests outraged the opposition, bringing about the end of his regime (della Porta 2017a). It is not surprising, therefore, that these two divergent pressures produce contradictory results, and empirical research indicates a radicalization of those groups most exposed to police violence in some cases and renunciation of unconventional forms of action in others (Wilson 1976). Strong repression is more likely to be successful when a cycle of protest has not yet been initiated, and solidarities around movement identities are therefore not yet strong enough; "indiscriminate repression is likely to provoke further popular mobilization only during the ascendant phase of the protest cycle" (Brokett 1995, pp. 131–132).

Institutional control strategies influence protest strategies especially. First, they affect the organizational models adopted within movements. This was the case with French republicanism in the nineteenth century, where "intensified repression typically reinforced the role of secret societies and informal centers of sociability like cafés, vintners, and cabarets" (Aminzade 1995, p. 42); on the other hand, "the extension of universal male suffrage and civil liberties as well as a new geography of representation fostered the development of more formal organization" (1995, p. 59). In more recent times, too, repression has led to a process of "encapsulation" of social movement organization, in some cases to the point of going underground (della Porta 1990, 1995; Neidhardt 1981). In the global justice movement, groups such as the Black Block that choose to use violent strategies, adopt a very fluid and semiclandestine form of organization that is resistant to police investigation. Social movement organizations in some movement areas in the United States tried to protect themselves from growing surveillance. Information collected from open source as well as infiltration (in the US, with power increased by the PATRIOT ACT) has been defined as

> *a policing tactic which aims to quell or weaken political activity. Technologies of surveillance include direct surveillance, such as observation and visits by officers, recording of automobile plate numbers, raids, questioning, and burglary; electronic* surveillance, such as phone taps, audio eavesdropping, tracking of e-mail, and monitoring of *Internet and other computer activity; use of video, photo, and car-tracking devices; undercover surveillance, including by police in disguise, and the use of informants; infiltrators, and agents provocateurs; and databasing and the sharing of databased information.*
>
> (Starr, Fernandez and Scholl 2011, p. 73)

Strategies of repression also influence repertoires of action. A comparative study of Germany and Italy (della Porta 1995), for instance, indicated that tough policing techniques tend to discourage peaceful mass protest and at the same time encourage the more radical fringes of protest. Radicalization among social movements in Italy in the 1970s coincided with a period of harsher repression during which the police killed a number of demonstrators at public marches. Moreover, the belief that the state was conducting a "dirty war" poisoned relationships between elected politicians and movement activists. In Germany, on the other hand, the reformist attitudes of the social democrat and liberal government and a tolerant, selective, and 'soft" style of protest policing were reflected in a comparatively lower level of radicalization in the social movement sector. In both countries the high point of repression coincided with a shrinking of the movements' more moderate wing, a decline that indirectly helped the most extreme elements to prevail, particularly in Italy during the 1970s. The lower levels of violence in the 1980s corresponded instead to an increasing tolerance of protest. In the global justice movement, escalation developed again in the course of physical interactions with the police forces deployed in order to block demonstrators from entering the part of the cities where IGO meetings were taking place.

Police intervention influences the very aims of protestors, whose focus shifts from single issues and policy demands to the "meta-issue" of protest itself. A process of politicization of protests has been noted all along the development of anti-austerity protests. From Latin America to southern Europe, repression of collective action on e.g. the rights to water in Cochababa, Bolivia, or in defense of the Gezi Park in Istanbul, Turkey, have escalated in massive movements after brutal police intervention (della Porta and Atak 2017). In 2011, the killing of protestors in Tunisia and Egypt created waves of solidarity that ended with the breakdown of the dictators (della Porta 2017a). In the same year, anti-austerity protests politicized in Spain and Greece as protestors were outraged at police repression (della Porta 2015a).

8.4   ALLIES AND SOCIAL MOVEMENTS

While opponents try to reduce movements' resources and opportunities, allies tend to increase them. The greater the closure of institutional opportunity, the more important is the presence of allies for movements gaining access to the decision-making process. Such allies come in a variety of forms. First, as already noted, the resource-mobilization approach has emphasized the role of "reform professionals" (bureaucrats from certain public agencies, charities, religious organizations, and so on) in helping some social movements. In the United States, for example, the churches, certain foundations, and the agencies involved in federal antipoverty programs supported the civil rights movement (McAdam 1982; Morris 1984). Religious associations and third-sector groups often participate in protest for social justice, against austerity, for migrant rights (della Porta 2018c). Focusing on progressive movements, the social science literature has looked especially at unions and left-wing parties as potential allies.

8.4.1   Unions and Movements

The trade unions have often been an important ally for emerging actors, such as the student movement or the women's movement, particularly in Europe but also, e.g., in Latin America. With a wide social base and very often privileged channels of access to institutional decision-makers (both directly through the public administration and indirectly through the political parties), the trade unions can increase the mobilization capacities and chances of success for social movements. The weaker the institutional recognition of workers' representatives in the workplace and the decision-making process, the greater will be their propensity to assume a political role, allying themselves with social movements and taking part in public protest. The more influential interest groups are, the smaller will be the space for relatively unorganized movements because "a well-resourced, coherently structured, and professionalized system of interest groups may also be able to prevent outside challengers from having access to the state. Moreover, highly institutionalized, encompassing arrangements of policy negotiations between the public administration and private interest associations will be both quite inaccessible to challengers and able to act" (Kriesi et al. 1995, p. 31).

According to this point of view, neocorporatism – that is, a model of interest representation with monopolistic, centralized interest organizations that participate in public decision-making – reduces the incidence of protest. Access to the institutional system of public decision making facilitates agreement between different social groups and the state without the need for noninstitutional forms of collective action. Both control over the formation of social demand (Schmitter 1981) and the capacity to satisfy that demand (Nollert 1995) would have the effect of discouraging protest. However, if a neocorporatist structure undoubtedly reduces strikes in industry, its effect on protest in other sectors is far from clear. In fact, guaranteeing privileges to powerful interests could lead to rebellion by their weaker rivals and thus to the rise of powerful new movements. On the other hand, neocorporatism could as easily create a tendency to incorporate emerging groups within the structure of concerted policy-making. A comparison between the American and German antinuclear movements revealed that the American system, with its multiple points of access and traditionally weak executive, favored legal strategies and pragmatic movements. The initial closure of the German state (traditionally assertive of its supremacy over civil society) toward interests that cut across its corporatist outlook favored strategies of direct action (Joppke 1993). However, "once new issues and interests pass the high hurdles of party and parliament, the German polity firmly institutionalizes them" (Joppke 1993, p. 201).

In the last few decades, research on unions has stressed their growing weakness, attributing it either to capital hypermobility and the resulting decline in national sovereignty or to post-Fordist fragmentation of workers. Recently, however, some more optimistic approaches have pointed at the persisting role of unions, capable of taking advantage of globalization and imposing a strengthening of workers' rights in countries where capital was invested. In particular, unions appear quite active in developing countries – as Silver (2003, p. 164) observes, "the deep crisis into which core labor movements fell in the 1980s was not immediately replicated elsewhere. On the contrary, in the late 1980s and 1990s, major waves of labor militancy hit 'showcases' of rapid industrialization in the Second and third Worlds." As with Fordism, initially considered a source of unavoidable defeat for the working class, post-Fordism would also present both challenges and opportunities for the workers' organization. In fact, the WTO protest in Seattle has been seen as a sign of the remobilization of labor and recent literature pointed at a revitalization of unions, as well as of movement unionism, as trade unions use horizontal forms of organizations and disruptive forms of actions within broader coalitions (Diani 2018; Robinson 2000).

8.4.2   Social Movements and Parties

Where social movement allies are concerned, it is on the political parties that, especially in Europe, attention has mainly focused. Although it has often been noted that parties are important for movements and vice versa, the literature on relations between the two is at best sparse. Reciprocal indifferences have been further fueled as research on parties moved away from concerns with the relations between parties and society – focusing on parties within institutions – and social movement studies mainly framed them as a social phenomenon whose political aspects had to be located outside of the political institutions. Research on contentious politics has indeed become very movement-centric, dismissing the existing reciprocal relationship between electoral and protest politics (Hutter 2014). At the same time, literature on political parties grew more and more biased toward institutions, forgetting about the linkages with society (della Porta 2015b).

Critiques of a vision of movements as outsiders have been voiced, however, within social movement studies. As Jack Goldstone suggested, institutional politics is permeated by social movements considered as "an essential element of normal politics in modern societies," which do not necessarily institutionalize or fade away. Rather, "parties and movements have become overlapping, mutually dependent actors in shaping politics to the point that long-established political parties welcome social movement support and often rely specifically on their association to win elections" (2003, p. 4).

Relations between parties and movements are various: "Movements compete with parties. Movements infiltrate parties. . . . Movements become parties" (Garner and Zald 1985, p. 137). Social movements have often addressed programmatic challenges to parties, by rising new issues, not yet represented in the party system; organizational challenges, by promoting a participatory model; electoral challenges, by raising support for some emerging topics in public opinion, and even succeeded in changing parties' programs and organization (della Porta 2007). In a recent contribution, McAdam and Tarrow (2010, 533) singled out six of types of relations between movements and parties:

> Movements introduce new forms of collective action that influence election campaigns. Movements join electoral coalitions or, in extreme cases, turn into parties themselves. Movements engage in proactive electoral mobilization. Movements engage in reactive electoral mobilization. Movements polarize political parties internally.

On the side of party studies, relations between parties and movements have been addressed as specific forms of relations with interest groups, in particular within reflections on organizational linkages. A linkage has been defined as "any means by which political leaders act in accordance with the wants, needs, and demands of the public in making public policy" (Luttbeg 1981, p. 3). Particularly important have been considered the relations between parties and interest organizations, as linkages through organizations allow for a better selection and aggregation of "relevant grievances into reasonably coherent packages of political demands, which then become the object of negotiation between organizational and party elites." This could prove very effective for the party, since "As long as organisational integration is high, organisation members may cast their vote according to their leaders' recommendation even if they disagree with individual elements of the deal, because their prime loyalty is to the organization" (Poguntke 2002, p. 7). Relations between parties and interest groups are said to co-evolve, adapting to each other, through competition and cooperation as the two actors see each other as means potentially useful for their ends, and thus try to influence each other through overlapping leadership or other forms of pressure – but also provide each other brokerage for reaching out of one's own networks as well as bridging identities (Heaney 2010).

When looking at party systems, a very first observation is that some social movements have *produced new parties (and party families)*: the labor movements arose from, or gave birth to, socialist parties; regionalist parties have been rooted in ethnic movements; confessional parties in religious movements and the Greens in environmental ones. As Tarrow (2015, p. 95) noted:

Many parties begin life as movements. Think of the labor movement that gave birth to social democratic parties in Western Europe; or the abolitionist movement that was at the core of the Republican party during and after the American Civil War; or the indigenous peoples' movements that produced ethnically-supported parties in Bolivia and Ecuador in recent decades. Movements frequently give rise to parties when movement activists transfer their activism to institutional politics.

Influentially, Lipset and Rokkan (1967) have located parties within social cleavages, in which they originate and which they contribute to consolidate. Social movements have, more or less harmonically, *allied* with parties even beyond stable organizational linkages. Linkages to movements can be stressed in the very name of the party, in the opening of participation to movement members, in support for movement claims, in the shared use of protest. The presence of overlapping membership at grassroots and leadership levels as well as the presence of movement activists in electoral lists testify for these ties. Party members may "engage in social movement activities themselves, thus promoting and leading to attitudinal changes in the party with respect to those themes at the core of the social movements' mobilizations" (Piccio 2012, p. 268). Indeed, "for a social movement to be more likely to have an impact on a party, a certain degree of overlap must exist between the party and the social movements' identities" (Piccio 2012, p. 268).

The traditional allies of the progressive social movements have mainly been the leftist parties (Kriesi 1989b; Kriesi et al. 1995; della Porta 1996a), and the radical left is considered as by far the most relevant party in protest politics (Hutter 2014; Kriesi 1989b: 296). As mediators between civil society and the state, the parties of the left need to mobilize public opinion and voters, so that the programs and membership of the institutional left have often been altered by interaction with movements (i.e., Piccio 2012). From the Labour Party in Great Britain to the Social Democrats in Germany, from the French socialists to the Italian communists, the programmes and members of the institutional left have changed following interactions with social movements and in response to increasing awareness on themes such as gender discrimination or environmental protection. Social movements have indeed been extremely sensitive to the characteristics of their allied political parties: they have often privileged action in society, leaving parties the job of bringing their claims into institutions. They have placed themselves on the political left–right axis and have constructed discourses compatible with the ideologies of their allies.

Movements-parties relations have been addressed with reference to *political cleavages*. Comparative research has indicated that, in general, the "old left" has been more disposed to support movements where exclusive regimes had for a long time hindered the moderation of conflicts on the left-right axis (della Porta and Rucht 1995; Kriesi et al. 1995, p. 68; Tarrow 1990). *Party divisions* within the traditional left have also been cited as influencing attitudes toward social movements. In particular, divisions on the left between a social-democratic (or socialist) and a communist party are said to increase the relevance of the working class vote, discouraging left-wing parties from addressing postmaterial issues (Kriesi 1991, 18). Differently, the global justice movement, stressing the traditional demands of social rights and justice, seems to have been more able to influence the institutional left in countries such as Italy, France, or Spain, where the moderate left feared the competition of more radical communist or Trotskyist parties (della Porta 2007). As center-left parties moved to the right, supporting neoliberal reform, radical left parties gain relevance as movement allies (della Porta, Fernandez et al. 2017).

Electoral competition is an important dimension in explaining the reaction of potential allies toward social movements as the propensity to support protest has been connected with electoral instability, which renders the winning of new votes particularly important. In fact, member-challenger coalitions are most probable in closely divided and competitive political situations (Piven and Cloward 1977, pp. 31–32; Tilly 1978, pp. 213–214). Alliances between parties and social movements can be facilitated when the electoral environment is more unstable (Piccio 2012). Additionally, the position of the left toward social movements is influenced by whether or not they are in *government:* when in opposition, social democrats take advantage of the push provided by social movements; when in power, on the other hand, they tend to be forced by budgetary constraints or coalition partners to limit their openness to emerging demands (Kriesi 1991, p. 19; Kriesi 1989b, pp. 296–297). Finally, availability toward changes could be different for *mainstream versus peripheral* parties, the latter being those who have little to no chance to achieve power (Kriesi 2015).

The borders between movements and parties are blurred in *movement parties*, a concept that refers to political parties that have particularly strong organizational and external links with social movements (della Porta, Fernandez et al. 2017). Movement parties emerge as a sort of hybrid between the two, when organizational and environmental linkages are very close: to different degrees, they have overlapping membership, co-organize various forms of collective action, fund each other, address similar concerns. As organizations, they participate in protest campaigns, but also act in electoral arenas. As social movements are networks of organizations and individuals, movement parties can be considered as part of them, as testified for by overlapping memberships as well as organizational and action links. According to Kitschelt, "Movement parties are coalitions of political activists who emanate from social movements and try to apply the organization and strategic practice of social movements in the arena of party competition" (2006, p. 280). Additionally, even if in different formats, movement parties aim at integrating the movement constituencies within their organizations. Movement parties also represent movements' claims, by channelling their concerns in the institutions. As for framing, "movement-based parties are more likely to be driven by ideological militancy than by pragmatic political considerations" (Tarrow 2015, p. 95). Moreover, even if using (also) an electoral logic, they tend to be supportive of protest, participating in campaigns together with other movement organizations, as "in terms of external political practice, movement parties attempt a dual track by combining activities within the arena of formal democratic competition with extra-institutional mobilization" (Kitschelt 2006, p. 281).

8.5 DISCURSIVE OPPORTUNITY AND THE MEDIA SYSTEM

Research on social movements demonstrated the explanatory power of the concept of political opportunity, but also pointed at the role of cultural variables in the perception of political opportunities and constraints, as well as in the choice of organizational models and repertoires of action. First, political opportunity approaches are criticized for failing to recognize that "cultural and strategic processes define and create the factors usually presented as 'structural'" (Goodwin and Jaspers 2004a, p. 27). Cultural elements filter in fact the external reality, so that the appearance of opportunities might pass unperceived; or alternatively, activists might perceive closed opportunities as being open (Kurzman 2004). Even earlier proponents of the concept of political opportunity structures have written that "Opportunities and threats are not objective categories, but depend on the kind of collective attribution that the classical agenda limited to framing of movement goals" (McAdam, Tarrow, and Tilly 2001, p. 45).

The debate, however, goes beyond the role of perceptions to address the restrictive effect that the focus on political opportunities has had on social movement studies (Goodwin and Jasper 2004b). The emphasis on the political has in particular obscured the role of discursive opportunities, such as the capacity of movements' themes to resonate with cultural values. The political opportunity structure has indeed been defined as "the playing field in which framing context occurs" (Gamson 2004, p. 249).

While they are also structural (in the sense that they are beyond the movements' sphere of immediate influence), discursive opportunities are distinct from political institutions (Koopmans 2004; Polletta 2004). Cultural environments define the resonance of movements' demands (Williams and Kubal 1999), with changes possible only in transitional times (Schudson 1989). The way in which the abortion issue was discussed in Germany and the United States resonated with general themes in their national political cultures (Ferree, Gamson, Gerhards, and Rucht 2002); the return of public opinion toward a general support of the public sphere (versus the private sphere) helped the development of the global justice movement (della Porta, Andretta et al. 2006) as well as the spreading of anti-austerity protests (della Porta 2015a).

Mass-media emerge then as particularly important for social movement development. In media studies, conditions and limits of media contribution to democratic participation have, however, not occupied a central place. When addressing the role of an active and autonomous public sphere, research on political communication has tended rather to stigmatize the commercialization and/or lack of political autonomy of the mass media as a serious challenge to the performance of a "power of oversight" over the elected politicians. Recent tendencies in the mass media – among which concentration, deregulation, digitalization, globalization, and the pluralization of the publics – tend to have ambivalent effects on democracy (Dahlgren 2009). Although various theorizations have mapped different types of public spheres (Gerhard and Neidhardt 1990), and research on political communication has traditionally stressed the role of different filters between the media-as-senders and the citizens-as-receivers (e.g. Deutsch 1964), research on political communication has mainly focused on the mass-media as a separate power. This focus on mass media also explains the limited attention given to social movements' channels of communication, such as alternative journals, publishers, radio, and the like.

Control of the media and of symbolic production therefore becomes both an essential premise for any attempt at political mobilization and an autonomous source of conflict. Even though it is debated to which extent protest events are first of all "newspaper demonstrations," i.e. oriented mainly at media coverage (Neveu 1999, p. 28), media are indeed the most obvious shaper of public sensitivity (Jasper 1997, p. 286). The success of protest action is influenced by the amount of media attention it receives, and this also affects the character of social movement organizations (Gitlin 1980). As Gamson (2004, p. 243) observed, "the mass media arena is the major site of context over meaning because all of the players in the policy process assume its pervasive influence – either it is justified or not."

Research on social movements and the media has traditionally addressed especially the limited capacity of social movements to influence the mass media, characterized by selection but also descriptive biases when covering protest (Gamson and Modigliani 1989; Gamson 2004). Focused mainly on the interaction between the mass media and social movements, research has repeatedly singled out media bias against social movements endowed with little social capital – in terms of relations and reputation as reliable sources – to be spent with journalists. Social movements have been, in fact, described as "weak" players in the mass-mediatic sphere, and the relationships between activists and journalists as competitive (Neveu 1999). General tendencies (journalistic preference for the visible and dramatic, for example, or reliance on authoritative sources of information) and specific characteristics of the media system (a greater or lesser degree of neutrality on the part of journalists, the amount of competition between the different media) both influence social movements. Evolutions toward depoliticization of the journalistic profession, or increasing commercialization (Neveu 1999) further reduce activists' access. The use of newspapers as a main source of information on protest events has pushed toward systematic analyses on the selection bias of the quality press. Comparing the coverage in national newspaper with that in regional ones or police records allowed to single out the overrepresentation of large demonstrations and violent ones, as well as of protests that use novel forms and that meet contingent issue cycles (della Porta 2009a, 2017a).

Research has also suggested that, when effective in producing newsworthy events, social movement organizations and activists have been said to do this at high costs, in terms of adaptation to the media logic. In his influential volume *The Whole World is Watching*, Gitlin (1980) described different steps in the relations with the media, going from lack of interest to cooptation. Beyond the media, discursive opportunities in the broader public are quoted as determinant of movements' relative success in agenda setting. As Charlotte Ryan observed long ago (1991), the focus on inequality in power of the different actors who intervene in the mass media has been useful in counterbalancing some naive assumptions of the (then dominant) gatekeeper organizational model, that underestimated the barriers of access to the news by weak actors. At the same time, however, it is risky to underestimate the capacity for agency by social movement organizations as well as the active role of the audiences in making sense of media messages (Ryan 1991).

Research on alternative media has instead paid attention to social movements as agents of democratic communication. Given changes in the technological and cultural opportunities, scholars in this field tend to stress more and more the blurring of the borders between senders and receivers, producers and users. Attention to agency has been stronger in research on the movement-near medias, variously defined as alternative, activist, citizen radical, autonomous etc. (for a review, Mattoni 2009, pp. 26–29). In Downing's definition (2001, p. 3), "radical alternative media constitute the most active form of the active audience and express oppositional strands, overt and covert, within popular cultures." They are "media, generally small scale and in many different forms, that express an alternative vision to hegemonic policies, priorities and perspectives" (Downing 2001, p. v).

While research on the mass-mediatic opportunities (or lack thereof) run parallel to the one on political opportunities, research on the radical media took some ideas from the resource mobilization approach in social movements, looking at movements' media as social movement organizations of a special type. Within media studies, analyses on alternative, or radical, media stressed especially the differences in the ways in which they produce news, as well as in the public they address. In general, they looked, at a micro level, at both the product as well as the (decentralized) practices of news-production. In this approach, radical alternative media are social movement organizations of a special type, constructing a movement public sphere. Their *raison d'être* is in the critique of the established media (Rucht 2004) and the promotion of the "democratization of information" (Cardon and Granjon 2003). In this way, they play an important role for democracy, both by expanding the range of information and ideas, being more responsive to the excluded, and impacting on participants' sense of the self. Doubts have been expressed, however, on their capacity to go beyond those who are already sympathetic to the cause, and reaching the general publics. Social movements do indeed develop different movement strategies to address the media (from abstention to attack, alternative, and adaptation, Rucht 2004). Efficient in circulating information between the activists, they have however to meet the uneasy task of reaching the mass media, if they want their message circulates outside movement–sympathetic circles (Bennet 2004).

Beyond the availability of technological and material resources, the complex visions of information rights, communication styles, knowledge creation shape the different strategies of social movement organizations (Milan 2008; Mattoni 2008, Fuster 2009). Some recent reflection and research on social movements and their communication practices have in fact challenged a structuralist view, focused on institutions, and a conception of alternative media as separated from the broader media field, and have looked more at their relations, norms, and vision. Research on alternative media started indeed to stress the agency of social movements and their communicative practices, as well as the integration of (or at least overlapping between) different actors and fields of action in media seen as arenas (Gamson 2004). Characteristics of these media were not only their critical, counter-hegemonic contents, but also their capacity to involve not only (or mainly) professional journalists, but also normal citizens in news production, given their horizontal links with their audience (Atkinson 2010). Participatory activists contribute to blur the borders between audience and producers, readers and writers through co-performance (Atkinson 2010, p. 41).

With the blurring of the borders between producers and receivers, not only citizens are active processors of media messages, but, as Lance Bennett observed, "People who have long been on the receiving end of one-way mass-communication are now increasingly likely to become producers and transmitters" (2003b, p. 34). This increased capacity of normal citizens and activists to produce information has been seen as a consequence of post-modern individualization, with an increasing fluidity and mobility of political identities (Bennett 2003b), but also specific changes in the media field, such as:

1. New ways of consuming media, which explicitly contest the social legitimacy of media power;
2. New infrastructures of production, which have an effect on who can produce news and in which circumstances;
3. New infrastructures of distribution, which change the scale and terms in which symbolic production in one place can reach other places (Couldry 2003, p. 44).

In fact, among the new trends in "communication power," Manuel Castells has noted that "the production of the message is self-generated, the definition of the potential receiver(s) is self-directed, and the retrieval of specific messages or content from the World Wide Web and electronic communication networks is self-selected" (2009, p. 55). In this way, "The media audience is transformed into a communicative subject increasingly able to redefine the process by which societal communication frames the culture of society" (2009, p. 116). A networking logic reflects, and at the same time contributes to, the spreading of embedded sets of values oriented toward the building of horizontal ties and decentralized coordination of autonomous units (Juris 2008) as well as reciprocal identification.

In recent reflections, the focus of attention is not so much (or no longer) on the abstract "power of the media," but more on the relations between media and publics: the ways in which "people exercise their agency in relation to media flows" (Couldry 2006, p. 27). Media practices include not only the practices of the media actors, but also more broadly what various actors do in relations with the media, including activist media practices. Not only "reading media imagery is an active process in which context, social location, and prior experience can lead to quite different decoding" (Gamson, Croteau, Hoynes and Sasson 1992, p. 375), but people participate more and more in the production of messages within a media environment (similar to Bourdieu's field) in which different spokepersons intervene and different types of medias interact. In Mattoni's definition (2009, p. 33), a media environment is an "open, unpredictable and controversial space of mediatization and communication, made up of different layers which continuously combine with one another due to the information flows circulating within the media environment itself." As she observed (2009, p. 34), "in complex and multilayered media environments individuals simultaneously play different roles, especially in particular situations of protest, mobilization and claims making." A continuous flow of communication between what Bennett (2004) conceptualized as micro, meso, and macro media also makes the boundaries between news production and news consumption more flexible.

Certainly, new technologies have transformed the ambitions and capacity for communication of social movements (see Chapter 6). In particular, internet is broadly used to mobilize for online through *electronic advocacy* (Hick and McNutt 2002, p. 8). Also, in part thanks to the internet, transnational campaigns have developed on several issues, aiming at transforming international norms (Bennett 2003a). Given their larger flexibility, social movement organizations have emerged as more open to experimentation and permeable to technological changes, with a more innovative and dynamic use of the internet. Given their low costs, the new technologies offers cheap means for communication beyond borders. Moreover, the internet has facilitated the development of epistemic communities and advocacy networks (Keck and Sikkink 1998) that produce and spread alternative information on various issues (Olesen 2005). This has been particularly important for the mobilization of transnational campaigns (Reitan 2007).

Beyond their instrumental use, the new technologies have been said to resonate with social movements' vision of democracy at the normative level. Fast and inexpensive communication allows for flexible organizational and more participatory structures (Smith 1997; Bennett 2003a). More in general, the internet

fits with the basic features of the kind of social movements emerging in the Information Age (...) To build an historical analogy, the constitution of the labor movement in the industrial era cannot be separated from the industrial factory as its organizational setting (...) the internet is not simply a technology: it is a communication media, and it is the material infrastructure of a given organizational form: the network.

(Castells 2001, pp. 135–136)

The use of the internet is "shaping the movement on its own web-like image," with hubs at the center of activities, and the spokes "that link to other centers, which are autonomous but interconnected" (Klein 2002, p. 16; see also Jordan 2002 and Juris 2008).

The internet has been also said to multiply public spaces for deliberation and therefore allowing for the creation of new collective identities (della Porta and Mosca 2005). In various campaigns and protest actions, online forums and mailing lists have hosted debates on various strategic choices as well as reflections on their effects a demonstration's success and failure among "distant" activists. Virtual communities have proved capable of developing a solidarity (Fuster 2010).

Research on the global justice movements and anti-austerity protests has confirmed the importance of social movement agency in determining the use of new technologies, as well as the blurring borders between news production and news consumption. First of all, there are differences, and even tensions, in the use of new technologies by various social movement organizations, reflecting different conceptions of democracy and communication even within the same social movement (della Porta 2009a and 2009b). Conceptions of democracy inside and outside the groups tend to filter the technological potentials of technological innovations, so pointing at different genres (Vedres, Bruszt, and Stark 2005) or styles (della Porta and Mosca 2005) in the politics on the web. This confirms that "deterministic assumptions are challenged by an awareness that technology is not a discrete artifact which operates externally to impact upon social relations" (Pickerill 2003, 23).

Contextual and organizational characteristics helped in fact to explain the strategic choices made by SMOs. Different SMOs tend to exploit different technological opportunities, producing websites endowed with different qualities that apparently reflect different organizational models. In particular, SMOs oriented toward more formal and hierarchical organizations seem to prefer a more traditional (and instrumental) use of the internet, while less formalized groups tend to use more interactive tools (and identity building) available online, as well as various forms of computer-mediated protest. Movement traditions as well as democratic conceptions also play some role in influencing the different qualities of the websites. Overall, less resourceful, informal, and newer SMOs tend to develop a more innovative use of the internet, while more resourceful, formal, and older groups tend to use it as a more conventional medium of communication (Mosca and della Porta 2009). Once again, the use of internet cannot be conceived in isolation from communication by other means. New media are part of the broader media environment. Many studies underline that face-to-face relationships are very important for the construction of virtual nets, which do not emerge spontaneously. In addition, the internet is often considered as something adding to existing relations, rather than as an alternative to them.

Summarizing, research on social movements with a focus on the old and new media has developed some important observations in terms of social movements' capacity of communication, participating in various ways in media arenas. Protest campaigns affect activists' perceptions of the media (Couldry 2000), and different social movements' uses of the media are influenced more by normative than by instrumental constraints.

8.6 SUMMARY

The institutional variables most frequently discussed have related to the formal openness of the decision-making process. Starting from the hypothesis that the greater the number of points of access, the more open the system, the relevance of the distribution of power and the availability of direct democracy have been discussed. Informal characteristics and, in particular, traditional strategies of interaction with challengers were considered as well as structural characteristics. In the last decades, devolution at the subnational level and more autonomous competences of the public bureaucracies (and, in particular, the judiciary) have increased the points of access, while the growing power of multinational corporations and IGOs have made access to decision makers more difficult. Neither of these (tendentially stable) dimensions, however, is well adapted to explaining conjunctural events such as the rise and decline of protest or the mobilizing capacity of social movements. As far as the consequences of collective action are concerned, the formal or informal openness of the decision-making system does not automatically privilege emergent demands because institutions are also potentially open to social movements' opponents. Although the effects of the stable political opportunity structure in terms of social movement success thus appear ambiguous, the effects on the strategies adopted by movements seem less equivocal. The greater the opportunities of access to the decision-making system, the more social movements tend to adopt moderate strategies and institutional channels.

The conjunctural characteristics of conflict and alliances have a significant influence on the emergence of protest and on mobilization potential. The strength of institutional opponents, together with movement/countermovement interaction, influence the rise of protest and movement strategies. The policing of protest and the styles of which have changed historically and spatially influence social movement trajectories and characteristics. Coercive strategies have often produced escalation. While democratic countries moved toward negotiated forms of control, recent global protests, although largely peaceful, have been met by tough policing. Forms of policing derive in part from police organizations and cultures; however, they are also sensitive to political opportunities. Under this label, diachronic, cross-national comparative research has discussed the characteristics and effects of four groups of variables relating to:

1. Political institutions
2. Political cultures
3. Behavior of opponents of social movements
4. Behavior of their allies

Alliances with the parties of the left and the trade unions have provided important resources for social movements and increased their chance of success in the past. As the decline of mass parties, and with them of party activism, challenge the potential alliances between parties and social movements new movement parties emerged.

If the concept of political opportunity has assumed a central role in social movement research, attention has been paid to subjective perceptions of reality. Recent research has begun to address the way in which cultural variables filter political opportunities, and discursive opportunities influence movements' strategies and chances of success. Pluralism of the mass media and the richness of meso-level media emerge as important conditions for the spread of movement messages. At the same time, new media channels and practices have been created, creating challenged and opportunities for movements in a complex media environment.

CHAPTER 9

The Effects of Social Movements

The financial crisis triggered a complex process of participatory, direct democracy in the first of the European countries that had been hit by it, Iceland. After a period of extraordinary economic growth between 2005 and 2007, the Icelandic people were heavily hit by a financial crash. Its consequences were immediately felt: 'in December of 2009 around 42% of mortgages and bank loans were in arrears and, between 2009 and 2013, an average number of three families per day saw their houses repossessed due to default' (Hallgrímsdóttir and Brunet-Jailly, 2015, p. 87). The crisis was, to a large extent, a result of the privatisation of banking (together with fisheries) in 2004. Since 2005, the three main Icelandic commercial banks (Landsbanki, Kaupthing and Glitnir) had expanded their activities, offering very high interest rates (above 15%). Landsbanki was particularly culpable, having established Icesave as a subsidiary branch that collected deposits, especially in the UK and the Netherlands. The profits were then reputedly used to support activities by bankers' political allies in center-right parties. With the collapse of Lehman Brothers, the commercial banks were unable to repay credits. As Ostaszewski (2013, p. 61) summarized, "The next piece of news was insolvency of Icelandic banks which meant the total collapse of the financial market. The Icelandic society faced bankruptcy. Almost immediately Icelandic krona depreciated against the euro by 50%, GDP shrank by 3%, unemployment rose from 1 to 9% and OMX15 Iceland stock index saw an unprecedented decline of 90%. The public debt-to-GDP ratio was 115%. Over 65% of Icelandic companies became insolvent."

Protests erupted then, unexpectedly in such a small country, involving a large part of a population whose experience with contentious politics was extremely limited. Indeed, the anti-austerity protestors reinvented the organizational formats they adopted as well as the action repertoire they used (della Porta 2017a). Opposing the government, which wanted to blame the global crisis, protesters spread a moral frame stigmatizing the political corruption of an octopus-like elite made up of businesspeople and politicians, which, they claimed, had acted out of greed against the tradition of solidarity of Icelanders. Started with a rock concert, called for by a tiny group, the mobilization spread quickly and massively. Public protest meetings in downtown Reykjavík became a regular occurrence, attracting a growing number of individuals, with a clear demand: that the ruling government, the chairman of the board of governors of the Central Bank, and the director of the Financial Supervisory Authority resigned (Bernburg 2016, p. 6). Protests empowered new visions within the very horizontal organizational format of a citizens' movement. On 20 January 2009, thousands of people gathered in front of the parliament in Reykjavík, remaining in the central square for three days:

> From the normally placid and consumption-obsessed population an anxious, angry protest movement emerged. A handful of organizers, mainly people like singers, writers and theatre directors who had been outside of politics, called for rallies in the main square in front of the parliament building to demand a change of government. Thousands of people, all age groups and distinctly middle-class, assembled in shoulder-to-shoulder numbers never seen before in Iceland. [...] For all the fear and anger the protestors also felt a sense of elated solidarity.
>
> (Wade and Sigurgeirsdóttir 2011, p. 693)

The protest had significant political effects. Especially, what came to be known as a Saucepan Revolution pushed the president Grímsson to call a referendum om the Icesave bill, which essentially upheld collective national responsibility for private banking debts (with a cost of approximately $17,000 for every man, woman, and child in a country of only 320,000), After a petition was signed by more than 60,000 citizens (about a quarter of the electorate) (Curtis et al. 2014, p. 722). Held in 2010, with a turnout of 62.7% of registered voters, the referendum returned a unanimous No vote (98.1%), rejecting the Icesave repayment deal. Similarly, a new referendum rejected the second Icesave bill: 75.3% of eligible voters participated, with 59.8% rejecting the proposal (Hallgrímsdóttir and Brunet-Jailly 2015).

Additionally, the protests also triggered a very particular constitutional process, prompted by and carried out through high levels of citizens involvement. After the humiliating double defeat of the Icelandic authorities regarding the Icesave issue, citizens demanded a new constitution to express the collective values of a post-crash Icelandic state and society (della Porta, Andretta et al. 2016, p. 49). On 14 November 2009, a network of liberal grassroots think-tanks, the Anthill, held a National Assembly, in Reykjavík. In a participatory fashion:

> The Anthill envisioned that it would draw on the collective intelligence of Icelandic citizens to accomplish two tasks: define the most important values in Icelandic society and produce a vision for the future of the country. These tasks were important in terms of policy, but the objective of the National Assembly was also procedural. The Thjodfundur process was meant to be an alternative national visioning process, providing an authentic space where citizens could participate in democracy.
>
> (Elkins et al. 2012)

The National Assembly saw the involvement of about 1,200 citizens, of whom 900 were randomly selected; 300 represented interest groups and government officials. The process was highly innovative in terms of its inclusivity and transversality of participants. In 2010, an act on a Constitutional Assembly was passed in the parliament, establishing an advisory group in charge of reviewing and rewriting the existing Constitution dating from 1944. Composed of 25 delegates, the Assembly was elected by the Icelandic citizens in order to examine the Constitution in addition to, with the consultancy of experts, drafting a legislative bill for a constitutional change to be submitted to the parliament. A National

Forum was to be held before the elections of the Constitutional
Assembly, including 1,000 participants of voting age, randomly
selected. Organised by a government Constitutional Committee
and facilitated by the parliament, the National Forum was held on
6 November 2010; 950 Icelanders participated. Eventually, 'the
National Forum channelled the existing social and political discourse surrounding Iceland's government and constitution into a
number of broad, but concise, recommendations' (Elkins et al.
2012). After a one-day meeting in October 2010, it issued a short
guideline about the desires for the new constitution, including the
public ownership of natural resources (Gylfason 2012, p. 12). The
parliament then appointed a seven-member Constitutional
Committee, including professionals such as lawyers, intellectuals
and scientists which issued a 700-page report with detailed ideas
about the content of the new constitution (Gylfason 2012, p. 13).

Representatives to the Constitutional Assembly were elected on
November 2010. It has been noted that: 'The election campaign
was exceptionally civilized, and quite different from parliamentary
election campaigns. [...] The elected representatives comprised a
diverse group of people of all ages with broad experience from
representatives on an individual basis from hundreds of scattered
candidates', including "almost every nook and cranny of national
life: doctors, lawyers, priests, and professors, yes, but also company
board members, a farmer, a champion for the rights of handicapped
persons, mathematicians, media people, erstwhile members of
parliament, a nurse, a philosopher, poets and artists, political
scientists, a theatre director, and a labor union leader, a good cross
section of society" (Gylfason, 2012, p. 12).

The constitutional body convened between April and July 2011.
After assessing the need for a new constitution, the council split
into three working groups in order to address the main issues,
which went from the definition of basic values to democratic
participation. Materials were published on its website with
presentation of assessments on the 1944 Constitution, the work of
the council, the material it received, and the draft constitution.
Sessions of the council were broadcast, and calls for proposals on
social media sites such as YouTube, Twitter, Facebook and Flickr
brought about a broad response. Three thousand suggestions were

posted on the council's Facebook page, the best of which were discussed on the website. Indeed, thanks to this participation in the drafting via social media the Iceland's draft constitution was described as "the world's first crowdsourced constitution" (Elkins et al. 2012). The main issues addressed were "the moral vacuum in the government, the role and accountability of the country's executives, and the lack of outlets for direct democratic participation" (Elkins et al. 2012). A draft constitution was approved unanimously and submitted to the parliament in July 2011. Even if it was not adopted by the Parliament, the constitutional process empowered the citizens and helped introducing new ideas in an intensely populated public sphere. The struggle for the approval of the constitution continued in fact for a long time (della Porta 2020).

This short account on the *crowdsourced* constitutional process in Iceland vividly illustrates some potential effects of citizens' mobilizations even in the most important constitutional moments. In social movement studies, an analysis of their effects is an integral part of the research on social movements as agents of social change. Different movements have achieved different degrees of success, and the determinants of their outcomes have been central to debates on social movements. A number of social movement characteristics have been frequently cited as particularly influential in this respect. In general, research has concentrated on such questions as: are movements that propose radical change more successful than those that propose moderate change or vice versa? Does violence work? Is a centralized and bureaucratic organization a help or a hindrance for social movements? While social movement studies have been slow to address the effects of contentious politics (concentrating attention rather on its causes and modalities), a growing body of literature has developed more recently to address these questions (Bosi et al. 2016, for a review). In what follows, we first consider the difficulties social movements (and analysts) face in identifying victorious strategies (9.1). Changes in policies (9.2) and in politics (9.3) will then be discussed. Sections 9.4 and 9.5 will finally address the role of social movements in promoting and deepening democracy.

9.1   SOCIAL MOVEMENT EFFECTS: SOME CAVEATS

Assessing the outcomes of movements is not easy: not only several actors contribute to define such outcomes, but even movements themselves are composite actors, endowed with various types of resources and using different strategies of protest, but also persuasion. Outcomes can moreover be planned and unplanned as well as being more or less favorable to the social movement itself. In this sense, a success is the positive "outcome of a resolved challenge" (Gamson 1990) at procedural or substantive levels. Research on movements' outcomes has indeed considered dimensions both internal and external to the movements. Internally, each wave of protests tends to change the material and symbolic resources available for specific movements and broader movement families. As for external impacts, social movements can achieve acceptance and be recognized as a legitimate counterpart from their opponents, i.e. procedural impacts, and/or they might obtain advantages and concessions according to their claims, i.e. substantial impacts (Kitschelt 1986). Movements might produce structural impacts by affecting the political institutions, and sensitizing impacts, by influencing the political debate (Kriesi 2004). Also culture, identity and subjectivity are influenced by waves of mobilization as social movements contribute to socialize new generations of citizens (Giugni et al. 1999; della Porta 2018a).

In one of the first and most influential studies on the effects produced by the strategies social movements adopt, William Gamson (1990) has linked success – when the demands of a challenger are met and consequent concessions are obtained – to a minimalist strategy (thinking small), the adoption of direct action, and a centralized and bureaucratic organization. Challenging this vision, other scholars have however pointed at radical claims and strategies as promising strategic choice under some circumstances as they might reinforce internal solidarity and favor the creation of alliances. Additionally, it has been pointed out that when organizations, including social movement organizations, become bureaucratized, the desire for organizational survival tends to prevail over declared collective objectives. According to Francis Fox Piven and Richard Cloward (1977, pp. xxi–xxii), the effort to build organizations is not only futile but also damaging as

> by endeavoring to do what they cannot do, organizers fail to do what they can do. During those brief periods in which people are roused to indignation, when they are prepared to defy the authorities to whom they ordinarily defer ... those who call themselves leaders do not usually escalate the momentum of the people's protest.

In addition, no particular strategic element can be evaluated in isolation and without taking into account the conditions within which social movements must operate (Burstein et al. 1995) and the presence of alliances or opponents in power (Cress and Snow 2000).

Indeed, the identification of a "strategy for success" is an arduous task for both activists and scholars as movement campaigns are characterized by multiple actors and forms of action: from marches to crowdsourced constitutional processes, such as in the Icelandic anti-austerity protests. The attribution of credit for obtaining substantive successes faces a series of obstacles, given the existence of such close relationships between a set of variables that it becomes impossible to identify cause and effect. For instance, socioeconomic, cultural, and political instances of globalization are the product of at the same time reactions to previous movements and adaptation to movement pressures, settling new resources and constraints for protest.

Most importantly, movements are never the sole actors to intervene on an issue. Rather, they do so in alliance with political parties and, not infrequently, with public agencies – as the Icelandic examples illustrate, up to the president of the republic. Thus, "the outcome of bargaining is not the result of the characteristics of either party, but rather is the function of their resources relative to each other, their relationships with third parties, and other factors in the environment" (Burstein, Einwohner, and Hollander 1995, p. 280). If the results obtained by social movements (or their failure to obtain them) have often been explained by environmental conditions, particularly the openness of political opportunities and the availability of allies, it is difficult nonetheless to identify which of the many actors involved in a given policy area are responsible for one reaction or another, establishing whether a given policy would have been enacted through other institutional actors anyway.

Fourth, the difficulties created by a plurality of actors add up to the difficulty of reconstructing the causal dynamics underlying particular public decisions. On the one hand, events are so intertwined that it is difficult to say which came first, particularly in moments of high mobilization. On the other, social movements demand long-term changes, but the protest cycle stimulates immediate incremental reforms. When social movements successfully place particular issues on the public agenda this "does not happen directly or even in a linear fashion. In fact, as their ideas are vulgarized and domesticated, the early risers in a protest cycle often disappear from the scene. But a portion of their message is distilled into common frameworks of public or private culture while the rest is ignored" (Tarrow 1994, p. 185). The evolution toward movements' aims is characterized by steps forward and steps back, moments in which public policy approaches the demands made by social movements and others in which the situation deteriorates.

Whether the results of protest should be judged in the short or in the long term represents a further problem. Social movements frequently obtain successes in the early phases of mobilization, but this triggers opposing interests and often a backlash in public opinion. Thus, while it is true that there is a broad consensus on many of the issues raised by social movements (peace, the defense of nature, improvements in the education system, equality), mobilization can nevertheless result in the polarization of public opinion. This normally produces a growth in movement support, but very often also a growth in opposition. Furthermore, movement success on specific demands frequently leads to the creation of countermovements: the development of neoliberalism as an ideology of the capitalist class has been explained as a reaction to the labor movement victories in terms of social rights (Sklair 1995). While the capacity of social movements to realize their general aims has been considered low, they have been seen as more effective in importing new issues into the public debate. Particularly when one is comparing different movements or countries, the problems outlined above hinder an evaluation of the relative effectiveness of particular movement strategies. While there is also a problem with the attribution of particular results to more institutionalized actors such as political parties and pressure groups, factors particular to social movements such as their distance from the levers of power, heterogeneous definition of their objectives, and organizational instability further complicate matters. In what follows, therefore, we will not attempt to identify winning strategies but, rather, to consider some of the consequences of the interaction between social movements and their environment, distinguishing effects at substantial and procedural level.

9.2   CHANGES IN PUBLIC POLICY

A first area for assessing the effects produced by social movements is that of actual policy. Generally, social movements are formed to express dissatisfaction with existing policy in a given area. Environmentalist groups have demanded intervention to protect the environment; pacifists have opposed the culture of war; students have criticized selection and authoritarianism in education; the feminist movement has fought discrimination against women; the world social forums criticized neoliberal globalization; protest during the financial crisis targeted austerity measures. Although it is usual to make a distinction between political and cultural movements – the first following a more instrumental logic, the second a more symbolic one – all movements tend to make demands on the political system.

First of all, some specific claims acquire high symbolic relevance, becoming nonnegotiable, as the basis for a movement's identity. For example, in many countries the feminist movement has been constructed around the nonnegotiable right of women to "choose" concerning childbirth; the halting of the installation of NATO nuclear missiles fulfilled a similar role for the peace movement. In the first case, mobilization was proactive, seeking to gain something new, the right to free abortion. In the second, it was reactive, seeking to block a decision (to install cruise missiles), which had already been taken. One of the founding organizations of the World Social Forum in Porto Alegre, ATTAC, emerged around the demands of a tax on transnational transactions; also present in Porto Alegre, the debt relief campaign asked for the foreign debt of poor countries to be totally written off. The constitutional process in Iceland had the highly symbolic meaning of refounding the country. In all cases, considerable changes in public policy were being demanded. Characteristic of these nonnegotiable objectives is their role in the social movements' definitions of themselves and of the external world (Pizzorno 1978). Demands whose symbolic value is very high, such as the Equal Rights Amendment in the case of the American feminist movement, remain central for a movement even when their potential effectiveness is questioned (Mansbridge 1986).

While nonnegotiable demands are particularly important in the construction of collective identities, social movements rarely limit themselves to just these. In the case of the global justice movement, the general aim of "building another possible world" has been articulated in specific requests, from the opposition to privatization of public services and public good (i.e., the campaign for free access to water) to the rights of national governments to organize the low-cost production of medicines in emergency cases; from the opposition to specific projects of dam construction to a democratic reform of the United Nations. Cooperating in global protest campaigns, ecological associations stressed the environmental unsustainability of neoliberal capitalism, trade unions the negative consequences of free trade on labor rights and levels of employment, feminist groups the suffering of women under cuts to the welfare state. Anti-austerity protests put forward claims on housing but also pensions and public services. Social movements "struggle within and with welfare systems, variously rising to challenge existing arrangements, contributing to changing them, defending existing provisions against attack, or seeking to implant their own direct means of solving welfare problems. But they do so discontinuously" (Barker and Levalette 2015, p. 715). From the global South to Europe, privatization, liberalization, and deregulation have been resisted by social movements, including unions, especially of the public services.

Considering public policies, the changes brought about by social movements may be evaluated by looking at the various phases of the decision-making process (Kolb 2007): the emergence of new issues; the writing and applying of new legislation; and the effects of public policies in alleviating the condition of those mobilized by collective action. Five levels of responsiveness to collective demands within the political system have been so traditionally distinguished:

> The notion of "access responsiveness" indicates the extent to which authorities are willing to hear the concerns of such a group ... If the demand ... is made into an issue and placed on the agenda of the political system, there has occurred a second type of responsiveness which can here be labeled "agenda responsiveness" ... As the proposal ... is passed into law, a third type of responsiveness is attained; the notion of 'policy responsiveness' indicates the degree to which those in the political system adopt legislation or policy congruent with the manifest demands of protest groups ... If measures are taken to ensure that the legislation is fully enforced, then a fourth type of responsiveness is attained: "output responsiveness" ... Only if the underlying grievance is alleviated would a fifth type of responsiveness be attained: "impact responsiveness."
>
> (Schumaker 1975, pp. 494–495)

So, for instance, the influence of environmental movements upon policy has been considered as more likely in the agenda-setting stages of policy formation, when policy preferences are still malleable (Olzak and Soule 2009). In this early stage, environmental movements can lobby elites and/or rise awareness in the public opinion). However, environmental campaigns are at times effective also in opposing policy changes: "environmental campaigners have resisted, and sometimes successfully obstructed the implementation of government policy. In some cases, the impact of the environmental movement appears clear, as, for example, in the case of the protests in Germany that disrupted the transport of nuclear waste" (Rootes and Nulman 2015, p. 733).

In general, research on social movements has concentrated on the production of legislation. Most "studies focus on policy responsiveness, fewer on access responsiveness, and very few on the political agenda, outputs, policy impact, or structural change" (Burstein et al. 1995, p. 285). Having identified a series of areas in which movements intervene, quantitative and qualitative analyses attempt to measure the response of parliaments and governments. An analysis of the concrete effects of social movements cannot stop, however, with the production of legislation. As noted in our discussion of social movements and political opportunities, different states have different capacities for implementing legislation, and it is precisely from the implementation of legislation that concrete gains are achieved. Even more relevant, transnational norms set in international agreements require laws to be enacted at the national level. As the cases of agreements on arms proliferation and land mines, or the Kyoto Agreement to control climate changes, indicate, very often superpowers (first of all, the United States) refuse to sign or implement international agreements. In order to evaluate the results produced by a social movement, therefore, it is also necessary to analyze how the laws or agreements they helped bring about are actually applied.

Real change, the effects produced by legislation however implemented, is even more difficult to judge. Laws that seek to meet certain of the demands of social movements may be limited in effect or even counterproductive, no matter how well implemented. As research on the effects of environmental movements has noted:

> *The striking thing about environmental movements is that despite their many successes, and justified celebration of their increasing influence in many policy arenas, the assault on the global environment proceeds at an unprecedented pace. Scarcely a week goes by without new evidence of continuing degradation of the global environment: the concentrations of greenhouse gases in the atmosphere are at unprecedentedly high levels and rising; tropical rainforests continue to be logged and burned so that the "lungs of the planet" are an ever smaller proportion of the surface area of the Earth; biodiversity continues to decline at an alarming rate; overfishing and acidification of the oceans increasingly endanger tropical reefs and marine ecology.*
>
> (Rootes and Nulman 2015, p. 740)

Talking about norms already implies considering that, alongside structural changes in the condition of those categories or social groups mobilized by collective action, cultural transformation is a further important element in achieving and consolidating new gains. Although it is true that all movements tend to call for legislative change, this is neither their only, nor even perhaps their primary, objective. Movements are in fact carriers of symbolic messages (Gamson 2004, p. 247): they aim to influence bystanders, spreading their own conception of the world, and they struggle to have new identities recognized. The effects of social movements are also connected with diffuse cultural change, the elaboration of "new codes" (Melucci 1982, 1984). Typically, new ideas emerge within critical communities, and are then spread via social movements – as Rochon (1998, p. 179) observes, "The task of translating the chronic problem as described by the critical community into an acute problem that will attract media attention is the province of social and political movements." It is useful, therefore, to look at a movement's sensitizing impact, i.e., the "possibility that a movement will provoke a sensitizing of some social actor in the political arena or the public arena, which goes in the direction of the goals of the movement" (Kriesi et al. 1995, p. 211).

Furthermore, social movements are more aware than some better-resourced actors of their need for public support. Since protest mobilization is short lived, social movements cannot content themselves with legislative reforms that can always be reversed later. They must ensure that support for their cause is so widely disseminated as to discourage any attempt to roll reforms back. As noted about the environmental movement:

> *By engaging the public, environmental movements have often been credited with setting the agenda for public policy on environmental matters, but in general their impact is perhaps better conceived not as agenda-setting so much as highlighting neglected issues, maintaining their salience, keeping public concern alive even at times when the attentions of policy makers are diverted elsewhere by other pressing issues such as those of economic crisis management, and pressing their advantage when windows of political opportunity are opened*

(Rootes and Nulman 2015, 734).

To cite another example, student protests against neoliberal universities in Chile or Canada were effective in sensitizing the public opinion to education as a public good (Smeltzer and Hearn 2015; della Porta, Cini and Guzman 2020).

It should be added that social movements do not aim only to change public opinion, but also seek to convince those responsible for implementing public policy, and change the values of political elites as well as those of the public. Although mass mobilization may temporarily convince political parties to pass a law, that law must also be implemented. In this case, too, social movements do not always have sufficient means of access to the less visible areas of policy implementation, and their chances of success therefore depend on influencing the public agencies responsible for implementing the laws that concern them. For instance, via direct contacts or brokers, experts within or near movements have been able to infiltrate the international advocacy community, and help spread dissent concerning neoliberal strategies within the political and nonpolitical elite.

9.3   SOCIAL MOVEMENTS AND PROCEDURAL CHANGES

Social movements do not limit their interventions to single policies. They frequently influence the way in which the political system as a whole functions: its institutional and formal procedures, elite recruitment, the informal configuration of power (Kitschelt 1986; Rucht 1992). Movements demand, and often obtain, decentralization of political power, consultation of interested citizens on particular decisions or appeals procedures against decisions of the public administration. They interact with the public administration, presenting themselves as institutions of "democracy from below" (Roth 1994): they ask to be allowed to testify before representative institutions and the judiciary, to be listened to as counterexperts, to receive legal recognition and material incentives.

Protest, only a small part of overall social movement activity, is undoubtedly considered important, but also ineffectual unless accompanied by other forms of political pressure and democratic control. Although contacts with government ministries and the public bureaucracy may not be seen on their own as particularly effective in influencing policy, they are considered useful for information-gathering and for countering the influence of pressure groups – so, e.g., the environmental movement has been able to counter anti-environmentalists by building alliances within the European Commission bureaucracy (Ruzza 2004). As we shall see in what follows, social movements increase the possibilities of access to the political system, both through *ad hoc* channels relating to certain issues and through institutions that are open to all noninstitutional actors.

Already the labor movement had pressured the nation-state toward increasing citizenship rights, at civil, political and social levels. In the late twentieth century, social movements have been able to introduce changes toward greater grassroots control over public institutions. In many European countries, administrative decentralization has taken place since the 1970s, with the creation of new channels of access to decision-makers. Various forms of participation in decision making have been tried within social movement organizations. If the rise of mass political parties has been defined as a "contagion from the left" and the power of the mass media as a "contagion from the right," the new social movements have been acclaimed as a "contagion from below" (Rohrschneider 1993). Social movements have brought about a pluralization of the ways in which political decisions are taken, pushed by cyclical dissatisfaction with centralized and bureaucratic representative democracy. In this sense, social movements have produced a change in political culture, in the whole set of norms and reference schemes that define the issues and means of action that are politically legitimate. Repertoires of collective action, which were once condemned and dealt with simply as public order problems, have slowly become acceptable (della Porta 1998a).

In many countries, direct democracy has been developed as a supplementary channel of access to those opened within representative democracy. On issues such as divorce, abortion, or gender discrimination, for example, the women's movement was in many cases able to appeal directly to the people using either popularly initiated legislation or referenda for the abrogation of existing laws or the implementation of transnational treaties. As in the Icelandic case, during the Great Recession, referenda have become an increasingly important instrument of direct expression for ordinary citizens, particularly on issues that are not directly related to the social cleavages around which political parties have formed. Referendum campaigns present social movements with an opportunity to publicize the issues that concern them, as well as the hope of being able to bypass the obstacle represented by governments hostile to their demands (della Porta, O'Connor et al. 2017).

Social movements also contribute to the creation of new arenas for the development of public policy. Expert commissions are frequently formed on issues raised by protest, and social movement representatives may be allowed to take part, possibly as observers. The "President's Commission on Campus Unrest," which William Scranton presided over in the United States (in 1970) is one example. Others are the commission led by Lord Scarman into rioting in the United Kingdom in the 1980s and the commission of inquiry set up on "Youth Protest in the Democratic State" in Germany (Willelms et al. 1993). After Seattle, commissions of independent experts have been set to investigate the social effects of globalization (such as a Parliamentary Commission in Germany) as well as the police behavior during transnational protest events (see the Seattle City Council Commission on the Seattle events). In Greece, the Truth Committee on Public Debt was established on April 4, 2015, by a decision of the president of the Hellenic Parliament to investigate into a debt that was considered as odious and illegitimate. Common to them all is the recognition that the problems they address are in some way extraordinary, and require extraordinary solutions. Although such expert commissions usually have a limited mandate and consultative power only, they enter a dialogue with public opinion through press contact and the publication of reports.

Besides commissions of enquiry, other channels of access are opened by the creation of consultative institutions on issues related to social movement demands. State ministries, local government bureaus, and other similar bodies now exist on women's or ecological issues in many countries, but also in IGOs. Such institutions, which are frequently set up on a permanent basis, have their own budgets and power to implement policies. Some regulatory administrative bodies have been established under the pressure of movement mobilizations, and see movement activists as potential allies (Amenta 1998). Also, as in the EU (Ruzza 2004), movement activists have been co-opted by specific public bodies as members of their staff (or vice versa). New opportunities for a "conflictual cooperation" develop within regulatory agencies that are set to implement goals that are also supported by movement activists (Giugni and Passy 1998, p. 85). The public administrators working in these institutions mediate particular social movement demands through both formal and informal channels and frequently ally themselves with movement representatives in order to increase the amount of public resources available in the policy areas over which they have authority. They tend to have frequent contacts with representatives of the social movements involved in their areas, the movement organizations taking on a consultancy role in many instances, and they sometimes develop common interests. Collaboration can take various forms: from consultation, to incorporation in committees, to delegation of power (Giugni and Passy 1998, p. 86; Diani 2015, p. ch. 8).

Informal negotiation has enabled some international governmental organizations to co-opt social movement associations that agree to work through discreet channels. Nongovernmental organizations have thus been accorded the status of actors, and on occasion important ones, in world governance, acknowledged as participants in the development of international norms (such as those on human rights) and on their implementation (Pagnucco 1996, p. 14). Besides a certain degree of institutional recognition, NGOs specializing in development assistance have received funding for the development programs they have presented, or for joining in projects already presented by national or international governments (O'Brien, Goetz, Scholte, and Williams 2000, p. 120). Many are also involved in managing funds earmarked for emergencies and humanitarian aid, which now make up more than half the projects of the World Bank (Brecher, Costello, and Smith 2000, p. 114). What is more, social movements have participated in institution-building at the international level (in particular, on human rights as well as environmental protection and, more recently, on refugee issues, della Porta 2018c), using their "soft power" in the form of knowledge and information (Smith 2004, p. 317).

In particular, social movement activists maintain direct contacts with decision-makers, participating in epistemic communities made up of representatives of governments, parties, and interest groups of various types and persuasions. In particular, NGOs critical of neoliberalist globalization have resorted to pressure both at the national and international levels, cultivating specific expertise. From human rights groups to environmentalists, epistemic communities – composed of activists and bureaucrats belonging to international organizations, as well as politicians from many countries – have won significant gains in a number of areas: for example, decontamination of radioactive waste, the establishment of an international tribunal on human rights violations, and a ban on antipersonnel mines (Khagram, Riker, and Sikkink 2002). Some NGOs have not only increased in size but also strengthened their influence on various stages of international policymaking (Sikkink and Smith 2002; Boli 1999). Their assets include an increasing credibility in public opinion and the consequent availability of private funding, as well their rootedness at the local level. Their specific knowledge, combined with useful contacts in the press, make many NGOs seem particularly reliable sources. At transnational level, "It is now widely recognized that civil society, from traditional international non-governmental organizations (INGOs) to transnational social movements, plays a significant role in global governance." Not only the very process of globalization enhanced a sense of common purpose but also "The widespread recognition of the transnational value of: human rights, civic participation, accountability, good governance and democracy, social empowerment, and gender equality, have enhanced the possibilities for CSOs [civil society organizations] to gain space and legitimacy in the international system beyond the traditional framework of state-based representation" (Marchetti 2015, p. 755).

Most important, so-called deliberative arenas have developed in the last two decades around the principle of participation of "normal citizens" in public arenas for debate, empowered by information and rules for high-quality communication. Research on co-management in public policies noted, if not a change in the paradigm, at least the experimentation with different bases of legitimacy through the incorporation of different points of view. Within the frame of "governing with the people," experiments with deliberative and participatory democracy in public decision-making have developed as ways of increasing the participation of citizens, creating high-quality communicative arenas and empowering citizens. The adopted formulas are, indeed, varied. In a study commissioned by the OECD, David Shand and Morten Arnberg's (1996) proposes a continuum of participation from minimal involvement to community control through regular referenda, with intermediary techniques such as consultation, partnership and delegation, in which control over developing policy options is handed to a board of community representatives within a framework specified by the government. Similarly, Patrick Bishop and Glyn Davis (2002) distinguish between consultation practices (interest group meetings, public meetings, discussion papers, public hearings); partnership (advisory boards, citizens' advisory committees, policy community fora, public inquiries); and controls (referenda, *community parliaments,* electronic voting). In fact, one could distinguish, with Graham Smith (2009), two main institutional formulas: the first is based on open assembly, and the second is oriented to the construction of a "mini-public," usually selected by lot.

As far as the *assembly model* is concerned, institutions of participatory democracy like neighbourhood assemblies or even thematic assemblies, neighborhood councils, consultation committees, strategic participatory plans now form part of local government in most democratic countries. In addition, user representatives are often admitted to the institutions that govern schools or other public services, which sometimes are even handed to citizens' groups to manage. The participatory budget promoted in Porto Alegre, a Brazilian city of 1,360,000 inhabitants, received particular attention. Throughout a long-term experiment, the participatory budget acquired an articulate and complex structure, oriented to achieving two main objectives: social equality and citizen empowerment in the allocation of part of the city budget. A fundamental criterion in the distribution of public funds was, in fact, the level of privation of public services and well-being in different neighborhoods. The organization of the process was oriented to controlling the limits of assemblies, in particular in terms of blocking decisions, without renouncing the advantages of direct democracy. Recognizing its success, the United Nations defined the participatory budget as one of the 40 "best practices" at global level (Allegretti 2003, p. 173).

As for the *mini-publics model*, from the beginning of the 1960s the idea of drawing lots as a democratic method of choosing representatives was implemented in citizen juries that emerged first in Germany and the United States and then in Denmark and France: small groups of citizens, drawn from population registers, met to express their opinion on some decisions. Similar to this is the *deliberative poll* model, which foresees informed deliberation among citizens selected to mirror some social characteristics of the population (Sintomer 2007, pp. 133 ff). While traditional surveys follow the logic of aggregation of individual preferences, deliberative polls – which may involve hundreds of people – aim to discover what public opinion would be if citizens had the possibility to study and discuss a certain theme.

Both types of experiments have proliferated at the national and, above all, the local level with aims that include effective problem-solving and equitable solutions as well as broad, deep, and sustained participation, improving managerial capacities, through greater transparency and the circulation of information, but also of transforming social relations, reconstructing social ties and capital of solidarity and trust and, from the political point of view, of democratizing democracy (Bacqué, Rey and Sintomer 2005; Font et al. 2014). In particular, the participatory budget has been credited with creating a positive context for deliberation fostering greater activism, networking associations, and working from a citywide orientation (Baiocchi 2002).

Several of these practices aim at reaching high deliberative quality in the sense that "all potentially affected groups have equal opportunity to get involved in the process and equal right to propose topics, formulate solutions, or critically discuss taken-for-granted approaches, and because decision-making is by exchange of argument" (Baccaro and Papadakis 2008). Even though the intensity of participation, its duration and influence, varies greatly between the various participatory devices, they do show the insufficiency of a merely representative conception of democracy.

But what exactly do these new arenas offer social movements? According to some authors, the presence of such channels of access presents more risks than advantages. In the first place, movements are induced to accept the shifting of conflict from the streets to less congenial arenas, where resources in which they are poor, such as technical or scientific expertise, are particularly important. The organization of a commission may be nothing more than a symbolic, elite gesture to constituencies and a means of delaying a decision until quieter times prevail (Lipsky 1965). Indeed, the creation of new procedures and institutional arenas can be seen as a means of co-opting movement elites and demobilizing the grassroots, if they are naive enough not to notice the deception (Piven and Cloward 1977, p. 53). Mistrust in the real independence of NGOs is indicated by the proliferation of such acronyms as GONGOs (government-organized NGOs), BONGOs (business-organized NGOs), and GRINGOs (government-run/initiated NGOs). NGOs are predominantly based in the north of the world (two-thirds of UN-registered NGOs have their headquarters in Europe and North America) (Sikkink 2002). Intergovernmental organizations have, furthermore, preferred dealing with larger, more top-heavy NGOs, that are less monitored by their base of support. While some NGOs were the first to mobilize against international financial institutions (in particular the World Bank, IMF, and WTO), protests developed due to skepticism regarding the efficacy of lobbying, coupled with a perception that large NGOs' reformist approach had failed (Brand and Wissen 2002). At a time of cutbacks in public spending, NGOs run the risk of being exploited to supplant an increasingly failing public service (Chandhoke 2002, p. 43). Moreover, adroitly manipulated experts can be used to legitimate as most "scientifically appropriate" those solutions that suit governments. Referenda address limited questions and mobilize public opinion only for very short periods; they also carry the risk that decisions will be made by the "silent majority," uninterested in (and uninformed about) the issues and problems raised by social movements, and therefore easily influenced by those with the most resources to devote to manipulating consensus. Some studies conclude that citizen participation in policy making increases efficiency, but others express doubts about its capacity to solve free-rider problems and produce optimal decisions or facilitate the achievement of the public good (Font et al. 2014). While assessments of the role of civil society organizations are often positive:

> [T]he normative competition at the global level is very intense. Any norm generates benefits and costs, it has beneficiaries and victims. As a matter of fact, in its implementation, the pro-CSOs norm has tended so far to favor by and large a specific set of organizations (big INGOs, strong transnational networks),

marginalizing less organized grassroots movements and small local groups. As a consequence, while still leaving windows of opportunities for mobilizations on different levels, overall, the current global governance scheme has been de facto selective in its interaction with civil society. Institutionalized, professional CSOs are part and parcel of the functional mode of governance insofar as they act as governance partners in the implementation of sector-comprehensive strategies on different policy levels or in the promotion of a pro-global integration agenda thereby providing alternative, deliberative paths for the re-legitimization of many international organizations.

(Marchetti 2015, pp. 763–764)

This might have perverse effect as, "the more international organizations seek professionalized NGOs, the less they will have bottom up civil society actors, which entails a diminution of the very legitimizing and communicative role of civil society" (Marchetti 2015, p. 764). In fact, international governmental organizations select campaigns (and frame their aims) so that they can claim some success, therefore enhancing their brand name (Bob 2005), being responsive to funders and supporters in the North and the West of the world.

In addition, participatory models of democracy are difficult to implement. The levels of effective participation, plurality, and efficacy of new arenas of decision making are varied and far from satisfactory. As for the pluralism of the new participatory arenas, since resources for collective mobilization are unequally distributed among social groups, poorer areas, and groups risk being excluded by the new institutions of policy making. Finally, in terms of empowerment, their effective capacity for decision making is often minimal: for various reasons, new channels of participation have usually been limited to "consultation" of citizens. If increasing participation allows for more visibility – and accountability – of policy making, parallel (and more effective) decision making seems to bypass public arenas.

The position of social movement organizations toward these experiments is, in fact, ambivalent. In particular, notwithstanding their resonance with the value promoted in these institutional experiments, social movements frequently criticized the results of "top-down" experiments as a merely symbolic representation of citizens' participation, responding to a renewed and more sophisticated consensus strategy (della Porta 2009a and 2009b). Critically, such experiments were considered elitist, but also useless and even dangerous in terms of cooptation. These processes were also labeled as artificial (not true experiments of a new democratic model) or "top-down" (promoted and implemented from the top of the political system). According to social movement activists, the "palaces of power" were not really opened to citizens' participation, but remained accessible only to the élites (in particular the economic ones). The criticism addresses especially the missing links between the consultation, deliberation, decision and monitoring phases, but also the technocratic distortion of the political debate, the pre-selection (by institutions) of relevant social actors to be involved in consultation, and in some cases the limited significance of the stakes (as signs of a too-cautious approach by the institutions) (della Porta 2013).

On the other hand, social movements have frequently been able to profit (partly through alliances with experts and policymakers) from the switching of decision-making to *ad hoc* commissions, certainly more open to public scrutiny than the normal arenas of policy implementation. New issues have been brought onto the public agenda through the work of such commissions (Willelms et al. 1993). Although social movements have not always been on the winning side in referenda, the latter have nonetheless contributed to putting new issues on the public agenda and to creating public sympathy for emergent actors. The ability to transform the rules of the political game, then, is a precondition for influencing public policy. In other words, procedural victories come (at least in part) before, and are indispensable for, successes on a more substantive level (Rochon and Mazmanian 1993). Enlarging policy making to encompass citizen participation – in the forms of auditing, people's juries, etc. – has often helped in solving problems created by local opposition to locally unwanted land use (LULU) (Bobbio and Zeppetella 1999; Bacqué, Rey and Sintomer 2005). As we have mentioned, the participatory emphasis on good governance, as well as its confidence in popular education (Baiocchi 2001), seems to have produced positive results in terms of empowerment of citizens as well as improvement of their quality of life. As Talpin (2015, p. 783) noted:

> *The involvement of social movements' organizations in participatory institutions has to face specific obstacles. First, their adversarial cognitive frames, seeing protest and bargaining as the means of promoting their cause, might not fit the more collaborative attitude required in democratic innovations. Also, activists might not acquire the skills required by participatory engagement: protest implies capacities other than the facilitation and organization of democratic processes. Finally, the most powerful SMOs might not be ready for engagement in institutions taking place mostly at the local level. Despite these hurdles, social movements' engagement in democratic innovations is considered a crucial condition for the success of participatory experiments.*

Social movements play a countervailing power within democratic innovations, counter-balancing the domination of more powerful groups within deliberative processes characterized by asymmetries in terms of knowledge and skills (Fung and Wright 2001). Additionally, social movements might increase public participation and make public authorities accountable toward the implementation of the results of democratic innovations (Talpin 2015, p. 784).

Summarizing, at a time in which tensions in democracies are increasing, democratic participation offers an important resource to reinvigorating democratic life. Institutional democratic innovations and social movements have long been identified as important in this effort. Yet, these phenomena have usually occurred and have been interpreted as independent from each other. We can conclude that:

> *Deliberative democracy and collective action have often been opposed as offering conflicting ways of constructing the common good, based on cooperative discussion on the one hand, and adversarial protest and negotiation on the*

other. Social movements have however shaped the inception and organization of democratic innovations to a large extent. Historically, the first wave of delibera-tive and participatory institutions appeared in the 1970s as a response to social movements' claims for a greater inclusiveness of the political process. Social movements also influence the way democratic innovations work, by partici-pating, or on the contrary boycotting, new forms of democratic engagement. Finally, social movements' internal democratic practices and reflections about the limits of informal decision making have inspired the field of deliberative democracy, which has, in turn, influenced collective action research.

(Talpin 2015, p. 781)

9.4   SOCIAL MOVEMENTS AND DEMOCRATIZATION

Social movements contribute to policy and procedures in different steps of democra-tization processes. Charles Tilly (2004a, p. 125) stresses in fact the existence of

a broad correspondence between democratization and social movements. Social movements originated in the partial democratization that set British subjects and North-American colonists against their rulers during the eigh-teenth century. Across the nineteenth century, social movements generally flourished and spread where further democratization was occurring and receded when authoritarian regimes curtailed democracy. The pattern continued during the first and twenty-first century: the maps of full-fledged institutions and social movements overlap greatly.

If democratization promotes democracy via the broadening of citizens' rights and the public accountability of ruling elites, most, but not all, social movements support democracy. In fact, in pushing for suffrage enlargement or the recognition of associa-tional rights, social movements contribute to democratization: "Gains in the democ-ratization of state processes are perhaps the most important that social movements can influence and have the greatest systemic impacts" (Amenta and Caren 2004, p. 265). This was not always the case, however: some movements – e.g., fascist and neo-fascist ones – denied democracy altogether, while others – e.g., some New Left move-ments in Latin America – had the unwanted effect of producing a backlash in democratic rights (Tilly 2004b). Identity politics, such as those driving ethnic con-flicts, often ended up in religious war and racial violence (Eder 2003).

Two different conceptions of the role played by social movements in the process of democratization have been singled out by Tilly (1993–1994, p. 1). According to a *populist approach* to democracy, emphasizing participation from below, "social move-ments contribute to the creation of a public space – social settings, separate both from governing institutions and from organizations devoted to production or reproduction, in which consequential deliberation over public affairs takes place – as well as sometimes contributing to transfers of power over states. Public space and transfers of power then supposedly promote democracy, at least under some conditions. An *elitist approach* assess instead that democratization must be a top-down process, while an excess of mobilization leads to new forms of authoritarianism, since the elites feel afraid of too many and too rapid changes.

Social movements contribute to democratization only under certain conditions. In particular, only those movements that explicitly demand increased equality and protection for minorities promote democratic development. In fact, looking at the process of democratization, it can be observed that collective mobilization has frequently created the conditions for a destabilization of authoritarian regimes, but at times it leads to an intensification of repression or the collapse of weak democratic regimes, particularly when social movements do not stick to democratic conceptions.

However, social movements often openly mobilized for democracy. In Africa and Asia, Latin America as well as in Eastern Europe, although in different forms, social movements asked for democratization, producing a final breakdown of fascist as well as socialist authoritarian governments. Studies on democratization have traditionally assigned a limited role to social movements and protest. Yet, in historical sociology, Barrington Moore Jr. (1966), R. Bendix (1964) and T. H. Marshall (1992) all recognized the impact of class struggles on early democratization.

Although the usual focus has been on the middle class as promoters of democratization, more recently, Dietrich Rueschemeyer, Evelyn Huber Stephens, and John D. Stephens (1992) pointed to the role of the working class in promoting democratization in the last two waves of democratization in Southern Europe, South America, and the Caribbean. In fact, "the working class was the most consistent democratic force" (1992, p. 8), "it was the subordinated classes that fought for democracy," so that "the chances of democracy, then must be seen as fundamentally shaped by the balance of class power" (1992, pp. 46–47). The middle class played instead an ambivalent role, pressing for their inclusion, but only occasionally (when weak) allying with the working class, in order to extend democracy to them as well. The growth of working classes is therefore pointed out as critical for the promotion of democracy as "a dense civil society establishes a counterweight to the state, so favoring democracy" (1992, p. 50).

While class analyses of democratization processes have been criticized for a "structuralist bias," the *transitologist* approach stresses instead agency, as well as a dynamic and processual vision of democratization, focusing on elite strategies and behavior. For O'Donnell and Schmitter, transitions from authoritarian rule are illustrations of "underdetermined social change, of large-scale transformations that occur when there are insufficient structural or behavioral parameters to guide and predict the outcome" (1986, p. 363).

It is, however, elite politics that count, as literature on recent democratization processes "emphasizes elite strategic choices, downplaying or ignoring the role of labor in democratization" (Collier 1999, p. 5). In this narrative, the heroism of the few drives the process, as it is the action of exemplary individuals that tests the capacity of the regime to resist (Bermeo 1990, p. 361). Stress is put on the role of leaders, often individuals, which are considered as especially relevant in periods of high uncertainties and indeterminacy and approaches are extremely state-centric, with privileged role accorded to institutional actors (Bermeo 1990, p. 361). While civil society is supposed to play an important role in promoting the transition process, these "resurrections of civil society" are seen as short disruptive moments when movements, unions, churches, and society in general push for the initial liberalization of a nondemocratic regime into a transition toward democracy (Karl 1990, p. 1). In their seminal work O'Donnell and Schmitter (1986, pp. 53–54) observed:

> *In some cases and at particular moments of the transition, many of these diverse layers of society may come together to form what we choose to call the popular upsurge. Trade unions, grass-roots movements, religious groups, intellectuals, artists, clergymen, defenders of human rights, and professional associations all support each other's efforts toward democratization and coalesce into a greater whole which identifies itself as the people.*

Although this is a moment of great expectations, 'regardless of its intensity and of the background from which it emerges, this popular upsurge is always ephemeral' (O'Donnell and Schmitter 1986, pp. 55–56). In an ideal-typical development of democratization, three stages are depicted: splits in the elite on how to legitimize the regime are followed by liberalization (as loosening of repression) initiated by the regime itself, that pushes the regime into a slippery slope, opening opportunities for social movements, among which the labor movement; finally, incumbents negotiate with moderated opposition party leaders (Ulfelder 2005). Mass mobilization "is typically seen as a relatively brief phase, quickly superseded by the next step. The emphasis from this perspective is thus on the process by which soft-line incumbents and moderate opposition party leaders reach some implicit or explicit agreement on a transition form an authoritarian regime" (Collier 1999, p. 6). Rather, transitology tends to consider movements and protest actors as manipulated by elites and focusing on very instrumentally defined purposes (see Przeworski 1991, p. 57; for a critique, Baker 1999). Even though the dynamic, agency-focused approach of transitology allowed for some interest in the role played by movements in democratization to develop, it did not focus attention on them, while calling for tactical moderation as political parties are called for negotiating pacts, mediating conflicts and sedating revolts.

In research on democratization process, however dominant, the "elitist" approach has not been unchallenged. The relevance of contention during democratization processes is stressed instead by social movement studies, which however flourished in (and on) established democracies, with less than rare attempts to look at social movements in democratization phases (for a review, Rossi and della Porta 2009). As Ulfelder (2005, p. 313) synthetized, "Various subsequent studies of democratic transitions have afforded collective actors a more prominent role, allowing for the possibility that mass mobilization has a substantial impact on the transition process and is sometimes the catalyst that sets a transition in motion." In fact, the balance of both participation by outsiders and contention in empirical cases varies in different paths of democratization (della Porta 2014; 2017a). Case studies have indicated that democratization is often linked to contentious dynamics, such as pro-democratic cycles of protest, and waves of strikes (cf. Foweraker and Landman 1997; Collier 1999; McAdam, Tarrow and Tilly 2001). They can affect different steps of the democratization process.

Protests have also developed under authoritarian regimes. Repertoire of resistance in authoritarian regimes involves a sort of duplicity in public discourse, with however the construction of some free spaces (from church to artistic spaces) within which "Members gather, talk, and sometimes take part in activities that push the limits of what the regime may define as acceptable" (Johnston 2015, p. 627). Creatively, oppositional activists engage in form of hidden protest, such as let telephone ringing at the same time in the same place, carrying toilette papers, bringing flowers to symbolic places, spraying graffiti. So, "small acts of protest and opposition are creatively carved out of situations where social control breaks down and islands of freedom are creatively and agentically claimed by dissident actors" (Johnston 2015, p. 618). Singing prohibited songs at public events or mobilizing at funerals of oppositional leaders are among these creative tactics.

Resistance is also used in what Bayat refers to as *nonmovements*. Collective actions of noncollective actors, these are not ideologically driven but rather aimed at redistribution and autonomy through the use of dissimulation, sabotage, and false compliance. So, "the story of nonmovements is the story of agency in the times of constraints" (Bayat 2010, p. 26). Everyday forms of resistance by the poor and the emarginated showed a capacity for resistance through a quiet encroachment of the ordinary: "a silent, patient, protracted and pervasive advancement of ordinary people on the propertied and powerful in order to survive hardships and better their lives" (Bayat 1997, p. 7). Threats to survival brought about an activation of those networks for collective action. The Arab Spring mobilized groups like the ones Bayat had studied in Iran. There, the squatters of the shantytowns who had mobilized to ask for basic services sometimes acquired them through illicit or do-it-yourself practices, tapping water and electricity, constructing roads, clinics, mosques, and libraries, forming their own associations and consumer cooperatives (Bayat 2010, p. 2). Similar was the resistance of the unemployed, often young, who protested, but also engaged in street vending and street services, putting up kiosks or stalls, as "their collective operation converted the street sidewalks into vibrant and colorful shopping places" (Bayat 2010, p. 3). As Bayat recalled, in the cases he studied, "vendors resisted the eviction policy in different ways. They organized street demonstrations, withstood the eviction agents on the spot, took legal actions, and publicized their plight in the press. The most enduring method was the everyday guerrilla-type tactic of 'sell and run'" (Bayat 2010, p. 149). These actions politicized in the face of a repression that comprised everyday harassment and extraordinary brutality. A street vendor, and his self-immolation, were in fact at the root of the Tunisian upheaval.

Some forms of action during the Arab Spring were based on what Bayat (2010) defined as the encroachment of everyday life with a sort of cosmopolitanism of the subalterns. Free spaces were constructed during practices of self-help among the poor and emarginated groups, which so often play an important role in resisting authoritarian and semi-authoritarian regimes. It was through the politicization of various forms of resistance that the streets then became a space for mobilization. As Bayat (2010, p. 220) noted, the Arab street was neither irrational nor dead; rather, the regimes' attempts to depoliticize social ties had a hyper-politicizing effect. The poor had built relations by occupying the same street, and coming together under common threats:

> *[C]onflict originates from the active use of public space by subjects who, in the modern states, are allowed to use it only passively – through walking, driving, watching – or in other ways that the state dictates. Any active or participative use infuriates officials, who see themselves as the sole authority to establish and control public order. Thus, the street vendors who proactively spread their businesses in the main alleyways; squatters who take over public parks, lands, or sidewalks; youth who control the street-corner spaces, street children who establish street communities; poor housewives who extend their daily household activities into alleyways; or protestors who march in the streets, all challenge the state prerogatives and thus may encounter reprisal*
>
> (Bayat 2010, p. 11).

Protests (especially, strikes) often constitute precipitating events that start *liberalization*, spreading the perception among the authoritarian elites that there is no choice other than opening the regime if they want to avoid an imminent or potential civil war or violent takeover of power by democratic and/or revolutionary actors (e.g. Bermeo 1997, Wood 2000). During liberalization, civil society organizations publicly (re) emerge in a much more visible fashion (O'Donnell and Schmitter 1986): trade unions, left-wing parties and urban movements, mainly in shantytowns and industrial districts, have often pushed for democracy, sometimes in alliance with transnational actors (e.g. in Latin America, as well as in Eastern Europe; Keck and Sikkink 1998; Glenn 2003).

During the *transition* to democracy, old (labor, ethnic) movements and new (women's, urban) movements have often participated in large coalitions asking for democratic rights as well as social justice (della Porta 2014, 2017a). The importance of protest in transition processes has been observed in Africa (Bratton and Van de Walle 1997), Latin America, and Southern Europe (Collier and Mahoney 1997; della Porta, Andretta et al. 2018). The mobilization of a pro-democracy coalition of trade unions, political parties, churches, and social movements has often been pivotal in supporting movements toward democracy in the face of contending countermovements pushing for the restoration of authoritarian/totalitarian regimes. The bargaining dynamic among elites interacts then with the increased intensity of protest (Casper and Taylor 1996, pp. 9–10; Glenn 2003, p. 104).

Social movements are also active during *consolidation*, a step that is generally considered to start with the first free and open elections, the end of the uncertainty period and/or the implementation of a minimum quality of substantive democracy (Linz and Stepan 1996; O'Donnell 1993, 1994; Rossi and della Porta 2009 for a review).

In some cases, this is accompanied by a demobilization of civil society organizations as energies are channeled into party politics; in others, however, demobilization does not occur. In fact, social movement organizations mobilized during liberalization and transition rarely totally disband; on the contrary, democratization often facilitates the development of social movement organizations (for example, the women's movement in Southern Europe, della Porta, Andretta et al. 2018). The presence of a tradition of mobilization, as well as movements that are supported by political parties, unions and religious institutions can facilitate the maintenance of a high level of protest, as in the Communist Party's promotion of shantytown dwellers' protests in Chile; the *Partido dos Trabalhadores* (PT) and part of the Roman Catholic Church with the rural movements and unions in Brazil; or the environmental movements in Eastern Europe. In this stage, movements might claim the rights of those who are excluded by *low-intensity democracies* and ask for a more inclusive democracy (i.e. peasants', employment, indigenous people and women's rights) and the end of authoritarian legacies. Furthermore, movements' networks play an important role in mobilizing against persistent exclusionary patterns and authoritarian legacies (Yashar 2005). Keeping elites under continuous popular pressure after transition can facilitate a successful consolidation (Karatnycky and Ackerman 2005). What is more, movements' alternative practices and values help to sustain and expand democracy (de Sousa Santos 2005).

9.5 NORMATIVE CONCEPTIONS OF DEMOCRACY IN MOVEMENT

The spread of new policy arenas has contributed to the realization of what has been considered one of the principal aims, if not the principal aim, of many (if not all) social movements: the development of a new conception of democracy. In fact, it has been claimed that social movements do not limit themselves to developing special channels of access for themselves but that, more or less explicitly, they expound a fundamental critique of conventional politics, thus shifting their endeavors from politics itself to metapolitics (Offe 1985). From this point of view, social movements affirm the legitimacy (if not the primacy) of alternatives to parliamentary democracy, criticizing both liberal democracy and the "organized democracy" of political parties: "The stakes and the struggle of the left and libertarian social movements thus invoke an ancient element of democratic theory that calls for an organization of collective decision making referred to in varying ways as classical, populist, communitarian, strong, grassroots, or direct democracy against a democratic practice in contemporary democracies labeled as realist, liberal, elite, republican, or representative democracy" (Kitschelt 1993, p. 15).

It is certainly the case that the idea of democracy developed by social movements since the 1960s rests on at least partially different foundations than representative democracy. According to the representative democracy model, citizens elect their representatives and exercise control through the threat of denying re-election at subsequent polls. The direct democracy favored by social movements rejects the principle of delegation, viewed as an instrument of oligarchic power, and asserts that representatives should be subject to recall at all times. Moreover, delegation is comprehensive in a representative democracy, where representatives decide on a whole range matters for citizens. In comparison, in a system of direct democracy, authority is delegated on an issue-by-issue basis. Whereas representative democracy envisages the creation of a specialized body of representatives, direct democracy opts for continual turnover. Representative democracy is based on formal equality (one person, one vote); direct democracy is participatory, the right to decide being recognized only in the case of those who demonstrate their commitment to the public cause. While representative democracy is often bureaucratic, with decision making concentrated at the top, direct democracy is decentralized and emphasizes that decisions should be taken as near as possible to ordinary people's lives.

The principle of an empowered participatory democracy links the traditional conception of participatory and direct democracy with political theorists' emerging interest in deliberative democracy – in particular, the quality of communication. Deliberative theories have developed from concerns with the functioning of representative institutions; however, scholars of deliberative democracy disagree on the locus of deliberative discussion, some being concerned with the development of liberal institutions, others with alternative public spheres free from state intervention (della Porta 2005b). The analysis of the communicative quality of democracy is central to the work of Jürgen Habermas (1996), who postulates a double-track process, with "informal" deliberation taking place outside institutions and then, as it becomes public opinion, affecting institutional deliberation. According to other authors, however, deliberations take place in voluntary groups especially (Cohen 1989). A strong supporter of the latter position and an expert in movement politics, John Dryzek (2000) has argued that social movements are best placed to build deliberative spaces that can keep a critical eye on public institutions. Jane Mansbridge (1996) has also argued that deliberation should take place in a number of enclaves, free from institutional power – including that of social movements themselves. If social movements nurture committed, critical attitudes toward public institutions, deliberative democracy requires citizens embedded in associative networks able to build democratic skills among their adherents (Offe 1997, p. 102–3). As the experiment of Porto Alegre indicates, in the movements for globalization from below, deliberative practices have indeed attracted a more or less explicit interest.

Trying to summarize various and not always coherent definitions, we suggest that participatory democracy is empowered when, under conditions of equality, inclusiveness, and transparency, a communicative process based on reason (the strength of a good argument) is able to transform individual preferences and reach decisions oriented to the public good (della Porta 2005a). Some of the dimensions of this definition (such as inclusiveness, equality, and visibility) echo those included in the participatory models we have described as typical of new social movements, while others (above all, the attention to the quality of communication) emerge as new concerns.

First, as in the movement tradition, empowered participatory democracy is inclusive: it requires that all citizens with a stake in the decisions be included in the process and be able to express their voice. This means that the deliberative process takes place under conditions of a plurality of values, where people have different perspectives on their common problems. Additionally, all participants are equals: deliberation takes place among free and equal citizens (Cohen 1989, p. 20). Moreover, the concept of transparency resonates with direct, participatory democracy. In Joshua Cohen's definition, a deliberative democracy is "an association whose affairs are governed by the *public* deliberation of its members" (1989, p. 17, emphasis added). In deliberative democratic theory, public debate strives to "replace the language of interest with the language of reason" (Elster 1998, p. 111): having to justify a position before a public forces one to look for justifications linked to common values and principles.

What is new in the conception of deliberative democracy, and in some of the contemporary movements' practices, is the emphasis on preference (trans)formation, with an orientation to the definition of the public good. In fact, "deliberative democracy requires the transformation of preferences in interaction" (Dryzek 2000, p. 79). It is "a process through which initial preferences are transformed in order to take into account the points of view of the others" (Miller 1993, p. 75). In this sense, deliberative democracy differs from conceptions of democracy as an aggregation of (exogenously generated) preferences. Some reflections on participatory democracy have also included practices of consensus: decisions must be approvable by all participants (unanimous) – in contrast with majoritarian democracy, where decisions are legitimated by votes. Deliberation (or even communication) is based on the belief that, while not giving up my perspective, I might learn if I listen to another (Young 1996). Consensus is, however, possible only in the presence of shared values and a common commitment to the construction of a public good (such as the common value of social justice in the participatory schema). In a deliberative model of democracy, "The political debate is organized around alternative conceptions of the public good," and above all, it "draws on identities and citizens' interests in ways that contribute to public building of public good" (Cohen 1989, pp. 18–19). A deliberative setting facilitates the search for a common end or good (Elster 1998).

Above all, deliberative democracy stresses reason: people are convinced by the force of the better argument. In particular, deliberation is based on horizontal flows of communication, multiple producers of content, wide opportunities for interactivity, confrontation on the basis of rational argumentation, and attitude to reciprocal listening (Habermas 1981, 1996). In this sense, deliberative democracy is discursive. According to Young, however, discourse does not exclude protest: "Processes of engaged and responsible democratic participation include street demonstrations and sit-ins, musical works and cartoons, as much as parliamentary speeches and letters to the editor" (2003, p. 119). Empowered participatory democracy has, in fact, been discussed as an alternative to top-down imposition of public decisions, which is increasingly seen as lacking legitimacy and becoming more difficult to manage, given both the increasing complexity of problems and the increasing ability of noninstitutionalized actors to make their voices heard.

As the global justice movement, but also the anti-austerity protest camps illustrate, movements experiment with participatory, discursive models of democracy both in their internal decision-making and in their interactions with political institutions. Internally, social movements have – with varying degrees of success – attempted to develop an organizational structure based on participation (rather than delegation), consensus-building (rather than majority vote), and horizontal networks (rather than centralized hierarchies) (della Porta 2015a).

As far as the social movements' critique of existing democracy is concerned, their search for an alternative cannot be considered to have concluded, with still open risks of producing oligarchies and charismatic leaderships, the very problems at the center of their critique of traditional politics. Although it maximizes responsiveness, the direct democracy model has weaknesses as far as representation and efficiency are concerned (Kitschelt 1993). Problems of efficiency affect the success of movement organizations themselves; problems of representation concern the legitimation of new forms of democracy. The refusal by social movements to accept the principles of representative democracy can undermine their image as democratic actors, particularly when they begin to take on official and semiofficial functions within representative institutions, assuming the form of parties or public interest groups. Social forums, bringing together heterogeneous actors, pay great attention to the quality of internal communication, but with unequal results.

These limitations notwithstanding, it should be recognized that social movements have helped to open new channels of access to the political system, contributing to the identification, if not the solution, of a number of representative democracy's problems. More generally, recent research has stressed the role social movements can play in helping to address two related challenges to democratic governance. On the input side, contemporary democracy faces a problem of declining political participation, at least in its conventional forms. The reduced capacity of political parties to bridge society and the state adds to this problem, while the commercialization of the mass media reduces their capacity to act as an arena for debating public decisions. On the other hand, the effectiveness of democracies in producing a just and efficient output is jeopardized, in part by the increasing risks in complex (and global) societies. The two problems are related, since weakening in the ability of institutional actors to intervene in the formation of collective identities reduces their capacity to satisfy (more and more fragmented) demands. As Fung and Wright (2001) have stressed, transformative democratic strategies are needed to combat the increasing inadequacy of liberal democracy to realize its goals of political involvement of the people, consensus through dialogue, and public policies aimed at providing a society in which all citizens benefit from the nation's wealth.

9.6 SUMMARY

Social movement mobilization has generated changes in a variety of areas. As far as public policy is concerned, a great deal of legislation has been produced on issues raised during protest campaigns. Any evaluation of the significance of the changes introduced by these laws requires analysis of their implementation as well as of transformations in the value system and in the behavior of both ordinary citizens and elites. Changes in public policy and public opinion have been accompanied by procedural changes, with the creation of new decision-making arenas no longer legitimated by the model of representative democracy. *Ad hoc* commissions, new government ministries, and local government committees constitute channels of access to the decision-making process frequently used by social movement organizations. Empowered participatory experiments have developed from the participatory agenda in Porto Alegre, characterized by attention to participation, good communication, and decisional power. Emphasis on participation over representation thus enriches the concept of democracy. In fact, with various degrees of success, social movements have recently paid attention to inclusive and equal participation, as well as consensus-building and good communication.

Although the variety of objectives, strategies, and actors involved in this process renders it difficult to identify winning strategies for new collective actors, it can, nevertheless, be said that in recent decades the structure of power in liberal democracies appears to have been transformed in the direction of greater recognition for new actors. Social movements have helped democratization in authoritarian regimes, but also contributed to more participatory approaches in representative democracies. However, with breaks and irregularities, democracy has brought about decreasing inequalities and protection from arbitrary government interventions (Tilly 2004a, p. 127). Can we say that, in struggling for democracy, social movements have succeeded in radically changing the power distribution in society? Many signs discourage one from excessive optimism. Protest goes in cycles, and what is won during peaks of mobilization may be once again jeopardized during moments of latency. The labor movement contributed to creating many social and political rights, but the neoliberal turn at the end of the twentieth century called into question the welfare state that had appeared to be an institutionalized achievement from the 1970s. Social inequalities are again on the rise. If protest is more and more accepted as "normal politics," some forms of contentious politics are more and more stigmatized as uncivilized in public opinion and are repressed by the police. Nevertheless, social movements continue to engage with political, social, cultural and economic institutions in a varieties of ways and, at times, with success.

References

Abăseacă, Raluca. 2018. "Collective Memory and Social Movements in Times of Crisis: The Case of Romania." *Nationalities Papers* 46(4): 671–684.

Abbott, Andrew. 1995. "Things of Boundaries." *Social Research* 62: 857–882.

Ackland, Robert and Mathieu O'Neil. 2011. "Online Collective Identity: The Case of the Environmental Movement." *Social Networks* 33(3): 177–190.

Ahmad, Akhlaq. 2014. "The Role of Social Networks in the Recruitment of Youth in an Islamist Organization in Pakistan." *Sociological Spectrum* 34(6): 469–488.

Ahmed, Saifuddin, Jaeho Cho, and Kokil Jaidka. 2017. "Tweeting India's Nirbhaya Protest: A Study of Emotional Dynamics in an Online Social Movement." *Social Movement Studies* 16(4): 447–465.

Ahrne, Göran and Nils Brunsson. 2011. "Organization Outside Organizations: The Significance of Partial Organization." *Organization* 18(1): 83–104.

Ahrne, Göran, Nils Brunsson, and David Seidl. 2016. "Resurrecting Organization by Going beyond Organizations." *European Management Journal* 34(2): 93–101.

Akram, Sadiya. 2014. "Recognizing the 2011 United Kingdom Riot sas Political Protest: A Theoretical Framework Based on Agency, Habitus and the Preconscious." *The British Journal of Criminology* 54(3): 375–392.

Alberici, Augusta Isabella and Patrizia Milesi. 2016. "Online Discussion, Politicized Identity, and Collective Action." *Group Processes & Intergroup Relations* 19(1): 43–59.

Alberoni, Francesco. 1984. *Movement and Institution*. New York: Columbia University Press.

Albertazzi, Daniele, Arianna Giovannini, and Antonella Seddone. 2018. "'No Regionalism Please, We Are Leghisti !' The Transformation of the Italian Lega Nord under the Leadership of Matteo Salvini." *Regional & Federal Studies* 28(5): 645–671.

Alexander, Peter. 2010. "Rebellion of the Poor: South Africa's Service Delivery Protests – a Preliminary Analysis." *Review of African Political Economy* 37(123): 25–40.

Alimi, Eitan Y. 2015. "Repertoires of Contention." Pp. 410–422 in *The Oxford Handbook of Social Movements*, edited by D. della Porta and M. Diani. Oxford: Oxford University Press.

Allegretti, Giovanni. 2003. *L'insegnamento di Porto Alegre. Autoprogettualità come paradigma urbano*. Firenze: Alinea.

Almeida, Paul and Chris Chase-Dunn. 2018. "Globalization and Social Movements." *Annual Review of Sociology* 44(1): 189–211.

Amenta, Edwin. 1998. *Bold Relief: Institutional Politics and the Origins of Modern American Policy*. Princeton, NJ: Princeton University Press.

Amenta, Edwin and Caren Neal. 2004. "The Legislative, Organizational, and Beneficiary Consequencesof State Oriented Challengers." Pp. 461–488 in *The Blackwell Companion to Social Movements*, edited by D. A. Snow, S. H. Soule, and H. Kriesi. Oxford, Blackwell.

Amenta, Edwin and Michael P. Young. 1999. "Democratic States and Social Movements. Theoretical Arguments and Hypotheses." *Social Problems* 46: 153–172.

Aminzade, Ronald. 1995. "Between Movement and Party: The Transformation of Mid-Nineteenth-Century French Republicanism." Pp. 167–198 in *The Politics of Social Protest: Comparative Perspectives on States and Social Movements*, edited by J. C. Jenkins and B. Klandermans. Minneapolis, MI: University of Minnesota Press.

Andersson, Linus. 2018. "What's Left of the Radical Left Online? Absence of Communication, Political Vision, and Community in Autonomist Web Milieus in Sweden." *New Media & Society* 20(1): 384–398.

Andretta, Massimiliano, Donatella della Porta, Lorenzo Mosca, and Herbert Reiter. 2002. *Global, Noglobal, New Global. La Protesta Contro Il G8 a Genova*. Roma: Laterza.

Andretta, Massimiliano, Donatella della Porta, Lorenzo Mosca, and Herbert Reiter. 2003. *Global – new global. Identität und Strategien der Antiglobalisierungsbewegung*. Frankfurt am Main: Campus Verlag.

Andretta, Massimiliano, Gianni Piazza and Anna Subirats. 2015. "Urban Dynamics and Social Movements." Pp. 200–215 in *The Oxford Handbook of Social Movements*, edited by D. della Porta and M. Diani. Oxford: Oxford University Press.

Andrews, Kenneth and Bob Edwards. 2004. "Advocacy Organizations in the US Political Process." *Annual Review of Sociology* 30: 479–506.

Anheier, Helmut K. 2003. "Movement Development and Organizational Networks." Pp. 49–74 in *Social Movements and Networks*, edited by M. Diani and D. McAdam. Oxford: Oxford University Press.

Anheier, Helmut K. and Nikolas Scherer. 2015. "Voluntary Actions and Social Movements" Pp. 494–510 in *The Oxford Handbook of Social Movements*, edited by D. della Porta and M. Diani. Oxford: Oxford University Press.

Anheier, Helmut K. and Nuno Themudo. 2002. "Organizational Forms of Global Civil Society: Implications of Going Global." Pp. 191–216 in *Global Civil Society 2002*, edited by M. Glasius, M. Kaldor and H. Ahheier. Oxford: Oxford University Press.

Anheier, Helmut, Marlies Glasius, and Mary Kaldor. 2001. "Introducing Global Civil Society." Pp. 3–22 in *Global Civil Society 2001*, edited by H. Anheier, M. Glasius, and Mary Kaldor. Oxford/New York: Oxford University Press.

Anria, Santiago. 2013. "Social Movements, Party Organization, and Populism: Insights from the Bolivian MAS." *Latin American Politics and Society* 55(3): 19–46.

Anria, Santiago. 2018. *When Movements Become Parties: The Bolivian MAS in Comparative Perspective*. Cambridge: Cambridge University Press.

Ansell, Christopher K. 1997. "Symbolic Networks: The Realignment of the French Working Class, 1887-1894." *American Journal of Sociology* 103(2): 359–390.

Arampatzi, Athina. 2017. "Contentious Spatialities in an Era of Austerity: Everyday Politics and 'struggle Communities' in Athens, Greece." *Political Geography* 60: 47–56.

Arampatzi, Athina and Walter J. Nicholls. 2012. "The Urban Roots of Anti-Neoliberal Social Movements: The Case of Athens, Greece." *Environment and Planning A* 44(11): 2591–2610.

Ariemma, Lisa and Judith Burnside-Lawry. 2016. "Transnational Resistance Networks: New Democratic Prospects? The Lyon-Turin Railway and No TAV Movement." *Research in Social Movements, Conflicts and Change* 39: 137–65.

Armstrong, Elizabeth A. 2002. *Forging Gay Identities: Organizing Sexuality in San Francisco, 1950-1994*. Chicago: University of Chicago Press.

Arrighi, Giovanni and Beverly J. Silver. 1999. *Chaos and Governance in the Modern World System*. Minneapolis/London: University of Minnesota Press.

Arrighi, Giovanni, Terence K. Hopkins, and Immanuel Wallerstein. 1989. *Antisystemic Movements*. London: Verso.

Arthur, Mikaila Mariel Lemonik. 2009. "Thinking Outside the Master's House: New Knowledge Movements and the Emergence of Academic Disciplines." *Social Movement Studies* 8(1): 73–87.

Ashraf, Ahmad. 1988. "Bazaar-Mosque Alliance: The Social Basis of Revolts and Revolutions." *International Journal of Politics, Culture, and Society* 1(4): 538–567.

Ashuri, Tamar and Yaniv Bar-Ilan. 2016. "How Flat Organizations Filter: Organizational Gatekeeping in a Networked Environment." *Information, Communication & Society* 19(10): 1411–1126.

Aslanidis, Paris. 2018. "Populism as a Collective Action Master Frame for Transnational Mobilization." *Sociological Forum* 33(2): 443–464.

Assoudeh, Eliot and Debra J. Salazar. 2017. "Movement Structure in an Authoritarian Regime: A Network Analysis of the Women's and Student Movements in Iran." *Research in Social Movements, Conflicts and Change* 41: 137–171.

Atkinson, Joshua D. 2010. *Alternative Media and Politics of Resistance*. Peter Lang: New York.

Atouba, Yannick and Michelle Shumate. 2010. "Interorganizational Networking Patterns Among Development Organizations." *Journal of Communication* 60: 293–317.

Aunio, Anna-Liisa and Suzanne Staggenborg. 2011. "Transnational Linkages and Movement Communities." *Sociology Compass* 5(5): 364–375.

Auyero, Javier. 2001. "Glocal Riots." *International Sociology* 16: 33–53.

Auyero, Javier. 2004. "When Everyday Life, Routine Politics, and Protest Meet." *Theory and Society* 33: 417–441.

Auyero, Javier. 2007. *Routine Politics and Violence in Argentina*. New York/Cambridge: Cambridge University Press.

Avramopoulou, Eirini. 2013. "*On the Fantasy of Dispossession.*" *Cultural Anthropology*, October. www.culanth.org/fijieldsights/400-on-the-fantasy-of-dispossession.

Ayres, Jeffrey M. 1998. *Defying Conventional Wisdom: Political Movements and Popular Contention against North American Free Trade*. Toronto: University of Toronto Press.

Baccaro, Lucio and Kostantinos Papadakis. 2008. "The promise and perils of participatory policy making." *IILS* 117: 1–69.

Bacqué, Marie-Hélène, Henri Rey, and Yves Sintomer, eds. 2005. *Gestion de proximité et démocratie participative*. Paris: La Découverte.

Baek, Young Min. 2010. "To Buy or Not to Buy: Who are Political Consumers? What do they Think and How do they Participate?" *Political Studies* 58(5): 1065–1086.

Bagguley, Paul. 1991. *From Protest to Acquiescence: Political Movements of the Unemployed*. London: Macmillan.

Bagguley, Paul. 1995. "Middle Class Radicalism Revisited." In *Social Change and the Middle Classes*, edited by T. Butler and M. Savage. London: UCL Press.

Baiocchi, Gianpaolo. 2001. "Participation, Activism, and Politics: The Porto Alegre Experiment and Deliberative Democratic Theory." *Politics and Society* 29: 43–72.

Baiocchi, Gianpaolo. 2002. "Synergizing Civil Society: State–Civil Society Regimes in Porto Alegre, Brazil." *Political Power and Social Theory* 15: 3–52.

Baker, Gideon. 1999. "The Taming Idea of Civil Society." *Democratization*, 6(3): 1–29.

Ballard, Richard, Adam Habib, and Imraan Valodia, eds. 2006. *Voices of Protest. Social Movements in Post-Apartheid South Africa*. Durban: University of KwaZulu-Natal Press.

Balsiger, Philip. 2014a. "Between Shaming Corporations and Proposing Alternatives: The Politics of an 'Ethical Shopping Map'." *Journal of Consumer Culture* 14(2): 218–235.

Balsiger, Philip. 2014b. *The Fight for Ethical Fashion. The Origins and Interactions of the Clean Clothes Campaign*. Farnham, Burlington VT: Ashgate.

Balsiger, Philip. 2015. "Managing Protest: The Political Action Repertoires of Corporations." Pp. 653–666 in *The Oxford Handbook of Social Movements*, edited by D. della Porta and M. Diani. Oxford: Oxford University Press.

Bandy, Joe and Jennifer Bickham-Mendez. 2003. "A Place of Their Own? Women Organizers in the Maquilas of Nicaragua and Mexico." *Mobilization* 8: 173–188.

Barbalet, Jack M. 1988. *Citizenship*. Milton Keynes: Open University Press.

Barker, Colin. 2013. "Class Struggle and Social Movements." Pp. 39–61 in *Marxism and Social Movements*, edited by C. Barker, L. Cox, J. Krinsky and A. G. Nilsen. Leiden: Brill.

Barker, Colin and Michael Lavalette. 2015. "Welfare Changes and Social Movements." Pp. 711–728 in *The Oxford Handbook of Social Movements*, edited by D. Della Porta and M. Diani. Oxford/New York: Oxford University Press.

Barker, Colin, Laurence Cox, John Krinsky, and Alf Gunvald Nilsen, eds. 2013. *Marxism and Social Movements*. Leiden: Brill.

Barnard-Wills, David. 2011. "'This is not a cyber war, it's a …?': Wikileaks, anonymous and the politics of hegemony." *International Journal of Cyber Warfare and Terrorism* 1(1): 13–23.

Barnes, Samuel H., Max Kaase, Allerbeck Klaus, Barbara Farah, Felix Heunks, Ronald Inglehart, Myron Kent Jennings, Hans-Dieter Klingemann, Alan Marsh, and Leopold Rosenmayr. 1979. *Political Action*. London/Newbury Park, CA: Sage.

Baron, David P. 2010. "Morally-Motivated Self-Regulation." *American Economic Review* 100(4): 1299–1329.

Barrington Moore, Jr. 1966. *Social Origins of Dictatorship and Democracy: Lord and Peasant in the Making of the Modern World*. Boston: Beacon Press.

Bartolini, Stefano. 2000. *The Political Mobilization of the European Left*. Cambridge, Cambridge University Press.

Bartolini, Stefano and Peter Mair. 1990. *Identity, Competition and Electoral Availability. The Stabilization of European Electorates*. Cambridge/New York: Cambridge University Press.

Bauman, Zygmunt. 2000. *Liquid Modernity*. Oxford: Polity.

Bauman, Zygmunt. 2007. *Liquid Times: Living in Times of Uncertainty*. Oxford: Polity.

Baumgarten, Britta. 2017. "The Children of the Carnation Revolution? Connections between Portugal's Anti-Austerity Movement and the Revolutionary Period 1974/1975." *Social Movement Studies* 16(1): 51–63.

Baumgarten, Britta, Priska Daphi, and Peter Ullrich, eds. 2014. *Conceptualizing Culture in Social Movement Research*. Basingstoke: Palgrave Macmillan.

Bayat, Asef. 1997. *Street Politics: Poor People's Movements in Iran*. New York: Columbia University Press.

Bayat, Asef. 2010. *Life as Politics*. Stanford, CA: Stanford University Press.

Bayat, Asef. 2012a. "The 'Arab Street.'" Pp. 73–84 in *The Journey to Tahrir: Revolution, Protest, and Social Change in Egypt*, edited by J. Sowers and C. Toensing. Verso.

Bayat, Asef. 2012b. "Politics in the City-Inside-Out." *City & Society* 24(2): 110–128.

Becker, Penny E. and Pawan Dhingra. 2001. "Religious Involvement and Volunteering: Implications for Civil Society." *Sociology of Religion* 62: 315–135.

Beer, William R. 1980. *The Unexpected Rebellion*. Ethnic Activism in Contemporary France. New York: Columbia University Press.

Beissinger, Mark R. 2002. *National Mobilization and the Collapse of the Soviet State*. New York/Cambridge: Cambridge University Press.

Beissinger, Mark R. 2015. "Contentious Collective Action and the Evolving Nation-State." Pp. 595–606 in *The Oxford Handbook of Social Movements*, edited by D. della Porta and M. Diani. Oxford: Oxford University Press.

Bell, Daniel. 1973. *The Coming of Post-industrial Society: A Venture in Social Forecasting*. New York: Basic Books.

Bendix, Reinhard.1964. *Nation Building and Citizenship*. New York: Wiley & Sons.

Benford, Robert D. and David A. Snow. 2000. "Framing Processes and Social Movements: An Overview and Assessment." *Annual Review of Sociology* 26: 611–639.

Bennani-Chraïbi, Mounia and Olivier Fillieule, eds. 2003. *Résistances et Protestations Dans Les Sociétés Musulmanes*. Paris: Presses de Sciences Po.

Bennett, Lance. 2003a. "Communicating global activism: strengths and vulnerabilities of networked politics." *Information, Communication & Society* 6(2): 143–168.

Bennett, Lance. 2003b. "New media power, the Internet and global activism." Pp. 17–37 in *Contesting Media Power. Alternative Media in a Networked World*, edited by N. Couldry and J. Curran. Lanham: Rowman and Littlefield.

Bennett, Lance. 2005. "Social Movements beyond Borders: Understanding Two Eras of Transnational Activism." Pp. 203–226 in *Transnational Protest and Global Activism*, edited by D. della Porta and S. Tarrow. Lanham: Rowman & Littlefield.

Bennett, Lance and Alexandra Segerberg. 2011. "Digital Media and the Personalization of Collective Action." *Information, Communication & Society* 14(6): 770–799.

Bennett, Lance and Alexandra Segerberg. 2013. *The Logic of Connective Action*. Cambridge/New York: Cambridge University Press.

Bennett, Lance and Alexandra Segerberg. 2015. "Communication in Movements." Pp. 367–382 in *Oxford Handbook of Social Movements*, edited by D. della Porta and M. Diani. Oxford/New York: Oxford University Press.

Berezin, Mabel. 2001. "Emotions and Political Identity." Pp. 83–91 in *Passionate Politics*, edited by J. Goodwin, J. M. Jasper, and F. Polletta. Chicago: Chicago University Press.

Berger, Peter Ludwig. 1999. "The Desecularization of the World: A Global Overview." Pp.1–18 in *The Desecularization of the World. Resurgent Religion and World Politics*, edited by P. L. Berger. Washington, D.C.: Ethics and Public Policy Center.

Berger, Peter L. and Thomas Luckmann. 1969. *The Social Construction of Reality: A Treatise in the Sociology of Knowledge*. London: Allen Lane.

Bergmann, Werner. 2002. "Exclusionary Riots: Some Theoretical Considerations." Pp. 161–183 in *Exclusionary Violence. Antisemitic Riots in Modern German History*, edited by C. Hoffmann et al. Ann Arbor: University of Michigan Press.

Bermeo, Nancy. 1990. "Review Article: Rethinking Regime Change" [Reviewed Works: "Transitions from Authoritarian Rule: Southern Europe" by Guillermo O'Donnell, Philippe C. Schmitter, and Laurence Whitehead; "Transitions from Authoritarian Rule: Latin America" by Guillermo O'Donnell, Philippe C. Schmitter, and Laurence Whitehead; "Transitions from Authoritarian Rule: Comparative Perspectives" by Guillermo O'Donnell, Philippe C. Schmitter, and Laurence Whitehead; "Transitions from Authoritarian Rule: Tentative Conclusions about Uncertain Democracies" by Guillermo O'Donnell and Philippe C. Schmitter]. *Comparative Politics* 22(3): 359–377.

Bermeo, Nancy. 1997. "Myths of Moderation: Confrontation and Conflict during Democratic Transition." *Comparative Politics* 29: 205–322.

Bernburg, Jón Gunnar. 2016. *Economic Crisis and Mass Protest: The Pots and Pans Revolution in Iceland*. New York: Routledge.

Bernstein, Mary. 1997. "Celebration and Suppression: The Strategic Uses of Identity by the Lesbian and Gay Movement." *The American Journal of Sociology* 103(3): 531–565.

Bertuzzi, Niccolò. 2017. "No Expo Network: A Failed Mobilization in a Post-Political Frame." *Social Movement Studies* 16(6): 752–756.

Beyerlein, Kraig and Kelly Bergstrand. 2016. "It Takes Two: A Dyadic Model of Recruitment to Civic Activity." *Social Science Research* 60: 163–180.

Bianchi, Marina and Maria Mormino. 1984. "Militanti Di Se Stesse. Il Movimento Delle Donne a Milano." Pp. 127–174 in *Altri codici. Aree di movimento nella metropoli*, edited by A. Melucci. Bologna: Il Mulino.

Billig, Michael. 1995. *Banal Nationalism*. London: Sage.

Bircham, Emma and John Charlton, eds. 2001. *Anti-Capitalism. A Guide to the Movement*. London/Sydney: Bookmarks Publications.

Bishop, Patrick and Glyn Davis. 2002. "Mapping Public Participation in Policy Choices." *Australian Journal of Public Administration* 61(1): 14–29.

Black, Simon. 2014. "'Street Music', Urban Ethnography and Ghettoized Communities." *International Journal of Urban & Regional Research* 38(2): 700–705.

Blanco, Ismael and Margarita León. 2017. "Social Innovation, Reciprocity and Contentious Politics: Facing the Socio-Urban Crisis in Ciutat Meridiana, Barcelona." *Urban Studies (Sage Publications, Ltd.)* 54(9): 2172–2188.

Blee, Kathleen M. 2002. *Inside Organized Racism: Women in the Hate Movement*. Berkeley, CA: University of California Press.

Blee, Kathleen M. 2007. "Ethnographies of the Far Right." *Journal of Contemporary Ethnographhy* 36(2): 119–128.

Blumer, Herbert. 1951. "Social Movements." Pp. 199–220 in *Principles of Sociology*, edited by A. McClung Lee. New York: Barnes & Nobles.

Bob, Clifford. 2005. *The Marketing of Rebellion: Insurgents, Media, and International Activism*. Cambridge: Cambridge University Press.

Bobbio, Luigi and Alberico Zeppetella, eds. 1999. *Perché proprio qui? Grandi opere e opposizioni locali*. Milano, Franco Angeli.

Boli, John and George Thomas, eds. 1999. *Constructing World Culture: International Nongovernmental Organizations Since 1875*. Stanford: Stanford University Press.

Boli, John. 1999. "Conclusion: World Authority Structures and Legitimations." Pp. 267–300 in *Constructing World Culture. International Nongovernmental Organizations since 1875*, edited by J. Boli and G. Thomas. Stanford: Stanford University Press.

Boltanski, Luc and Eva Chiappello. 2005. *The New Spirit of Capitalism*. London: Verso.

Boltanski, Luc and Laurent Thevenot. 1999. "The Sociology of Critical Capacity." *European Journal of Social Theory* 2: 359–377.

Bosi Lorenzo, Marco Giugni, and Katrin Uba, eds. 2016. *The consequences of Social Movements*. Cambridge: Cambridge University Press.

Bosi, Lorenzo and Stefan Malthaner. 2015. "Political Violence." Pp. 439–451 in *The Oxford Handbook of Social Movements*, edited by D. della Porta and M. Diani. Oxford: Oxford University Press.

Boström, Magnus, Michele Micheletti, and Peter Oosterveer, eds. 2019. *The Oxford Handbook of Political Consumerism*. Oxford/New York: Oxford University Press.

Bourdieu, Pierre. 1977. *Outline of a Theory of Practice*. Cambridge/New York: Cambridge University Press.

Bourdieu, Pierre. 1984. *Distinction*. Cambridge, MA: Harvard University Press.

Bourdieu, Pierre. 1992. "The Practice of Reflexive Sociology." Pp. 218–260 in *An Invitation to Reflexive Sociology*, P. Bourdieu and L. J. D. Wacquant, Chicago: University of Chicago Press.

Bozcalı, Fırat and Yoltar Çağrı. 2013. "A Look at Gezi Park from Turkey's Kurdistan." *Cultural Anthropology*, October. www.culanth.org/fijieldsights/396-a-look-atgezi-park-from-turkey-s-kurdistan.

Brand, Ulrich, and Markus Wissen. 2002. "Ambivalenzen praktischer Globalisierungskritik: Das Bispiel Attac." *Kurswechsel* 3: 102–113.

Bratton, Michael, and Nicolas van de Walle 1992. "Popular Protest and Political Reform in Africa." *Comparative Politics* 24(4): 419–442.

Braunstein, Ruth, Todd Nicholas Fuist, and Rhys H. Williams. 2017. *Religion and Progressive Activism: New Stories About Faith and Politics*. New York: NYU Press.

Brecher, Jeremy, and Tim Costello, eds. 1990. *Building Bridges: The Emerging Grassroots Coalition of Labor and Community*. New York: Monthly Review Press.

Brecher, Jeremy, Tim Costello, and Brendan Smith. 2000. *Globalization from Below: The Power of Solidarity*. Boston: South End Press.

Breines, Wini. 1980. "Community and Organization: The New Left and Michels' 'Iron Law.'" *Social Problems* 27(4): 419–429.

Brenner, Neil, Peter Marcuse, and Margit Mayer, eds. 2012. *Cities for People, Not for Profit: Critical Urban Theory and The Right To The City*. London: Taylor & Francis.

Brissette, Martha B. 1988. "Tax Protest and Tax Reform: A Chapter in The History of The American Political Process." *Journal of Law and Politics* 5: 187–208.

Broadbent, Jeffrey and Vicky Brockman. 2011. *East Asian Social Movements: Power, Protest, and Change in a Dynamic Region*. New York: Springer.

Brokett, Charles D. 1995. "A Protest-Cycle Resolution of the Repression/Popular-Protest Paradox." Pp. 117–144 in *Repertoires and Cycles of Collective Action*, edited by M. Traugott. Durham, NC: Duke University Press.

Bromley, David G. 2016. "Categorizing Religious Organizations." Pp. 17–24 in *The Oxford Handbook of New Religious Movements*, edited by J. R. Lewis and I. B. Tollefsen. New York/Oxford: Oxford University Press.

Brown, Gavin and Helen Yaffe. 2013. "Non-Stop Against Apartheid: Practicing Solidarity Outside the South African Embassy." *Social Movement Studies* 12(2): 227–234.

Brym, Robert, Melissa Godbout, Andreas Hoffbauer, Gabe Menard, and Tony Huiquan Zhang. 2014. "Social Media in the 2011 Egyptian Uprising." *The British Journal of Sociology* 65(2): 266–292.

Brysk, Alison. 2000. *From Tribal Village to Global Village: Indian Rights and International Relations in Latin America*. Stanford: Stanford University Press.

Buchanan, James. 1965. "An Economic Theory of Clubs." *Economica* 32: 1–14.

Buechler, Steven M. 2004. "The Strange Career of Strain and Breakdown Theories of Collective Action." Pp. 47–66 in *The Blackwell Companion to Social Movements*, edited by D. A. Snow, S. H. Soule, and H. Kriesi. Oxford: Blackwell.

Buechler, Steven M. 2011. *Understanding Social Movements: Theories from the Classical Era to the Present*. New York: Paradigm.

Burstein, Paul. 1998. "Interest Organizations, Political Parties, and the Study of Democratic Politics." Pp. 39–56 in *Social Movements and American Political Institutions*, edited by A. Costain and A. McFarland. Lanham: Rowman & Littlefield.

Burstein, Paul, Rachel L. Einwohner, and Jocelyn A. Hollander. 1995. "The Success of Political Movements: A Bargaining Perspective." Pp. 275–295 in *The Politics of Social*

Protest, edited by J. C. Jenkins and B. Klandermans. Minneapolis: University of Minnesota Press.

Byrd, Scott C. and Lorien Jasny. 2010. "Transnational Movement Innovation and Collaboration: Analysis of World Social Forum Networks." *Social Movement Studies* 9(4): 355–372.

Caiani, Manuela and Linda Parenti. 2016. *European and American Extreme Right Groups and the Internet*. Oxford: Routledge.

Calhoun, Craig. 1982. *The Question of Class Struggle: Social Foundations of Popular Radicalism during the Industrial Revolution*. Oxford: Blackwell.

Calhoun, Craig. 1993. "New Social Movements of the Early 19th Century." *Social Science Journal* 17: 385–427.

Calhoun, Craig, ed. 1994a. *Social Theory and the Politics of Identity*. Oxford: Blackwell.

Calhoun, Craig. 1994b. *Neither Gods nor Emperors : Students and the Struggle for Democracy in China*. Berkeley & Los Angeles, CA: University of California Press.

Calhoun, Craig. 1998. "Community without Propinquity Revisited: Communications Technology and the Transformation of the Urban Public Sphere." *Sociological Inquiry* 68(3): 373–397.

Cameron, James E. and Shannon L. Nickerson. 2009. "Predictors of Protest Among Anti-Globalization Demonstrators." *Journal of Applied Social Psychology* 39(3): 734–761.

Caniglia, Beth. 2001. "Informal Alliances vs. Institutional Ties: The Effects of Elite Alliances on Environmental TSMO Networks." *Mobilization: An International Quarterly* 6(1): 37–54.

Cardon, Domenique, and Fabien Granjou. 2003. "Peut-on se liberer des formats media-tiques? Le mouvement alter-mondialisation et l'Internet." *Mouvements* 25: 67–73.

Carroll, William K. and Robert S. Ratner. 1996. "Master Framing and Cross-Movement Networking in Contemporary Social Movements." *Sociological Quarterly* 37(4): 601–625.

Carson, Rachel. 1962. *Silent Spring*. Boston, MA: Houghton Mifflin.

Casanova, José. 2001. "Civil Society and Religion: Retrospective Reflections on Catholicism and Prospective Reflections on Islam." *Social Research* 68(4): 1042–1080.

Casper, Gretchen and Michelle M. Taylor. 1996. *Negotiating Democracy: Transitions from Authoritarian Rule*. Pittsburgh: University of Pittsburgh Press.

Castells, Manuel. 1972. *La Question Urbaine*. Paris: Maspero.

Castells, Manuel. 1977. *La Question Urbaine*. Paris: Maspero.

Castells, Manuel. 1983. *The City and the GrassRoots*. London: E. Arnold.

Castells, Manuel. 1996. *The Information Age. Vol. I: The Rise of the Network Society*. Oxford/Cambridge, MA: Blackwell.

Castells, Manuel. 1997. *The Information Age. Vol. II: The Power of Identity*. Oxford/Cambridge, MA: Blackwell.

Castells, Manuel. 2001. *The Internet Galaxy: Reflections on the Internet, Business and Society*. Oxford: Oxford University Press.

Castells, Manuel. 2012. *Networks of Outrage and Hope. Social Movements in the Internet Age*. Cambridge: Polity.

Catanzaro, Raimondo and Luigi Manconi, eds. 1995. *Storie Di Lotta Armata*. Bologna: il Mulino.

Cento Bull, Anna and Bryn Jones. 2006. "Governance and Social Capital in Urban Regeneration: A Comparison between Bristol and Naples." *Urban Studies* 43: 767–786.

Cernison, Matteo. 2019. *Social Media Activism: Water as a Common Good*. Amsterdam: Amsterdam University Press.

Cerulo, Karen. 1997. "Cerulo, Karen. 1997. 'Reframing Sociological Concepts for a Brave New (Virtual?) World." *Sociological Inquiry* 67: 48–58.

Cerulo, Karen and Janet M. Ruane. 1998. "Coming Together: New Taxonomies for the Analysis of Social Relations." *Sociological Inquiry* 68: 398–425.

Chandhoke, Neera. 2002. "The Limits of Global Civil Society." Pp. 35–53 in *Global Civil Society 2002*, edited by M. Glasius, M. Kaldor, and H. Ahheier. Oxford: Oxford University Press.

Chenoweth, Erica and Maria J. Stephan. 2011. *Why Civil Resistance Works: The Strategic Logic of Nonviolent Conflict*. New York: Columbia University Press.

Chironi, Daniela. 2019. "Generations in the Feminist and LGBT Movements in Italy: The Case of Non Una Di Meno." *American Behavioral Scientist* 0002764219831745.

Chironi, Daniela and Raffaella Fittipaldi. 2017. "Social Movements and New Forms of Political Organization: Podemos as a Hybrid Party." *PARTECIPAZIONE E CONFLITTO* 10(1): 275–305.

Christopoulou, Nadina and Mary Leontsini. 2017. "Weaving Solidarity: Migrant Women's Organisations in Athens." *Journal of Intercultural Studies* 38(5): 514–529.

Cinalli, Manlio. 2003. "Socio-Politically Polarized Contexts, Urban Mobilization and the Environmental Movement: A Comparative Study of Two Campaigns of Protest in Northern Ireland." *International Journal of Urban and Regional Research* 27(1): 158–177.

Cini Lorenzo, Daniela Chironi, Eliska Drapalova and Federico Tomasello. 2017. Towards a Critical theory of Social Movements: An Introduction." *Anthropological Theory* 17(4): 429–452.

Clark, Janine. 2004. "Social Movement Theory and Patron-Clientelism. Islamic Social Institutions and the Middle Classes in Egypt, Jordan, and Yemen." *Comparative Political Studies* 37: 941–968.

Clayton, Dewey M. 2018. "Black Lives Matter and the Civil Rights Movement: A Comparative Analysis of Two Social Movements in the United States." *Journal of Black Studies* 49(5): 448–480.

Coddou, Marion. 2017. "Sanctified Mobilization: How Political Activists Manage Institutional Boundaries in Faith-Based Organizing for Immigrant Rights." *Research in Political Sociology* 24: 25–65.

Cohen, Joshua. 1989. "Deliberation and Democratic Legitimacy." Pp. 17–34 in *The Good Polity*, edited by A. Hamlin and P. Pettit. Oxford: Blackwell.

Coleman, Gabriella. 2011. Anonymous: from the lulz to collective action. The new everyday: a media commons project (http://mediacommons.futureofthebook.org/tne/pieces/anonymous-lulz-collective-action).

Coleman, Gabriella. 2013. *Anonymous in Context: The Politics and Power behind the Mask.* 3. Waterloo, CA: CIGI.

Coleman, James. 1990. *Foundations of Social Theory*. Cambridge, MA: Belknap.

Collier, Ruth B. 1999. *Paths toward Democracy: The Working Class and Elites in Western Europe and South America*. Cambridge: Cambridge University Press.

Collier, Ruth B. and James Mahoney. 1997. "Adding Collective Actors to Collective Outcomes." *Comparative Politics* 29(3): 285–303.

Colomb, Claire and Johannes Novy, eds. 2017. *Protest and Resistance in the Tourist City*. London: Routledge.

Cotgrove, Stephen, and Andrew Duff. 1980. "Environmentalism, Middle-class Radicalism and Politics." *Sociological Review* 28: 333–351.

Couldry, Nick. 2000. *The Place of Media Power. Pilgrims and Witnesses of the Media Age*. London: Routledge.

Couldry, Nick. 2003. "Beyond the hall of mirrors? Some theoretical reflections on the global contestation of media power." Pp. 39–55 in *Contesting Media Power. Alternative Media in a Networked World*, edited by N. Couldry and J. Curran. Lanham: Rowman and Littlefield.

Couldry, Nick. 2006. *Listening Beyond the Echoes. Media, Ethics and Agency in an Uncertain World*. New York: Paradigm.

Cox, Laurence and Alf Gunvald Nilsen. 2013. "What Would a Marxist Theory of Social Movements Look Like?" Pp. 63–82 in *Marxism and Social Movements*, edited by C. Barker, L. Cox, J. Krinsky, and A. G. Nilsen. Leiden: Brill.

Cox, Laurence and Cristina Flesher Fominaya. 2013. "European Social Movements and Social Theory. A Richer Narrative?" in *Understanding European Movements*, edited by C. F. Fominaya and L. Cox. London: Routledge.

Creasap, Kimberly. 2012. "Social Movement Scenes: Place-Based Politics and Everyday Resistance." *Sociology Compass* 6(2): 182–191.

Cress, Daniel and David A. Snow. 1996. "Mobilization at the Margins: Resources, Benefactors, and the Viability of Homeless Social Movement Organizations." *American Sociological Review* 61: 1089–1109.

Cress, Daniel M. and David A. Snow. 2000. "The Outcomes of Homeless Mobilization: The Influence of Organization, Disruption, Political Mediation, and Framing." *American Journal of Sociology* 105(4): 1065–1104.

Crompton, Rosemary. 1993. *Class and Stratification: An Introduction to Current Debates*. Cambridge: Polity Press.

Crossley, Nick. 1999. "Working Utopias and Social Movements: An Investigation Using Case Study Materials from Radical Mental Health Movements in Britain." *Sociology-the Journal of the British Sociological Association* 33(4): 809–830.

Crossley, Nick. 2002. *Making Sense of Social Movements*. Buckingham: Open University Press.

Crossley, Nick. 2006. *Contesting Psychiatry: Social Movements in Mental Health*. London: Routledge.

Crossley, Nick. 2011. *Towards Relational Sociology*. London: Routledge.

Crossley, Nick. 2015. *Networks of Sound, Style and Subversion. The Punk and Post-Punk Worlds of Manchester, London, Liverpool and Sheffield, 1975–80*. Manchester: Manchester University Press.

Crouch, Colin. 1999. *Social Change in Western Europe*. Oxford: Oxford University Press.

Crouch, Colin. 2004. *Post Democracy*. London: Polity.

Culpepper, P. D. 2010. *Quiet Politics and Business Power: Corporate Control in Europe and Japan*. Cambridge: Cambridge University Press.

Cunningham, David. 2003. "State versus Social Movement: FBI Counterintelligence against the New Left." Pp. 45–77 in *States, parties, and social movements*, edited by J. Goldstone. Cambridge/New York: Cambridge University Press.

Curtis, K. Amber, Joseph Jupille, and David Leblang. 2014. "Iceland on the Rocks: The Mass Political Economy of Sovereign Debt Resettlement." *International Organization* 68(3): 721–740.

Curtis, Russell L. and Louis A. Zurcher. 1973. "Stable Resources of Protest Movements: The Multi-Organizational Field." *Social Forces* 52(1): 353–368.

Curtis, Russell L. and Louis A. Zurcher. 1974. "Social Movements: An Analytical Exploration of Organizational Forms." *Social Problems* 21(3): 356–370.

d'Ovidio, M. and A. Cossu. 2017. "Culture Is Reclaiming the Creative City: The Case of Macao in Milan, Italy." *City, Culture and Society* 8: 7–12.

Dahlgren, Peter. 2009. *Media and Political Engagement. Citizens, Communication and Democracy*. Cambridge: Cambridge University Press.

Dalton, Russell J. 1988. *Citizen Politics in Western Democracies*. Chatham, NJ: Chatham House.

Dalton, Russell J. 1994: *The Green Rainbow: Environmental Groups in Western Europe*. New Haven: Yale University Press.

Dalton, Russell J. 2015. *The Good Citizen: How a Younger Generation is Reshaping American Politics*. Irvine: University of California.

Dalton, Russell J. 2017. *The Participation Gap: Social Status and Political Inequality*. Oxford: Oxford University Press.

Dalton, Russell J. 2018. *Political Realignment*. Oxford/New York: Oxford University Press.

Dalton, Russell J., Scott C. Flanagan, and Paul A. Beck, eds. 1984. *Electoral Change in Advanced Industrial Democracies: Dealignment or Realignment?* Princeton: Princeton University Press.

Damen, Marie-Louise. 2013. "Political Alignments and Cleavages." In *The Wiley-Blackwell Encyclopedia of Social and Political Movements*, edited by D. A. Snow, D. della Porta, B. Klandermans, and D. McAdam. Hoboken, New Jersey: Wiley-Blackwell.

Daphi, Priska. 2017. *Becoming a Movement. Identity, Narrative, and Memory in the European Global Justice Movement*. London/New York: Rowman & Littlefield.

Dauvergne, Peter and Genevieve LeBaron. 2014. *Protest, Inc.: The Corporatization of Activism*. Cambridge, England: Polity Press.

Davenport, Christian. 1995. "Multi-Dimensional Threat Perception and State Repression: An Inquiry into Why States Apply Negative Sanctions." *American Journal of Political Science* 39(3): 683–713.

Davies, James. 1969. "The J-Curve of Rising and Declining Satisfactions as Cause of Some Great Revolutions and a Contained Rebellion." Pp. 690–730 in *Violence in America*, edited by H. D. Graham and T. R. Gurr. New York: Praeger.

Davis, Gerald F., Calvin Morrill, Hayagreeva Rao, and Sarah Soule. 2008. "Introduction: Social Movements in Organizations and Markets." *Administrative Science Quarterly* 53: 389–394.

de la Porte, Caroline and Elke Heins. 2015. "A New Era of European Integration? Governance of labour market and social policy since the sovereign debt crisis." *Comparative European Politics* 13(1): 8–28.

de Sousa Santos Boaventura. ed. 2005. *Democratizing Democracy*, London: Verso.

Dee, E. T. C. 2018. "Institutionalization as Path to Autonomy: An Anarchist Social Center in Brighton." *Space & Culture* 21(2): 192–204.

Delamata, Gabriela. 2004. *Los Barrios Desbordados: Las Organizaciones de Desocupados Del Gran Buenos Aires*. Buenos Aires: Eudeba.

della Porta, Donatella. 1990. *Il terrorismo di sinistra*. Bologna: il Mulino.

della Porta, Donatella. 1995. *Social Movements, Political Violence and the State*. Cambridge/New York: Cambridge University Press.

della Porta, Donatella. 1996a. *Movimenti collettivi e sistema politico in Italia, 1960–1995*. Bari: Laterza.

della Porta, Donatella. 1996b. "Social Movements and the State: Thoughts on the Policing of Protest." Pp. 62–92 in *Comparative Perspectives on Social Movements. Political Opportunities, Mobilizing Structures, and Cultural Framing*, edited by D. McAdam, J. McCarthy, and M. N. Zald. Cambridge/New York: Cambridge University Press.

della Porta, Donatella. 1998a. "The Political Discourse on Protest Policing." In *How Movements Matter*, edited by M. Giugni, D. McAdam, and C. Tilly. Minneapolis: University of Minnesota Press.

della Porta, Donatella. 1998b. "Police Knowledge and the Public Order in Italy." Pp. 1–32 in *Policing Protest: The Control of Mass Demonstrations in Western Democracies*, edited by D. della Porta and H. Reiter. Minneapolis: University of Minnesota Press.

della Porta, Donatella. 2004a. "Europeanization and Social Movements." In *Sociology of Europe*, edited by G. Bettin. Bologna: Monduzzi.

della Porta, Donatella. 2004b. "Démocratie en mouvement: les manifestants du Forum Social Européen, des liens aux réseaux." *Politix* 68: 49–77.

della Porta, Donatella. 2005a. "Deliberation in Movement: Why and How to Study Deliberative Democracy and Social Movements." *Acta politica*, 40(3): 336–350.

della Porta, Donatella. 2005b. "Making the Polis: Social Forums and Democracy in the Global Justice Movement." *Mobilization* 10(1): 73–94.

della Porta, Donatella. 2006. "From Corporatist Unions to Protest Unions? On the (Difficult) Relations between Organized Labour and New Social Movements." Pp. 71–95 in *The Diversity of Democracy. Corporatism, Social Order and Political Conflict*, edited by C. Crouch and W. Streek. Cheltenham: Edward Elgar Publishing.

della Porta, Donatella. 2008. "Eventful Protest, Global Conflicts." *Distinktion: Scandinavian Journal of Social Theory* 17: 26–27.

della Porta, Donatella. 2013. *Can Democracy Be Saved? Participation, Deliberation and Social Movements*. Cambridge: Polity.

della Porta, Donatella. 2014. *Mobilizing for Democracy*. Oxford: Oxford University Press.

della Porta, Donatella. 2015a. *Social Movements in Times of Austerity*. Cambridge: Polity.

della Porta, Donatella. 2015b. *I partiti politici*. Bologna: Il Mulino.

della Porta, Donatella. 2016. *Where Did the Revolution Go? Contentious Politics and the Quality of Democracy*. Cambridge: Cambridge University.

della Porta, Donatella. 2017a. *Where Did the Revolution Go?* Cambridge: Cambridge University Press.

della Porta, Donatella. 2017b. "Political Economy and Social Movement Studies." *Anthropological Theory* 17(4): 453–473.

della Porta, Donatella. 2018a. "1968 – The Resonant Memory of a Rebellious Year." *Contention* 6(2): 1–18.

della Porta, Donatella. 2018b. "Protests as Critical Junctures: Some Reflections towards a Momentous Approach to Social Movements." *Social Movement Studies* (online) DOI: 10.1080/14742837.2018.1555458.

della Porta Donatella. 2018c. "Contentious Moves: Mobilising for Refugees' Rights." Pp. 1–38 in *Solidarity Mobilizations in the 'Refugee Crisis'*, edited by D. della Porta. London: Palgrave.

della Porta Donatella. 2020. *How Social Movements Can Save Democracy*. Cambridge: Polity.

della Porta Donatella, ed. 2004c. *Comitati di cittadini e democrazia urbana*. Cosenza: Rubbettino.

della Porta Donatella, ed. 2007. *The Global Justice Movement*. Boulder, CO: Paradigm.

della Porta Donatella, ed. 2009a. *Another Europe*. New York/London: Routledge.

della Porta Donatella, ed. 2009b. *Democracy in Social Movements*. London: Palgrave.

della Porta Donatella and Kivanc Atak. 2017. "The Spirit of Gezi. A Relational Approach to Eventful Protest and Its Challenges." Pp. 31–59 in *Global Diffusion of Protest. Riding the Protest Wave in the Neoliberal Crisis*, edited by D. della Porta. Amsterdam: Amsterdam University Press.

della Porta Donatella, Lorenzo Cini, and Cesar Guzman. 2020. *Students Movements against Neoliberal Universities*. Bristol: Bristol University Press.

della Porta Donatella, Massimiliano Andretta, Tiago Fernandes, Eduardo Romanos, and Markos Vogiatzoglou. 2018. *Legacies and Memories in Movements: Justice and Democracy in Southern Europe*. Oxford: Oxford University Press.

della Porta Donatella, Michael Keating, Gianpaolo Baiocchi, Colin Crouch, Sheila Jasanoff, Erika Kraemer-Mbula, Dina Kiwan, Abby Peterson, Kenneth M. Roberts, Philippe C. Schmitter, Alberto Vannucci, Antoine Vauchez, and Asanga Welikala. 2018. "The Paradoxes of Democracy and the Rule of Law." Pp. 373–410 in IPSP (Ed.), *Rethinking Society for the 21st Century: Report of the International Panel on Social Progress*. Cambridge: Cambridge University Press.

della Porta, Donatella and Alice Mattoni, eds. 2014. *Spreading Protests. Social Movements at Times of Crisis*. Colchester, UK: ECPR Press.

della Porta, Donatella and Dieter Rucht. 1995. "Left-libertarian Movements in Context: Comparing Italy and West Germany, 1965–1990." Pp. 229–272 in *The Politics of Social Protest. Comparative Perspectives on States and Social Movements*, edited by J. C. Jenkins and B. Klandermans. Minneapolis: University of Minnesota Press.

della Porta, Donatella and Dieter Rucht. 2002a. "The Dynamics of Environmental Campaigns." *Mobilization* 7: 1–14.

della Porta, Donatella and Dieter Rucht, eds. 2002b. "Special Issue: Comparative Environmental Campaigns." *Mobilization* 7: 1–98.

della Porta, Donatella and Elena Pavan. 2017. "Repertoires of Knowledge Practices: Social Movements in Times of Crisis." *Qualitative Research in Organizations and Management: An International Journal* 12(4): 297–314.

della Porta, Donatella and Gianni Piazza. 2008. *Le Ragioni Del No. Le Campagne Contro La Tav in Val Di Susa e Il Ponte Sullo Stretto*. Milano: Feltrinelli.

della Porta, Donatella and Herbert Reiter. 1998. "Introduction: The Policing of Protest in Western Democracies." Pp. 1–32 in *Policing Protest: The Control of Mass Demonstrations in Western Democracies*, edited by D. della Porta and H. Reiter. Minneapolis: University of Minnesota Press.

della Porta, Donatella and Herbert Reiter 2004a. *Polizia e protesta. L'ordine pubblico dalla Liberazione ai "no global"*. Bologna: il Mulino.

della Porta, Donatella and Herbert Reiter. 2004b. *La protesta e il controllo. Movimenti e forze dell'ordine nell'era della globalizzazione*. Milano: Berti/Altreconomia.

della Porta, Donatella and Lorenzo Mosca. 2005. "Global-net for Global Movements? A Network of Networks for a Movement of Movements." *Journal of Public Policy* 25(1): 165–190.

della Porta, Donatella and Manuela Caiani. 2006. *Quale Europa? Europeizzazione, identità e conflitti*. Bologna: Il Mulino.

della Porta, Donatella and Manuela Caiani. 2009. *Social Movements and Europeanization*. Oxford: Oxford University Press.

della Porta, Donatella and Maria Fabbri. 2016. "Producing Space in Action. The Protest Campaign against the Construction of the Dal Molin Military Base." *Social Movement Studies* 15(2): 180–196.

della Porta, Donatella and Mario Diani, eds. 2015. *The Oxford Handbook of Social Movements*. Oxford: Oxford University Press.

della Porta, Donatella and Mario Diani. 2004a. "'No to the War with No Ifs or Buts': Protests Against the War in Iraq." Pp. 200–2018 in *Italian Politics Yearbook 2004*, edited by S. Fabbrini and V. Della Sala. New York: Berghahn.

della Porta, Donatella and Mario Diani. 2004b. *Movimenti senza protesta? L'ambientalismo in Italia*. Bologna: il Mulino (with the collaboration of Massimiliano Andretta).

della Porta, Donatella and Mario Diani. 2006. *Social Movements*. Oxford: Blackwell.

della Porta, Donatella and Massimiliano Andretta. 2002. "Changing Forms of Environmentalism in Italy: The Protest Campaign against the High-Speed Railway System." *Mobilization* 1: 59–77.

della Porta, Donatella and Olivier Fillieule. 2004. "Policing Social Protest." Pp. 217–241 in *The Blackwell Companion to Social Movements*, edited by D. A. Snow, S. H. Soule, and H. Kriesi. Oxford: Blackwell.

della Porta, Donatella and Sidney Tarrow, eds. 2005. *Transnational Protest and Global Activism*. Lanham, MD: Rowman & Littlefield.

della Porta, Donatella and Sidney Tarrow. 1987. "Unwanted Children. Political Violence and the Cycle of Protest in Italy, 1966-1973." *European Journal of Political Research* 14: 607–632.

della Porta, Donatella, Abby Peterson and Herbert Reiter. 2006. *The Policing of Transnational Protest*. Aldershot: Ashgate.

della Porta, Donatella, Francis O'Connor, Martin Portos and Anna Subirats. 2017. *Social Movements and Referendums from Below: Direct Democracy in the Neoliberal Crisis*. Bristol: Policy Press.

della Porta, Donatella, Joseba Fernandez, Hara Kouki, and Lorenzo Mosca. 2017. *Movement Parties in Times of Austerity*. Cambridge: Polity.

della Porta, Donatella, Massimiliano Andretta, Lorenzo Mosca, and Herbert Reiter. 2006. *Globalization From Below: Transnational Activists and Protest Networks*. Minneapolis, MN: University of Minnesota Press.

della Porta, Donatella, Massimiliano Andretta, Tiago Fernandes, Francis O'Connor, Eduardo Romanos, Markos Vogiatzoglou. 2016. *Late Neoliberalism and its Discontents in the Economic Crisis: Comparing Social Movements in the European Periphery*. Cham, Switzerland: Palgrave Macmillan.

Den Hond, Frank, Frank G. A. De Bakker, and Nikolai Smith. 2015. "Social Movements and Organizational Analysis." Pp. 291–305 in *Oxford Handbook of Social Movements*, edited by D. della Porta and M. Diani. Oxford/New York: Oxford University Press.

DeNardo, James. 1985. *Power in Numbers: The Political Strategy of Protest and Rebellion*. Princeton, NJ: Princeton University Press.

Deseriis, Marco. 2013. "Is Anonymous a new form of Luddism? A comparative analysis of industrial machine breaking, computer hacking, and related rhetorical strategies." *Radical History Review* 117: 33–48.

Deutsch, Karl W. 1964. *The Nerves of Government*. Models of Political Communication. New York: Free Press.

Di Feliciantonio, Cesare. 2017. "Spaces of the Expelled as Spaces of the Urban Commons? Analysing the Re-Emergence of Squatting Initiatives in Rome." *International Journal of Urban & Regional Research* 41(5): 708–725.

Di Gregorio, Monica. 2012. "Networking in Environmental Movement Organisation Coalitions: Interest, Values or Discourse?" *Environmental Politics* 21(1): 1–25.

Di Nunzio, Daniele and Emanuele Toscano. 2011. *Dentro e Fuori Casapound. Capire il Fascismo del Terzo Millennio*. Roma: Armando.

Diakoumakos, George. 2015. "Post-Materialism in Greece and the Events of December 2008." *Journal of Modern Greek Studies* 33(2): 293–316.

Diani, Mario. 1992. "The Concept of Social Movement." *Sociological Review* 40(1): 1–25.

Diani, Mario. 1995. *Green Networks. A Structural Analysis of the Italian Environmental Movement*. Edinburgh: Edinburgh University Press.

Diani, Mario. 1996. "Linking Mobilization Frames and Political Opportunities: Insights from Regional Populism in Italy." *American Sociological Review* 61: 1053–1069.

Diani, Mario. 1997. "Social Movements and Social Capital: A Network Perspective on Movement Outcomes." *Mobilization* 2: 129–147.

Diani, Mario. 2000a. "Simmel to Rokkan and Beyond: Elements for a Network Theory of (New) Social Movements." *European Journal of Social Theory* 3: 387–406.

Diani, Mario. 2000b. "Social Movement Networks Virtual and Real." *Information, Communication and Society* 3: 386–401.

Diani, Mario. 2003. "Leaders or Brokers?" Pp. 105–122 in *Social Movements and Networks*, edited by M. Diani and D. McAdam. Oxford/New York: Oxford University Press.

Diani, Mario. 2009. "The Structural Bases of Protest Events. Multiple Memberships and Networks in the February 15th 2003 Anti-War Demonstrations." *Acta Sociologica* 52: 63–83.

Diani, Mario. 2011. "Networks and Internet into Perspective." *Swiss Political Science Review* 17(4): 469–74.

Diani, Mario. 2012. "Interest Organizations in Social Movements: An Empirical Exploration." *Interest Groups & Advocacy* 1(1): 26–47.

Diani, Mario. 2013. "Organizational Fields and Social Movement Dynamics." Pp. 145–168 in *The Future of Social Movement Research: Dynamics, Mechanisms, and Processes*, edited by J. van Stekelenburg, C. Roggeband, and B. Klandermans. Minneapolis, MN: University of Minnesota Press.

Diani, Mario. 2015. *The Cement of Civil Society: Studying Networks in Localities*. Cambridge/New York: Cambridge University Press.

Diani, Mario. 2018. "Unions as Social Movements or Unions in Social Movements?" Pp. 43–65 in *Social Movements and Organized Labor. Passions and Interests*, edited by J. Groete and C. Wagemann. London/New York: Routledge.

Diani, Mario and Caelum Moffatt. 2016. "Modes of Coordination of Collective Action in the Middle-East: Has the Arab Spring Made a Difference?" Pp. 27–45 in *Contention, Regimes, and Transition*, edited by E. Alimi, A. Sela, and M. Sznajder. Oxford/New York: Oxford University Press.

Diani, Mario and Doug McAdam, eds. 2003. *Social Movements and Networks*. Oxford/New York: Oxford University Press.

Diani, Mario and Francesca Forno. 2003. "Italy." Pp. 135–165 in *Environmental Protest in Western Europe*, edited by C. Rootes. Oxford: Oxford University Press.

Diani, Mario and Giovanni Lodi. 1988. "Three In One: Currents in the Milan Ecology Movement." *International Social Movement Research* 1: 103–124.

Diani, Mario and Ivano Bison. 2004. "Organizations, Coalitions, and Movements." *Theory and Society* 33(3–4): 281–309.

Diani, Mario and Katia Pilati. 2011. "Interests, Identities, and Relations: Drawing Boundaries in Civic Organizational Fields." *Mobilization* 16: 265–282.

Diani, Mario and Maria Kousis. 2014. "The Duality of Claims and Events: The Greek Campaign Against the Troika's Memoranda and Austerity, 2010–2012." *Mobilization* 19(4): 387–404.

Diani, Mario and Paolo R. Donati. 1999. "Organizational Change in Western European Environmental Groups: A Framework for Analysis." *Environmental Politics* 8: 13–34.

Diani, Mario, Dieter Rucht, Ruud Koopmans, Pamela Oliver, Verta Taylor, Doug McAdam, and Sidney Tarrow. 2003. "Book Symposium on: Dynamics of Contention." *Mobilization* 8: 109–141.

Diani, Mario, Henrik Ernstson, and Lorien Jasny. 2018. "'Right to the City' and the Structure of Civic Organizational Fields: Evidence from Cape Town." *VOLUNTAS: International Journal of Voluntary and Nonprofit Organizations* 29: 637–652.

DiMaggio, Paul and Walter W. Powell. 1983. "The Iron Cage Revisited: Institutional Isomorphism and Collective Rationality in Organizational Fields." *American Sociological Review* 48: 147–160.

Dioun, Cyrus. 2018. "Negotiating Moral Boundaries: Social Movements and the Strategic (Re)Definition of the Medical in Cannabis Markets." *Research in the Sociology of Organizations* 56: 53–82.

Dixon, M. and V. J. Roscigno. 2003. "Status, Networks, and Social Movement Participation: The Case of Striking Workers." *American Journal of Sociology* 108(6): 1292–1327.

Dobusch, Leonhard and Dennis Schoeneborn. 2015. "Fluidity, Identity, and Organizationality: The Communicative Constitution of *Anonymous*: Fluidity, Identity, and Organizationality." *Journal of Management Studies* 52(8): 1005–1035.

Dodson, Kyle. 2011. "The Movement Society in Comparative Perspective." *Mobilization: An International Quarterly* 16(4): 475–494.

Doerr, Nicole, Alice Mattoni, and Simon Teune. 2015. "Visuals in Social Movements." Pp. 557–566 in *Oxford Handbook of Social Movements*. Vol. Nicole Doerr, Alice Mattoni, and Simon Teune, edited by D. della Porta and M. Diani. Oxford/New York: Oxford University Press.

Doherty, Brian. 1998. "Opposition to Road-Building." *Parliamentary Affairs* 51: 370–383.

Domaradzka, Anna. 2018. "Urban Social Movements and the Right to the City: An Introduction to the Special Issue on Urban Mobilization." *VOLUNTAS: International Journal of Voluntary and Nonprofit Organizations* 29(4): 607–620.

Domaradzka, Anna and Filip Wijkstrom. 2016. "Game of the City Re-Negotiated: The Polish Urban Re-Generation Movements as an Emerging Actor in a Strategic Action Field." *Polish Sociological Review* 3: 291–308.

Donati, Paolo R. 1992. "Political Discourse Analysis." Pp. 136–167 in *Studying collective action*, edited by M. Diani and R. Eyerman. London/Newbury Park: Sage.

Downing, John D.H. 2001. *Radical media: Rebellious communication and social movements*. Thousand Oaks, CA: Sage.

Doyle, Timothy. 2005. *Environmental Movements*. New Brunswick: Rutgers University Press.

Drury, John, Steve Reicher, and Clifford Stott. 2003. "Transforming the Boundaries of Collective Identity: From the 'Local' Anti-Road Campaign to 'Global' Resistance?" *Social Movement Studies: Journal of Social, Cultural and Political Protest* 2(2): 191–212.

Dryzek, John S. 2000. *Deliberative Democracy and Beyond*. New York: Oxford University Press.

Durand Ochoa, Ursula. 2014. *The Political Empowerment of the Cocaleros of Bolivia and Peru*. London: Palgrave.

Duyvendak, Jan Willem, and James M. Jasper, eds. 2015. *Breaking Down the State: Protestors Engaged*. Amsterdam: Amsterdam University Press.

Earl, Jennifer. 2010. "The Dynamics of Protest-Related Diffusion on the Web." *Information, Communication & Society* 13(2): 209–225.

Earl, Jennifer. 2011. "Political Repression: Iron Fists, Velvet Gloves, and Diffuse Control." *Annual Review of Sociology* 37: 261–284.

Earl, Jennifer and Kathrin Kimport. 2011. *Digitally Enabled Social Change Activism in the Internet Age*. Boston, MA: MIT Press.

Earl, Jennifer and R. Kelly Garrett. 2017. "The New Information Frontier: Toward a More Nuanced View of Social Movement Communication." *Social Movement Studies* 16(4): 479–493.

Earl, Jennifer, Lauren Copeland, and Bruce Bimber. 2017. "Routing around organizations: Self-directed political consumption." *Mobilization* 22(2): 131–153.

Earl, Jennifer, Sarah H. Soule, and John McCarthy. 2003. "Protest Under Fire? Explaining the Policing of Protest." *American Sociological Review* 68: 581–606.

Eckstein, Susan, ed. 2001. *Power and Popular Protest: Latin American Social Movements*. Berkeley: University of California Press.

Eder, Klaus. 1993. *The New Politics of Class. Social Movements and Cultural Dynamics in Advanced Societies*. Newbury Park/London: Sage.

Eder, Klaus. 1995. "Does Social Class Matter in the Study of Social Movements? A Theory of Middle Class Radicalism." Pp. 21–54 in *Social Movements and Social Classes*, edited by L. Maheu. London/Thousand Oaks: Sage.

Eder, Klaus. 2003. "Identity Mobilization and Democracy: An Ambivalent Relation." Pp. 61–80 in *Social Movements and Democracy*, edited by Pedro Ibarra. New York: Palgrave.

Eder, Klaus. 2015. "Social Movements in Social Theory." Pp. 31–49 in *The Oxford Handbook of Social Movements*, edited by D. della Porta and M. Diani. Oxford: Oxford University Press.

Edwards, Bob and John D. McCarthy. 2004. "Strategy Matters: The Contingent Value of Social Capital in the Survival of Local Social Movement Organizations." *Soc. Forces* 83(2): 621–651.

Edwards, Bob, Michael Foley, and Mario Diani, eds. 2001. *Beyond Tocqueville: Social Capital, Civil Society, and Political Process in Comparative Perspective,*. Hannover, NH: University Press of New England.

Edwards, Gemma. 2014. "Infectious Innovations? The Diffusion of Tactical Innovation in Social Movement Networks, the Case of Suffragette Militancy." *Social Movement Studies* 13(1): 48–69.

Eggert, Nina and Marco Giugni. 2015. "Migration and Social Movements." Pp. 159–172 in *Oxford Handbook of Social Movements*, edited by D. della Porta and M. Diani. Oxford: Oxford University Press.

Eggert, Nina. 2014. "The Impact of Political Opportunities on Interorganizational Networks: A Comparison of Migrants' Organizational Fields." *Mobilization: An International Quarterly* 19(4): 369–386.

Eggert, Nina and Katia Pilati. 2014. "Networks and Political Engagement of Migrant Organisations in Five European Cities." *European Journal of Political Research* n/a-n/a.

Eidson, John R., Dereje Feyissa, Veronika Fuest, Markus V. Hoehne, Boris Nieswand, Günther Schlee, and Olaf Zenker. 2017. "From Identification to Framing and Alignment: A New Approach to the Comparative Analysis of Collective Identities." *Current Anthropology* 58(3): 340–351.

Einwohner, Rachel. 2006. "Identity Work and Collective Action in a Repressive Context: Jewish Resistance on the 'Aryan Side' of the Warsaw Ghetto." *Social Problems* 53(1): 38–56.

Eisinger, Peter K. 1973. "The Conditions of Protest Behavior in American Cities." *American Political Science Review* 67: 11–28.

Elbert, Rodolfo and Pablo Pérez. 2018. "The Identity of Class in Latin America: Objective Class Position and Subjective Class Identification in Argentina and Chile." *Current Sociology* 66(5): 724–747.

Eliasoph, Nina. 2013. *The Politics of Volunteering*. Cambridge: Polity Press.

Elkins Zachary, Tom Ginsburg, and James Melton. 2012. "A Review of Iceland's Draft Constitution." *The Comparative Constitutions Project*. Available online at: http://comparativeconstitutionsproject.org/wp-content/uploads/CCP-Iceland-Report.pdf?6c8912

Elliott, Thomas, Jennifer Earl, and Thomas V. Maher. 2017. "Recruiting Inclusiveness: Intersectionality, Social Movements, and Youth Online." *Research in Social Movements, Conflicts & Change* 279–311.

Ellis, Stephen and Ineke van Kessel, eds. 2009. *Movers and Shakers. Social Movements in Africa*. Leiden/Boston: Brill.

Elster, Jon. 1998. "Deliberation and Constitution Making." Pp. 97–122 in *Deliberative Democracy*, edited by J. Elster. Cambridge: Cambridge University Press.

Epstein, Barbara. 1991. *Political Protest and Cultural Revolution: Nonviolent Direct Action in the 1970s and 1980s*. Berkeley: University of California.

Etzioni, Amitai. 1975. *A Comparative Analysis of Complex Organizations*. New York: Free Press.

Evans, Peter. 2000. "Fighting Marginalization with Transnational Networks." *Contemporary Sociology* 29: 230–241.

Evcimen, Gamze. 2017. "Anti-Capitalist Muslims in Turkey: The Gezi Park Resistance and Beyond." Pp. 67–84 in *Domestic and Regional Uncertainties in the New Turkey*, edited by O. Tufekci, A. Chiriatti, and H. Tabak. Newcastle upon Tyne: Cambridge Scholars Publishing.

Everton, Sean F. 2015. "Networks and Religion: Ties That Bind, Loose, Build Up, and Tear Down." *Journal of Social Structure* 16: 1–34.

Eyerman, Ron and Andrew Jamison. 1991. *Social Movements: A Cognitive Approach*. Cambridge: Polity Press.

Eynaud, Philippe, Maïté Juan, and Damien Mourey. 2018. "Participatory Art as a Social Practice of Commoning to Reinvent the Right to the City." *VOLUNTAS: International Journal of Voluntary and Nonprofit Organizations* 29(4): 621–636.

Fagan, Adam and Petr Jehlicka. 2003. "Contours of the Czech Environmental Movement: A Comparative Analysis of Hnuti Duha (Rainbow Movement) and Jihoceske Matky (South Bohemian Mothers)." *Environmental Politics* 12(2): 49–70.

Fantasia, Rick. 1989. *Cultures of Solidarity: Consciousness, Action, and Contemporary American Workers*. Berkeley/London, CA: University of California Press.

Fantasia, Rick and Judith Stepan-Norris. 2004. "The Labor Movement in Motion." Pp. 555–575 in *The Blackwell Companion to Social Movements*, edited by D. A. Snow, S. H. Soule, and H. Kriesi. Oxford: Blackwell.

Farro, Antimo L. and Deniz Günce Demirhisar. 2014. "The Gezi Park Movement: A Turkish Experience of the Twenty-First-Century Collective Movements." *International Review of Sociology* 24(1): 176–189.

Favre, Pierre, ed. 1990. *La Manifestation*. Paris: Presses de la Fondation Nationale des Sciences Politiques.

Favretto, Ilaria and Xavier Itçaina, eds. 2016. *Protest, Popular Culture and Tradition in Modern and Contemporary Western Europe*. London: Palgrave Macmillan.

Featherstone, Mike. 1987. "Lifestyle and Consumer Culture." *Theory, Culture and Society* 4: 54–70.

Fernandez, Roberto M. and Doug McAdam. 1989. "Multiorganizational Fields and Recruitment to Social Movements." *International Social Movement Research* 2: 315–343.

Fernández-Savater, Amador, Cristina Flesher Fominaya, Luhuna Carvalho, Çiğdem, Hoda Elsadda, Wiam El-Tamami, Patricia Horrillo, Silvia Nanclares, and Stavros Stavrides. 2017. "Life after the Squares: Reflections on the Consequences of the Occupy Movements." *Social Movement Studies* 16(1): 119–151.

Ferree, Myra Marx and Carol McClurg Mueller. 2004. "Feminism and the Women's Movement: A Global Perspective." Pp. 576–607 in *The Blackwell Companion to Social Movements*, edited by D. A. Snow, S. Soule, and H. Kriesi. Oxford: Blackwell.

Ferree, Myra Marx, William Gamson, Juergen Gerhards, and Dieter Rucht. 2002. *Shaping Abortion Discourse: Democracy and the Public Sphere in Germany and the United States*. Cambridge and New York: Cambridge University Press.

Fillieule, Olivier and Erik Neveu, eds. 2019. *Activists Forever? Long-Term Impacts of Political Activism in Various Contexts. Cambridge*; New York: Cambridge University Press.

Fillieule, Olivier and Guya Accornero. 2016. *Social Movement Studies in Europe*. The State of the Art. New York/Oxford: Berghahn Books.

Fillieule, Olivier, ed. 1993. *Sociologie de la protestation. Les formes de l'action collective dans la France contemporaine*. Paris: L'Harmattan.

Fishman, Robert M. 2013. "How Civil Society Matters in Democratization: Theorizing the Iberian Divergence." *Paper presented at the Conference of CES*. Amsterdam, June: 25–27.

Fishman, Robert M. 2014. "Networks and Narratives in the Making of Civic Practice. Lessons from Iberia." Pp. 159–180 in *Varieties of Civic Innovation*, edited by J. Girouard. Nashville: Vanderbilt University Press.

Flam, Helena. 2015. "Micromobilization and Emotions." Pp. 264–276 in *The Oxford Handbook of Social Movements*, edited by D. della Porta and M. Diani. Oxford: Oxford University Press.

Flam, Helena, ed. 1994a. *States and Anti-Nuclear Movements*. Edinburgh: Edinburgh University Press.

Flam, Helena. 1994b. "Political Responses to the Anti-Nuclear Challenge: II. Democratic Experiences and the Use of Force." Pp. 329–354 in *States and Antinuclear Movements*, edited by H. Flam. Edinburgh: Edinburgh University Press.

Flesher Fominaya, Cristina. 2010. "Creating Cohesion from Diversity: The Challenge of Collective Identity Formation in the Global Justice Movement." *Sociological Inquiry* 80(3): 377–404.

Flesher Fominaya, Cristina. 2014. *Social Movements and Globalization*. Basingstoke: Palgrave.

Flesher Fominaya, Cristina. 2015. "Debunking Spontaneity: Spain's 15-M/ Indignados as Autonomous Movement." *Social Movement Studies* 14(2): 142–163.

Flesher Fominaya, Cristina. 2016. "Cultural Barriers to Activist Networking: Habitus (in) action in Three European Transnational Encounters." *Antipode Journal* 48(1): 151–171.

Flesher Fominaya, Cristina. 2019. "Collective Identity in Social Movements: Assessing the Limits of a Theoretical Framework." Pp. 429–445 in *The Wiley Blackwell Companion to Social Movements*, edited by D. A. Snow, S. Soule, H. Kriesi, and H. McCammon. Oxford: Wiley Blackwell.

Flesher Fominaya, Cristina and Kevin Gillan. 2017. "Navigating the Technology-Media-Movements Complex." *Social Movement Studies* 16(4): 383–402.

Florea, Ioana, Agnes Gagyi, and Kerstin Jacobsson. 2018. "A Field of Contention: Evidence from Housing Struggles in Bucharest and Budapest." *VOLUNTAS: International Journal of Voluntary and Nonprofit Organizations* 29(4): 712–724.

Follesdal, Andreas. 2004. "Political Consumerism as Chance and Challenge." Pp. 3–20 in *Politics, Products and Markets: Exploring Political Consumerism Past and Present,* edited by M. Micheletti, A. Follesdal, and D. Stolle. New Brunswick, NJ: Transaction Publishers.

Font, Joan, Donatella della Porta, and Yves Sintomer, eds. 2014. *Participatory Democracy in Southern Europe*. New York: Rowman and Littlefield.

Forno, Francesca and Paolo R. Graziano. 2014. "Sustainable community movement organisations." *Journal of Consumer Culture* 14(2): 139–157.

Foucault, Michel. 1977. *Discipline and Punish*. New York: Pantheon.

Foweraker, Joe and Todd Landman. 1997. *Citizenship Rights and Social Movements*. Oxford: Oxford University Press.

Franzini, Maurizio and Mario Pianta. 2016. *Disuguaglianze. Quante sono, come combatterle*. Roma-Bari: Laterza.

Franzosi, Roberto. 2004. *From Words to Numbers*. Cambridge: Cambridge University Press.

Fraser, Nancy. 2014. "Behind Marx's Hidden Abode." *New Left Review* 86: 55–72.

Freschi, Anna Carola. 2000. "Comunità virtuali e partecipazione. Dall'antagonismo ai nuovi diritti." *Quaderni di Sociologia* 23: 85–109.

Friedman, Debra and Doug McAdam. 1992. "Identity Incentives and Activism: Networks, Choices and the Life of a Social Movement." Pp. 156–173 in *Frontiers of Social Movement Theory*, edited by A. Morris and C. Mueller. New Haven, CT: Yale University Press.

Fung, Archon and Erik Olin Wright. 2001. "Deepening Democracy: Innovations in Empowered Participatory Governance." *Politics and Society* 29: 5–41.

Fuster Morell, Mayo. 2010. "Participation in Online Creation Communities: Ecosystemic Participation?" Pp. 270–295 in *Vol. Conference Proceedings of JITP 2010: The Politics of Open Source*. Amherst, Mass.: University of Massachussets.

Galaskiewicz, Joseph. 1985. "Interorganizational Relations." *Annual Review of Sociology* 11: 281–304.

Gambetti, Zeynep. 2013. "The Politics of Visibility." *Cultural Anthropology*, www.culanth.org/fieldsights/401-the-politics-of-visibility

Gamson, Josh. 1989. "Silence, Death, and the Invisible Enemy: AIDS Activism and Social Movement "Newness"." *Social Problems* 36: 351–367.

Gamson, William. A. 1990. *The Strategy of Social Protest* (2nd edition). Belmont, CA: Wadsworth (original edition 1975).

Gamson, William A. 1992. "The Social Psychology of Collective Action." Pp. 29–50 in *Frontiers of Social Movement Theory*, edited by A. Morris and Carol Mueller. New Haven, CT: Yale University Press.

Gamson, William A. 2004. "Bystanders, Public Opinion and the Media." Pp. 242–261 in *The Blackwell Companion to Social Movements*, edited by D. A. Snow, S. H. Soule, and H. Kriesi. Oxford: Blackwell.

Gamson, William A. and André Modigliani. 1989. "Media Discourse and Public Opinion on Nuclear Power." *American Journal of Sociology* 95: 1–37.

Gamson, William A. and David S. Meyer. 1996. "Framing Political Opportunity." Pp. 275–290 in *Comparative Perspective on Social Movements. Political Opportunities, Mobilizing*

Structures, and Cultural Framing, edited by D. McAdam, J. McCarthy, and M. N. Zald. Cambridge/New York: Cambridge University Press.

Gamson, William A., David Croteau, William Hoynes, and Theodore Sasson. 1992. "Media Images and the Social Construction of Reality." *Annual Review of Sociology* 18: 373–393.

Gamson, William, Bruce Fireman, and Steve Rytina. 1982. *Encounters with Unjust Authority*. Homewood, Ill.: Dorsey Press.

Garner, Roberta and Mayer N. Zald. 1985. "The political economy of social movement sectors." Pp. 119–145 in *The Challenge of Social Control: Citizenship and Institutions in Modern Society*, edited by D. G. Suttles and M. N. Zald. Norwood (N. J.): Ablex Publishing Corporation.

Gastón, Pablo. 2018. "Contention Across Social Fields: Manipulating the Boundaries of Labor Struggle in the Workplace, Community, and Market." *Social Problems* 65(2): 231–250.

Gawerc, Michelle. 2016. "Constructing a Collective Identity Across Conflict Lines: Joint Israeli-Palestinian Peace Movement Organizations." *Mobilization: An International Quarterly* 21(2): 193–212.

Geary, Dick. 1981. *European Labour Protest 1848–1939*. New York: St Martin's Press.

Geary, Dick. 1989. "Introduction." In *Labour and Socialist Movements in Europe Before 1914*, edited by D. Geary. Oxford/New York: Berg.

Gerbaudo, Paolo. 2012. *Tweets and the Streets: Social Media and Contemporary Activism*. London: Pluto Press.

Gerhard, Jürgen and Friedhelm Neidhardt, ed. 1990. "Strukturen und Funktionen moderner Oeffentlighkeit: Fragestellung und Ansaetze." *WZB discussion paper FS III*: 90–101.

Gerlach, Luther. 1971. "Movements of Revolutionary Change. Some Structural Characteristics." *American Behavioral Scientist* 43: 813–836.

Ghaziani, Amin. 2014. "Measuring Urban Sexual Cultures." *Theory and Society* 43(3–4): 371–393.

Ghaziani, Amin, Verta Taylor, and Amy Stone. 2016. "Cycles of Sameness and Difference in LGBT Social Movements | Annual Review of Sociology." *Annual Review of Sociology* 42: 165–183.

Giddens, Anthony. 1983. "La società europea negli anni ottanta: Divisioni di classe, conflitto di classe e diritti di cittadinanza." Pp. 153–200 in *Le società complesse*, edited by G. Pasquino. Bologna: il Mulino.

Giddens, Anthony. 1990. *The Consequences of Modernity*. Cambridge/Stanford, CA: Polity Press/Stanford University Press.

Giglou, Roya Imani, Christine Ogan, and Leen d'Haenens. 2018. "The Ties That Bind the Diaspora to Turkey and Europe during the Gezi Protests." *New Media & Society* 20(3): 937–955.

Girling, John. 2004. *Social Movements and Symbolic Power: Radicalism, Reform and the Trial of Democracy in France*. New York: Palgrave Macmillan Press.

Gitlin, Todd. 1980. *The Whole World is Watching: Mass Media in the Making and Unmaking of the New Left*. Berkeley/Los Angeles, CA: University of California Press.

Giugni, Marco. 1996. "Federalismo e movimenti sociali." *Rivista italiana di scienza politica* 26: 147–171.

Giugni, Marco and Florence Passy. 1998. "Contentious Politics in Complex Societies: New Social Movements between Conflict and Cooperation." Pp. 81–107 in *From Contention to Democracy*, edited by M. Giugni, D. McAdam, and C. Tilly. Lanham, MD: Rowman and Littlefield.

Giugni, Marco and Florence Passy, eds. 2001. *Political Altruism? Solidarity Movements in International Perspective*. Lanham, MD: Rowman and Littlefield.

Giugni, Marco, Doug McAdam, and Charles Tilly, eds. 1999. *How Movements Matter*. Minneapolis: University of Minnesota Press.

Glenn, John K. 1999. "Competing Challengers and Contested Outcomes to State Breakdown: The Velvet Revolution in Czechoslovakia." *Social Forces* 78(1): 187–211.

Glenn, John K. 2003. "Contentious Politics and Democratization." *Political Studies* 51(1): 103–120.

Goh, Kian. 2018. "Safe Cities and Queer Spaces: The Urban Politics of Radical LGBT Activism." *Annals of the American Association of Geographers* 108(2): 463–477.

Goldfrank, Benjamin. 2011. *Deepening Local Democracy in Latin America: Participation, Decentralization, and the Left*. University Park (PA): Pennsylvania State University Press.

Goldstein, Robert J. 1983. *Political Repression in 19th Century Europe*. London: Croom Helm.

Goldstone, Jack A. 2015. "Demography and social movements." Pp. 146–158 in *The Oxford handbook of social movements*, edited by D. della Porta and M. Diani. Oxford, England: Oxford University Press.

Goldthorpe, John H. 1982. "On the Service Class, Its Formation and Future." In *Social Class and the Division of Labour*, edited by A. Giddens and G. Mackenzie. Cambridge: Cambridge University Press.

Gongaware, Timothy B. 2010. "Collective Memory Anchors: Collective Identity and Continuity in Social Movements." *Sociological Focus* 43(3): 214–239.

Gonzalez-Bailon, Sandra. 2017. *Decoding the Social World: Data Science and the Unintended Consequences of Communication*. Boston, MA: MIT Press.

Gonzalez-Bailon, Sandra and Ning Wang. 2016. "Networked Discontent: The Anatomy of Protest Campaigns in Social Media." *Social Networks* 44: 95–104.

Goodwin, Jeff. 2011. "Why We Were Surprised (Again) by the Arab Spring." *Swiss Political Science Review* 17(4): 452–456.

Goodwin, Jeff and James M. Jasper. 1999. "Caught in a Winding, Snarling Vine: The Structural Bias of Political Process Theory." *Sociological Forum* 14(1): 27–54.

Goodwin, Jeff and James M. Jasper. 2004a. "Caught in a Winding. Snarling Vine: The Structural Bias of Political Process Theory." Pp. 3–30 in *Rethinking Social Movements. Structure, Meaning and Emotions*, edited by J. Goodwin and J. M. Jasper. Lanham, MD: Rowman and Littlefield.

Goodwin, Jeff and James M. Jasper. 2004b. "Trouble in Paradigms." Pp. 75–93 in *Rethinking Social Movements. Structure, Meaning and Emotions*, edited by J. Goodwin and J. J. Jasper. Lanham, MD: Rowman and Littlefield.

Goodwin, Jeff and Rene Rojas. 2015. "Revolutions and Regime Change." Pp. 793–804 in *The Oxford Handbook of Social Movements*, edited by D. della Porta and M. Diani. Oxford, England: Oxford University Press.

Goodwin, Jeff, James M. Jasper, and Francesca Polletta, eds. 2001. *Passionate Politics*. Chicago: Chicago University Press.

Gould, Roger V. 1995. *Insurgent Identities*. Chicago: Chicago University Press.

Gouldner, Alvin. 1979. *The Future of Intellectuals and the Rise of the New Class*. New York: Continuum.

Graeber, David, 2012. *The Democracy Project: A History. A Crisis. A Movement*. London, Allen Lane.

Grasso, Maria T. 2016. *Generations, Political Participation and Social Change in Western Europe*. London: Routledge.

Grasso, Maria T. and Marco Giugni. 2016. "Do Issues Matter? Anti-Austerity Protests' Composition, Values, and Action Repertoires Compared." *Research in Social Movements, Conflicts and Change* 39: 31–58.

Grasso, Maria T. and Marco Giugni. 2018. "Political Values and Extra-Institutional Political Participation: The Impact of Economic Redistributive and Social Libertarian Preferences on Protest Behaviour." *International Political Science Review* 0192512118780425.

Grazioli, Margherita and Carlotta Caciagli. 2018. "Resisting to the Neoliberal Urban Fabric: Housing Rights Movements and the Re-Appropriation of the 'Right to the City' in Rome, Italy." *VOLUNTAS: International Journal of Voluntary and Nonprofit Organizations* 29(4): 697–711.

Greenfield, Liah. 1992. *Nationalism: Five Roads to Modernity*. Cambridge, MA: Harvard University Press.

Gulati, Ranjay and Martin Gargiulo. 1999. "Where Do Interorganizational Networks Come From?" *American Journal of Sociology* 104: 1439–1493.

Gurak, Laura J. and John Logie. 2003. "Internet Protests, from Text to Web." Pp. 25–46 in *Cyberactivism. Online Activism in Theory and Practice*, edited by M. McCaughey and M. D. Ayers. London: Routledge.

Gurr, Ted R. 1970. *Why Men Rebel*. Princeton, NJ: Princeton University Press.

Gurr, Ted R. and Barbara Harff. 1994. *Ethnic Conflict in World Politics*. Boulder, CO: Westview Press.

Gusfield, Joseph. 1963. *Symbolic Crusade*. Urbana: University of Illinois Press.

Gusfield, Joseph. 1989. "Constructing Ownership of Social Problems: Fun and Profit in the Welfare State." *Social Problems* 36: 431–441.

Gutiérrez Sanín Francisco and Elisabeth Jean Wood. 2014. "What Should We Mean By 'Pattern of Political Violence'? Repertoire, Targeting, Frequency and Technique." *Paper presented at the annual meeting of the American Political Science Association*. Washington D.C., August 29.

Gylfason, Thorvaldur. 2012. "From Collapse to Constitution: The Case of Iceland." *CESifo Working Paper Series N. 3770*. Available online at: http://ssrn.com/abstract=2034241

Haas, Peter M. 1992. "Epistemic Communities and International Policy Coordination." *International Organization* 2: 1–35.

Haas, Peter M. 2015. *Epistemic Communities, Constructivism, and International Environmental Politics*. New York/London: Routledge.

Habermas, Jürgen. 1976. *Legitimation Crisis*. London: Heinemann.

Habermas, Jürgen. 1981. *Theorie des kommunikativen Handelns*. Frankfurt am Main: Suhrkamp.

Habermas, Jürgen. 1987. *The Theory of Communicative Action*. Cambridge: Polity Press.

Habermas, Jürgen. 1996. *Between Facts and Norms: Contribution to a Discursive Theory of Law and Democracy*. Cambridge, MA: MIT Press.

Hall, Peter and David Soskice, eds. 2001. *Varieties of Capitalism*. Oxford: Oxford University Press.

Hallgrímsdóttir, Helga Kristin and Emmanuel Brunet-Jailly. 2014. "Contentious politics, grassroots mobilization and the Icesave dispute. Why Iceland did not 'play nicely'." *Acta Sociologica* 58(1): 79–93.

Hampton, Keith and Barry Wellman. 2003. "Neighboring in Netville: How the Internet Supports Community and Social Capital in a Wired Suburb." *City & Community* 2: 277–311.

Hancock, Landon E., ed. 2016. "Narratives of Identity in Social Movements, Conflicts and Change." *Research in Social Movements, Conflicts and Change* 40.

Harvey, David. 2003. "The Right to the City." *International Journal of Urban and Regional Research* 27(4): 939–941.

Harvey, David. 2005. *A Brief History of Neoliberalism*. Oxford: Oxford University Press.

Haug, Christoph. 2013. "Organizing Spaces: Meeting Arenas as a Social Movement Infrastructure between Organization, Network, and Institution." *Organization Studies* 34(5–6): 705–732.

Haunss, Sebastian and Darcy Leach. 2009. "Scenes and Social Movements." Pp. 255–276 in *Culture, Social Movements, and Protest*, edited by H. Johnston. Burlington, VT/Aldershot UK: Ashgate Publishers.

Hayes-Conroy, Allison and Deborah G. Martin. 2010. "Mobilising Bodies: Visceral Identification in the Slow Food Movement." *Transactions of the Institute of British Geographers* 35(2): 269–281.

He, Shenjing and Desheng Xue. 2014. "Identity Building and Communal Resistance against Landgrabs in Wukan Village, China." *Current Anthropology* 55(S9): S126–137.

Heaney, Michael T. 2010. "Linking political parties and interest groups." Pp. 568–587 in *The Oxford Handbook of American Political Parties and Interest Groups*, edited by L. S. Maisel, J. M. Berry and G. C. Edwards III. Oxford, Oxford University Press.

Hechter, Michael. 1975. *Internal Colonialism: The Celtic Fringe in Bristish National Development 1536-1966*. London: Routledge and Kegan.

Heery, Edmund, Steve Williams, and Brian Abbott. 2012. "Civil Society Organizations and Trade Unions: Cooperation, Conflict, Indifference." *Work, Employment & Society* 26(1): 145–160.

Heideman, Laura. 2017. "Cultivating Peace: Social Movement Professionalization and Ngoization in Croatia." *Mobilization* 22(3): 345–362.

Heins, Elke and Caroline de la Porte. 2015. "The Sovereign Debt Crisis, the EU and Welfare State Reform." *Comparative European Politics* 13(1): 1–7.

Held, David and Anthony McGrew. 2000. *The Global Transformation Reader: An Introduction*. Cambridge: Polity Press.

Held, David, Anthony McGrew, David Goldblatt, and Jonathan Perraton. 1999. *Global Transformations*. Cambridge: Polity Press.

Hendrikx, Bas, Stefan Dormans, Arnoud Lagendijk, and Mike Thelwall. 2017. "Understanding the Geographical Development of Social Movements: A Web-Link Analysis of Slow Food." *Global Networks* 17(1): 47–67.

Hensby, Alexander. 2016. "Open Networks and Secret Facebook Groups: Exploring Cycle Effects on Activists' Social Media Use in the 2010/11 UK Student Protests." *Social Movement Studies* 16: 466–478.

Hermida, Alberto and Víctor Hernández-Santaolalla. 2018. "Twitter and Video Activism as Tools for Counter-Surveillance: The Case of Social Protests in Spain." *Information, Communication & Society* 21(3): 416–433.

Hess, Andreas. 2007. "The Social Bonds of Cooking." *Cultural Sociology* 1(3): 383–407.

Hess, David and Martin Brian. 2006. "Repression, Backfire, and The Theory of Transformative Events." *Mobilization: An International Quarterly* 11(2): 249–267.

Hetland, Gabriel and Jeff Goodwin. 2013. "The Strange Disappearance of Capitalism from Social Movement Studies." Pp. 83–102 in *Marxism and Social Movements*, edited by C. Barker, L. Cox, J. Krinsky, and A. G. Nilsen. Leiden: Brill.

Hick, Steven and John McNutt, 2002. "Communities and Advocacy on the Internet: A Conceptual Framework." Pp. 3–18 in *Advocacy, Activism and the Internet*, edited by S. Hick and J. McNutt. Chicago: Lyceum Books.

Hill, Tim, Robin Canniford, and Peter Millward. 2018. "Against Modern Football: Mobilising Protest Movements in Social Media." *Sociology* 52(4): 688–708.

Hirschman, Albert O. 1982. *Shifting Involvements: Private Interests and Public Action*. Princeton, NJ: Princeton University Press.

Hobsbawm, Eric. 1952. "The Machine Breakers." *Past and Present* 1: 57–70.

Hobsbawm, Eric and Terence Ranger, eds. 1983. *The Invention of Tradition*. Cambridge: Cambridge University Press.

Hoffman, Lily M. 1989. *The Politics of Knowledge: Activist Movements in Medicine and Planning*. Albany, NY: SUNY Press.

Hoffman, Michael and Amaney Jamal. 2014. "Religion in the Arab Spring: Between Two Competing Narratives." *The Journal of Politics* 76(3): 593–606.

Holland, Dorothy, Gretchen Fox, and Vinci Daro. 2008. "Social Movements and Collective Identity: A Decentered, Dialogic View." *Anthropological Quarterly* 81(1): 95–126.

Howard, Philip and Muzammil Hussain. 2013. *Democracy's Fourth Wave? Digital Media and the Arab Spring*. Oxford/New York: Oxford University Press.

Hoyng, Rolien. 2014. "Place Brands, Nonbrands, Tags and Queries: The Networks of Urban Activism in the Creative City Istanbul." *Cultural Studies* 28(3): 494–517.

Hughes, Joanne, Andrea Campbell, and Richard Jenkins. 2011. "Contact, Trust and Social Capital in Northern Ireland: A Qualitative Study of Three Mixed Communities." *Ethnic and Racial Studies* 34(6): 967–985.

Hughes, Neil. 2018. "'Tourists Go Home': Anti-Tourism Industry Protest in Barcelona." *Social Movement Studies* 17(4): 471–477.

Hunt, Lynn. 1984. *Politics, Culture, and Class in the French Revolution*. Berkeley, CA: University of California Press.

Hunt, Scott A., Robert D. Benford, and David A. Snow. 1994. "Identity Fields: Framing Processes and the Social Construction of Movement Identities." Pp. 185–208 in *New Social Movements: From Ideology to Identity*, edited by E. Larana, H. Johnston, and J. Gusfield. Philadelphia: Temple University Press.

Hutter, Sven. 2014. *Protesting Culture and Economics in Western Europe: New Cleavages in Left and Right Politics*. Minneapolis, University of Minnesota Press.

Imig, Doug and Sidney Tarrow, eds. 2001a. *Contentious Europeans: Protest and Politics in an Emerging Polity*. Lanham, MD: Rowman & Littlefield.

Imig, Doug, and Sidney Tarrow. 2001b. "La contestation politique dans l'Europe en formation." Pp. 195–223 in *L'action collective en Europe*, edited by R. Balme, D. Chabanet, and V. Wright. Paris: Presses De Science Po.

Inglehart, Ronald. 1977. *The Silent Revolution: Changing Values and Political Styles among Western Publics*. Princeton: Princeton University Press.

Inglehart, Ronald. 1990. *Culture Shift in Advanced Industrial Society*. Princeton, NJ: Princeton University Press.

Inglehart, Ronald and Christian Welzel. 2005. *Modernization, Cultural Change and Democracy*. Cambridge: Cambridge University Press.

Isin, Engin F. and Bryan S. Turner, eds. 2002. *Handbook of Citizenship Studies*. London: Sage.

Jamison, Andrew, Ron Eyerman, and Jacqueline Cramer. 1990. *The Making of the New Environmental Consciousness: A Comparative Study of the Environmental Movements in Sweden, Denmark and the Netherlands*. Edinburgh: Edinburgh University Press.

Jarvis, Jason L. 2014. "Digital image politics: the networked rhetoric of Anonymous." *Global Discourse: An Interdisciplinary Journal of Current Affairs and Applied Contemporary Thought Publication* 4(2–3): 1–24.

Jasper, James M. 1997. *The Art of Moral Protest*. Chicago: University of Chicago Press.

Jasper, James M. 2018. *The Emotions of Protest*. Chicago: University of Chicago Press.

Jasper, James M. and Aidan McGarry. 2015. "Introduction: The Identity Dilemma, Social Movements, and Contested Identity." Pp. 65–84 in *The Identity Dilemma*, edited by A. McGarry and J. M. Jasper. Philadelphia: Temple University Press.

Jasper, James M. and Francesca Polletta. 2019. "The Cultural Context of Social Movements." Pp. 63–78 in *The Wiley Blackwell Companion to Social Movements*, edited by D. A. Snow, S. Soule, H. Kriesi, and H. McCammon. Oxford: Wiley Blackwell.

Jasper, James M. and Jane D. Poulsen. 1995. "Recruiting Strangers and Friends: Moral Shocks and Social Networks in Animal Rights and Anti-Nuclear Protests." *Social Problems* 42: 493–512.

Jasper, James M., and Jan Willem Duyvendak, eds. 2015. *Players and Arenas: The Interactive Dynamics of Protest*. Amsterdam: Amsterdam University Press.

Jasper, James M., Michael Young, and Elke Zuern. 2018. "Character Work in Social Movements." *Theory & Society* 47(1): 113–131.

Jenkins, J. Craig and Bert Klandermans. 1995. "The Politics of Social Protest." Pp. 3–13 in *The Politics of Social Protest: Comparative Perspectives on States and Social Movements*, edited by J. C. Jenkins and B. Klandermans. Minneapolis: University of Minnesota Press.

Johnston, Hank. 1991. *Tales of Nationalism: Catalonia, 1939–1979*. New Brunswick, NJ: Rutgers University Press.

Johnston, Hank. 2002. "Verification and Proof in Frame and Discourse Analysis." Pp. 62–91 in *Methods of Social Movement Research*, edited by B. Klandermans and S. Staggenborg. Minneapolis/London: University of Minnesota Press.

Johnston, Hank. 2015. "The Game's Afoot": Social Movements in Authoritarian States." Pp. 753–766 in *The Oxford Handbook of Social Movements*, edited by D. della Porta and M. Diani. Oxford: Oxford University Press.

Johnston, Hank and Eitan Alimi. 2013. "A Methodology Analyzing for Frame Dynamics: The Grammar of Keying Battles in Palestinian Nationalism." *Mobilization: An International Quarterly* 18(4): 453–474.

Jones, Candace, William S. Hesterly, and Stephen P. Borgatti. 1997. "A General Theory of Network Governance: Exchange Conditions and Social Mechanisms." *Academy of Management Review* 22: 911–945.

Joppke, Christian. 1993. *Mobilizing against Nuclear Energy: A Comparison of Germany and the United States*. Berkeley/Los Angeles: University of California Press.

Jordan, Grant and William Maloney. 1997. *The Protest Business?* Manchester: Manchester University Press.

Jordan, Tim. 2002. *Activism! Direct Action, Hacktivism and the Future of Society*. London: Reaktion Books.

Juris, Jeffrey S. 2008. *Networking Futures: The Movements against Corporate Globalization*. Durham, NC: Duke University Press.

Juris, Jeffrey S. 2012. "Reflections on #Occupy Everywhere: Social Media, Public Space, and Emerging Logics of Aggregation." *American Ethnologist* 39(2): 259–279.

Kanellopoulos, Kostas, Konstantinos Kostopoulos, Dimitris Papanikolopoulos, and Vasileios Rongas. 2016. "Competing Modes of Coordination in the Greek Anti-Austerity Campaign, 2010–2012." *Social Movement Studies* 16: 101–118.

Kaplan, Jeffrey and Helene Lööw, eds. 2002. *The Cultic Milieu: Oppositional Subcultures in an Age of Globalization*. Walnut Creek, CA: Alta Mira Press.

Karakayalí, Serhat, and Özge Yaka. 2014. "The Spirit of Gezi: The Recomposition of Political Subjectivities in Turkey." *New Formations: A Journal of Culture/theory/ politics* 83(1): 117–138.

Karatnycky, Adrian and Peter Ackerman. 2005. *How Freedom Is Won. From Civic Resistance to Durable Democracy*. New York: Freedom House.

Karl, Terry Lynn. 1990. "Dilemmas of Democratization in Latin America." *Comparative Politics* 23(1): 1–21.

Keck, Margeret, and Kathryn Sikkink. 1998. *Activists Beyond Borders*. Ithaca, NY: Cornell University Press.

Kenny, Bridget C. 2005. "Militant Divisions, Collective Possibilities: Lessons for Labour Mobilization from South African Retail Sector Workers." *Divisions Chez Les Militants, Possibilités Collectives: Les Leçons Pour Une Mobilisation Du Mouvement Ouvrier Tirées Du Secteur Des Petits Commerçants En Afrique Du Sud*. 38(1/2): 156–183.

Kerbo, Harold R. 1982. "Movements of 'Crisis' and Movements of 'Affluence' A Critique of Deprivation and Resource Mobilization Theories." *Journal of Conflict Resolution* 26(4): 645–663.

Kertzer, David. 1988. *Rituals, Politics, and Power*. New Haven: Yale University Press.

Kertzer, David. 1996. *Politics and Symbols: The Italian Communist Party and the Fall of Communism*. New Haven, CT: Yale University Press.

Ketelaars, Pauline. 2017. "Tracing Protest Motives: The Link Between Newspaper Coverage, Movement Messages, and Demonstrators' Reasons to Protest." *Sociological Forum* 32(3): 480–500.

Khagram, Sanjeev, James Riker, and Kathryn Sikkink, eds. 2002: *Reconstructing World Politics: Transnational Social Movements, Networks and Norms*. Minneapolis: University of Minnesota Press.

Khamis, Sahar and Katherine Vaughn. 2011. "Cyberactivism in the Egyptian Revolution: How Civic Engagement and Citizen Journalism Tilted the Balance." *Arab Media & Society* (14).

Killian, Lewis. 1964. "Social Movements." Pp. 426–445 in *Handbook of Modern Sociology*, edited by R. E. Farris. Chicago: Rand McNally.

King, Brayden G. 2008a. "A Social Movement Perspective of the Stakeholder Collective Action and Influence." *Business and Society* 47: 21–49.

King, Brayden G. 2008b. "A Political Mediation Model of Corporate Response to Social Movement Activism." *Administrative Science Quarterly* 53: 395–421.

King, Leslie and Julianne Busa. 2017. "When Corporate Actors Take over the Game: The Corporatization of Organic, Recycling and Breast Cancer Activism." *Social Movement Studies* 16(5): 549–563.

Kioupkiolis, Alexandros. 2016. "Podemos: The Ambiguous Promises of Left-Wing Populism in Contemporary Spain." *Journal of Political Ideologies* 21(2): 99–120.

Kitschelt, Herbert. 1985. "New Social Movements in West Germany and the United States." *Political Power and Social Theory* 5: 273–342.

Kitschelt, Herbert. 1986. "Political Opportunity Structures and Political Protest: Anti-Nuclear Movements in Four Democracies." *British Journal of Political Science* 16: 57–85.

Kitschelt, Herbert. 1993. "Social Movements, Political Parties, and Democratic Theory." *The Annals of the AAPSS* 528: 13–29.

Kitschelt, Herbert. 2006. "Movement Parties." Pp. 278–290 in *Handbook of Party Politics*, edited by R. S. Katz and W. J. Crotty. London/Thousand Oaks: Sage.

Kitts, James A. 2000. "Mobilizing in Black Boxes: Social Networks and SMO Participation." *Mobilization* 5: 241–257.

Klandermans, Bert, Hanspeter Kriesi, and Sidney Tarrow, eds. 1988. *From Structure to Action: Comparing Social Movement Research across Cultures*. Greenwich, CT: JAI Press.

Klein, Naomi. 1999. *No Logo*. New York: HarperCollins.

Klein, Naomi. 2002. *Fences and Windows: Dispatches From the Front Lines of the Globalization Debate*. London: Flamingo.

Knoke, David. 1990. *Organizing for Change*. Hawthorne, NY: Aldine de Gruyter.

Kolb, Felix. 2007. *Protest and Opportunities*. Frankfurt, Germany/New York, NY: Campus.

Koopmans, Ruud. 2004. "Political Opportunity Structure: Some Splitting to Balance the Lumping." Pp. 61–74 in *Rethinking Social Movements: Structure, Meaning and Emotions*, edited by J. Goodwin and J. M. Jasper. Lanham, MD: Rowman and Littlefield.

Koopmans, Ruud and Jan Willem Duyvendak. 1995. "The Political Construction of the Nuclear Energy Issue and Its Impact on the Mobilization of Anti-Nuclear Movements in Western Europe." *Social Problems* 42: 201–218.

Koopmans, Ruud and Paul Statham. 1999. "Political Claims Analysis: Integrating Protest Event and Political Discourse Approaches." *Mobilization* 4: 203–221.

Koopmans, Ruud and Paul Statham. 2010. *The Making of a European Public Sphere: Media Discourse and Political Contention*. Cambridge/New York: Cambridge University Press.

Kornhauser, William. 1959. *The Politics of Mass Society*. Glencoe, Ill.: Free Press.

Kotronaki, Loukia. 2013. "Les Mobilisations Des Indignés: Politique Du Conflit et Politique Conventionnelle Aux Années Du Mémorandum En Grèce." *Pôle Sud* 38: 53–70.

Kotronaki Loukia and Seraphim Seferiades. 2012. "Along the Pathways of Rage: The Space-Time of an Uprising." Pp. 157–170 in *Violent Protest, Contentious Politics, and the Neoliberal State*, edited by S. Seferiades, London and New York: Routledge.

Kousis, Maria and Charles Tilly. 2004. "Introduction: Economic and Political Contention in Comparative Perspective." Pp. 1–11 in *Economic and Political Contention in Comparative Perspective*, edited by M. Kousis and C. Tilly. Boulder, CO: Paradigm Publishers.

Kováts, Eszter. 2018. "Questioning Consensuses: Right-Wing Populism, Anti-Populism, and the Threat of 'Gender Ideology.'" *Sociological Research Online* 23(2): 528–538.

Kowalewski, David and Paul D. Schumaker. 1981. "Protest Outcomes in the Soviet Union." *Sociological Quarterly* 22: 57–68.

Kriesi, Hanspeter. 1988. "Local Mobilization for the People's Petition of the Dutch Peace Movement." *International Social Movement Research* 1: 41–81.

Kriesi, Hanspeter. 1989a. "New Social Movements and the New Class in the Netherlands." *American Journal of Sociology* 94(5): 1078–1116.

Kriesi, Hanspeter. 1989b. "The Political Opportunity Structure of the Dutch Peace Movement." *West European Politics* 12: 295–312.

Kriesi, Hanspeter. 1991. "The Political Opportunity Structure of New Social Movements." *Discussion Paper FS III: 91–103*. Berlin: Wissenschaftszentrum.

Kriesi, Hanspeter. 1993. *Political Mobilization and Social Change: The Dutch Case in Comparative Perspective*. Aldershot: Avebury.

Kriesi, Hanspeter. 1995. "The Political Opportunity Structure of New Social Movements: Its Impact on Their Mobilization." Pp. 167–198 in *The Politics of Social Protest* J. C. Jenkins and B. Klandermans. Minneapolis/London: University of Minnesota Press/ UCL Press.

Kriesi, Hanspeter. 1996. "The Organizational Structure of New Social Movements in a Political Context." Pp. 152–184 in *Comparative Perspective on Social Movements. Political Opportunities, Mobilizing Structures, and Cultural Framing*, edited by D. McAdam, J. McCarthy, and M. N. Zald. Cambridge/New York: Cambridge University Press.

Kriesi, Hanspeter. 2004. "Political Context and Opportunity." Pp. 67–90 in *The Blackwell Companion to Social Movements*, edited by D. A. Snow, S. H. Soule, and H. Kriesi. Oxford: Blackwell.

Kriesi, Hanspeter. 2015. "Party system, political system and social movements." Pp. 667–680 in *The Oxford Handbook on Social Movements*, edited by D. della Porta and M. Diani. Oxford, Oxford University Press.

Kriesi, Hanspeter and Takis S. Pappas, eds. 2015. *European Populism in the Shadow of the Great Recession*. Colchester: ECPR Press.

Kriesi, Hanspeter, Edgar Grande, Martin Dolezal, Marc Helbling, Dominic Hoeglinger, Swen Hutter, and Bruno Wuest. 2012. *Political Conflict in Western Europe*. Cambridge/ New York: Cambridge University Press.

Kriesi, Hanspeter, Edgar Grande, Romain Lachat, Martin Dolezal, Simon Bornschier, and Timotheos Frey. 2008. *West European Politics in the Age of Globalization*. Cambridge/ New York: Cambridge University Press.

Kriesi, Hanspeter, Ruud Koopmans, Jan Willem Duyvendak, and Marco Giugni. 1995. *New Social Movements in Western Europe*. Minneapolis/London: University of Minnesota Press.

Krinsky, John and Nick Crossley. 2014. "Social Movements and Social Networks: Introduction." *Social Movement Studies* 13(1): 1–21.

Kuhar, Roman, and David Paternotte. 2017. *Anti-Gender Campaigns in Europe: Mobilizing against Equality*. Lanham, MD: Rowman and Littlefield.

Kühle, Lene and Lasse Lindekilde. 2009. *Radicalisation among Young Muslims in Aarhus*. Aarhus: Aarhus: Centre for Studies in Islamism and Radicalisation (CIR).

Kurzman, Charles. 2004. "The Poststructuralist Consensus in Social Movement Theory." Pp. 111–120 in *Rethinking Social Movements: Structure, Meaning and Emotions*, edited by J. Goodwin and J. M. Jasper. Lanham, MD: Rowman and Littlefield.

Laclau, Ernesto. 2005. *On Populist Reason*. London: Verso.

Lahusen, Christian. 2004. "Joining the Cocktail Circuit: Social Movement Organizations at the European Union." *Mobilization* 9: 55–71.

Lash, Scott and John Urry. 1987. *The End of Organized Capitalism.* Cambridge: Polity.

Latouche, Serge. 1989. *L'occidentalisation du monde: Essai sur la signification, la portée et les limites de l'uniformisation planétaire.* Paris: La Découverte.

Lavine, Marc, J. Adam Cobb, and Christopher J. Roussin. 2017. "When Saying Less Is Something New: Social Movements and Frame-Contraction Processes." *Mobilization* 22(3): 275–292.

Leca, Bernard. 2018. "Les « gilets Jaunes » : Forces et Faiblesses d'une Organisation En Essaim." *The Conversation.* Retrieved January 24, 2019 (http://theconversation.com/les-gilets-jaunes-forces-et-faiblesses-dune-organisation-en-essaim-108195).

Lee, Francis L. F. 2018. "Internet Alternative Media, Movement Experience, and Radicalism: The Case of Post-Umbrella Movement Hong Kong." *Social Movement Studies* 17(2): 219–233.

Leenders, Reinoud. 2012. "Collective Action and Mobilization in Dar'a: An Anatomy of the Onset of Syria's Popular Uprising." *Mobilization* 17(4): 419–434.

Lefebvre, Henri. 1968. *Le Droit à La Ville.* Paris: Anthropos.

Lemieux, Vincent. 1997. "Réseaux et Coalitions." *L'Année Sociologique* 47(1): 55–72.

Lemieux, Vincent. 1998. *Les Coalitions. Liens, Transactions et Controles.* Paris: Puf.

Lenox, Michael J. and Charles E. Eesley. 2009. "Private Environmental Activism and the Selection and Response of Firm Targets." *Journal of Economics & Management Strategy* 18: 45–73.

Levi, Margaret and David Olson. 2000. "The Battles in Seattle." *Politics & Society* 28(3): 309–329.

Levitsky, Steven and Kenneth M. Roberts. 2011a. "Latin America's "left turn": a framework for analysis." Pp. 1–28 in *The Resurgence of the Latin American Left*, edited by S. Levitsky and K. M. Roberts. Baltimore, Johns Hopkins University Press.

Levitsky, Steven and Kenneth M. Roberts. 2011b. "Conclusion: Democracy, Development, and the Left." Pp. 399–427 in *The Resurgence of the Latin American Left*, edited by S. Levitsky and K. M. Roberts. Baltimore, Johns Hopkins University Press.

Lichterman, Paul. 1995. *The Search for Political Community: American Activists Reinventing Commitment.* Cambridge/New York: Cambridge University Press.

Lichterman, Paul. 2008. "Religion and the Construction of Civic Identity." *American Sociological Review* 73: 83–104.

Light, Ryan. 2015. "Like Strangers We Trust: Identity and Generic Affiliation Networks." *Social Science Research* 51: 132–144.

Lijphart, Arend. 1969. "Consociational Democracy." *World Politics* 21(2): 207–225.

Lijphart, Arend. 1999. *Patterns of Democracy. Government Forms and Performance in Thirty-Six Countries.* New Haven and London: Yale University Press.

Lindekilde, Lasse and Lene Kühle. 2015. "Religious Revivalism and Social Movements." Pp. 173–1184 in *The Oxford Handbook of Social Movements, edited by* D. della Porta and M. Diani. Oxford, England: Oxford University Press.

Lindgren, Elaine H. 1987. "The Informal-Intermittent Organization: A Vehicle for Successful Citizen Protest." *Journal of Applied Behavioral Research* 23: 397–412.

Linz, Juan J. and Alfred Stepan. 1996. *Problems of Democratic Transition and Consolidation*. Baltimore, MD: Johns Hopkins Press.

Lipset, Seymour M. and Stein Rokkan, eds. 1967. *Party Systems and Voter Alignments*. New York: Free Press.

Lipsky, Michael. 1965. *Protest and City Politics*. Chicago: Rand McNally & Co.

Lipsky, Michael. 1970. "Introduction." Pp. 1–7 in *Law and Order: Police Encounters*, edited by M. Lipsky. New York: Aldine Publishing Company.

Livesay, Jeff. 2002. "The Duality of Systems: Networks as Media and Outcomes of Movement Mobilization." *Current Perspectives on Social Theory* 22: 185–221.

Lo, Clarence Y. H. 1982. "Countermovements and Conservative Movements in the Contemporary US." *Annual Review of Sociology* 8: 107–134.

Lo, Clarence Y. H. 1990. *Small Property, Big Government: Social Origins of the Property Tax Revolt*. Berkeley, CA: University of California Press.

Loader, Brian D. and Dan Mercea. 2011. "Networking Democracy?" *Information, Communication & Society* 14(6): 757–769.

Lofland, John. 1989. "Consensus Movements: City Twinnings and Derailed Dissent in the American Eighties." *Research in Social Movements, Conflict and Change* 11: 163–189.

Lofland, John. 1996. *Social Movement Organizations*. New York: Aldine de Gruyter.

Longard, Shelby. 2013. "The Reflexivity of Individual and Group Identity within Identity-Based Movements: A Case Study." *Humanity & Society* 37(1): 55–79.

López, Miguel Angel Martínez. 2017. "Squatters and Migrants in Madrid: Interactions, Contexts and Cycles." *Urban Studies (Sage Publications, Ltd.)* 54(11): 2472–2489.

Lotan, Gilad, Erhardt Graeff, Mike Ananny, Devin Gaffney, Ian Pearce, and Danah Boyd. 2011. "The Revolutions Were Tweeted: Information Flows During the 2011 Tunisian and Egyptian Revolutions." *International Journal of Communication* 5: 1375–1405.

Loukakis, Angelos, Johannes Kiess, Maria Kousis, and Christian Lahusen. 2018. "Born to Die Online? A Cross-National Analysis of the Rise and Decline of Alternative Action Organizations in Europe." *American Behavioral Scientist* 62(6): 837–855.

Lowi, Theodor. 1971. *The Politics of Disorder*. New York: Norton.

Luce, Stephanie. 2014. *Labor Movements: Global Perspectives*. Cambridge: Polity Press.

Lumley, Robert. 1990. *States of Emergency. Cultures of Revolt in Italy from 1968 to 1978*. London: Verso.

Luttbeg, Norman R. 1981. *Public Opinion and Public Policy: Models of Political Linkage*. Itasca (Ill.): F. E. Peacock Publishers, 3rd edn.

Maddison, Sarah and Emma Partridge. 2014. "Agonism and Intersectionality: Indigenous Women, Violence and Feminist Collective Identity" edited by L. M. Woehrle. *Research in Social Movements, Conflicts and Change* 37: 27–52.

Madi-Sisman, Ozlem. 2013. "The Arab Spring for Women: A Missed Opportunity? [2013]." *Turkish Review (Spring 2013)*.

Madrid, Raul. L. 2009. "The Origins of the Two Lefts in Latin America." *Political Science Quarterly* 125(4): 1–23.

Mansbridge, Jane. 1986. *Why We Lost the ERA*. Chicago: University of Chicago Press.

Mansbridge, Jane. 1996. "Using Power/Fighting Power: The Polity." Pp. 46–66 in *Democracy and Difference: Contesting the Boundaries of the Political*, edited by S. Benhabib. Princeton, N.J., Princeton University Press.

Marchetti, Raffaele. 2015. "The Conditions for Civil Society Participation in International Decision Making." Pp. 753–766 in *The Oxford Handbook of Social Movements*, edited by D. della Porta and M. Diani. Oxford: Oxford University Press.

Marks, Gary 1989. *Union in Politics: Britain, Germany and the United States in the Nineteenth and Early Twentieth Century*. Princeton: Princeton University Press.

Marks, Gary and Doug McAdam. 1998. "Social Movements and the Changing Political Opportunity in the European Community." In *Social Movements in a Globalizing World*, edited by D. della Porta, H. Kriesi, and D. Rucht. New York/London: Longman.

Marshall, Thomas H. 1992. "Citizenship and Social Class." Pp. 3–51 in *Citizenship and Social Class*, edited by T. H. Marshall, and H. D. Bottomore. London: Pluto Press.

Martín, Irene. 2015. "Podemos y otros modelos de partido-movimiento." *Revista Española de Sociología* 24: 107–114.

Martìnez, Miguel. 2013. "The Squatters' Movement in Europe: A Durable Struggle for Social Autonomy in Urban Politics." *Antipode* 45(4): 866–887.

Martinez-Alier, Joan, Leah Temper, Daniela Del Bene, and Arnim Scheidel. 2016. "Is There a Global Environmental Justice Movement?" *The Journal of Peasant Studies* 43(3): 731–755.

Marx, Gary T. 1979. "External Efforts to Damage or Facilitate Social Movements: Some Patterns, Explanations, Outcomes and Complications." Pp. 94–125 in *The Dynamics of Social Movements*, edited by J. McCarthy and M. N. Zald. Cambridge, MA: Winthrop Publishing.

Marx, Gary T. and James Wood. 1975. "Strands of Theory and Research in Collective Behaviour." *Annual Review of Sociology* 1: 363–428.

Massa, Felipe G. 2017. "Guardians of the Internet: Building and Sustaining the Anonymous Online Community." *Organization Studies (01708406)* 38(7): 959–988.

Mathivet, Charlotte and Shelley Buckingham. 2009. "The Abahlali BaseMjondolo Shack Dwellers Movement and the Right to the City in South Africa." Retrieved January 3, 2017 (http://base.d-p-h.info/es/fiches/dph/fiche-dph-8059.html).

Mattoni, Alice. 2009. "Multiple Media Practices in Italian Mobilizations Against Precarity of Work." *PhD Thesis*. Florence: European University Institute.

Mayer, Margit. 2009. "The 'Right to the City' in the Context of Shifting Mottos of Urban Social Movements." *City* 13: 362–374.

Mayer, Margit. 2012. "The 'Right to the City' in Urban Social Movements." Pp. 63–85 in *Cities for People Not for Profit: Critical Urban Theory and the Right to the City*, edited by N. Brenner, P. Marcuse, and M. Mayer. New York: Routledge.

McAdam, Doug. 1982. *Political Process and the Development of Black Insurgency: 1930–1970*. Chicago: University of Chicago Press.

McAdam, Doug. 1986. "Recruitment to High-Risk Activism: The Case of Freedom Summer." *American Journal of Sociology* 92(1): 64–90.

McAdam, Doug. 1988. *Freedom Summer*. New York: Oxford University Press.

McAdam, Doug. 1994. "Culture and Social Movements." Pp. 36–57 in *New Social Movements: From Ideology to Identity*, edited by E. Larana, H. Johnston, and J. Gusfield. Philadelphia: Temple University Press.

McAdam, Doug. 2003. "Beyond Structural Analysis: Toward a More Dynamic Understanding of Social Movements." Pp. 281–298 in *Social Movements and Networks*, edited by M. Diani and D. McAdam. Oxford: Oxford University Press.

McAdam, Doug and Dieter Rucht. 1993. "The Cross-national Diffusion of Movement Ideas." *The Annals of the AAPSS* 528: 56–74.

McAdam, Doug and Roberto M. Fernandez. 1990. "Microstructural Bases of Recruitment to Social Movements." *Research in Social Movements, Conflict and Change* 12: 1–33.

McAdam, Doug and Ronnelle Paulsen. 1993. "Specifying the Relationship Between Social Ties and Activism." *American Journal of Sociology* 99(3): 640–667.

McAdam, Doug and Sidney Tarrow. 2005. "Scale Shift in Transnational Contention." Pp. 121–150 in *Transnational Protest & Global Activism*, edited by D. della Porta and S. Tarrow. Lanham, MD: Rowman and Littlefield Publishers Inc.

McAdam, Doug and Sidney Tarrow. 2010. "Ballots and Barricades: on the Reciprocal Relationship between Elections and Social Movements." *Perspectives on Politics* 8(2): 529–542.

McAdam, Doug and William H. Jr Sewell. 2001. "It's about Time: Temporality in the Study of Social Movements and Revolutions." Pp. 89–125 in *Silence and Voice in the Study of Contentious Politics*, edited by R. R. Aminzade, J. A. Goldstone, D. McAdam, E. J. Perry, W. H. Jr. Sewell, S. Tarrow, C. Tilly. Cambridge: Cambridge University Press.

McAdam, Doug, Sidney Tarrow, and Charles Tilly. 2001. *Dynamics of Contention*. Cambridge: Cambridge University Press.

McAteer, Emily and Simone Pulver. 2009. "The Corporate Boomerang: Shareholder Transnational Advocacy Networks Targeting Oil Companies in the Ecuadorian Amazon." *Global Environmental Politics* 9(1): 1–30.

McCarthy, John D. and Mark Wolfson. 1992. "Consensus Movements, Conflict Movements, and the Cooptation of Civic and State Infrastructures." Pp. 273–298 in *Frontiers of Social Movement Theory*, edited by A. Morris and C. Mueller. New Haven, CT: Yale University Press.

McCarthy, John D. and Mayer N. Zald. 1987. *Social Movements in an Organizational Society*. New Brunswick: Transaction.

McCarthy, John D., Patrick Rafail, and Ashley Gromis. 2013. "Recent Trends in Public Protest in the U.S.A.: The Social Movement Society Thesis Revisited." Pp. 369–396 in *The Future of Social Movement Research: Dynamics, Mechanisms, and Processes*, edited by J. van Stekelenburg, C. Roggeband, and B. Klandermans. Minneapolis, MN: University of Minnesota Press.

McCarthy, John, Clark McPhail, and Jackie Smith. 1996. "Images of Protest: Dimensions of Selection Bias in Media Coverage of Washington Demonstrations, 1982 and 1991." *American Sociological Review* 61: 478–499.

McCorkel, Jill and Jason Rodriquez. 2009. "'Are You an African?' The Politics of Self-Construction in Status-Based Social Movements." *Social Problems* 56(2): 357–384.

McDonald, Kevin. 2002. "From Solidarity to Fluidarity: Social Movements Beyond 'Collective Identity'. The Case of Globalization Conflicts." *Social Movement Studies* 1: 109–128.

McDonald, Kevin. 2015. "From Indymedia to Anonymous: Rethinking Action and Identity in Digital Cultures." *Information, Communication & Society* 18: 968–982.

McDonnell, Mary-Hunter and Brayden G. King. 2013. "Keeping up Appearances: Reputational Threat and Impression Management after Social Movement Boycotts." *Administrative Science Quarterly* 58(3): 387–419.

McGarry, Aidan and James M. Jasper, eds. 2015. *The Identity Dilemma*. Philadelphia: Temple University Press.

McPhail, Clark, David Schweingruber, and John D. McCarthy. 1998. "Policing Protest in the United States: From the 1960s to the 1990s." Pp. 49–69 in *Policing Protest: The Control of Mass Demonstrations in Western Democracies*, edited by D. della Porta and H. Reiter. Minneapolis: University of Minnesota Press.

McPherson, Miller. 1983. "An Ecology of Affiliation." *American Sociological Review* 48: 519–532.

McPherson, Miller, Pamela A. Popielarz, and Sonia Drobnic. 1992. "Social Networks and Organizational Dynamics." *American Sociological Review* 57: 153–170.

Meadows, Donella H., Jorgen Randers, and William W. Behrens. 1972. *The Limits to Growth*. London: Earth Island.

Mello, Brian. 2018. "The Islamic State: Violence and Ideology in a Post-Colonial Revolutionary Regime." *International Political Sociology* 12(2): 139–155.

Melucci, Alberto. 1982. *L'invenzione del presente: Movimenti, identità, bisogni individuali*. Bologna: il Mulino.

Melucci, Alberto, ed. 1984. *Altri codici: Aree di movimento nella metropoli*. Bologna: il Mulino.

Melucci, Alberto. 1989. *Nomads of the Present: Social Movements and Individual Needs in Contemporary Society*. London: Hutchinson.

Melucci, Alberto. 1995. "The Process of Collective Identity." Pp. 41–63 in *Social Movements and Culture*, edited by H. Johnston and B. Klandermans. Minneapolis/London: University of Minnesota Press/UCL Press.

Melucci, Alberto. 1996. *Challenging Codes*. Cambridge/New York: Cambridge University Press.

Meyer, David S. and Sidney Tarrow, eds. 1998. *The Social Movement Society: Contentious Politics for a New Century*. Lanham: Rowman & Littlefield.

Meyer, David S. and Suzanne Staggenborg. 1996. "Movements, Countermovements and the Structure of Political Opportunities." *American Journal of Sociology* 101(1): 628–660.

Micheletti, Michele. 2003. *Political Virtue and Shopping: Individuals, Consumerism, and Collective Action*. Palgrave: Macmillan.

Micheletti, Michele and Stolle, Dietlind. 2015. "Consumer Strategies in Social Movements." Pp. 478–493 in *The Oxford Handbook of Social Movements*, edited by D. della Porta and M. Diani. Oxford: Oxford University Press.

Milan, Stefania. 2015. "From Social Movements to Cloud Protesting: The Evolution of Collective Identity." *Information, Communication & Society* 18(8): 887–900.

Milan, Stefania and Arno Hintz. 2013. "Networked Collective Action and the Institutionalized Policy Debate: Bringing Cyberactivism to the Policy Arena?" *Internet & Policy* 5: 7–26.

Miliband, Ralph. 1989. *Divided Societies: Class Struggle in Contemporary Capitalism*. Oxford: Clarendon Press.

Miller, David. 1993. "Deliberative Democracy and Social Choice." Pp. 74–92 in *Prospects for Democracy*, edited by D. Held. Cambridge: Polity Press.

Minkoff, Debra. 1995. *Organizing for Equality*. New Brunswick: Rutgers University Press.

Mische, Ann. 2003. "Cross-Talk in Movements: Reconceiving the Culture-Network Link." Pp. 258–80 in *Social Movements and Networks*, edited by M. Diani and D. McAdam. Oxford: Oxford University Press.

Mische, Ann. 2008. *Partisan Publics*. Princeton, NJ: Princeton University Press.

Mische, Ann. 2011. "Relational Sociology, Culture, and Agency." Pp. 80–97 in *The Sage Handbook of Social Network Analysis*, edited by P. Carrington and J. Scott. London: Sage.

Mitchell, Don and Lynn A. Staeheli. 2005. "Permitting Protest: Parsing the Fine Geography of Dissent in America." *International Journal of Urban and Regional Research* 29(4): 796–813.

Mizruchi, Mark S. 1996. "What Do Interlocks Do? An Analysis, Critique and Assessment of Research on Interlocking Directorates." *Annual Review of Sociology* 22: 271–298.

Moaddel, Mansoor. 2002. "Ideology as Episodic Discourse: The Case of the Iranian Revolution." *American Sociological Review* 57: 353–579.

Moghadam, Valentine M. 2000. "Transnational Feminist Networks – Collective Action in an Era of Globalization." *International Sociology* 15(1): 57–85.

Monier, Elizabeth Iskander and Annette Ranko. 2013. "The Fall of the Muslim Brotherhood: Implications for Egypt." *Middle East Policy* 20(4): 111–123.

Monterde, Arnau, Antonio Calleja-López, Miguel Aguilera, Xabier E. Barandiaran, and John Postill. 2015. "Multitudinous Identities: A Qualitative and Network Analysis of the 15M Collective Identity." *Information, Communication & Society* 18(8): 930–950.

Monticelli, Lara and Donatella della Porta. 2019. "The Successes of Political Consumerism as a Social Movement". Pp.773–792 in *Oxford Handbook of Political Consumerism*, edited by M. Boström, M. Micheletti, and P. Oosterveer. Oxford/New York: Oxford University Press.

Moody, Kim. 1997. *Workers in a Lean World*. London: Verso.

Moore, Tod. 2017. "The Transformation of the Occusphere." *Social Identities* 23(6): 674–687.

Moran, Niall. 2017. "Collective Identities and Formal Ideologies in the Irish Grassroots Pro-Asylum Seeker Movement." *Irish Journal of Sociology* 25(1): 48–72.

Morgan, Jane. 1987. *Conflict and Order: The Police and Labour Disputes in England and Wales: 1900–1939*. Oxford: Clarendon Press.

Morris, Aldon. 1984. *The Origins of the Civil Rights Movement: Black Communities Organizing for Change*. New York: Free Press.

Morris, Aldon. 2000. "Charting futures for sociology. Social organization reflections on social movement theory. Criticisms and proposals." *Contemporary Sociology* 29(3): 445–454.

Morris, Aldon and Cedric Herring. 1987. "Theory and Research in Social Movements: A Critical Review." *Annual Review of Political Science* 2: 137–198.

Motta, Renata. 2015. "Transnational Discursive Opportunities and Social Movement Risk Frames Opposing GMOs." *Social Movement Studies* 14(5): 576–595.

Mudde, Cas. 2017. "Populism: An Ideational Approach." in *The Oxford Handbook of Populism, Oxford Handbooks*, edited by C. Rovira Kaltwasser, P. A. Taggart, P. Ochoa Espejo, and P. Ostiguy. Oxford: Oxford University Press.

Mudu, Pierpaolo. 2014. "Ogni Sfratto Sarà una Barricata: Squatting for Housing and Social Conflict in Rome." Pp. 136–163 in *The Squatters' Movement in Europe. Commons and Autonomy as Alternative to Capitalism*, edited by SQEK, C. Cattaneo, and M. Martìnez. London: PlutoPress.

Muir, Jenny. 2011. "Bridging and Linking in a Divided Society: A Social Capital Case Study from Northern Ireland." *Urban Studies* 48(5): 959–976.

Munck, Gerardo L. 2001. "The Regime Question." *World Politics* 54(1): 119–145.

Nagle, John. 2013. "'Unity in Diversity': Non-Sectarian Social Movement Challenges to the Politics of Ethnic Antagonism in Violently Divided Cities." *International Journal of Urban and Regional Research* 37(1): 78–92.

Nakano, Dana Y. 2013. "An Interlocking Panethnicity: The Negotiation of Multiple Identities among Asian American Social Movement Leaders." *Sociological Perspectives* 56(4): 569–595.

Neidhardt, Friedhelm. 1981. "Über Zufall, Eigendynamik und Institutionalisierbarkeit absurder Prozesse. Notizen am Beispiel der Entstehung und Einrichtung einer terroristischen Gruppe." Pp. 243–257 in *Soziologie in weltbürgerlicher Absicht*, edited by H. von Alemann and H. P. Thurn. Opladen: Westdeutscher Verlag.

Nepstad, Sharon E. 2011. *Nonviolent Revolutions: Civil Resistance in the Late 20th Century*. New York: Oxford University Press.

Nepstad, Sharon E. 2004. *Convictions of the Soul: Religion, Culture, and Agency in the Central America Solidarity Movement*. New York: Oxford University Press.

Nepstad, Sharon E. and Christian Smith. 1999. "Rethinking Recruitment to High-Risk/Cost Activism: The Case of Nicaragua Exchange." *Mobilization: An International Quarterly* 4: 25–40.

Neveau, Eric, 1999. "Media, mouvements sociaux, espace public." *Reseaux* 98: 17–85.

Nez, Héloïse. 2011. "No es un botellón, es la revolución! Le mouvement des indignés à Puerta del Sol, Madrid", *Mouvements*. http://www.mouvements.info/No-es-unbotellon-es-la-revolucion.html

Nez, Héloïse. 2012. "Délibérer au sein d'un mouvement social: ethnographie des assemblées des Indignés à Madrid." *Participations* 3: 79–101.

Nicholls, Walter and Justus Uitermark. 2017. *Cities and Social Movements. Immigrant Rights Activism in the United States, France, and the Netherlands 1970–2015*. Oxford/Malden, MA: Wiley Blackwell.

Nicholson, Michael. 1998. *International Relations: A Concise Introduction*. New York: New York University Press.

NION. 2010. "Not in Our Name! Jamming the Gentrification Machine: A Manifesto." *City* 14(3): 323–325.

Nollert, Michael. 1995. "Neocorporatism and Political Protest in the Western Democracies: A Cross-National Analysis." Pp. 138–164 in *The Politics of Social Protest: Comparative Perspectives on States and Social Movements*, edited by J. C. Jenkins and B. Klandermans. Minneapolis: University of Minnesota Press.

Noonan, Rita. 1995. "Women Against the State: Political Opportunities and Collective Action Frames in Chile's Transition to Democracy." *Sociological Forum* 19: 81–111.

Norris, Pippa. 2002. *Democratic Phoenix*. Cambridge/New York: Cambridge University Press.

Norris, Pippa and Ronald Inglehart. 2002. Islam & the West: Testing the Clash of Civilizations Thesis. SSRN Scholarly Paper. ID 316506. Rochester, NY: Social Science Research Network.

Norris, Pippa and Ronald Inglehart. 2004. *Sacred and Secular*. Cambridge/New York: Cambridge University Press.

Norris, Pippa and Ronald Inglehart. 2019. *Cultural Backlash: Trump, Brexit and Authoritarian-Populism*. Cambridge/New York: Cambridge University Press.

Novy, Johannes and Claire Colomb. 2013. "Struggling for the Right to the (Creative) City in Berlin and Hamburg: New Urban Social Movements, New 'Spaces of Hope'?" *International Journal of Urban & Regional Research* 37(5): 1816–1838.

O'Donnell, Guillermo. 1993. "On the State, Democratization and some Conceptual Problems." *Working Paper Series No. 92*. Notre Dame: The Helen Kellogg Institute for International Studies, University of Notre Dame.

O'Donnell, Guillermo. 1994. "Delegative Democracy?" *Journal of Democracy* 5(1): 56–69.

O'Donnell, Guillermo and Philippe C. Schmitter. 1986. *Transitions from Authoritarian Rule: Tentative Conclusions about Uncertain Democracies*. Baltimore, MD: Johns Hopkins University Press.

Oaten, Alexander. 2014. "The Cult of the Victim: An Analysis of the Collective Identity of the English Defence League." *Patterns of Prejudice* 48: 331–349.

Oberschall, Anthony. 1973. *Social Conflict and Social Movements*. Englewood Cliffs, NJ: Prentice Hall.

Oberschall, Anthony. 1980. "Loosely Structured Collective Conflict: A Theory and an Application." *Research in Social Movements, Conflict and Change* 3: 45–54.

Oberschall, Anthony. 1993. *Social Movements: Ideologies, Interests, and Identities*. New Brunswick, NJ/London: Transaction.

Offe, Claus. 1985. "New Social Movements: Changing Boundaries of the Political." *Social Research* 52: 817–868.

Offe, Claus. 1997. "Microaspects of Democratic Theory: What Makes for the Deliberative Competence of Citizens?" Pp. 81–104 in *Democracy's Victory and Crisis*, edited by A. Hadenius. New York: Cambridge University Press.

Ohlemacher, Thomas. 1996. "Bridging People and Protest: Social Relays of Protest Groups Against Low-Flying Military Jets in West Germany." *Social Problems* 43: 197–218.

Okamoto, Dina. 2003. "Toward a Theory of Panethnicity: Explaining Asian American Collective Action." *American Sociological Review* 68(6): 811–842.

Okamoto, Dina. 2010. "Organizing across Ethnic Boundaries in the Post–Civil Rights Era: Asian American Panethnic Coalitions." Pp. 143–169 in *Strategic Alliances: New Studies of Social Movement Coalitions*, edited by N. Van Dyke and H. McCammon. Minneapolis, MN: University of Minnesota Press.

Okechukwu, Amaka. 2014. "Shadows of Solidarity: Identity, Intersectionality, and Frame Resonance." *Research in Social Movements, Conflicts & Change* 37: 153–180.

Olesen, Thomas. 2004. "The Transnational Zapatista Solidarity Network: An Infrastructure Analysis." *Global Networks* 4(1): 89–107.

Olesen, Thomas. 2005. *International Zapatismo: The Construction of Solidarity in the Age of Globalization*. London: Zed Books.

Oliver, Pamela. 1989. "Bringing the Crowd Back In: The Nonorganizational Elements of Social Movements." *Research in Social Movements, Conflict and Change* 11: 1–30.

Oliver, Pamela and David A. Snow. 1995. "Social Movements and Collective Behavior." Pp. 571–599 in *Sociological Perspectives on Social Psychology*, edited by K. Cook, G. A. Fine, and J. House. Boston, MA: Allyn and Bacon.

Oliver, Pamela and Hank Johnston. 2000. "What a Good Idea! Ideologies and Frames in Social Movement Research." *Mobilization: An International Quarterly* 5(1): 37–54.

Olzak, Susan. 1992. *The Dynamics of Ethnic Competition and Conflict*. Stanford, CA: Stanford University Press.

Olzak Susan and Sarah A. Soule. 2009. "Cross-Cutting Influences of Protest and Congressional Legislation in the Environmental Movement." *Social Forces* 88(1): 201–225.

Omi, Michael and Howard Winant. 1994. *Racial Formation in the United States: From 1960s to 1990s*. New York: Routledge.

Opp, Karl-Dieter. 1989. *The Rationality of Political Protest*. Boulder, CO: Westview Press.

Örs, İlay Romain. 2014. "Genie in the Bottle: Gezi Park, Taksim Square, and the Realignment of Democracy and Space in Turkey." *Philosophy & Social Criticism*, 0191453714525390.

Ortoleva, Peppino. 1988. *Saggio sui movimenti del 68 in Europa e in America*. Rome: Editori Riuniti.

Osa, Maryjane. 2003. *Solidarity and Contention. Networks of Polish Opposition*. Minneapolis, MN: University of Minnesota Press.

Ostaszewski, Piotr. 2013. "Iceland – Political Implications of the Financial Crisis of 2008 and the Road to Change in the Economic Policy and in the Model of Democracy." *Forum Scientiae Oeconomia* 1(1): 55–74.

Ostiguy, Pierre. 2017. "Populism: A Socio-Cultural Approach." in *The Oxford handbook of populism, Oxford handbooks*, edited by C. Rovira Kaltwasser, P. A. Taggart, P. Ochoa Espejo, and P. Ostiguy. Oxford: Oxford University Press.

Padovani, Claudia and Andrew Calabrese, eds. 2014. *Communication Rights and Global Justice*. Basingstoke: Palgrave.

Pagnucco, Ron. 1996. "Social Movement Dynamics during Democratic Transition and Consolidation: A Synthesis of Political Process and Political Interactionist Theories." *Research on Democracy and Society* 3: 3–38.

Pakulski, Jan. 1995. "Social Movements and Class: The Decline of the Marxist Paradigm." Pp. 55–86 in *Social Movements and Social Classes*, edited by L. Maheu. London/ Thousand Oaks: Sage.

Panebianco, Angelo. 1988. *Political Parties: Organization and Power*. Cambridge/New York: Cambridge University Press.

Parla, Ayşe. 2013. "Protest and the Limits of the Body." *Cultural Anthropology*, October. www.culanth.org/fieldsights/403-protest-and-the-limits-of-the-body.

Parnell, Susan and Edgar Pieterse. 2010. "The 'Right to the City': Institutional Imperatives of a Developmental State: Institutional Imperatives of a Developmental State." *International Journal of Urban and Regional Research* 34(1): 146–162.

Parsa, Misagh. 2013. "Iranian Islamic Revolution of 1979." in *The Wiley-Blackwell Encyclopedia of Social and Political Movements*. Blackwell Publishing Ltd.

Passerini, Luisa. 1996. *Autobiography of a Generation: Italy, 1968*. Hanover, N.H: University Press of New England.

Passy, Florence. 2003. "Social Networks Matter. But How?" Pp. 21–48 in *Social Movements and Networks*, edited by M. Diani and D. McAdam. Oxford: Oxford University Press.

Passy, Florence and Gian-Andrea Monsch. 2014. "Do Social Networks Really Matter in Contentious Politics?" *Social Movement Studies* 13(1): 22–47.

Pavan, Elena. 2012. *Frames and Connections in the Governance of Global Communications: A Network Study of the Internet Governance Forum*. Lanham, MD: Rowman & Littlefield.

Perasović, Benjamin and Marko Mustapić. 2018. "Carnival Supporters, Hooligans, and the 'Against Modern Football' Movement: Life within the Ultras Subculture in the Croatian Context." *Sport in Society* 21(6): 960–976.

Perez, Marcos Emilio. 2018. "Becoming a Piquetero: Working-Class Routines and the Development of Activist Dispositions." *Mobilization* 23(2): 237–253.

Perry, Francesca. 2016. "Right to the City: Can This Growing Social Movement Win over City Officials?" *The Guardian*, April 19.

Perz, Bertrand. 2015. "The Austrian Connection: SS and Police Leader Odilo Globocnik and His Staff in the Lublin District." *Holocaust & Genocide Studies* 29(3): 400–430.

Peterson, Abby and Mattias Wahlström. 2015. "Repression: The Governance of Domestic Dissent." Pp. 634–652 in *The Oxford Handbook on Social Movements*, edited by D. della Porta and M. Diani. Oxford, Oxford University Press.

Pianta, Mario. 2001. "Parallel Summits of Global Civil Society." Pp. 169–195 in *Global Civil Society 2001*, edited by H. Anheier, M. Glasius, and M. Kaldor. Oxford: Oxford University Press.

Pianta, Mario. 2002. "Parallel Summits: an Update." Pp. 371–377 in *Global Civil Society*, edited by H. K. Anheier, M. Glasius, and M. Kaldor. Oxford: Oxford University Press.

Piccio, Daniela. R. 2012. "Party Responses to Social Movements. A Comparative Analysis of Italy and the Netherlands in the 1970s and 1980s." *PhD Thesis*. Firenze: European University Institute.

Pickerill, Jenny. 2003. *Cyberprotest. Environmental Activism Online*. Manchester: Manchester University Press.

Pickvance, Chris G. 1985. "The Rise and Fall of Urban Movements and the Role of Comparative Analysis." *Society And Space* 3: 31–53.

Pickvance, Chris G. 1986. "Concepts, Contexts and Comparison in the Study of Urban Movements: A Reply to M. Castells." *Society and Space* 4: 221–231.

Piketty, Thomas. 2014. *Capital in the Twenty-First Century*. Cambridge: Harvard University Press.

Piven, Frances Fox and Richard A. Cloward. 1977. *Poor People's Movements*. New York: Pantheon.

Piven, Frances Fox and Richard A. Cloward. 1992. "Normalizing Collective Protest." Pp. 301–325 in *Frontiers in Social Movement Theory*, edited by A. Morris and C. McClurg Mueller. New Haven: Yale University Press.

Piven, Frances Fox and Richard A. Cloward. 2000. "Power Repertoires and Globalization." *Politics and Society* 28: 413–430.

Pizzorno, Alessandro. 1978. "Political Exchange and Collective Identity in Industrial Conflict." Pp. 277–298 in *The Resurgence of Class Conflict in Western Europe*, edited by C. Crouch and A. Pizzorno. New York: Holmes and Meier.

Pizzorno, Alessandro. 1993. *Le radici della politica assoluta*. Milano: Feltrinelli.

Pizzorno, Alessandro. 1996. "Decisioni o Interazioni? La Micro-Descrizione Del Cambiamento Sociale." *Rassegna Italiana Di Sociologia* 37: 107–132.

Pizzorno, Alessandro. 2008. "Rationality and Recognition." Pp. 162–174 in *Approaches in the social sciences*, edited by D. della Porta and M. Keating. Cambridge: Cambridge University Press.

Podolny, Joel M. and Karen L. Page. 1998. "Network Forms of Organization." *Annual Review of Sociology* 24: 57–76.

Poguntke, Thomas. 2002. "Party Organizational Linkage: Parties without Firm Social Roots?" Pp. 43–62 in *Political Parties in the New Europe: Political and Analytical Challenges*, edited by K. R. Luther and F. Müller-Rommel. Oxford: Oxford University Press.

Polletta, Francesca. 1999. "'Free Spaces' in Collective Action." *Theory and Society* 28(1): 1–38.

Polletta, Francesca. 2002. *Freedom Is an Endless Meeting: Democracy in American Social Movements*. Chicago: Chicago University Press.

Polletta, Francesca. 2004. "Culture Is Not Just in Your Head." Pp. 97–110 in *Rethinking Social Movements: Structure, Meaning and Emotions*, edited by J. Goodwin and J. M. Jasper. Lanham, Rowman and Littlefield.

Polletta, Francesca and Beth Gharrity Gardner. 2015. "Narrative and Social Movements." Pp. 534–548 in *Oxford Handbook of Social Movements*, edited by D. della Porta and M. Diani. Oxford/New York: Oxford University Press.

Polletta, Francesca and James M. Jasper. 2001. "Collective Identity and Social Movements." *Annual Review of Sociology* 27: 283–305.

Powell, Walter W. 1990. "Neither Markets nor Hierarchy: Network Forms of Organization." *Research in Organizational Behavior* 12: 295–336.

Prakash, Sanjeev and Per Selle, eds. 2004. *Investigating Social Capital. Comparative Perspectives on Civil Society, Participation, and Governance*. New Delhi: Sage.

Priante, Anna, Michel L. Ehrenhard, Tijs van den Broek, and Ariana Need. 2018. "Identity and Collective Action via Computer-Mediated Communication: A Review and Agenda for Future Research." *New Media & Society* 20(7): 2647–2669.

Pribble, Jenny and Evelyne Huber. 2011. "Social policy and redistribution: Chile and Uruguay." pp. 117–138 in *The Resurgence of the Latin American Left*, edited by S. Levitsky and K. M. Roberts. Baltimore, Johns Hopkins University Press.

Princen, Thomas and Matthias Finger. 1994. "Introduction." Pp. 1–25 in *Environmental NGOs in World Politics: Linking the Local and the Global*, edited by T. Princen and M. Finger. London: Routledge.

Pruijt, Hans. 2007. "Urban Movements." Pp. 5115–5119 in *Encyclopaedia of Sociology*, edited by G. Ritzer. Malden: Blackwell.

Przeworski, Adam. 1991. *Democracy and the Market*. Cambridge: Cambridge University Press.

Putnam, Robert. 2000. *Bowling Alone: The Collapse and Revival of American Community*. New York: Simon & Schuster.

Qi, Xiaoying. 2017. "Social Movements in China: Augmenting Mainstream Theory with Guanxi." *Sociology* 51(1): 111–126.

Raco, Mike. 2003. "Governmentality, Subject-building, and the Discourses and Practices of Devolution in the UK." *Transactions of the Institute of British Geographers* 28: 75–95.

Ravetto-Biagioli, Kriss. 2013. "Anonymous: social as political." *Leonardo Electronic Almanac* 19(4): 178–195.

Reifer, Thomas Ehrlich. 2004. *Globalization, Hegemony & Power*. London: Paradigm.

Reiner, Robert. 1998. "Policing, Protest, and Disorder in Britain." Pp. 35–48 in *Policing Protest: The Control of Mass Demonstrations in Western Democracies*, edited by D. della Porta and H. Reiter. Minneapolis: University of Minnesota Press.

Reitan, Ruth. 2007. *Global Activism*. New York/London: Routledge.

Reiter, Herbert. 1998. "Police and Public Order in Italy, 1944–1948. The Case of Florence." Pp. 143–165 in *Policing Protest: The Control of Mass Demonstrations in Western Democracies*, D. della Porta and H. Reiter. Minneapolis: University of Minnesota Press.

Richardson, Dick and Chris Rootes, eds. 1995. *The Green Challenge: The Development of Green Parties in Europe. London*; New York: Routledge.

Ritter, Daniel P. 2015a. "Civil Resistance." Pp. 467–477 in *The Oxford Handbook of Social Movements*, edited by D. della Porta and M. Diani. Oxford: Oxford University Press.

Ritter, Daniel P. 2015b. *The Iron Cage of Liberalism: International Politics and Unarmed Revolutions in the Middle East and North Africa*. Oxford: Oxford University Press.

Ritzer, George. 2000. *The McDonaldization of Society: New Century Edition*. Thousand Oaks, CA: Pine Forge.

Robbins, Thomas. 1988. *Cults, Converts & Charisma*. London: Sage.

Roberts, Kenneth M. 2015. *Changing Course in Latin America: Party Systems in the Neoliberal Era*. New York: Cambridge University Press.

Robertson, Roland. 1992. *Globalization: Social Theory and Global Culture*. London: Sage Publications.

Robinson, Ian. 2000. "Neoliberal Restructuring and U.S. Unions: Toward Social Movement Unionism?" *Critical Sociology* 26(1–2): 109–138.

Rochon, Thomas R. 1988. *Between Society and State: Mobilizing for Peace in Western Europe*. Princeton: Princeton University Press.

Rochon, Thomas R. 1998. *Culture Moves: Ideas, Activism, and Changing Values*. Princeton: Princeton University Press.

Rochon, Thomas R. and Daniel A. Mazmanian. 1993. "Social Movements and the Policy Process." *The Annals of the AAPSS* 528: 75–87.

Rohrschneider, Robert. 1993. "Impact of Social Movements on the European Party System." *The Annals of the American Academy of Political and Social Sciences* 528: 157–170.

Rokkan, Stein. 1970. *Citizens, Elections, Parties*. Oslo: Universitetforlaget.

Rokkan, Stein. 1999. "Cleavages and Their Political Translation." Pp. 278–302 in *State Formation, Nation Building and Mass Politics in Europe. The Theory of Stein Rokkan*, edited by P. Flora, S. Kuhnle and D. Urwin. Oxford: Oxford University Press.

Roman Etxebarrieta, Gorka. 2018. "El Rock Radical Vasco. La Constitución de Los Sujetos Políticos a Través de La Música." *Basque Radical Rock. Constituting the Political Subjects through the Music.* (64): 24–40.

Romanos, Eduardo. 2014. "Evictions, Petitions and Escraches: Contentious Housing in Austerity Spain." *Social Movement Studies* 13(2): 296–302.

Roos, Jerome E. and Leonidas Oikonomakis. 2014. "They Don't Represent Us! The Global Resonance of the Real Democracy Movement from the Indignados to Occupy." Pp.

117–133 in *Spreading Protest: Social Movements in Times of Crisis*, edited by D. della Porta and A. Mattoni. Colchester; ECPR PRESS.

Rootes, Christopher. 1995. "A New Class? The Higher Educated and the New Politics." Pp. 220–235 in *Social Movements and Social Classes*, edited by L. Maheu. London/ Thousand Oaks: Sage.

Rootes, Christopher, ed. 2003. *Environmental Protest in Western Europe*. Oxford: Oxford University Press.

Rootes Christopher and Eugene Nulman. 2015. "The Impacts of Environmental Movements." Pp. 729–742 in *The Oxford Handbook of Social Movements*, edited by D. della Porta and M. Diani. Oxford: Oxford University Press.

Rootes, Christopher and Robert J. Brulle. 2013. "Environmental Movements." Pp. 413–419 in *The Wiley-Blackwell Encyclopedia of Social and Political Movements*. Oxford/ Malden, MA: Blackwell.

Rose, Fred. 2000. *Coalitions across the Class Divide*. Ithaca, NY: Cornell University Press.

Rose, Richard. 1984. *Understanding Big Government*, London: Sage.

Roseneil, Sasha. 1995. *Disarming Patriarchy*. Milton Keynes: Open University Press.

Rosenthal, Naomi, David McDonald, Michele Ethier, Meryl Fingrutd, and Roberta Karant. 1997. "Structural Tensions in The Nineteenth Century Women's Movement." *Mobilization: An International Quarterly* 2(1): 21–46.

Rosenthal, Naomi, Meryl Fingrutd, Michele Ethier, Roberta Karant, and David McDonald. 1985. "Social Movements and Network Analysis: A Case Study of Nineteenth-Century Women's Reform in New York State." *American Journal of Sociology* 90(5): 1022–1054.

Rossi, Federico M. 2017. *The Poor's Struggle for Political Incorporation*. Cambridge/New York: Cambridge University Press.

Rossi, Federico and Donatella della Porta. 2009. "Social Movements, Trade Unions and Advocacy Networks." Pp. 172–195 in *Democratization*, edited by C. Haerpfer, P. Bernhagen, R. Inglehart, and R. Welzel. Oxford: Oxford University Press.

Rossi, Federico M. and Marisa von Bülow, eds. 2015. *Social Movement Dynamics: New Perspectives on Theory and Research from Latin America*. Farnham, UK/Burlington, VT: Ashgate.

Roth, Roland. 1994. *Demokratie von unten: Neue soziale Bewegungen auf dem Wege zur politischen Institution*. Köln: Bund Verlag.

Rovira Kaltwasser, Cristóbal, Paul A. Taggart, Paulina Ochoa Espejo, and Pierre Ostiguy, eds. 2017. *The Oxford Handbook of Populism*. Oxford: Oxford University Press.

Rucht, Dieter, ed. 1991. *Research on Social Movements: The State of the Art in Western Europe and the USA*. Frankfurt: Campus.

Rucht, Dieter. 1990. "The Strategies and Action Repertoire of New Movements." Pp. 156–175 in *Challenging the Political Order: New Social Movements in Western Democracies*, edited by R. J. Dalton and M. Kuechler. Cambridge: Polity Press.

Rucht, Dieter. 1992. "Studying the Effects of Social Movements: Conceptualization and Problems." *Paper presented at the Joint Sessions of the European Consortium for Political Research*. Limerick, March 30–April 4.

Rucht, Dieter. 1994. *Modernisierung und Soziale Bewegungen.* Frankfurt am Main: Campus.

Rucht, Dieter. 1995. "Parties, Associations and Movements as Systems of Political Interest Intermediation." Pp. 103–125 in *Political Parties in Democracy*, edited by J. Thesing and W. Hofmeister. Sankt Augustin: Konrad-Adenauer-Stiftung.

Rucht, Dieter. 1999. "Linking Organization and Mobilization: Michels's Iron Law of Oligarchy Reconsidered." *Mobilization: An International Quarterly* 4(2): 151–169.

Rucht, Dieter. 2003a. "Media Strategies and Media Resonance in Transnational Protest Campaigns." Paper presented at the conference Transnational Processes and Social Movements. Bellagio, Italy, July 22–26.

Rucht, Dieter, ed. 2003b. *Berlin, 1. Mai 2002: Politische Demonstrationsrituale.* Opladen: Leske + Budrich.

Rucht, Dieter. 2004. "The Quadruple "A": Media Strategies of Protest Movements since the 1960s." Pp. 29–56 in *Cyberprotest: New Media, Citizens and Social Movements*, edited by W. van de Donk, B. Loader, P. Nixon, and D. Rucht. London: Routledge.

Rudig, Wolfgang. 1990. *Anti-Nuclear Movements.* London: Longman.

Rudig, Wolfgang and Georgios Karyotis. 2013. "Beyond the Usual Suspects? New Participants in Anti-Austerity Protests in Greece." *Mobilization: An International Quarterly* 18(3): 313–330.

Rueschemeyer, Dietrich, Evelyn Huber Stephens, and John D. Stephens. 1992. *Capitalist Development and Democracy.* Chicago: University of Chicago Press.

Runciman, Carin. 2015. "The Decline of the Anti-Privatisation Forum in the Midst of South Africa's 'Rebellion of the Poor'." *Current Sociology* 63(7): 961–979.

Rupp, Leila J. and Verta Taylor. 1987. *Survival in the Doldrums: The American Women's Rights Movement, 1945 to the 1960s.* Columbus, OH: Ohio State University Press.

Rupp, Leila J. and Verta Taylor. 2003. *Drag Queens at the 801 Cabaret.* Chicago: University of Chicago Press.

Russett, Bruce and Harvey Starr. 1996. *World Politics: The Menu for Choice.* New York: W. H. Freeman and Co.

Russo, Antonio Paolo and Alessandro Scarnato. 2018. "'Barcelona in Common': A New Urban Regime for the 21st-Century Tourist City?" *Journal of Urban Affairs* 40(4): 455–474.

Russo, Chandra. 2014. "Allies Forging Collective Identity: Embodiment and Emotions on the Migrant Trail." *Mobilization* 19(1): 67–82.

Ruzza, Carlo. 2004: *Europe and Civil Society: Movement Coalitions and European Governance.* Manchester: Manchester University Press.

Ryan, Charlotte. 1991. *Prime Time Activism. Media Strategies for Grassroots Organizing.* Boston: South End.

Saab, Rim, Charles Harb, and Catherine Moughalian. 2017. "Intergroup Contact as a Predictor of Violent and Nonviolent Collective Action: Evidence From Syrian Refugees and Lebanese Nationals." *Peace & Conflict* 23(3): 297–306.

Salet, Wilhelm. 2007. "Framing Strategic Urban Projects." Pp. 3–19 in *Framing Strategic Urban Projects. Learning from Current Experiences in European Urban Regions*, edited by W. Salet and E. Gualini. London: Routledge.

Samuelson, Paul. 1954. "The Pure Theory of Public Expenditure." *Review of Economics and Statistics* 36: 387–389.

Sandell, Rickard. 1999. "Organizational Life Aboard the Moving Bandwagons: A Network Analysis of Dropouts from a Swedish Temperance Organization, 1896–1937." *Acta Sociologica* 42: 3–15.

Sandell, Rickard and Charlotte Stern. 1998. "Group Size and the Logic of Collective Action: A Network Analysis of a Swedish Temperance Movement 1896–1937." *Rationality and Society* 10: 327–345.

Sartori, Giovanni. 1970. "Concept Misformation in Comparative Politics." *American Political Science Review* 64: 1033–1052.

Sassen, Saskia. 1991. *The Global City*. Princeton, NJ: Princeton University Press.

Sassen, Saskia. 2000. *Cities in a World Economy*. Thousand Oaks: Pine Forge Press, 117–138.

Sassen, Saskia. 2014. *Expulsions*. Cambridge, MA: Harvard University Press.

Saunders, Clare. 2008. "Double-Edged Swords? Collective Identity and Solidarity in the Environment Movement." *British Journal of Sociology* 59(2): 227–253.

Saunders, Clare. 2013. *Environmental Networks and Social Movement Theory*. London: Bloomsbury.

Saunders, Clare. 2014. "Insiders, Thresholders, and Outsiders in West European Global Justice Networks: Network Positions and Modes of Coordination." *European Political Science Review* 6(02): 167–189.

Scharpf, Fritz W. 1984. "Economic and Institutional Constraints of Full-Employment Strategies: Sweden, Austria, and West Germany." Pp. 257–290 in *Order and Conflict in Contemporary Capitalism*, edited by J. H. Goldthorpe. Oxford: Clarendon Press.

Scharpf, Fritz W. 2011. "Monetary Union, Fiscal Crisis and Pre-emption of Democracy." *ZSE* 9(2): 163–198.

Schmitt-Beck, Rüdiger. 1989. "Organizational Interlocks Between New Social Movements and Traditional Elites." *European Journal of Political Research* 17: 583–598.

Schmitter, Philippe. 1981. "Interest Intermediation and Regime Governability in Contemporary Western Europe and North America." Pp. 287–327 in *Organized Interests in Western Europe: Pluralism, Corporatism, and the Transformation of Politics*, edited by S. Berger. Cambridge/New York: Cambridge University Press.

Schock, Kurt. 2005. *Unarmed Insurrections: People Power Movements in Nondemocracies*. Minneapolis: University of Minnesota Press.

Schoene, Matthew. 2017. "Urban Continent, Urban Activism? European Cities and Social Movement Activism." *Global Society* 31(3): 370–391.

Schou, Arild. 1997. "Elite Identification in Collective Protest Movements: A Reconsideration of the Reputational Method with Application to the Palestinian Intifada." *Mobilization* 2: 71–86.

Schradie, Jen. 2018. "The Digital Activism Gap: How Class and Costs Shape Online Collective Action." *Social Problems* 65(1): 51–74.

Schudson, Michael. 1989. "How Culture Works: Perspectives from Media Studies on the Efficacy of Symbols." *Theory and Society* 18: 153–180.

Schumaker, Paul D. 1975. "Policy Responsiveness to Protest Group Demands." *The Journal of Politics* 37: 488–521.

Schurman, Rachel. 2004. "Fighting "Frankenfoods: Industrial Opportunity Structures and the Efficacy of the Anti-Biotech Movement in Western Europe." *Social Problems* 51(2): 243–268.

Schuster, Federico L., German Pérez, Sebastian Pereyra, Melchor Armesto, Martin Armelino, Analia Garcia, Ana Natalucci, Melina Vazquez, and Patricia Zipcioglu. 2006. *Transformaciones de La Protesta Social En Argentina 1989-2003*. Instituto Gino Germani-UBA Buenos Aires.

Scott, Alan. 1990. *Ideology and the New Social Movements*. London: Unwin Hyman.

Seel, Benjamin, Matthew Paterson, and Brian Doherty, eds. 2000. *Direct Action in British Environmentalism*. London: Routledge.

Seferiades, Seraphim. 2013. "Greece at a Crossroads. Roots, Dilemmas, Prospects." *Pôle Sud* 38: 5–14.

Sewell, William H. 1992. "A Theory of Structure: Duality, Agency, and Transformation." *American Journal of Sociology* 98(1): 1–29.

Sewell, William H. Jr. 1996. "Three Temporalities: Toward an Eventful Sociology." Pp. 245–280 in *The Historic Turn in the Human Sciences*, edited by T. J. McDonald. Ann Arbor: University of Michigan Press.

Shand, David and Morten Arnberg. 1996. "Background Paper." *Responsive Government: Service Quality Initiatives*, Paris: Organization for Economic Cooperation and Development (OECD).

Sharp, Gene. 2005. *Waging Nonviolent Struggle: 20th Century Practice and 21st Century Potential*. Boston: Extending Horizons Books.

Shemtov, Ronit. 1999. "Taking Ownership of Environmental Problems." *Mobilization* 4: 91–106.

Shepard, Benjamin. 2016. *Rebel Friendships: "Outsider" Networks and Social Movements*. Basingstoke: Palgrave Macmillan.

Sheptycki, James W. E. 2005. "Policing Protest When Politics Go Global. Comparing Public Order Policing in Canada and Bolivia." *Policing and Society* 15(3): 327–352.

Sikkink, Kathryn. 2002. "Reconstructing World Politics: The Limits and Asymmetries of Soft Power." Pp. 301–317 in *Reconstructing World Politics: Transnational Social Movements, Networks and Norms*, edited by S. Khagram, J. V. Riker, and K. Sikkink. Minneapolis: University of Minnesota Press.

Silver, Beverly J. 2003. *Forces of Labor: Workers' Movements and Globalization Since 1870*. Cambridge: Cambridge University Press.

Silver, Beverly J. and Sahan Savas Karatasli. 2015. "Historical Dynamics of Capitalism and Labor Movement." Pp. 133–145, in *Oxford Handbook of Social Movements*, edited by D. della Porta and M. Diani. Oxford: Oxford University Press.

Simmel, Georg. 1955. "The Web of Group Affiliations." Pp. 125–95 in *Conflict & the Web of Group Affiliations*. New York: Free Press.

Simmons, Jonathan. 2018. "'Not That Kind of Atheist': Scepticism as a Lifestyle Movement." *Social Movement Studies* 17(4): 437–450.

Simpson, Cohen R. 2015. "Multiplexity and Strategic Alliances: The Relational Embeddedness of Coalitions in Social Movement Organisational Fields." *Social Networks* 42: 42–59.

Singer, Peter W. 2004. *Corporate Warriors: The Rise of the Privatized Military Industry.* Ithaca, NY: Cornell University Press.

Sintomer, Yves. 2007. *Le Pouvoir au Peuple: Jury citoyens, tirage au sort, et démocratie participative.* Paris: La Découverte.

Sklair, Laskie. 1995. "Social Movements and Global Capitalism." *Sociology* 29: 495–512.

Skocpol, Theda. 1979. *States and Social Revolutions.* Cambridge/New York: Cambridge University Press.

Skocpol, Theda and Vanessa Williamson. 2016. *The Tea Party and the Remaking of Republican Conservatism.* New York/Oxford: Oxford University Press.

Smelser, Neil J. 1962. *Theory of Collective Behavior.* New York: Free Press.

Smeltzer, Sandra and Alison Hearn. 2015. "Student Rights in an Age of Austerity? 'Security', Freedom of Expression and the Neoliberal University." *Social Movement Studies* 14(3): 352–358.

Smilde, David. 2005. "A Qualitative Comparative Analysis of Conversion to Venezuelan Evangelicalism: How Networks Matter." *Am. J. Sociol.* 111(3): 757–796.

Smith, Anthony D. 1981: *The Ethnic Revival.* Cambridge: Cambridge University Press.

Smith, Anthony D. 1986. *The Ethnic Origins of Nations.* Oxford: Blackwell.

Smith, Graham. 2009. *Democratic Innovations: Designing Institutions for Citizen Participation.* Cambridge: Cambridge University Press.

Smith, Jackie and Dawn Wiest. 2012. *Social Movements in the World-System.* New York: Russell Sage.

Smith, Jackie. 1997. "Characteristics of the Modern Transnational Social Movement Sector." Pp. 42–58 in *Transnational Social Movements and Global Politics*, edited by J. Smith, C. Chatfield, and R. Pagnucco. Syracuse, NY: Syracuse University Press.

Smith, Jackie. 1999. "Transnational Organizations." *In Encyclopedia, of Violence, Peace, and Conflict* 3: 591–602.

Smith, Jackie. 2001. "Globalizing Resistance: The Battle of Seattle and the Future of Social Movements." *Mobilization* 6: 1–20.

Smith, Jackie. 2004. "Transnational Processes and Movements." Pp. 311–335 in *The Blackwell Companion to Social Movements*, edited by D. A. Snow, S. H. Soule and H. Kriesi. Oxford: Blackwell.

Smith, Jackie. 2008. *Social Movements for Global Democracy.* Baltimore: John Hopkins University Press.

Smith, Jackie, Basak Gemici, Samantha Plummer, and Melanie M. Hughes. 2018. "Transnational Social Movement Organizations and Counter-Hegemonic Struggles Today." *Journal of World-Systems Research* 24(2): 372–402.

Snow, David A. 2004. "Framing Processes, Ideology, and Discursive Fieds." Pp. 380–412 in *The Blackwell Companion to Social Movements*, edited by D. A. Snow, S. Soule, and H. Kriesi. Oxford: Blackwell.

Snow, David A. 2005. "Social Movements as Challenges to Authority: Resistance to an Emerging Conceptual Hegemony?" in *Authority in Contention*, edited by D. J. Myers and D. Cress. New York: Elsevier.

Snow, David A. and Robert D. Benford. 1992. "Master Frames and Cycles of Protest." Pp. 133–155 in *Frontiers of Social Movement Theory*, edited by A. Morris and C. Mueller. New Haven, CT: Yale University Press.

Snow, David A., Burke E. Rochford, Steven Worden, and Robert Benford. 1986. "Frame Alignment Processes, Micromobilization, and Movement Participation." *American Sociological Review* 51: 464–481.

Snow, David A., Louis Zurcher, and Sheldon Ekland-Olson. 1980. "Social Networks and Social Movements: A Microstructural Approach to Differential Recruitment." *American Sociological Review* 45: 787–801.

Snow, David A., Sarah Soule, Hanspeter Kriesi, and Holly McCammon. 2019a. "Mapping and Opening Up the Terrain." Pp. 1–16 in *The Wiley Blackwell Companion to Social Movements*, edited by D. A. Snow, S. Soule, H. Kriesi, and H. McCammon. Oxford: Blackwell.

Snow, David A., Sarah Soule, Hanspeter Kriesi, and Holly McCammon, eds. 2019b. *The Wiley Blackwell Companion to Social Movements*. Oxford: Blackwell.

Somers, Margaret. 1994. "The Narrative Constitution of Identity. A Relational and Network Approach." *Theory and Society* 23(5): 605–649.

Sommier, Isabelle. 2003. *Le renouveau des mouvements contestataires à l'heure de la mondialisation*. Paris: Flammarion.

Soule, Sarah A. 2004. "Diffusion Process Within and Across Movements." Pp. 294–310 in *The Blackwell Companion to Social Movements*, edited by D. A. Snow, S. H. Soule, and H. Kriesi. Oxford: Blackwell.

Soule, Sarah A. 2009. *Contentious and Private Politics and Corporate Social Responsibility*. Cambridge: Cambridge University Press.

Soule Sarah A. and Brayden King. 2015. "Market Business, and Social Movements" Pp. 696–710 in *The Oxford Handbook on Social Movements*, edited by D. della Porta and M. Diani. Oxford, Oxford University Press.

Soule, Sarah A. and Jennifer Earl. 2005. "A Movement Society Evaluated: Collective Protest in the United States, 1960–1986." *Mobilization*, 345–364.

Sowers, Jeannie and Chris Toensing, eds. 2012. *The Journey to Tahrir: Revolution, Protest, and Social Change in Egypt*. Verso.

Soysal, Yasemine N. 1994. *Limits of Citizenship: Migrants and Postnational Membership in Europe*. Chicago: Chicago University Press.

Srinivasan, Ramesh. 2011. "London, Egypt and the Nature of Social Media." *The Washington Post*.

Staggenborg, Suzanne. 1991. *The Pro-Choice Movement: Organization and Activism in the Abortion Conflict*. New York: Oxford University Press.

Stamatov, Peter. 2002. "Interpretive Activism and the Political Uses of Verdi's Operas in the 1840s." *American Sociological Review* 67(3): 345–366.

Standing, Guy. 2011. *The Precariat: The New Dangerous Class*. London: Bloomsbury Publishing.

Stanton, Jessica A. 2013. "Terrorism in the Context of Civil War." *The Journal of Politics* 75(4): 1009–1022.

Stark, Rodney and William S. Bainbridge. 1980. "Networks of Faith: Interpersonal Bonds and Recruitment to Cults and Sects." *American Journal of Sociology* 85: 1376–1395.

Stevenson, Rachel and Nick Crossley. 2014. "Change in Covert Social Movement Networks: The 'Inner Circle' of the Provisional Irish Republican Army." *Social Movement Studies* 13(1): 70–91.

Stier, Sebastian, Lisa Posch, Arnim Bleier, and Markus Strohmaier. 2017. "When Populists Become Popular: Comparing Facebook Use by the Right-Wing Movement Pegida and German Political Parties." *Information, Communication & Society* 20(9): 1365–1388.

Stiglitz, Joseph E. 2012. *The Price of Inequality*. New York: Norton and Co.

Stoddart, Mark C. J. and David Tindall. 2010. "'We've Also Become Quite Good Friends': Environmentalists, Social Networks and Social Comparison in British Columbia, Canada." *Social Movement Studies* 9(3): 253–271.

Stolle, Dietlind and Marc Hooghe. 2004. "Consumers as Political Participants? Shifts in Political Action Repertoires in Western Societies." Pp. 265–288 in *Politics, Products and Markets: Exploring Political Consumerism Past and Present*, edited by M. Micheletti, A. Follesdal, and D. Stolle. New Brunswick, NJ: Transaction Publishers.

Stott, Clifford, John Drury, and Steve Reicher. 2017. "On the Role of a Social Identity Analysis in Articulating Structure and Collective Action: The 2011 Riots in Tottenham and Hackney." *British Journal of Criminology* 57(4): 964–981.

Strand, David and John W. Meyer. 1993. "Institutional Conditions for Diffusion." *Theory and Society* 22: 487–511.

Strauss, Anselm. 1947. "Research in Collective Behavior: Neglect and Need." *American Sociological Review* 12: 352–354.

Streeck, Wolfgang. 2010. "E pluribus Unum? Varieties and commonalities of capitalism." *MPIFGF, Discussion Paper* 10/12.

Streeck, Wolfgang. 2011. "The Crisis in Contest. Democratic Capitalism and Its Contradictions." *MPIFGF, Discussion Paper* 11/15.

Stryker, Sheldon, Timothy J. Owens, and Robert W. White. 2000. *Self, Identity, and Social Movements*. Minneapolis: University of Minnesota Press.

Suh, Chan S., Ion Bogdan Vasi, and Paul Y. Chang. 2017. "How Social Media Matter: Repression and the Diffusion of the Occupy Wall Street Movement." *Social Science Research* 65: 282–93.

Swidler, Ann. 1986. "Culture in Action: Symbols and Strategies." *American Sociological Review* 51: 273–286.

Talpin, Jean-Pierre. 2015. "Democratic Innovations." Pp. 782–792 in *The Oxford Handbook of Social Movements*, edited by D. della Porta and M. Diani. Oxford: Oxford University Press.

Tan, Anna and David A. Snow. 2015. "Cultural Conflicts and Social Movements." Pp. 513–533 in *Oxford Handbook of Social Movements*, edited by D. della Porta and M. Diani. Oxford/New York: Oxford University Press.

Tan, Er-Win. 2018. "Overcoming the Challenge of Fake News." *IAFOR Journal of Arts & Humanities* 5(2): 23–38.

Tarrow, Sidney. 1983. "Struggling to Reform: Social Movements and Policy Change during Cycles of Protest." *Western Societies Paper 15*. Ithaca: Cornell University.

Tarrow, Sidney. 1989. *Democracy and Disorder: Protest and Politics in Italy, 1965–1975.* Oxford/New York: Oxford University Press.

Tarrow, Sidney. 1990. "The Phantom at the Opera: Political Parties and Social Movements of the 1960s and the 1970s in Italy." Pp. 251–273 in *Challenging the Political Order: New Social Movements in Western Democracies*, edited by R. J. Dalton and M. Kuechler. Cambridge: Polity Press.

Tarrow, Sidney. 1994. *Power in Movement: Social Movements, Collective Action and Politics.* New York/Cambridge: Cambridge University Press.

Tarrow, Sidney. 1998. *Power in Movement* (2nd Ed.). New York/Cambridge: Cambridge University Press.

Tarrow, Sidney. 2005. *The New Transnational Activism.* Cambridge: Cambridge University Press.

Tarrow, Sidney. 2008. "Charles Tilly and the Practice of Contentious Politics." *Social Movement Studies* 7(3): 225–246.

Tarrow, Sidney. 2011. *Power in Movement* (3rd Ed.). New York/Cambridge: Cambridge University Press.

Tarrow, Sidney. 2012. *Strangers at the Gate. Movements and States in Contentious Politics.* Cambridge: Cambridge University Press.

Tarrow, Sidney. 2015. "Contentious Politics." Pp. 86–107 in *The Oxford Handbook of Social Movements*, edited by D. della Porta and M. Diani. Oxford: Oxford University Press.

Tavory, Iddo and Nina Eliasoph 2013. "Coordinating Futures: Toward a Theory of Anticipation." *The American Journal of Sociology* 118(4): 908–942.

Taylor, Verta. 1989. "Social Movement Continuity: The Women's Movement in Abeyance." *American Sociological Review* 54: 761–775.

Taylor, Verta and Nancy Whittier. 1992. "Collective Identity in Social Movement Communities: Lesbian Feminist Mobilization." Pp. 104–132 in *Frontiers of Social Movement Theory*, edited by A. Morris and C. Mueller. New Haven, CT: Yale University Press.

Taylor, Verta and Nella van Dyke. 2004. "Get up, stand up: Tactical repertoires of social movements." Pp. 262–293 in *The Blackwell companion to social movements*, edited by S. David A., S. A. Soule, and H. Kriese. Malden, MA: Blackwell Publishing.

Tejerina, Benjamín, Ignacia Perugorría, Tova Benski, and Lauren Langman. 2013. "From indignation to occupation: A new wave of global mobilization." *Current Sociology* 61(4): 377–392.

Temper, Leah, Federico Demaria, Arnim Scheidel, Daniela Del Bene, and Joan Martinez-Alier. 2018. "The Global Environmental Justice Atlas (EJAtlas): Ecological Distribution Conflicts as Forces for Sustainability." *Sustainability Science* 13(3): 573–584.

Therborn, Göran. 2013. *The Killing Fields of Inequality*. Cambridge: Polity.

Therborn, Göran. 2014. "New Masses? Social Bases of Resistance." *New Left Review* 85: 7–16.

Thompson, Edward P. 1963. *The Making of the English Working Class*. London: Penguin.

Thompson, Edward P. 1971. "The Moral Economy of the English Crowds in the Eighteenth Century." *Past and Present* 50(1): 76–136.

Thompson, John B. 1995. *The Media and Modernity*. Cambridge: Cambridge University Press.

Tilly, Charles. 1978. *From Mobilization to Revolution*. Reading, MA: Addison-Wesley.

Tilly, Charles. 1984a. *Big Structures, Large Processes, Huge Comparisons*. New York: Russell Sage.

Tilly, Charles. 1984b. "Social Movements and National Politics." Pp. 297–317 in *State-Making and Social Movements: Essays in History and Theory*, edited by C. Bright and S. Harding. Ann Arbor: University of Michigan Press.

Tilly, Charles. 1986. *The Contentious French*. Cambridge MA: Harvard University Press.

Tilly, Charles. 1986. *The Contentious French*. Cambridge, MA: Harvard University Press.

Tilly, Charles. 1993. *European Revolutions 1492–1992*. Oxford/Cambridge, MA: Blackwell.

Tilly, Charles. 1994. "Social Movements as Historically Specific Clusters of Political Performances." *Berkeley Journal of Sociology* 38: 1–30.

Tilly, Charles. 2003. *The Politics of Collective Violence*. Cambridge: Cambridge University Press.

Tilly, Charles. 2004a. *Social Movements 1768-2004*. Boulder, CO: Paradigm.

Tilly, Charles. 2004b. *Contention and Democracy in Europe 1650–2000*. Cambridge: Cambridge University Press.

Tilly, Charles. 2005. *Identities, Boundaries, and Social Ties*. Boulder, CO: Paradigm.

Tilly, Charles. 2008. *Explaining Social Processes*. Boulder, CO: Paradigm Publishers.

Tilly, Charles, Louise Tilly, and Richard Tilly. 1975. *The Rebellious Century 1830–1930*. Cambridge, MA: Harvard University Press.

Tindall, David. 2004. "Social Movement Participation Over Time: An Ego-Network Approach to Micro-Mobilization." *Sociological Focus* 37: 163–184.

Tindall, David. 2015. "Networks as Constraints and Opportunities." Pp. 231–245 in *Oxford Handbook of Social Movements*, edited by D. della Porta and M. Diani. Oxford/New York: Oxford University Press.

Tosini, Domenico. 2010. "Al-Qaeda's Strategic Gamble: The Sociology of Suicide Bombings in Iraq." *Canadian Journal of Sociology-Cahiers Canadiens De Sociologie* 35: 271–308.

Touraine, Alain. 1977. *The Self-Production of Society*. Chicago: University of Chicago Press.

Touraine, Alain. 1981. *The Voice and the Eye: An Analysis of Social Movements*. Cambridge: Cambridge University Press.

Touraine, Alain. 1985. "An Introduction to the Study of Social Movements." *Social Research* 52: 749–788.

Touraine, Alain. 1987. *The Workers' Movement*. Cambridge/New York: Cambridge University Press.

Traugott, Mark. 1995. "Barricades as Repertoire: Continuities and Discontinuities in the History of French Contention." Pp. 43–56 in *Repertoires and Cycles of Collective Action*, edited by M. Traugott. Durham, NC: Duke University Press.

Turam, Berna. 2015. *Gaining Freedoms: Claiming Space in Istanbul and Berlin*. Stanford, CA: Stanford University Press.

Turner, Bryan. 1988. *Status*. Milton Keynes: Open University Press.

Turner, Ralph. 1994. "Ideology and Utopia after Socialism." Pp. 79–100 in *New Social Movements: From Ideology to Identity*, edited by E. Larana, H. Johnston, and J. Gusfield. Philadelphia: Temple University Press.

Turner, Ralph and Lewis Killian. 1987 [1957]. *Collective Behavior*. Englewood Cliffs, NJ: Prentice-Hall.

Uitermark, Justus. 2017. "Complex Contention: Analyzing Power Dynamics within Anonymous." *Social Movement Studies* 16(4): 403–417.

Ulfelder, Jay. 2005. "Contentious Collective Action and the Breakdown of Authoritarian Regimes." *International Political Science Review* 26(3): 311–334.

Urry, John. 1995. "Rethinking Class." Pp. 169–181 in *Social Movements and Social Classes*, edited by L. Maheu. London/Thousand Oaks: Sage.

Uysal, Aysen. 2005. "Organisation du maintien de l'ordre et repression policière en Turquie." Pp. 257–280 in *Maintien de l'ordre et police des foules*, edited by D. della Porta and O. Fillieule. Paris: Presses de Science Po.

Vala, Carsten T. and Kevin J. O'Brien. 2007. "Attraction without Networks: Recruiting Strangers to Unregistered Protestantism in China." *Mobilization* 12(1): 79–94.

Valiente, Celia. 2015. "Social Movements in Abeyance in Non-Democracies: The Women's Movement in Franco's Spain." *Research in Social Movements, Conflicts & Change* 38: 259–290.

Valocchi, Stephen. 2009. "The Importance of Being 'We': Collective Identity and the Mobilizing Work of Progressive Activists in Hartford, Connecticut." *Mobilization: An International Quarterly* 14(1): 65–84.

Valocchi, Stephen. 2012. "Activism as a Career, Calling, and Way of Life." *Journal of Contemporary Ethnography* 42(2): 169–200.

Valocchi, Stephen. 2017. "Capitalisms and Gay Identities: Towards a Capitalist Theory of Social Movements." *Social Problems* 64(2): 315–331.

Van Aelst, Peter and Stefaan Walgrave. 2004. "New Media, New Movements? The Role of the Internet in Shaping the 'Anti-Globalization' Movement." Pp. 97–122 in *CyberProtest*, edited by W. Van de Donk, B. D. Loader, P. G. Nixon, and D. Rucht. London: Routledge.

Van Cott, Donna L. 2008. *Radical Democracy in the Andes*. New York, Cambridge University Press.

Van de Donk, Wim, Brian D. Loader, Paul G. Nixon, and Dieter Rucht. 2004. *CyberProtest*. London: Routledge.

Van Dyke, Nella and Bryan Amos. 2017. "Social Movement Coalitions: Formation, Longevity, and Success." *Sociology Compass* 11(7): n/a-N.PAG.

Van Dyke, Nella and Holly McCammon, eds. 2010. *Strategic Alliances: New Studies of Social Movement Coalitions*. Minneapolis, MN: University of Minnesota Press.

van Haperen, Sander, Walter Nicholls, and Justus Uitermark. 2018. "Building Protest Online: Engagement with the Digitally Networked #not1more Protest Campaign on Twitter." *Social Movement Studies* 17(4): 408–423.

Van Laer, Jeroen. 2017. "The Mobilization Dropout Race: Interpersonal Networks and Motivations Predicting Differential Recruitment in a National Climate Change Demonstration." *Mobilization: An International Quarterly* 22(3): 311–329.

Vasi, Ion Bogdan and Brayden G. King. 2012. "Social Movements, Risk Perceptions, and Economic Outcomes." *American Sociological Review* 77: 573–596.

Vedres, Balazs, Laszlo Bruszt, and David Stark. 2005. "Shaping the web of civic participation: civil society web sites in Eastern Europe." *The Journal of Public Policy* 25: 149–163.

Vegh, Sandor. 2003. "Classifying Forms of Online Activism." Pp. 71–95 in *Cyberactivism: Online Activism in Theory and Practice*, edited by M. McCaughey and M. D. Ayers. London: Routledge.

Vestergren, Sara, John Drury, and Eva Hammar Chiriac. 2017. "The Biographical Consequences of Protest and Activism: A Systematic Review and a New Typology." *Social Movement Studies* 16(2): 203–221.

Vicari, Stefania. 2014. "Networks of Contention: The Shape of Online Transnationalism in Early Twenty-First Century Social Movement Coalitions." *Social Movement Studies* 13(1): 92–109.

Vogiatzoglou, Markos. 2018. "Trade Unions in Greece: Protest and Social Movements in the Context of Austerity Politics." Pp. 193–210 in *Social Movements and Organized Labor. Passions and Interests*, edited by J. Groete and C. Wagemann. Farnham, UK/ Burlington, VT: Ashgate.

Waddington, David. 1992. *Contemporary Issues in Public Disorder: A Comparative and Historical Approach*. London: Routledge.

Waddington, David. 2008. "The Madness of the Mob: Explaining the "Irrationality" and Destructiveness of Crowd Violence." *Sociology Compass* 2(2): 675–687.

Waddington, David. 2015. "Riots." Pp. 423–438 in *The Oxford Handbook of Social Movements*, edited by D. della Porta and M. Diani. Oxford: Oxford University Press.

Waddington, David and Mike King. 2005. "The Disorderly Crowd: From Classical Psychological Reductionism to Socio-contextual Theory – The Impact on Public Order Policing Strategies." *Howard Journal* 44: 490–503.

Waddington, Peter Anthony James. 1994. *Liberty and Order: Policing Public Order in a Capital City*. London: UCL Press.

Wade Robert. H. and Silla Sigurgeirsdottir. 2011. "Iceland's meltdown: the rise and fall of international banking in the North Atlantic." *Brazilian Journal of Political Economy* 31(5): 684–697.

Wagner-Pacifici, Robin and E. Colin Ruggero. 2018. "Temporal blindspots in Occupy Philadelphia." *Social Movement Studies*, DOI: 10.1080/14742837.2018.1474096.

Walder, Andrew G. 2009. "Political Sociology and Social Movements." *Annual Review of Sociology* 35: 393–412.

Waldman, Linda. 2007. "When Social Movements Bypass the Poor: Asbestos Pollution, International Litigation and Griqua Cultural Identity." *Journal of Southern African Studies* 33: 577–600.

Walgrave, Stefaan and Dieter Rucht, eds. 2010. *The World Says No to War: Demonstrations Against the War in Iraq*. Minneapolis: University of Minnesota Press.

Walgrave, Stefaan and Jan Massens. 2000. "The Making of the White March: The Mass Media as Mobilizing Alternative to Movement Organizations." *Mobilization* 5: 217–239.

Walgrave, Stefaan, Lance Bennett, Jeroen Van Laer, and Christian Breunig. 2011. "Multiple Engagements and Network Bridging in Contentious Politics: Digital Media Use of Protest Participants." *Mobilization* 16(3): 325–349.

Walker, Jack. 1991. *Mobilizing Interest Groups in America: Patrons, Professions, and Social Movements*. Ann Arbor, MI: University of Michigan Press.

Wall, Derek. 1999. *Earth First! And the Anti-Roads Movement*. London: Routledge.

Wallerstein, Immanuel. 1974. *The Modern World System: Capitalist Agriculture and the Origins of the European World Economy in the Sixteenth Century*. New York: Academic Press.

Wallerstein, Immanuel. 1990. "Antisystemic Movements: History and Dilemma." In *Transforming the Revolution*, edited by A. G. Frank, G. Arrighi, S. Amin, and I. Wallerstein. New York: Monthly Review Press.

Wallis, Roy. 1977. *The Road to Total Freedom*. New York: Columbia University Press.

Wallis, Roy and Steve Bruce. 1986. *Sociological Theory, Religion and Collective Action*. Belfast: Queen's University Press.

Walton, John and David Seddon. 1994. *Free Markets and Food Riots: The Politics of Global Adjustement*. Oxford: Blackwell.

Wang, Dan, Alessandro Piazza, and Sarah A. Soule. 2018. "Boundary-Spanning in Social Movements: Antecedents and Outcomes." *Annual Review of Sociology* 44: 167–187.

Wellman, B. 2001. "Computer Networks As Social Networks." *Science* 293(5537): 2031–2034.

Werner, Timothy. 2012. *Public Forces and Private Politics in American Big Business*. Cambridge: Cambridge University Press.

Westphal, Joana. 2018. "Violence in the Name of God? A Framing Processes Approach to the Islamic State in Iraq and Syria." *Social Movement Studies* 17(1): 19–34.

Weyland, Kurt. 2017. "Populism: A Political Strategic Approach." in *The Oxford Handbook of Populism, Oxford Handbooks*, edited by C. Rovira Kaltwasser, P. A. Taggart, P. Ochoa Espejo, and P. Ostiguy. Oxford: Oxford University Press.

White, Harrison. 2008. *Identity and Control. How Social Formations Emerge*. Princeton, NJ: Princeton University Press.

Whittier, Nancy. 1995. *Feminist Generations: The Persistence of the Radical Women's Movement*. Philadelphia: Temple University Press.

Whittier, Nancy. 1997. "Political Generations, Micro-Cohorts, and the Transformation of Social Movements." *American Sociological Review* 62(5): 760–778.

Whittier, Nancy. 2004. "The Consequences of Social Movements for Each Other." Pp. 531–551 in *The Blackwell Companion to Social Movements*, edited by D. A. Snow, S. H. Soule, and H. Kriesi. Oxford: Blackwell.

Wickham, Carrie Rosefsky. 2002. *Mobilizing Islam: Religion, Activism, and Political Change in Egypt*. New York: Columbia University Press.

Wickham, Carrie Rosefsky. 2013. *The Muslim Brotherhood: Evolution of an Islamist Movement*. Princeton, NJ: Princeton University Press.

Wijk, Jakomijn van, Wouter Stam, Tom Elfring, Charlene Zietsma, and Frank den Hond. 2013. "Activists and Incumbents Tying for Change: The Interplay Between Agency, Culture and Networks in Field Evolution." *Academy of Management Journal* 56: 358–386.

Wilkin, Peter. 2018. "The Rise of 'Illiberal' Democracy: The Orbánization of Hungarian Political Culture." *Journal of World-Systems Research* 24(1): 5–42.

Willelms, Helmut, Marianne Wolf, and Roland Eckert. 1993. *Unruhen und Politikberatung: Funktion, Arbeitweise, Ergebnisse und Auswirkung von Untersuchungskommissionen in der USA, Grossbritannien und der Bundesrepublik Deutschlands*. Opladen: Westdeutscher Verlag.

Williams, Dana M. 2018a. "Contemporary Anarchist and Anarchistic Movements." *Sociology Compass* 12(6): 1–1.

Williams, Dana M. 2018b. "Happiness and Freedom in Direct Action: Critical Mass Bike Rides as Ecstatic Ritual, Play, and Temporary Autonomous Zones." *Leisure Studies* 37(5): 589–602.

Williams, Rhys H. 2004. "The Cultural Contexts of Collective Action." Pp. 91–115 in *The Blackwell Companion to Social Movements*, edited by D. A. Snow, S. Soule, and H. Kriesi. Oxford: Blackwell.

Williams, Rhys H. and Timothy J. Kubal. 1999. "Movement Frames and Cultural Environment: Resonance, Failure and Boundaries of the Legitimate." *Research in Social Movements, Conflict and Change* 21: 225–248.

Wilson, James Q. 1973. *Political Organizations*. New York: Basic Books.

Wilson, John. 1976. "Social Protest and Social Control." *Social Problems* 24: 469–481.

Wilson, John. 2000. "Volunteering." *Annual Review of Sociology* 26: 215–240.

Winegard, Jessica. 2012. "Taking out the Trash: Youth Clean up Egypt after Mubarak." Pp. 64–69 in *The Journey to Tahrir: Revolution, Protest, and Social Change in Egypt*, edited by J. Sowers and C. Toensing. London: Verso.

Wisler, Dominique and Hanspeter Kriesi. 1998. "Decision making and Style in Protest Policing. The Cases of Geneva and Zurich." Pp. 91–116 in *Policing Protest: The Control of Mass Demonstrations in Western Democracies*, edited by D. della Porta and H. Reiter. Minneapolis/London: University of Minnesota Press/UCL Press.

Wood, Elisabeth Jean. 2000. *Forging Democracy from Below: Insurgent Transitions in South Africa and El Salvador. Cambridge Studies in Comparative Politics.* Cambridge, UK; New York: Cambridge University Press.

Wood, Elisabeth Jean. 2015. "Social Mobilization and Violence in Civil War and their Social Legacies." Pp. 452–466 in *The Oxford Handbook of Social Movements*, edited by D. della Porta and M. Diani. Oxford: Oxford University Press.

Wood, Michael and Michael Hughes. 1984. "The Moral Basis of Moral Reform: Status Discontent vs. Culture and Socialization as Explanations of Anti-Pornography Social Movement Adherence." *American Sociological Review* 49: 86–99.

Wright, Erik O. 1985. *Classes*. London: Verso.

Wright, Steve. 2004. "Informing, Communicating and ICTs in Contemporary Anti-Capitalist Movements." Pp. 77–94 in *CyberProtest*, edited by W. Van de Donk, B. D. Loader, P. G. Nixon, and D. Rucht. London: Routledge.

Yangzom, Dicky. 2016. "Clothing and Social Movements: Tibet and the Politics of Dress." *Social Movement Studies* 15(6): 622–633.

Yashar, Deborah J. 1996. "Contesting Citizenship: Indigenous Movements and Democracy in Latin America." *Comparative Politics* 31: 23–42.

Yashar, Deborah J. 2005. *Contesting Citizenship in Latin America: The Rise of Indigenous Movements and the Postliberal Challenge.* New York: Cambridge University Press.

Yashar, Deborah J. 2011. "The left and citizenship rights." In *The Resurgence of the Latin American Left*, edited by S. Levitsky and K. M. Roberts. Baltimore, Johns Hopkins University Press.

Yécora, Fernando 2015. "Elecciones 20-D: el análisis de los resultados." *Debate* 21: 21 December.

Yörük, Erdem and Yüksel Murat. 2014. "Class and Politics in Turkey's Gezi Protests." *New Left Review* 89(Sept.-Oct.): 103–123.

Young, Iris Marion. 1996. "Communication and The Other: Beyond Deliberative Democracy." Pp. 120–35 in *Democracy and Difference: Contesting the Boundaries of the Political*, edited by S. Benhabib. Princeton: Princeton University Press.

Zald, Mayer N. 2000. "Ideologically Structured Action: An Enlarged Agenda for Social Movement Research." *Mobilization*, 1–16.

Zald, Mayer N. and Bert Useem. 1987. "Movement and Countermovement Interaction: Mobilization, Tactics, and State Involvement." Pp. 247–272 in *Social Movements in an Organizational Society*, edited by M. N. Zald and J. D. McCarthy. New Brunswick, NJ: Transaction Books.

Zald, Mayer N. and Roberta Ash. 1966. "Social Movement Organizations: Growth, Decay and Change." *Social Forces* 44: 327–340.

Zamponi, Lorenzo. 2018. *Social Movements, Memory and Media: Narrative in Action in the Italian and Spanish Student Movements.* Basingstoke: Palgrave Macmillan.

Zengin, Aslı. 2013. "What Is Queer about Gezi?" *Cultural Anthropology*, October. www.culanth.org/fijieldsights/407-what-is-queer-about-gezi.

Zhuo, Xiaolin, Barry Wellman, and Justine Ju. 2011. "The First Internet Revolt?" *Peacemagazine.Org.* Retrieved (http://www.peacemagazine.org/archive/v27n3p06.htm).

Zielonka, Jan. 2018. *Counter-Revolution. Liberal Europe in Retreat.* Oxford; New York: Oxford University Press.

Zietsma, Charlene, Peter Groenewegen, Danielle M. Logue, and C. R. (Bob) Hinings. 2017. "Field of Fields? Building the Scaffolding for Cumulation of Research on Institutional Fields." *Academy of Management Annals* 11: 391–450.

Zolberg Aristide R. 1995. "Response: Working-Class Dissolution." *International Labor and Working-Class History* 47(Spring): 28–38.

Zuk, Piotr and Pawel Zuk. 2017. "An 'Ordinary Man's' Protest: Self-Immolation as a Radical Political Message in Eastern Europe Today and in the Past." *Social Movement Studies* 17: 610–617.

Index

Social Movements: An Introduction, Third Edition. Donatella della Porta and Mario Diani.
© 2020 John Wiley & Sons Ltd. Published 2020 by John Wiley & Sons Ltd.